Schiedsgerichte unter
staatlicher Kontrolle

Schriftenreihe der August Maria Berges Stiftung für Arbitrales Recht

Herausgegeben von Dr. Hubertus W. Labes

Band 8

PETER LANG
Frankfurt am Main · Berlin · Bern · Bruxelles · New York · Oxford · Wien

Jörn Schämann

Schiedsgerichte unter staatlicher Kontrolle

Das englische Recht und das UNCITRAL-Modellgesetz

PETER LANG
Europäischer Verlag der Wissenschaften

Die Deutsche Bibliothek - CIP-Einheitsaufnahme

Schämann, Jörn:

Schiedsgerichte unter staatlicher Kontrolle : das englische Recht und das UNCITRAL-Modellgesetz / Jörn Schämann. - Frankfurt am Main ; Berlin ; Bern ; Bruxelles ; New York ; Oxford ; Wien : Lang, 2001
(Schriftenreihe der August-Maria-Berges-Stiftung für Arbitrales Recht ; Bd. 8)
Zugl.: Münster (Westfalen), Univ., Diss., 2000
ISBN 3-631-37481-X

D 6
ISSN 1435-4748
ISBN 3-631-37481-X

Meinen Eltern

Vorwort

In der vorliegenden Schrift verfolgt ihr Verf. das Ziel, das Verhältnis zwischen staatlicher Gerichtsbarkeit einerseits und Schiedsgerichtsbarkeit andererseits am Beispiel des englischen Schiedsverfahrensrechts und des UNCITRAL-Modellgesetzes über die internationale Handelsschiedsgerichtsbarkeit zu untersuchen. Wie bekannt, stand das UNCITRAL-Modellgesetz bei der Schaffung des englischen *Arbitration Act 1996* — wenn auch in geringem Umfang — Pate. Auf rechtsvergleichendem Wege (englisches Schiedsverfahrensrecht *versus UN-CITRAL-Model Act*) prüft der Verfasser folglich die Frage, welche Befugnisse einerseits das englische Schiedsverfahrensrecht und andererseits das UN-CITRAL-Modellgesetz den staatlichen Gerichten gewähren, um unterstützend oder korrigierend in ein Schiedsverfahren einzugreifen. Diese Untersuchung soll es dem Verf. am Ende seiner Schrift ermöglichen, die Frage zu beantworten, in welcher Weise die Balance zwischen staatlichen und schiedsrichterlichen Befugnissen optimiert werden kann. Die Kardinalfrage, die in dieser Schrift gestellt wird, lautet also: Bei welcher Aufteilung von Befugnissen unter diesen beiden Gerichtsbarkeiten wäre ein Optimum für ein reibungsloses Funktionieren des schiedsrichterlichen Verfahrens erreicht?

Dabei untersucht der Verf., was das englische Recht anbetrifft, nicht nur den seit 1997 geltenden *Arbitration Act 1996*, sondern auch das englische Schiedsverfahrensrecht seit dessen Ursprüngen im ausgehenden Mittelalter, d. h. einschließlich der Vorgänger des *Arbitration Act 1996*, nämlich der entsprechenden *Acts* von 1950, 1975 und 1979.

Das englische Schiedsverfahrensrecht ist insoweit deshalb besonders interessant, weil englische staatliche Gerichte zunächst bis zum Ende des 19. Jahrhunderts kaum derartige Eingriffs- und Kontrollbefugnisse in eine damals allerdings erst gering entwickelte Schiedsgerichtsbarkeit besaßen. Die englischen Gerichte wurden dann aber durch die verschiedenen *Arbitration Acts* mit Befugnissen solcher Art reichlich ausgestattet und behielten diese Befugnisse uneingeschränkt bis zum *Arbitration Act 1979*. Als später in den 80er Jahren eine Revision des englischen Schiedsverfahrensrechts als dringlich erschien und eine Übernahme des in der Zwischenzeit ausgearbeiteten *UNCITRAL-Model Act* diskutiert wurde, spielte die Problematik, wieviel Eingriffs- und Kontrollbefugnisse den staatlichen Gerichten eingeräumt werden sollten, wiederum eine große Rolle.

Der Verf. gelangt zu den folgenden Ergebnissen: Im Vergleich zum *UN-CITRAL-Model Act* reichen die Eingriffs- und Kontrololbefugnisse der englischen staatlichen Gerichte auch nach dem *Arbitration Act 1996* immer noch recht weit. Der Verf. bezweifelt daher zu Recht, ob die Regelungen in dem neuen Gesetz von 1996 als optimal bezeichnet werden können. An Hand vieler einzelner Regelungskomplexe in jenem Gesetz erläutert er seine These.

Für die Praxis der internationalen Schiedsgerichtsbarkeit ergibt sich hieraus folgendes: Schon vor dem Inkrafttreten des *Arbitration Act 1996* galt das englische Schiedsverfahrensrecht für kontinentaleuropäische Juristen als eine Besonderheit, mit der man nicht ganz vertraut war. London kam damals aus der Sicht kontinentaleuropäischer Juristen als Schiedsort für internationale Schiedsverfahren zwar in Frage, aber in der Regel nur dann, wenn das englische Schiedsverfahrensrecht durch die Vereinbarung abbedungen war, daß die ICC- oder eine andere institutionelle Schiedsordnung gelten sollte. Denn ein kontinentaleuropäischer Jurist konnte sich niemals dessen sicher sein, die Besonderheiten des englischen Schiedsverfahrensrechts in genügendem Umfang zu überblicken. Insbesondere konnte man nicht wissen, ob man wegen der Eingriffsbefugnisse der englischen staatlichen Gerichte entweder punktuell oder, in einem Anfechtungsverfahren, insgesamt im Endergebnis nicht doch vor den englischen staatlichen Gerichten landen würde.

Nach dem Inkrafttreten des *Arbitration Act 1996* hat sich an dieser Einschätzung zwar einiges geändert. In wesentlichen Punkten ist es jedoch bei dieser Beurteilung geblieben. Zwar sind die Eingriffsbefugnisse der englischen staatlichen Gerichte durch diesen *Act* erheblich beschnitten worden. Der eigentliche "Pferdefuß" blieb aber erhalten: Sofern nur einige nicht allzu schwere Voraussetzungen erfüllt sind, ist die Anfechtung eines Schiedsspruchs vor dem zuständigen staatlichen Gericht *(High Court)* gemäß Sec. 69 des *Act* immer noch möglich, und diesem Gericht ist eine - allerdings eingeschränkte - "révision au fond" des Schiedsspruchs gestattet. Hat man also einen obsiegenden Schiedsspruch unter vielen Mühen und Kosten vor dem Schiedsgericht erstritten, so muß man damit rechnen, daß die unterlegene Partei die Sache erneut vor das staatliche Gericht bringt. Dort müssen alle Fragen gegebenenfalls neu verhandelt werden.

Diese wenigen Bemerkungen sollen die praktische Bedeutung der vorliegenden Schrift kennzeichnen: Wer sich für London oder für einen anderen englischen Ort als Sitz seines Schiedsgerichts entscheidet, sollte vorher nicht nur einen kurzen, sondern einen längeren Blick in sie hineingeworfen haben. Aber abgesehen von der praktischen Bedeutung dieser Schrift gebühren ihrem Verfasser Anerkennung und Dank dafür, daß er die große allgemeine Problematik „Autonomie des Schiedsverfahrens *versus* Eingriffs- und Kontrollbefugnisse der staatlichen Gerichte“ an einem bedeutenden Beispiel auch theoretisch thematisiert hat.

Otto Sandrock

Vorwort des Verfassers

Die Arbeit ist das Ergebnis von Studienaufenthalten an der Victoria University of Wellington, der University of New South Wales, der University of British Columbia sowie an der Staatsbibliothek Berlin. Die gewonnenen Einblicke gehen über den Inhalt der Arbeit hinaus.

Die Arbeit wurde im Frühjahr 2000 von der Rechtswissenschaftlichen Fakultät der Westfälischen Wilhelms-Universität Münster als Dissertation angenommen. Rechtsprechung und Literatur befinden sich auf dem Stand von August 1999.

Stellvertretend für all diejenigen, welche mich im Aus- und Inland unterstützt haben, danke ich Dean Joost Blom und Rob von der UBC, Dr. Holger D. Müller, LL.M. (UBC) und Dr. Joken Dierksmeier, LL.M. (Edin.); Jens danke ich nicht nur für die Finanzierung.

Der August Maria Berges Stiftung für Arbitrales Recht bin ich sehr für die Aufnahme in die Schriftenreihe und die großzügige Unterstützung verpflichtet.

Mein besonderer Dank gilt meinem Doktorvater Professor Dr. Otto Sandrock, LL.M. (Yale) für seine Förderung auch über diese Arbeit hinaus.

Frankfurt am Main, im Dezember 2000 — Jörn Schämann

Inhaltsverzeichnis

Literaturverzeichnis

Abromson, E. J.	The English Arbitration Act of 1979: A Symbiotic Relationship between the Courts and Arbitration Tribunals, Suffolk Transnat'l L.J. 1980, 73
Barker, Robert	Judicial Review of English Arbitration in the Wake of Nema and Evia, Virg.J.Int'l L. 1983, 434
Bartos, Harald	Internationale Handelsschiedsgerichtsbarkeit, Verfahrensprinzipien, Diss. Trier, Frankfurt 1984
Barrington, Louise	One Small Step Backward?: A Comment on the Ken-Ren Cases, Am.Rev.Int.Arb. 1995, 65
Bentil, Kodvo	Making England a More Attractive Venue for International Arbitration by Less Judicial Oversight, J.Int'l Arb. 1988, 49
Berger, K.P.	Arbitration as a Source of Inspiration for Comparative Law, Legal Teaching and the Transnational Negotiation Process, in: Böckstiegel (Hrsg.), Arbitration and Act of State, Köln/Berlin/Bonn/München 1997, S. 99; zitiert: Berger, in: Böckstiegel (Hrsg.)
—	Aufgaben und Grenzen der Parteiautonomie in der Internationalen Wirtschaftsschiedsgerichtsbarkeit, RIW 1994, 12
—	Das neue deutsche Schiedssverfahrensrecht, DZWir 1998, 45
— (Hrsg.)	Einführung in das neue deutsche Schiedsverfahrensrecht, in: Berger (Hrsg.), Das neue deutsche Schiedsverfahrensrecht / The New German Arbitration Law, RWS-Dokumentation Nr. 21, Köln 1998, 3; zitiert: Schiedsverfahrensrecht

—	Germany Adopts the UNCITRAL Model Law, Int'l Arb.L.Rev. 1998, 121
—	International Economic Arbitration, Deventer 1993; zitiert: International Economic Arbitration
—	Internationale Wirtschaftsschiedsgerichtsbarkeit, Berlin/New York 1992
—	The Modern Trend towards Exclusion of Recourse against Transnational Arbitral Awards: A European Perspektive, Fordham Int'l L.J. 1989, 605
— (Hrsg.)	Transnational Law in Commercial Legal Practice, Münster 1999; zitiert: Transnational Law
Bernstein, Ronald	Arbitration and the Courts, Arbitration 1993, 4
—	Handbook of Arbitration Practice, 2. Aufl., London 1993; zitiert: Bernstein, Handbook, 2. Aufl.
Bernstein/Tackaberry/ Marriott/Wood	Handbook of Arbitration Practice, 3. Auflage, London 1998; zitiert: Bernstein, Handbook
Bingham, L.J.	Reasons and Reasons for Reasons: Differences Between a Court Judgment and an Arbitration Award, Arb.Int'l 1985, 141
Böckstiegel, K.H.	Public Policy and Arbitrability, in: Sanders (Hrsg.), ICCA Congress Series No. 3, Comparative Arbitration Practice and Public Policy in Arbitration, Niederlande 1987, S. 177; zitiert: Böckstiegel, in: Sanders (Hrsg.)
Boyd, Stewart	The Chartered Institute Annual Conference 1984: Innovation and Reform in the Law of Arbitration, Arbitration 1985, 440
—	The Role of National Law and the National Courts in England, in: Lew (Hrsg.) Contemporary Problems in International Arbitration, London 1986, S. 149; zitiert: Boyd, in: Lew (Hrsg.), Contemporary Problems
Boyd/Veeder	Le Développement du Droit Anglais de l'Arbitrage Depuis la Loi de 1979, Revue Arbitrage 1991, 209

Branson, D.P.	The Ken-Ren Case: It is an Ado Where More Aid is Less Help, Arb.Int'l 1994, 313
Briner, Robert	Domestic Arbitration: Practice in Continental Europe and its Lesson for Arbitration in England, Arb.Int'l 1997, 155
Broches, Aaron	Commentary on the UNCITRAL Model Law on International Commercial Arbitration, Deventer/ Boston 1990
Buchanan, Mark	Public Policy and International Commercial Arbitration, Am.Bus.L.J. 1988/89, 511
Calavros, Constantin	Das UNCITRAL-Modellgesetz über die Internationale Handelsschiedsgerichtsbarkeit, Bielefeld 1988
Campbell, John	Lives of the Chief Justices, 3. Aufl., Band 3, Northport 1894
Carbonneau, Thomas	A Comment on the 1996 United Kingdom Arbitration Act, Tulane Mar.L. J. 1997, 131
—	Arbitral Adjudication: A Comparative Assessment of its Remedies and Substantive Status in Transnational Commerce, Tex.Int.L.J. 1984, 33
Carlston, K.L.	Theory of the Arbitration Process, L.C.P. 1952, 631
Charles, Stephen	Appeals From Arbitration Awards, Arbitrator 1988, 105
—	Natural Justice and Alternative Dispute Resolution, Law Institute Journal 1986, 1079
Chatterjee, Charles	Legal Aspects of Severability of Arbitration Clauses: An English Perspective, Arb. & Disp.Res.J. 1996, 297
Chitty on Contracts	Chitty on Contracts, General Principles, 27. Aufl., London 1994; zitiert: Chitty on Contracts

Clark/Lange	Recent Changes in English Arbitration Practice Widen Opportunities for More Effective International Arbitrations, Bus.L. 1980, 1623
Collins, Lawrence	Dicey and Morris on the Conflict of Laws, 12. Aufl., London 1993
—	The Law Governing the Agreement and Procedure in International Arbitration in England, in: Lew (Hrsg.) Contemporary Problems in International Arbitration, London 1986, S. 126; zitiert: Collins, in: Lew (Hrsg.), Contemporary Problems
Cole, T.R.	Public Policy Exception to the New York Convention on the Recognition and Enforcement of Arbitral Awards, Ohio St.J.Disp.Res. 1986, 365
Comish, Alan	Arbitration at Common Law before the First (English) Arbitration Act 1698, Arbitration 1990, 194
Commercial Court Committee	Report on Arbitration, Cmnd 7284 (1978) (Donaldson Report), London 1978; zitiert: Donaldson Report
Commercial Court Committee - Sub-Committee on Arbititration	Final Report, London 1985; zitiert: Commercial Court Committee, Final Report
Conrick, B.J.	"Where the Kings Writ Does Not Run", 1 Queensland Institute of Technology Law Journal 1985, 1
Craig, William	Uses and Abuses of Appeal from Awards, Arb.Int'l 1988, 174
Cremades, Bernardo	Should Arbitrators Maintain Their Independence or Would it be Desirable for them to have Closer Links with the Courts in their Respective Countries?, Arbitration 1978, 83
Davenport, Brian	The Ken-Ren Case: Much Ado Nothing Very Much, Arb.Int'l 1994, 303
David, René	Arbitration in International Trade, Deventer 1985

Davidson, Fraser	International Commercial Arbitration - The United Kingdom and UNCITRAL Model Law, J.B.L. 1990, 480
—	The New Arbtration Act - A Model Law?, J.B.L. 1997, 101
—	The Relationship Between Arbitration and the Courts in Scotland and England, Civ.Just.Q. 1993, 372
Davis, R.K.F.	The Quest for Speed and Finality in Arbitration Proceedings - Does the Uniform Commercial Arbitration Act Go Far Enough?, Build. & Constr.L. 1989, 290
Delaume, George	Court Intervention in Arbitral Proceedings, in: Carbonneau (Hrsg.), Resolving Transnational Disputes Through International Arbitration, Charlottsville 1984, 195; zitiert: Delaume, in Carbonneau (Hrsg.)
Departmental Advisory Committee on Arbitration Law	1996 Report on the Arbitration Bill, London 1996, veröffentlicht in Arb.Int'l 1997, 275; zitiert: DAC, 1996-Report
—	A Report on the UNCITRAL Model Law on International Commercial Arbitration, London 1989; zitiert: Mustill-Report
—	Consultation Document on Commencement of the Arbitration Act 1996, Great Britain 1996
Deshpande, V.S.	Enforcement of Foreign Awards in India, U.K. and U.S.A., J.Int'l Arb. 1987, 41
—	Jurisdiction Over 'Foreign' and 'Domestic' Awards in the New York Convention 1958, Arb.Int'l 1991, 123
De Vries, Henry	International Commercial Arbitration: A Contractual Substitute for National Courts?, Tulane L.Rev. 1982, 42

Dierksmeier, Jochen — Der Kauf einer englischen "Private Limited Company", Heidelberg 1997

Diplock, L.J. — The 1978 Alexander Lecture: The Case Stated - its Use and Abuse, Arbitration 1978, 107

Dockray, Martin — The Inherent Jurisdiction to Regulate Civil Proceedings, L.Q.Rev. 1997, 120

Donaldson, John — Commercial Arbitration - 1979 and After, C.L.P. 1983, 1

Dore, Isaak — Arbitration and Conciliation Under the UNCITRAL Rules: A Textual Analysis, Dordrecht 1986

Editors, The, of Arbitration International — Editors Note, Arbitration International 1992, 241

El-Ahdab, M.O. — Le Centre Arab d'Arbitrage Commercial a Rabat, Revue de L'Arbitrage 1989, 631

Esplugues, Carlos — 'National Intervention' in International Commercial Arbitration, R.Gen. 1988, 81

Evans, Anthony — Court Intervention in Maritime Arbitration, Arb. & Disp.Res.J. 1999, 40

— — Some Thoughts on Adoption of the UNCITRAL Model Law, Arbitration 1987, 121

Ferguson, Robert — The Adjudication of Commercial Disputes and the Legal System in Modern England, Brit.J.Law & Soc. 1980, 141

Fleischhauer, C.-A. — UNCITRAL Model Law on International Commercial Arbitration, Arb.J. 1986, 17

Gaillard, Emmanuel — The Use of Comparative Law in International Commercial Arbitration, in: Sanders (Hrsg.), ICCA Congress Series No. 4, Deventer/Boston 1988, 283; zitiert: Gaillard, in: Sanders (Hrsg.), ICCA Series No.4

Gibson-Jarvie/Hawker — A Guide to Commercial Arbitration under the 1979 Act, London, 1980

Goldstajn, Aleksander — The Relationship Between International Commercial Arbitration and National Adjudication, in: Voskuil/Wade (Hrsg.), Hague-Zagreb Essays 4 on the Law of International Trade, Den-Haag 1983, S. 297; zitiert: Goldstajn, in: Voskuil/Wade (Hrsg.), Hague-Zagreb Essays 4

Goodhart, A.L. — Appeals on Questions of Fact, Law Quar.Rev. 1955, 402

Goodman, Ronald — UNCITRAL Model Law on International Commercial Arbitration: Divergent Approaches in England and Scotland - A Question of Appeal?, Bus.L. 1990, 250

Gottwald, Peter — Die Sachliche Kontrolle internationaler Schiedssprüche durch staatliche Gerichte, Beiträge zum internationalen Verfahrensrecht und zur Schiedsgerichtsbarkeit - Festschrift Heinrich Nagel, Münster 1987, S. 54; zitiert: Gottwald, in: FS Nagel

Granzow, J.H. — Das UNCITRAL-Modellgesetz über die internationale Handelsschiedsgerichtsbarkeit von 1985, Hamburg 1987

Gross, Peter — Separability Comes of Age in England: Harbour v. Kansa and Clause 3 of the Draft Bill, Arb.Int'l 1995, 85

Habscheid, Walther — Das Problem der Kompetenz-Kompetenz der Schiedsgerichte, SJZ 1982, 321

— Zur Frage der Kompetenz-Kompetenz der Schiedsgerichte, in: Grunsky (Hrsg.), Festschrift für Fritz Baur, Tübingen 1981, S. 425; zitiert: Habscheid, in: FS Baur

Hacking, L.J. — The "Stated Case" Abolished: The United Kingdom Arbitration Act of 1979, Int'l Lawy. 1980, 95

— U.K. Arbitration Act (1979) and U.K. State Immunity Act (1978), Int'l Bus.Lawy. 1980, 161

—	Where We Are Now: Trends and Developments Since the Arbitration Act (1979), J.Int'l Arb. 1985, 7
Hailsham, Quintin (Hrsg.)	Halsbury's Laws of England, 4. Aufl., Band 2, London 1991, zitiert: Halsbury's, Band 2
Harnik, Hans	Recognition and Enforcement of Foreign Arbitral Awards, Am.J.Comp.L. 1983, 703
Harris/Meisel	Public Policy and the Enforcement of International Arbitration Awards: Controlling the Unruly Horse, Lloyd's Mar. & Com.L.Q. 1998, 568
Harris/Planterose/Tecks	The Arbitration Act 1996, London 1996
Hepburn, Samantha	Natural Justice and Commercial Arbitration, Aust.Bus.L.Rev. 1993, 43
Herrmann, A.H.	The Draft English Bill: Pulling the Wrong Punches, Arb.Int'l 1994, 185
Herrmann, Gerold	For an UNCITRAL Model Restatement of Arbitration Law in the UK, Arb.Int'l 1988, 62
—	Overcoming Regional Differences: Arbitral Practice, Comparative Law and the Approximation of Laws, in: Sanders (Hrsg.), ICCA Congress Series No. 4, Deventer/Boston 1988, S. 291; zitiert: Herrmann, in: Sanders (Hrsg.), ICCA Series No. 4
—	The Arbitration Agreement as the Foundation of Arbitration and its Recognition by the Courts, ICCA Congress Series No. 6, S. 41; zitiert: Herrmann, in: Sanders (Hrsg.), ICCA Congress Series No. 6
—	The Role of the Courts Under the UNCITRAL Model Law Script, in: Lew (Hrsg.), Contemporary Problems in International Arbitration, London 1986, S. 164; zitiert: Herrmann, in: Lew (Hrsg.), Contemporary Problems
—	The UNCITRAL Model Law on International Commercial Arbitration: Introduction and General

	Provisions, in: Sarcevic (Hrsg.), Essays on International Arbitration, London/Dordrecht 1989, S. 3; zitiert: Herrmann, in: Sarcevic (Hrsg.)
—	The UNCITRAL Model Law - its Background, Salient Features and Purposes, Arb. Int'l 1985, 1
—	UNCITRAL's Work Towards a Model Law on International Commercial Arbitration, Pace L.Rev. 1983, 537
Hill, Jonathan	Some Private International Law Aspects of the Arbitration Act 1996, I.C.L.Q. 1997, 274
—	The Jurisdiction of the Courts to Grant Interim Measures in Support of Arbitration Proceedings, Lloyd's Mar. & Com.L.Q. 1992, 310
—	The Scope of the Doctrine of Separability, Lloyd's Mar. & Com.L.Q. 1992, 306
Holtzmann/Neuhaus	A Guide to the UNCITRAL Model Law on International Commercial Arbitration - Legislative History and Commentary, Deventer/Boston 1988
Hong Kong Law Reform Commission	Report on the Adoption of the UNCITRAL Model Law of Arbitration (Topic 17) Hong Kong 1987; zitiert: Hong Kong Law Reform Commission, Report
Hoyle, Mark	Preventing a Defendant From Leaving the Jurisdiction of the English Courts, Business L.R. 1988, 251
Hüßlein-Stich, Gabriele	Das UNCITRAL Modellgesetz über die internationale Handelsschiedsgerichtsbarkeit, Köln 1990
Hunter, Martin	Arbitration Procedure in England: Past, Present and Future, Arb.Int'l 1985, 82
—	Judicial Assistance for the Arbitrator, in: Lew (Hrsg.), Contemporary Problems in International Arbitration, London 1986, S. 195; zitiert: Hunter, in: Lew (Hrsg.), Contemporary Problems

—	UNCITRAL Model Law - Which Road Should London Take?, Arbitration 1984, 288
Hunter/Landau	The English Arbitration Act 1996 - Text and Notes, Den Haag/London/Boston 1998
International Chamber of Commerce	Guide to Arbitration, Paris 1983; zitiert: ICC, Guide
Jaffe, Paul	Judicial Supervision of Commercial Arbitration in England, Arbitration 1989, 184
—	The Judicial Trend Toward Finality of Commercial Arbitral Awards in England, Tex.Int'l L.J. 1989, 67
Jones, Timothy	Judicial Interpretation of the Arbitration Act 1996, Arbitration 1999, 35
Kaplan, Neill	The Model Law in Hong Kong - Two Years On, Arb.Int'l 1992, 223
Kendall, M.T.	Barristers' Independence and Disclosure, Arb.Int'l 1992, 287
Kerr, Michael	Arbitration and the Courts - The UNCITRAL Model Law, I.C.L.Q. 1985, 1
—	Commercial Dispute Resolution - The Changing Scene, in: Bos/Brownlie (Hrsg.), Liber Amicorum for Lord Wilberforce, S. 111; zitiert: Kerr, in: Bos/Brownlie
—	International Arbitration v. Litigation, J.B.L. 1980, 164
Kornblum, Udo	"Ordre Public Transnational", "Ordre Public International" und "Ordre Public Interne" im Recht der Privaten Schiedsgerichtsbarkeit, Beiträge zum internationalen Verfahrensrecht und zur Schiedsgerichtsbarkeit - Festschrift Heinrich Nagel, Münster 1987, S. 140 ff; zitiert: Kornblum, in: FS Nagel
Landau, Toby	The Effect of the New English Arbitration Act on Institutional Arbitration, J.Int'l Arb. 1996, 113
Lawrence, Roland	Appeal to the Court, N.L.J. 1983, 623

Lew, Julian — Determination of Arbitrators' Jurisdiction and the Public Policy Limitations on that Jurisdiction, in: ders. (Hrsg.), Contemporary Problems in International Arbitration, London 1986, S. 75; zitiert: Lew, in: ders. (Hrsg.), Contemporary Problems

— — The Recognition and Enforcement of Arbitration Awards in England, Int'l.Law. 1976, 425

Lewis, Charles — Leave to Appeal Under the Arbitration Act 1979, Lloyd's Mar. & Com.L.Q. 1982, 271

Lionnet, Klaus — Should the Procedural Law Applicable to International Arbitration be Denationalised or Unified? - The Answer of the UNCITRAL Model Law, J.Int'l Arb. 1991, 5

— — The UNCITRAL Model Law: A German Perspective, Arb.Int'l 1990, 343

Littman, Mark — England Reconsiders "The Stated Case", Int'l Law. 1979, 253

Loble/Mendelblatt — National Report: England and Wales, in: Association Internationale des Jeunes Avocats (Hrsg.), Evidence in International Arbitration Proceedings, London 1994, S. 113; zitiert: Loble/Mendelblatt, in: National Report

Lord/Salzedo — Guide to the Arbitration Act 1996, Great Britain 1996

MacFarlane, Thomas — Appeal from an Arbitral Award: Section 1 of the Arbitration Act 1979, B.L.R. 1983, 154

Malek, Ali — Judicial Review of Arbitration Awards after The Nema, N.L.J. 1981, 1302

Mann, F.A. — Lex Facit Arbitrum, in: Sanders (Hrsg.), International Arbitration - Liber Amicorum for Martin Domke, Den Haag 1967, S. 157; zitiert: Mann, in: Sanders (Hrsg.), International Arbitration

— — Private Arbitration and Public Policy, Civ.Just. Quart 1985, 257

Manson, Keith	The Inherent Jurisdiction of the Court, Aust.L.J. 1983, 449
Marriot, Arthur	Changes in Arbitration Law and Practice, Arbitration 1993, 41
—	The New Arbitration Bill, Arbitration 1996, 97
Marshall, Enid	Revocation of Arbitrator's Authority Under Arbitration Act 1950, s. 1, J.B.L. 1984, 46
Martinez, Ramona	Recognition and Enforcement of International Arbitral Awards Under the United Nations Convention of 1958, Int'l.Law. 1990, 487
Maxwell, Karen	The English Court's Assistance to Overseas Arbitration - Muddy Waters in the Arbitration Act 1996, Arb.Int'l 1997, 431
Mayer, Pierre	Seeking the Middle Ground of Court Control: A Reply to I.N. Duncan Wallace, Arb.Int'l 1991, 311
Meisel, Frank	The Changing Role of the High Court in Relation to Supervision of Commercial Arbitrations, Cahiers de Droit 1984, 653
Melis, Werner	Arbitration and the Courts, in: Sanders (Hrsg.), UNCITRAL's Projekt for a Model Law on International Commercial Arbitration, Deventer 1984, S. 83
Menzies, Ian	1996 And All That, Arb. & Disp.Res.J. 1997, 197
Merkin, Robert	Arbitration Act 1996 - An Annotated Guide, London 1996; zitiert: Merkin, Arbitration Act 1996
—	Arbitration Law, London 1991
Metzger, E.F.	Competénce-Compétence des Arbitres et Endépendance de la Convention Arbitrale dans la Convention dite Européenne sur l' Arbitrage Commercial International de 1961, in: Associazione Italiana per l' Arbitrato (Hrsg.) Commercial Arbitration: Essays in Memoriam, Eugenion Minoli, Turin 1974, 315; zitiert: Metzger, in: Commercial Arbitration

Michell, Paul — The Mareva Injunction in Aid of Foreign Proceedings, Osgoode Hall L.J. 1996, 741

Miller, Francis — Arbitration Act 1996 - The Proceedings in Parliament, Westminster, Arbitration 1996, 250

Murray, John — The UNCITRAL Model Law and Judicial Control of Arbitration in Scotland, Arb.Int'l 1993, 97

Mustill, Michael — Arbitration: History and Background, J.Int'l Arb. 1989, 43

— Comments and Conclusions, in: ICC International Court of Arbitration (Hrsg.), Conservatory and Provisional Measures in International Arbitration, Paris 1993, S. 118; zitiert: Mustill, in: ICCA

— Contemporary Problems in International Commercial Arbitration: A Response, Int'l Bus.Lawy. 1989, 161

— Delays in Arbitration: the Role of the Court, Arbitration 1986, 163

— Distinctive Features of English Commercial Arbitration, Arkiv for Sjorett 1976-77, 321

— Keynote Speach, in: Sanders (Hrsg.), ICCA Congress Series No. 6, Boston - Deventer 1993, S. 13; zitiert: Mustill, in: Sanders (Hrsg.)

— Transnational Arbitration in English Law, C.L.P. 1984, 133

Mustill/Boyd — Commercial Arbitration, 2. Aufl., London - Edinburgh 1989; zitiert: Mustill/Boyd

Nathan, K.V. — Arbitrate or Litigate - Powers of the Court, Arbitration 1989, 285

Neill, Patrick — New Zealand and the UNCITRAL Model Law, Arb.Int'l 1990, 271

New York State Bar Association, International Litigation Committee, Commercial and Federal Litigation Section — Report: The UNCITRAL Model Law on International Commercial Arbitration, N.Y.U.J.Int'l Law & Pol. 1990, 87; zitiert: New York State Bar Association

Nöcker, Thomas — Das Recht der Schiedsgerichtsbarkeit in Kanada, Heidelberg 1988

North/Fawcett (Hrsg.) — Cheshire & North Private International Law, 11. Aufl., London 1987

Okekeifere, Andrew — The UNCITRAL Model Law and the Problem of Delay in International Commercial Arbitration, J.Int'l Arb. 1996, 125

Parc, William — Judicial Controls in the Arbitral Process, Arb.Int'l 1989, 231

— — Judicial Supervision of Transnational Commercial Arbitration: The English Arbitration Act 1979, Harvard Int.L.J.1980, 87

— — The Influence of National Legal Systems on International Commercial Arbitration: Recent Developments in English Arbitration Law, in: Carbonneau (Hrsg.), Resolving Transnational Disputes Through International Arbitration - Sixth Socol Colloquium, Charlottesville 1984, S. 80; zitiert: Parc, in: Carbonneau (Hrsg.), Recent Developments

— — The Lex Loci Arbitri and International Commercial Arbitration, I.C.L.Q. 1983, 21

Parc/Paulsson — The Binding Force of International Arbitral Awards, Virg.J.Int'l L. 1983, 253

Parker of Waddington, L.J. — The Development of Commercial Arbitration, J.B.L. 1959, 213

— — The History and Development of Commercial Arbitration, Jerusalem 1959

Parker School of Foreign and Comparative Law	Commercial Arbitration: An International Bibliography, Deventer-New York 1992
Paulsson, Jan	Arbitration Unbound: An Award Detached from the Law of its Country of Origin, I.C.L.Q 1981, 358
—	Delocalisation of International Commercial Arbitration: When and Why it Matters, I.C.L.Q. 1983, 53
Potter, Patrick	International Commercial Arbitration in the United States: Considering Whether to Adopt UNCITRAL's Model Law, Mich.J.Int'l L. 1989, 912
Quigley, Leonard	Accession by the United States to the United Nations Convention on the Recognition and Enforcement of Foreign Arbitral Awards, Y.L.J. 1961, 1049
Rawlings, Jonathan	A Mandatory Stay, Arb.Int'l 1997, 421
Redfern, Alan	Arbitration and the Courts: Interim Measures of Protection - Is the Tide About to Turn?, Tex.Int'l L.J. 1995, 71
—	England as Forum for the Arbitration of International Construction Disputes, Int'l Constr.L.Rev., 258
—	The Arbitration Act 1996: A Major Opportunity for the International Arbitrator, Arb. & Disp.Res.J. 1997, 172
Redfern/Hunter	Law and Practice of International Commercial Arbitration, 2. Aufl., London 1991
Rhodes, Peter	Judicial Review of Commercial Arbitration, H.K.L.J. 1984, 159
Roebuck, Derek	The Myth of Judicial Jealousy, Arb.Int'l 1994, 395
Rogers, Andrew	Commercial Dispute Resolution: Litigation, Diskussion Paper, Sydney 1988
—	The Extra-Territorial Reach of the Mareva Injunction, Lloyd's Mar. & Com.L.Q. 1991, 231

—	The UNCITRAL Model Law: An Australian Perspective, Arb. Int'l 1990, 348
Rokison, Kenneth	"... Pastures New" - The 1997 Freshfield Lecture, Arb.Int'l 1988, 361
—	The Sources and Limits of the Arbitrator's Powers in England, in: Lew (Hrsg.), Contemporary Problems in International Arbitration, London 1986, S. 86; zitiert: Rokison, in: Lew (Hrsg.), Contemporary Problems
—	Towards More Effective Arbitration - A View from Counsel, Arbitration 1980, 88
Rosen, Janet	Arbitration Under Private International Law: the Doctrins of Separability and Competence de la Competence, Fordham Int'l.L.J. 1994, 599
Rutherford/Sims	Arbitration Act 1996: A Practical Guide, London 1996
Samuel, Adam	Arbitration Statutes in England and the USA, Arb. & Disp.Res.J. 1999, 2
—	Jurisdictional Problems in International Commercial Arbitration: A Study of Belgian, Dutch, English, French, Swedish, Swiss, U.S. and West German Law, Zürich 1989
—	Developments in English Arbitration Law Since the 1984 Antaios Decision, J.Int'l Arb. 1988, 9
—	Separability in English Law - Should an Arbitration Clause be Regarded as an Agreement Separate and Collateral to a Contract in Which it is Contained?, J.Int'l Arb. 1986, 95
—	The 1979 Arbitration Act - Judicial Review of Arbitration Awards on the Merits in England, J.Int'l Arb. 1985, 53
—	The Recognition and Enforcement of Foreign Judgments and Arbitral Awards in England with a Comparative Look at the United States of America,

in: Knoepfler (Hrsg.), Le Juriste Suisse Face au Droit et aux Jugements Étrangers, S. 107; zitiert: Samuel, in: Knoepfler (Hrsg.)

Sanders, Pieter — A Twenty Year Review of the Convention on the Recognition and Enforcement of Foreign Arbitral Awards, Int'l Law. 1979, 269

— L'Autonomie de la Clause Compromissoire, in: ICC (Hrsg.), Hommage à Frederic Eisenmann, Paris 1978, S. 31; zitiert: Sanders, in: Eisenmann

— L'Intervention du Juge dans la Procédure Arbitrale, Revue Arbitrage 1980, 238

— The New Arbitration Act 1979, Arbitration 1980, 11

Sandrock, Otto — Dispute Resolution in International Business Transactions, in: Norton (Hrsg.), Public International Law and the Future World Order, Liber Amicorum in Honor of A.J. Thomas Jr., Littleton/Col. 1987, S. 8-1; zitiert: Sandrock, in: Norton (Hrsg.)

— Handbuch der Internationalen Vertragsgestaltung, Ein Leitfaden für den Abschluß von Verträgen im Internationalen Wirtschaftsverkehr, Heidelberg 1980; zitiert: Sandrock, Internationale Vertragsgestaltung

— The Place of Arbitration and the Law Applicable to the Merits of the Dispute, in: Storme/de Ly (Hrsg.), The Place of Arbitration, Third International Symposium on the Law of International Commercial Arbitration, Ghent, 30-31 May 1991, Ghent 1992, S. 89; zitiert: Sandrock, in: Storme/de Ly

— Über Sinn und Methode zivilistischer Rechtsvergleichung, Frankfurt 1966; zitiert: Rechtsvergleichung

— Zügigkeit und Leichtigkeit versus Gründlichkeit, Internationale Schiedsverfahren in der Bundesrepublik Deutschland - Zugleich zu BGH v. 26.09.1985 - III ZR 16/84, JZ 1986, 370

— Zur Prozeßkostensicherheit in internationalen Schiedsverfahren, in: Festschrift für Hans Friedhelm Gaul zum 70. Geburtstag, Bielefeld 1997, S. 607; zitiert: Sandrock, in: FS Gaul

Sandrock/Hentzen Enforcing Foreign Arbitral Awards in the Federal Republic of Germany: The Example of a United States Award, Transnat'l Law. 1989, 49

Sandrock/Nöcker Einstweilige Maßnahmen internationaler Schiedsgerichte: bloße Papiertieger?, Jahrbuch für die Praxis der Schiedsgerichtsbarkeit Bd. 1 (1987), S. 74

Saville, Mark An Answer to Some Criticisms of the Arbitration Act 1996, Arb. & Disp.Res.J. 1997, 155

— The Arbitration Act 1996, Lloyd's Mar. & Com.L.Q. 1997, 502

— The Origin of the New English Arbitration Act 1996: Reconciling Speed with Justice in the Decisionmaking Process, Arb.Int'l 1997, 237

Schlosser, Peter Das Recht der Internationalen Privaten Schiedsgerichtsbarkeit, Tübingen 1975; zitiert: Schlosser, Schiedsgerichtsbarkeit

— The Competence of Arbitrators and of Courts, Arb.Int'l 1992, 189

Schmitthoff, Clive Arbitration - The Next Step in the United Kingdom, Arb.Int'l 1988, 67

— Commercial Law in a Changing Economic Climate, 2. Aufl., London 1981, S. 64; zitiert: Schmitthoff, Commercial Law

— Finality of Arbitral Awards and Judicial Review, in: Lew (Hrsg.), Contemporary Problems in International Arbitration, London 1986, S. 230; zitiert:

	Schmitthoff, in: Lew (Hrsg.), Contemporary Problems
—	Schmitthoff's Export Trade - The Law and Practice of International Trade, 9. Aufl., London 1990; zitiert: Schmitthoff, Export Trade
—	The Jurisdiction of the Arbitrator, in: Schultsz/v.d. Berg (Hrsg.), The Art of Arbitration: Essays on International Arbitration - Liber Amicorum Pieter Sanders, Deventer 1982, S. 285; zitiert: Schmitthoff, in: Schultsz/v.d. Berg
—	The Reform of the English Law of Arbitration, J.B.L. 1977, 305
—	The Supervisory Jurisdiction of the English Court, in: Sanders (Hrsg.) International Arbitration - Liber Amicorum for Martin Domke, Den Haag 1967, S. 289; zitiert: Schmitthoff, in: Sanders (Hrsg.)
—	The United Kingdom Arbitration Act 1979, Yearbook of Commercial Arbitration 1980, S. 231; zitiert: Schmitthoff, Yearbook 1980
Schwab, Karl Heinz	Schiedsgerichtsbarkeit, 3.Aufl., München 1979, S. 186 f
Schwebel, S.M.	The Hersch Lauterpacht Memorial Lectures - International Arbitration: Three Salient Problems, Cambridge 1987
Scott, John	Removal of an Arbitrator for Misconduct: The Remedy for Breach of Natural Justice, Constr. L.J. 1989, 185
Semple, Walter	The UNCITRAL Model Law and Provisional Measures in International Commercial Arbitration, Arb. & Disp.Res.L.J. 1994, 269
—	The UNCITRAL Model Law and the United Kingdom, Arbitration 1990, 95

Shenoi, Allan — Arbitration - Judicial Review of "One-Off" Arbitration Restricted in Great Britain Pursuant to 1979 Arbitration Act, Tex.Int'l L.J. 1982, 258

Shenton, David — Attachments and Other Interim Court Remedies in Support of Arbitration, Int'l Bus.Lawy. 1984, 101

— — The Enforcement of International Commercial Arbitral Awards in English Courts, Int'l Bus.Lawy. 1980, 35

Shenton/Toland — London as a Venue for International Arbitration: The Arbitration Act 1979, Law & Pol'y.Int'l.Bus. 1980, 643

Sheridan, Peter — Stay of Proceedings: the New Law in Construction, Arb. & Disp.Res L.J. 1997, 208

Sleightholme, James — The Arbitration Act 1996: A Commentary, Business L.R. 1997, 159

Smedresmann, Peter — The Arbitration Act 1979, J.Mar.L. & Com. 1979-80, 319

Sonnauer, Heinz — Die Kontrolle der Schiedsgerichte durch die staatlichen Gerichte, Köln/Berlin/Bonn/München 1992

Stalev, Zhivko — Interim Measures of Protection in the Context of Arbitration, in: Sanders (Hrsg.), ICCA Congress Series No. 6, Deventer-Boston 1993, S. 103; zitiert: Stalev, in: Sanders (Hrsg.), ICCA Congress Series No. 6

Starke, L.G. — Inherent Jurisdiction of Courts in Procedural Matters Regardless of the Relevant Applicable Statute, Aust.L.J. 1981, 47

Staughton, Christopher — Arbitration Act 1979 - A Pragmatic Compromise, New L.J. 1979, 920

Steyn, Johan — Arbitration and the Courts: Arbitration Systems in England and Wales and Recent Changes in Arbitration Law, Arbitration 1980, 146

— Englands Response to the UNCITRAL Model Law, Arb.Int'l, 1

— Arbitration in England: The Current Issues, Int'l Bus.Lawy. 1987, 432

— Remedies Against the Reluctant Respondent: The Position Under English Law, Arb.Int'l 1989, 294

— Towards a New English Arbitration Act, Arb.Int'l 1991, 17

Street, Laurence — Court Review of Awards - An Australian Perspective, The Institute of Arbitrators, Australia International Arbitration Conference, Discussion Paper, Sydney 1988, S. 1; zitiert: Street, Court Review of Awards

Strohbach, Heinz — Composition of the Arbitral Tribunal and Making of the Award, in: Sanders (Hrsg.), ICCA Congress Series No. 2, Deventer-Boston 1984, S. 103; zitiert: Strohbach, in: Sanders (Hrsg.), ICCA Congress Series No. 2

Sturges, W.A. — Arbitration - What is it?, N.Y.U.L.R. 1960, 1031

Svernlöv, Carl — The Evolution of Separability in England: Now Virtually Complete?, J.Int'l Arb. 1992, 115

— What Isn't Ain't: the Current Status of the Doctrine of Separability, J.Int'l Arb. 1991, 37

Szurski, Tadeusz — Arbitration Agreement and Competence of the Arbitral Tribunal, in: Sanders (Hrsg.), ICCA Congress Series No. 2, Deventer-Boston 1984, 53; zitiert: Szurski, in: Sanders (Hrsg.), ICCA Congress Series No. 2

Thieffry, Jean — Commentaire, in: Antaki/Prujiner (Hrsg.), Actes du 1e Colloque sur l'Arbitrage Commercial International, Montréal 1986, S. 379; zitiert: Thieffry, in: Antaki/Prujiner (Hrsg.)

Thomas, Rhidian — An Appraisal of the Arbitration Act 1979, Lloyd's Mar. & Com.L.Q. 1981, 199

—	International Commercial Arbitration Agreements and the Enforcement of Foreign Arbitral Awards - A Commentary on the Arbitration Act 1975, Lloyd's Mar. & Com.L.Q. 1981, 17
—	Power of Court to Extend Time for Commencing Arbitration Proceedings, Lloyd's Mar. & Com.L.Q. 1981, 529
—	Removals of Arbitrators by the Court, Arbitration 1982, 136
—	The Antaios: The Nema Guidelines Reconsidered, J.B.L. 1985, 200
—	The Judicial Supervision of Arbitral References Involving an Allegation of Fraud, Civ.Just.Q. 1990, 381
Trappe, Johannes	Links Between Arbritrators and the Court, Arbitration 1978, 69
Uff/Keating	Should England Reconsider the UNCITRAL Model Law or Not?, Arb.Int'l 1994, 179
Ungar, Kenneth	The Enforcement of Arbitral Awards under UNCITRALS Model Law on International Commercial Arbitration, Colum.J.Transnat'l L. 1987, 717
Van den Berg, Albert	The New York Arbitration Convention of 1958, Deventer 1981
Veeder, V.V.	National Report: England, in: ICC, International Handbook on Commercial Arbitration, 23. Ergänzung, Paris/New York März 1997; zitiert: Veeder, England
Wagoner, David	Interim Relief in International Arbitration, Arbitration 1996, 131
Wallace, Duncan	Control by Courts: A Plea for More, Not Less, Arb.Int'l 1990, 253
—	First Impressions of the 1996 Arbitration Act, Int'l Constr.L.Rev. 1997, 71

Walton/Vitoria — Russel on the Law of Arbitration, 20. Aufl., London 1982; zitiert: Russel on Arbitration

Warren, Derrill — The Concept of 'Null and Void' in International Arbitration, Arb.J. 1990, 57

Weiss, Andrew — The Status of the UNCITRAL Model Law on International Commercial Arbitration Vis-A-Vis the ICC, LCIA and UNCITRAL Arbitration Rules: Conflict or Complement, Syracuse.J.Int'l L. & Com. 1986, 367

Wetter, Gillis — The Importance of Having a Connection, Arb. Int'l 1987, 329

— — The Mustill Committee Report on the UNCITRAL Model Law, Arb.Int'l 1990, 268

Whiteley, Miranda — Stays and Summary Judgment Under the Arbitration Act 1996 - The Halki, 1998 Lloyd's Mar. & Com.L.Q. 1998, 164

Wilberforce, L. — Resolving International Commercial Disputes: The Alternatives, in: Paterson/Thompson (Hrsg.), UNCITRAL Arbitration Model in Canada, S. 7; zitiert: Wilberforce, in: Paterson/Thompson (Hrsg.)

Willoughby/Connal — The Mareva Injunction: A Cruel Tyranny, E.I.P.R 1997, 479

Varady, Tibor — On Appointing Authorities in International Commercial Arbitration, Emory J.Int.Disp.Res. 1988, 311

Voskuil/Freedberg-Swartzburg — Composition of the Arbitral Tribunal, in : Sarcevic (Hrsg.), Essays on International Commercial Arbitration, London/Dordrecht 1989, S. 64; zitiert: Voskuil/Freedberg-Swartzburg, in: Sarcevic (Hrsg.)

Zekos, Georgios — The Role of Courts in Commercial and Maritime Arbitration Under English Law, J.Int'l Arb. 1998, 51

Zicherman, David — The Use of Pre-Judgment Attachments and Temporary Injunctions in International Commercial Arbitration Proceedings: A Comparative Analysis of the British and American Approaches, Univ. of Pittsburgh L.Rev. 1989, 667

Zweigert/Kötz — An Introduction to Comparative Law, 2. Aufl., Oxford 1993

Entscheidungsregister

Aden Refinery Co. Ltd. v. Ugland Management Co. Ltd. ("The Ugland Obo One") [1987] Q.B. 650, 651, 656

Agro Company of Canada Ltd. v. Richmond Shipping Ltd. [1972] 2 Lloyd's Rep. 355

Aiden Shipping Co. Ltd. v. Interbulk Ltd. ("The Vimeira (No 2)") [1985] 2 Lloyd's Rep. 377, 400

Antaios Compania Naviera S.A. v. Salen Rederierna A.B. ("The Antaios") [1985] A.C. 191

Antaios, The, siehe Antaios Compania Naviera S.A. v. Salen Rederierna A.B.

Arab African Energy Corporation Ltd. v. Olieprodukten Nederland B.V. [1983] 2 Lloyd's Rep. 419

Ashville Investments Ltd. v. Elmer Contractors Ltd. [1988] 2 All E.R. 577

Babanaft International Co. S.A. v. Avant Petroleum Inc. ("The Oltenia"), [1982] 2 Lloyd's Rep. 99, 106

Bache v. Billingham (1894) 1 Q.B. 107

Baleares, The, siehe Geogas S.A. v. Trammo Gas Ltd.

Bank Mellat v. Helleniki Techniki S.A. [1984] Q.B. 291, 301

Beswick v. Beswick [1968] A.C. 58

BKMI Industrieanlagen v. Dutco [1994] A.D.R.L.J. 36

Bremer Handesgesellschaft m.b.H. v. Ets Soules et Cie and Anthony Scott [1985] 1 Lloyd's Rep. 160, 164

Bremer Vulkan Schiffbau und Maschinenfabrik v. South India Shipping Corpn. Ltd. ("The Bremer Vulkan") [1979] 3 All E.R. 194; [1980] 1 All E.R. 420; [1981] A.C. 909, 979, 980

Bremer Vulkan, The, siehe Bremer Vulkan Schiffbau und Maschinenfabrik v. South India Shipping Corpn. Ltd.

Bulk Oil (Zug) A.G. v. Sun International Ltd. and Sun Oil Trading Co. [1983] 2 Lloyd's Rep 587, 589; [1984] 1 Lloyd's Rep. 655, 657

Bulk Oil (Zug) A.G. v. Trans-Asiatic Oil Ltd. S.A. [1973] 1 Lloyd's Rep. 129

B.V.S. S.A. and Another v. Kerman Shipping Co. S.A. ("The Kerman") [1982] 1 W.L.R. 166, 171

Caledonian Insurance Co. v. Gilmour [1893] A.C. 85

Champsey Bhara & Co. v. Jivraj Balloo Spinning and Weaving Co. [1923] A.C. 480, 487

Channel Tunnel Group Ltd. & France Manche S.A. v. Balfour Beatty Construction Ltd. [1992] 2 W.L.R. 741, 757

Christopher Brown Ltd. v. Genossenschaft Österreichischer Waldbesitzer Holzwirtschaftsbetriebe Registrierte Genossenschaft mbH [1954] 1 Q.B. 8, 12, 13

City Centre Properties (ITC Pensions) Ltd. v. Matthew Hall & Co. Ltd. [1969] 1 W.L.R. 772, 779

Clough v. County Livestock Insurance Association Ltd. (1916) 85 L.J.K.B. 1185

Coastal States Trading (UK) Ltd. v. Mebro Mineralölhandels GmbH [1986] 1 Lloyd's Rep. 465, 467

Compagnie Européenne de Céreals S.A. v. Tradax Export S.A. [1986] 2 Lloyd's Rep 301.

Consolidated Investment and Contracting Co. v. Saponaria Shipping Co. Ltd. ("The Virgo") [1978] 2 Lloyd's Rep. 167

Cook v. Catchpole (1864) 11 L.T. 264

Coppée-Lavalin S.A./N.V. v. Ken-Ren Chemicals and Fertilisers Limited [1994] 2 All E.R. 449, 470, 471

Czarnikow v. Roth, Schmidt & Co. [1922] 2 K.B. 478.

Dallal v. Bank Mellat [1986] Q.B. 441

Dalmia Dairy Industries Ltd. v. National Bank of Pakistan [1978] 2 Lloyd's Rep. 223, 284, 286

Derry v. Peek (1889) 14 App.Cas. 337

D/S A/S Idaho v. Peninsular and Oriental Steam Navigation Co. ("The Strathnewton") [1982] 2 Lloyd's Rep. 296, 348

Eastcheap Dried Fruit Co. v. NV Gebroeders Catz Handelsvereeniging [1962] 1 Lloyd's Rep. 283

Empresa Cubana de Fletes v. Kissavos Shipping Co. S.A. ("The Agathon") (No. 2) [1984] 1 Lloyd's Rep. 183, 192

Ets. Soules & Cie v. International Trade Development Co. Ltd. [1979] 2 Lloyd's Rep. 122

Exormisis Shipping S.A. v. Oonsoo, The Democratic Peoples Republic of Korea and The Korean Foreign Transportation Corporation (No 1) [1975] 1 Lloyd's Rep 432

Faghirzadeh v. Rudolf Wolff (SA) (Pty) Ltd. [1977] 1 Lloyd's Rep 630, 639

Freeman & Sons Ltd. v. Chester RDC [1911] 1 K.B. 783

Geogas S.A. v. Trammo Gas Ltd. ("The Baleares") [1993] 1 Lloyd's Rep. 215, 231

Glafki Shipping Co. S.A. v. Pinions Shipping Co. No. 1 ("The Maira") [1982] 1 Lloyd's Rep. 257, 261)

Goddard v. Grey (1870) 6 Q.B. 139

Granvias Oceanicas Armadora S.A. v. Jibsen Trading Co. ("The Kavo Peiratis") [1977] 2 Lloyd's Rep. 344, 349
Grech v. Board of Trade (1923) 130 L.T. 15
Green v. Howell [1910] 1 Ch. 495
Green Star Shipping Co. v. London Assurance (1928) 31 Ll.L.R. 4
Hagop Ardahalian v. Unifert International S.A. ("The Ellissar") [1984] 2 Lloyd's Rep. 84
Halfdan Grieg & Co. A/S v. Sterling Coal and Navigation Corpn. ("The Lysland") [1973] 1 Q.B. 843, 863
Harbour Assurance Co. (UK) Ltd. v. Kansa General International Assurance Co. Ltd. [1993] 3 All E.R. 897
Hardwick Game Farm v. Suffolk Agricultural and Poultry Producers Association [1964] 2 Lloyd's Rep. 227
Hayter v. Nelson [1990] 2 Lloyd's Rep 265
Hersent v. United Towing Co. Ltd. ("The Tradesman") [1961] 2 Lloyd's Rep. 183
Heyman v. Darwins Ltd. [1942] 1 All E.R. 337
Hodgkinson v. Fernie (1857) 3 C.B.N.S. 189
Holgate v. Killik (1861) 7 H & N 418, 422
ICCO International Corpn. Co N.V. v. Interbulk Ltd. [1984] 2 Lloyd's Rep. 66, 75
International Bulk Shipping and Services v. Minerals and Metals Trading Corpn. of India [1996] 1 All E.R. 1017
Islamic Republic of Iran Shipping Lines v. Royal Bank of Scotland [1987] 1 Lloyd's Rep. 266
Islamic Republic of Iran Shipping Lines v. Zannis Compania Naviera S.A. [1991] 2 Lloyd's Rep. 265
Ismail v. Polish Ocean Lines [1976] 1 Q.B. 893
Italmare Shipping Co. v. Ocean Tanker Co. Inc. ("The Rio Sun") [1982] 1 W.L.R. 158, 162
Japan Line Ltd. v. Aggeliki Charis Compania Maritima S.A. ("The Angelic Grace") [1980] 1 Lloyd's Rep. 288.
Joe Lee Ltd. v. Lord Dalmeny [1927] 1 Ch. 300
Johnson v. Latham (1851) 20 L.J.Q.B. 236
J.T. Stratford & Sons Ltd. v. Lindley [1967] Lloyd's Rep. 133
Kent v. Elstob (1802) 3 East 18
Kerman, The, siehe B.V.S. S.A. and Another v. Kerman Shipping Co. S.A.
Kianta Osakeyhtio v. Britain and Overseas Trading Co. Ltd. [1954] 1 Lloyd's Rep. 247
Kill v. Hollister (1746) 1 Wils. 129

King v. Thomas Mc Kenna [1991] 1 All E.R. 653
K/S Norjarl A/S v. Hyundai Heavy Industries Co. Ltd. [1991] 3 All E.R. 211
Liberian Shipping Corpn. v. A. King & Sons Ltd. ("The Pegasus") [1967] 1 Lloyd's Rep. 302, 307, 309
Libra Shipping & Trading Corpn. Ltd. v. Northern Sales Ltd. ("The Aspen Trader") [1981] 1 Lloyd's Rep. 273
London and North Western and Great-Western Joint Rly. Companies v. Billington [1899] A.C. 79
London and North Western Rly. Co. v. Jones [1915] 2 K.B. 35
Mabanaft GmbH v. Consentino Shipping Company S.A. ("The Achillet") [1984] 2 Lloyd's Rep. 191, 192
MacPherson Train & Co Ltd. v. J. Milhem & Sons [1955] 2 Lloyd's Rep. 59
Mareva Compania Naviera S.A. v. International Bulk Carriers Limited [1975] 2 Loyd's Rep. 509.
Michael I. Warde v. Feedex International Inc. [1984] 1 Lloyd's Rep. 310, 311
Middlemiss and Gould v. Hartlepool Corpn. [1973] 1 All E.R. 172, 175
Miller's Timber Trust Co. Ltd. v. Plywood Factory Julius Potempa Ltd. (1939) 63 Ll.L.R. 184
Minister of Materials v. Steel Bros. & Co. Ltd. [1952] W.N. 114
Modern Engineering (Bristol) Ltd. v. C. Miskin & Son Ltd. [1981] 1 Lloyd's Rep. 135
Moran v. Lloyd's [1983] 2 All E.R. 20
Moscow V/O Exportkhleb v. Helmville Ltd. ("The Jocelyne") [1977] 2 Lloyd's Rep. 121
Navario Salvors Ltd. v. Navarino Recovery Ltd. (1925) 23 Ll.L.R. 36
Nema, The, siehe Pioneer Shipping Ltd. v. B.T.P. Tioxide Ltd.
Newgate v. Degelder (1666) 2 Keb. 10
Ninemia Maritime Corpn. v. Trave Schiffahrtsgesellschaft m.b.H. und Co. KG ("The Niedersachsen") [1983] 2 Lloyd's Rep. 600, 605
Northern Regional Health Authority v. Derek Crouch Construction Co. Ltd. [1984] 26 Build.L.R. 1
Obaseki Bros. v. Reif & Son [1952] 2 Lloyd's Rep. 264
Oltenia, The, siehe Babanaft International Co. S.A. v. Avant Petroleum Inc.
Oppenheim & Co. v. Mahomed Haneef [1922] 1 A.C. 482, 487
Orion Compania Espanola de Seguros v. Belfort Maatschappij voor Algemene Verzekeringeen [1962] 2 Lloyd's Rep. 257
Overseas Union Insurance Ltd. v. AA Mutual International Insurance Co. Ltd. [1988] 2 Lloyd's Rep. 63, 70, 71
Pan Atlantic Group Inc. v. Hassneh Insurance Co. of Israel Ltd. [1992] 2 Lloyd's Rep. 120

Pando Compania Naviera S.A. v. Filmo SAS [1975] Q.B. 742
Payne & Routh v. Hugh Baird & Sons (1921) 9 Ll.L.R. 167
Petraco (Bermuda) Ltd. v. Petromed International S.A. [1988] 2 Lloyd's Rep. 357
Phillip Alexander Securities and Futures Ltd. v. Bamberger, Urteil vom 12. Juli 1996, auzugsweise veröffentlicht in der Times vom 22. Juli 1996.
Pickethall v. Merhyr Tydvil Local Board (1886) 2 TLR 805
Pioneer Shipping Ltd. v. B.T.P. Tioxide Ltd. ("The Nema") [1980] 1 Lloyd's Rep. 519; [1982] A.C. 724
Pratt v. Swanmore Builders Ltd. and Baker [1980] 2 Lloyd's Rep. 504, 509, 512
President of India v. Jadranska Slobodna Plovidba [1992] 2 Lloyd's Rep. 274
Prodexport State Company for Foreign Trade v. E. D. & F. Mann Ltd. [1972] 2 Lloyd's Rep. 375 , 382; [1973] Q.B. 389, 395
Radford v. Hair and Others [1971] 1 Ch. 758
Radio Publicity (Universal) Ltd. v. Compagnie Luxembourgeoise de Radiodifusion [1936] 2 All E.R. 721
Re Boks & Co. and Peters Rushton & Co. Ltd. [1919] K.B. 491, 497
Re Fuerst Bros. & Co Ltd. and Stephenson [1951] 1 Lloyd's Rep. 429
Rena K, The [1979] 1 All E.R. 397, 407
Re Keighley, Maxsted & Co. and Durant & Co. [1893] 1 Q.B. 405
Re Montgomery Jones & Co. and Liebenthal & Co. (1898) 78 L.T.R. 406
Re Smith and Service and Nelson & Sons (1890) 25 Q.B.D. 545, 553
Richco International Ltd. v. Alfred C. Toepfer International ("The Bonde") [1991] 1 Lloyd's Rep. 136
River Plates Produkts Netherlands B.V. v. Etablissement Coargrain [1982] 1 Lloyd's Rep. 628
Rotheray & Sons Ltd. v. Carlo Bedarida & Co [1961] 1 Lloyd's Rep. 220
RS Hartley Ltd. v. Provincial Insurance Co Ltd. [1957] 1 Lloyd's Rep. 121
Russel v. Russel (1880) 14 Ch.D. 471
Schiffahrtsagentur Hamburg Middle East v. Virtue Shipping Corp. of Monrovia [1981] 1 Lloyd's Rep. 533, 538
Scott v. Avery (1856) 5 H.L.Cas. 811
Skips A/S Nordheim and Others v. Syrian Petroleum Co. Ltd. and Petrofina S.A. ("The Varenna") [1983] 2 Lloyd's Rep. 592, 597
Slade v. Metrodent Ltd. [1953] Q.B. 112
Soleimany v. Soleimany (19. Februar 1998), The Times, 3. März 1998
Spurrier v. La Cloche [1902] A.C. 446
Stinnes Interoil GmbH v. Halcoussis & Co ("The Yanxilas") [1982] 2 Lloyd's Rep. 445

Stockport Metropolitan Borough Council v. O'Reilly [1983] 2 Lloyd's Rep. 70, 78, 79

Succula and Pomona Shipping Co. Ltd. v. Harland and Wolff Ltd. [1980] 2 Lloyd's Rep. 381, 384

Thomas v. Countryside Council for Wales [1994] 4 All E.R. 853

Timmerman's Graan-En Maal Handel En Maalderij B.V. v. Sachs [1980] 1 Lloyd's Rep. 194

Toronto Rly Co. v. National British and Irish Millers Insurance Co. Ltd. (1914) 20 Com.Cas. 1

Tritonia Shipping Inc. v. South Nelson Forest Products Corpn. [1966] 1 Lloyd's Rep. 114

Vasso (owners) v. Vasso (cargo owners) ("The Vasso") [1983] 2 Lloyd's Rep. 346

Veritas Shipping Corpn. v. Anglo-Canadian Cement Ltd. [1966] 1 Lloyd's Rep. 76.

Vinava Shipping Co. Ltd. v. Finelvet A.G. ("The Chrysalis") [1983] 1 Lloyd's Rep. 503, 506

Vinior's Case (1610) 8 Co.Rep. 80

Voest-Alpine Aktiengesellschaft v. Ken-Ren Chemicals and Fertilisers Limited [1994] 2 All E.R. 449

Vosnoc Ltd. v. Transglobal Projects Ltd. [1998] 1 W.L.R. 101

Wallis v. Hirsh (1856) 1 C.B. 316

Westacre Investments Inc. v. Judoimport-SDPR Co. Ltd. and Others [1998] 2 Lloyd's Rep. 111

Wickham v. Harding (1859) 28 L.J.Ex. 215

Willesford v. Watson (1873) 8 Ch.App. 473, 480

Williams v. Wallis and Cox [1914] 2 K.B. 478, 485

Woodall v. Pearl Assurance Co. Ltd. [1919] 1 K.B. 593

Abkürzungsverzeichnis[1]

A.C.	Law Reports, Appeal Cases
A.D.R.J.	Alternative Dispute Resolution Journal
All E.R.	All England Law Reports
Am.Bus.L.J.	American Business Law Journal
Am.J.Comp.L.	American Journal of Comparative Law
Am.Rev.Int.Arb.	American Review of International Arbitration
App.Cas.	Appeal Cases, English Law Reports
Arb. & Disp.Res.L.J.	The Arbitration and Dispute Resolution Law Journal
Arb.J.	Arbitration Journal
Arb.Int'l	Arbitration International
Aust.Bus.L.Rev.	Australian Business Law Review
Aust.L.J.	Australian Law Journal
B.L.R.	Business Law Reports
Brit.J.Law & Soc.	British Journal of Law and Society
Build. & Constr.L.	Building and Construction Law
Build.L.R.	Builders Law Reports
Business L.R.	Business Law Review
Bus.L.	Business Lawyer
C.B.	Manning, Granger and Scott's English Common Bench Reports
C.B.N.S.	Manning, Granger and Scott's English Common Bench Reports
Ch.	Law Reports, Chancery
Ch.App.	English Law Reports, Chancery Appeals
Ch.D.	English Law Reports, Chancery Division
Civ.Just.Q.	Civil Justice Quarterly

1 Im Abkürzungsverzeichnis sind nur solche Abkürzungen gesondert aufgeführt, die nicht im
1) Kirchner, Hilbert, Abkürzungsverzeichnis der Rechtssprache, 4. Aufl., Berlin 1993, bzw.,
2) Duden, Rechtschreibung der deutschen Sprache und der Fremdwörter, 20. Aufl., Mannheim 1991
enthalten sind.

C.L.P.	Current Legal Problems
Colum.J.Transnat'l.Law	Columbia Journal of Transnational Law
Com.Cas.	Commercial Cases
Constr.L.J.	Construction Law Journal
Emory J.Int.Disp.Res.	Emory Journal of International Dispute Resolution
Doc.	Document
E.I.P.R.	European Intellectual Property Review
Fordham Int'l.L.J.	Fordham International Law Journal
Harvard Int.L.J.	Harvard International Law Journal
H.K.L.J.	Hong Kong Law Journal
H.L.Cas.	Clark's House of Lords Cases
H & N	Hurlstone and Norman's English Exchequer Reports
I.C.L.Q.	International and Comparative Law Quarterly
Int'l Bus.Lawy.	Internatioal Business Lawyer
Int'l Constr.L.Rev.	International Construction Law Review
Int'l.Law.	International Lawyer
J.	Justice
J.B.L.	Journal of Business Law
J.Int'l Arb.	Journal of International Arbitration
Law Inst.J.	Law Institute Journal
J.Mar.L. & Com.	Journal of Maritime Law and Commerce
K.B.	English Law Reports, Kings Bench
Keb.	Keble's English Kings Bench Reports
Law & Pol'y.Int'l.Bus.	Law and Policy in International Business
Law Quar.Rev.	Law Quarterly Review
L.C.P.	Law and Contemporary Problems
L.J.	Lord Justice
L.J.Ex.	Law Journal Reports, Exchequer Division, New Series
L.J.K.B.	Law Journal Reports, Kings Bench
Ll.L.R.	Lloyd's List Law Reports
Lloyd's Mar. & Com.L.Q.	Lloyd's Maritime and Commercial Law Quarterly
Lloyd's Rep.	Lloyd's (List) Law Reports
L.Q.Rev.	Law Quarterly Review
L.R.	Law Reports
L.T.	Law Times Journal
L.T.R.	Law Times Reports
Mich.J.Int'l L.	Michigan Journal of International Law

New L.J.	New Law Journal
N.Y.U.J.Int'l Law & Pol.	New York University Journal of International Law and Politics
Ohio St.J.Disp.Res.	Ohio State Journal of Dispute Resolution
Osgoode Hall L.J.	Osgoode Hall Law Journal
Pace L.Rev.	Pace Law Review
Q.B.D.	Law Reports, Queen's Bench Division
Q.B.	Queen's Bench Report, England
Queensland Inst.Techn.L.J.	Queensland Institute of Technology Law Journal
R.Gen.	Revue Générale de Droit
s	section
SJZ	Schweizerische Juristenzeitung
ss	sections
Suffolk Transnat'l L.J.	Suffolk Transnational Law Journal
Syracuse.J.Int'l L. & Com.	Syracuse Journal of International Law and Commerce
Tex.Int'l L.J.	Texas International Law Journal
TLR	Times Law Reports
Transnat'l Law.	Transnational Lawyer
Tulane L.Rev.	Tulane Law Review
Tulane Mar.L.J.	Tulane Maritime Law Journal
UN	United Nations
Univ. of Pittsburgh L.Rev.	University of Pittsburgh Law Review
v.	versus
Virg.J.Int'l L.	Virginia Journal of International Law
Wils.	Wilson's English Kings Bench Reports
W.L.R.	Weekly Law Reports
W.N.	Weekly Notes of English Law Reports
Y.L.J.	Yale Law Journal

Einleitung

Der 31. Januar 1997 wird als schicksalsreicher Tag in die Geschichte des englischen Schiedsrechts eingehen. An diesem Tag trat in England der *Arbitration Act* 1996 in Kraft. Der weltweit von Schiedsfachkreisen mit Spannung erwartete *Act* ersetzt nunmehr die *Arbitration Acts* 1950, 1975 und 1979. Bei einer durchschnittlichen "Lebensdauer" englischer Schiedsgesetze von über zwanzig Jahren wird der neue *Act* damit auf unabsehbare Zeit über das Schicksal Englands - vor allem Londons - als Standort internationaler Schiedsverfahren entscheiden.

England ist an einem entscheidenden Punkt in seiner traditionsreichen Geschichte als Anbieter von *arbitration-services* angelangt. Standen die Engländer zunächst an vorderster Front der Förderung der internationalen Schiedsgerichtsbarkeit,[1] sieht sich das englische Schiedsverfahrensrecht seit den siebziger Jahren erheblicher in- und ausländischer Kritik ausgesetzt.[2] Vor allem die als zu weitgehend empfundenen Eingriffsbefugnisse der staatlichen Gerichte[3] stoßen weltweit auf teils erhebliche Ablehnung. Bereits in den siebziger Jahren hatte diese Kritik den englischen Gesetzgeber zum Einlenken gezwungen. Der damals erlassene *Arbitration Act* 1979 vermochte es jedoch nicht, die Kritik ganz verstummen zu lassen.[4] Zu halbherzig war der Reformansatz. England verlor gegenüber anderen, progressiveren Anbieterstaaten von Schiedsverfahren an Boden. Es überrascht deshalb nicht, wenn die englische "Schiedsindustrie" ehrgeizige Erwartungen an den neuen *Act* von 1996 hat.[5] Er soll das Image der englischen Schiedsgerichtsbarkeit für ausländische Parteien aufpolieren und wieder im alten Glanz erstrahlen lassen. Ganz nüchtern formuliert: er soll ein Kassenschlager werden.[6]

Die Engländer sehen sich auf dem Markt der Schiedsgerichtsbarkeit in jüngerer Zeit einer ernstzunehmenden Konkurrenz ausgesetzt. Die Tatsache, daß dieser

---

1 Abromson, Suffolk Transnat'l L.J. 1980, 75.

2 Vgl. statt anderer Samuel, J.Int'l Arb. 1985, 53; Staughton, New L.J. 1979, 920.

3 Soweit nachfolgend der (alleinstehende) Begriff „Gericht(e)“ verwendet wird, sind die staatlichen Gerichte gemeint. Schiedsgerichte dagegen werden stets als solche bezeichnet.

4 Steyn, Arb. Int'l 1991, 17.

5 Harris/Planterose/Tecks, S. IV ff.

6 Samuel, Arb. & Disp. Res. L.J. 1999, 2 ("*There will presumably now follow [...] the circus by which English practitioners will seek to sell the legislation to overseas customers.*").

Markt sehr lukrativ sein kann, ist auch anderen Nationen nicht verborgen geblieben. Die letzten Jahre haben weltweit eine "Flut" von Schiedsrechtsreformen mit sich gebracht.[7] Im Mittelpunkt dieser Reformen steht das am 21. Juni 1985 von der Generalversammlung der Vereinten Nationen verabschiedete UNCITRAL Modellgesetz über die Internationale Handelsschiedsgerichtsbarkeit (nachfolgend: Modellgesetz).[8] 34 Länder und Staaten haben das Modellgesetz zwischenzeitlich unter mehr oder wenigen großen Abänderungen[9] in innerstaatliches Recht übernommen. Das Modellgesetz stellt eines der modernsten und - mit Blick auf das Thema dieser Arbeit - konsequentesten Schiedsverfahrensgesetze überhaupt dar. Anders als das englische Recht schränkt das Modellgesetz die Eingriffsbefugnisse der Gerichte erheblich ein. Vierzehn Jahre nach seiner Verabschiedung hat das Modellgesetz durch seine internationale Akzeptanz einen einzigartigen Stellenwert, ja eine "Marktführerschaft" erreicht. Zu Recht wurde es deshalb auch als "*benchmark by which the quality of national arbitration laws is judged*" bezeichnet.[10]

Die Qualität und der Erfolg eines Schiedsgesetzes wird ganz wesentlich durch das Verhältnis zwischen Schieds- und staatlicher Gerichtsbarkeit bestimmt.[11] Dieses Verhältnis entscheidet über den Grad der Autonomie, welcher der Schiedsgerichtsbarkeit eingeräumt wird. Damit verbunden ist zwangsläufig aber auch eine Entscheidung über den staatlichen Justizgewährungsanspruch der Schiedsparteien.[12] Denn in dem Maße, in dem die Schiedsgerichtsbarkeit wirklich autonom ist, wird den Parteien der Gang vor die staatlichen Gerichte verwehrt. Hier liegt erhebliches Konfliktpotential: wie weit muß die schiedsgerichtliche Autonomie gehen, damit die Schiedsgerichtsbarkeit den an sie gerichteteten Erwartungen - etwa hinsichtlich von Zügigkeit und Wirtschaftlichkeit - gerecht werden kann?[13] Wie weit darf sie (noch) gehen, ohne die Gefahr von unkontrol-

---

7 Berger, Internationale Wirtschaftsschiedsgerichtsbarkeit, S. 1 ff.

8 Einleitend Goodman, Bus.L. 1990, 250; Lionnet, Arb.Int'l 1990, 343; Murray, Arb.Int'l 1993, 97; New York State Bar Association, N.Y.U.L.J.Int'l L. & Pol. 1990, 87; Potter, Mich.J.Int'l L. 1989, 912; Rogers, Arb.Int'l 1990, 348 ff; Weiss, Syracuse.J.Int'l L. & Com. 1986, 367.

9 Anders als internationale Konventionen ist ein Modellgesetz vom rezipierenden Staat in beliebiger Weise abänderbar, um so den besonderen Erfordernissen des jeweiligen Staates gerecht zu werden.

10 Steyn, Arb.Int'l 1994, 3.

11 Mustill/Boyd, S. 1.

12 Vgl. Sonnauer, S. 25.

13 Zu den Vorteilen der Schiedsgerichtsbarkeit vgl. die Ausführungen bei Sandrock, Internationale Vertragsgestaltung, S. 885 ("Ein Wort über die Bedeutung und Vorteile der Schiedsgerichtsbarkeit im internationalen Handelsverkehr zu verlieren, hie-

liertem Machtmißbrauch heraufzubeschwören?[14] Kein Schiedsrecht wäre vollständig ohne die Beantwortung dieser Fragen. Die Ausgestaltung der staatlichen Befugnisse ist ein Bereich zentraler Bedeutung. Hieran zeigt sich, "wes Geistes Kind" das entsprechende Schiedsrecht wirklich ist. Daran erweist sich auch, ob Schiedsvereinbarung und -spruch nach dem jeweils anwendbaren Recht das Papier wert sind, auf dem sie stehen.

Die Frage nach dem "richtigen" Verhältnis von staatlicher und Schiedsgerichtsbarkeit läßt sich nicht abstrakt beantworten. Ein entsprechender Versuch wird im Rahmen dieser Arbeit auch nicht unternommen. Vielmehr soll anhand einer konkreten rechtsvergleichenden Untersuchung des Modellgesetzes sowie des alten und neuen englischen Rechts ermittelt werden, erstens, welche Änderungen das neue englische Recht gegenüber dem alten gebracht hat und zweitens, wie das neue englische Recht im Vergleich zum Modellgesetz zu beurteilen ist.[15]

Ein Rechtsvergleich zwischen Modellgesetz und englischem Recht bietet sich wie kein zweiter in diesem Bereich an.[16] Das liegt vor allem an dem polarisierenden Charakter, der dem englischen Recht einerseits und dem Modellgesetz andererseits zugeschrieben wird. Während das Modellgesetz dafür bekannt ist, daß es die Befugnisse der Gerichte in einschneidender Weise beschränkt, genießt das englische Schiedsrecht traditionell einen gegenteiligen Ruf. Offen zutage trat dieser Konflikt spätestens mit Englands Absage an das Modellgesetz.[17] Hier prallten zwei Schiedsrechtsphilosophien aufeinander, wie sie unterschiedlicher kaum hätten sein können.

Indem nach dem "richtigen" Maß staatlicher Kontrollbefugnisse gefragt wird und danach, welches in diesem Punkt das überlegene System ist, hat die vorlie-

---

ße Eulen nach Athen zu tragen.") m.w.N.; Wilberforce, in: Paterson/Thompson (Hrsg.), S. 7.

14 Vgl. auch Berger, Fordham Int'l L.J.1989, 608.

15 Gaillard, in: Sanders (Hrsg.), S. 283 führt zum Nutzen von Rechtsvergleichen auf dem Gebiet der Schiedsgerichtsbarkeit das Folgende an:
"International Commercial Arbitration has radically transformed the role of comparative law. Not long ago, comparative law was perceived to be an academic discipline. Its primary function was to provoke reflection on various legal systems and could at its best lead to legislative reform. International commercial arbitration revolutionized the field, transforming comparative law into an eminently practical and often lucrative discipline. Indeed, in many instances important international commercial litigations are won based on the resolution of issues of comparative law."
Vgl. auch Berger, in: Böckstiegel (Hrsg), S. 309 ff; Sandrock, Rechtsvergleichung.

16 Das neue deutsche Schiedsverfahrensrecht ist nicht Gegenstand dieser Arbeit. Vgl. hierzu statt anderer Berger, DZWir 1998, 45 ff; ders., Int'l Arb.L.Rev. 1998, 121 ff; ders. (Hrsg.), Schiedsverfahrensrecht, S. 3 ff.

17 Vgl. *infra* Teil II, Kapitel 3.

gende Arbeit einen rechtstheoretischen Ansatz. Die Arbeit wendet sich gleichwohl in erster Linie an den Praktiker und Anwender des Modellgesetzes[18] und des englischen *Arbitration Acts* 1996. So ist Voraussetzung für die Beantwortung der zuvor aufgeworfenen Frage eine systematische Untersuchung der einschlägigen Vorschriften und der Rechtsprechung.

Der Schwerpunkt der Untersuchung liegt auf dem englischen Recht. Dessen Darstellung weist, soweit es um das alte englische Recht geht, dabei notwendigerweise auch rechtshistorische Aspekte auf. Eine Darstellung und Untersuchung des neuen englischen Rechts wäre ohne eine solche des alten englischen Rechts nicht möglich. Wie im weiteren Verlauf deutlich werden wird, ist der *Arbitration Act* 1996 zu einem Großteil ohnehin nur ein konsolidierendes *restatement* des alten englischen Rechts. Um das neue englische Recht zu verstehen, muß in vielen Fällen deshalb etwa auf die Rechtsprechung zu den entsprechenden Vorschriften des alten Rechts zurückgegriffen werden.[19] Die Änderungen, die der *Arbitration Act* 1996 bringt, sind zudem nur vor dem Hintergrund des alten Rechts zu beurteilen. Bei der Darstellung des neuen englischen Rechts wird dabei auf das alte verwiesen, soweit keine Änderungen erfolgt sind.

Die Arbeit ist in drei Teile untergliedert. Teil I enthält eine kurze theoretische Grundlagendiskussion über den Umfang staatlicher Kontrollbefugnisse bei Schiedsverfahren. Die Ausführungen dienen in erster Linie der Darstellung des grundlegenden Problems der "richtigen" Balance von schiedsgerichtlicher Autonomie und staatlichen Eingriffsbefugnissen. Hier wird zudem zur Bedeutung des nationalen Rechts für internationale Schiedsverfahren Stellung bezogen. Teil II gibt einen - wiederum kurzen - Überblick darüber, wie sich die staatlichen Kontrollbefugnisse im englischen Recht entwickelt haben. Teil III der Arbeit enthält den eigentlichen Rechtsvergleich. Die jeweiligen staatlichen Kontrollbefugnisse werden chronologisch, dem Gang des Verfahrens entsprechend, untersucht. Der Aufbau innerhalb der einzelnen Kapitel ist dabei stets der gleiche. Zunächst wird die entsprechende Regelung des Modellgesetzes untersucht. Vor diesem Hintergrund folgt dann die Untersuchung zunächst des alten und dann des neuen englischen Rechts.[20]

---

18 Mit "Anwendern" des Modellgesetzes sind die Anwender der jeweiligen staatlichen Gesetze, durch welche das Modellgesetz übernommen wurde, gemeint.

19 Bernstein, Handbook, S. 32: "*It is [...] inevitable that the courts will draw on the rich body of precedent which exists when interpreting the new provisions.*"

20 Wie nachfolgend deutlich werden wird, ist das englische Recht umfangreicher als das Modellgesetz. Es kommt deshalb vor, daß bestimmten Regelungen im englischen Recht kein entsprechendes Pendant im Modellgesetz gegenübersteht. In diesen Fällen beschränkt sich der Rechtsvergleich auf das alte und neue englische Recht.

Teil I
Rechstheoretische Grundlagen

Kapitel 1
Das Verhältnis von staatlicher und Schiedsgerichtsbarkeit

Mustill/Boyd beginnen die Einleitung zu ihrem Werk mit folgender Feststellung:[21]

> "The law of private arbitration is concerned with the relationship between the courts and the arbitral process."

Diese Feststellung hat bis heute nichts an Gültigkeit verloren. Ihre Aktualität wird durch die weltweiten dynamischen Entwicklungen auf dem Gebiet des Schiedsverfahrensrechts bestätigt.[22] Kaum ein anderes Thema der Schiedsgerichtsbarkeit hat in Literatur und Rechtsprechung soviel Aufmerksamkeit erfahren wie dasjenige des Verhältnisses von staatlicher und Schiedsgerichtsbarkeit,[23] kaum ein anderes wurde so kontrovers diskutiert und kein anderes hat nach wie vor so wenig Aussicht auf eine allseits überzeugende Antwort.[24]

Die Bedeutung des Verhältnisses zwischen staatlicher und Schiedsgerichtsbarkeit erschließt sich vor dem Hintergrund der Rechtsnatur von Schiedsverfahren.[25] Diese wird zwar in erster Linie durch die Privatautonomie der Parteien bestimmt. Doch kann die Schiedsgerichtsbarkeit erst im Zusammenwirken mit der staatlichen Gerichtsbarkeit Bedeutung haben.[26] Zwar ist theoretisch eine klare Trennung durchaus denkbar. Die Folge aber wäre eine Verkümmerung der Bedeutung der Schiedsgerichtsbarkeit. Aufgrund des staatlichen Machtmonopols sind es unweigerlich die staatlichen Gerichte, die einer Schiedsvereinbarung erforderlichenfalls die nötigen "Zähne" verleihen.

---

21 Mustill/Boyd, S. 1.
22 Vgl. Einleitung.
23 Vgl. nur die über 1.000 Quellenangaben zu diesem Thema in Parker School, S. 471 - 549.
24 Vgl. Einleitung.
25 Zur Rechtsnatur der Schiedsgerichtsbarkeit vgl. Sonnauer, Jurisdictional Problems, S. 31 ff; David, S. 77 f; Sturges, N.Y.U.L.R. 1960, 1031; Carlston, L.C.P. 1952, 631.
26 Bartos, Internationale Handelsschiedsgerichtsbarkeit, S. 19.

Mustill/Boyd umschreiben die Konsequenzen einer strikten Trennung von staatlicher und Schiedsgerichtsbarkeit wie folgt:[27]

"Whilst recognising the right of parties to agree that their disputes should be decided by arbitration, the law would do nothing to enforce the agreement, to reinforce the procedure at its points of potential weakness, or to protect the parties against the risk of procedural or substantive injustice. English law came close to taking up this position in late medieval times; but no modern developed state can afford such a detached attitude."

Die Funktionsfähigkeit der Schiedsgerichtsbarkeit hängt somit immer auch von ihrem Verhältnis zur staatlichen Gerichtsbarkeit ab.

Kapitel 2
Die Bedeutung des nationalen Rechts für internationale Schiedsverfahren

Zwangsläufig stellt sich die Frage nach dem auf die staatlichen Kontroll- und Eingriffsbefugnisse anwendbaren Recht.[28]

Ursprünglich war anerkannt, daß die *lex locus arbitri* maßgeblich über die Befugnisse der staatlichen Gerichte in der Schiedsgerichtsbarkeit bestimmt.[29] Dies aber wurde von Stimmen in der Literatur zunehmend kritisiert.[30] Es wurde gefordert, inter- oder auch transnational genannte Schiedsverfahren losgelöst von der *lex locus arbitri* zu beurteilen.[31] Diese stünde oftmals lediglich in einem rein willkürlichen oder zufälligen Zusammenhang mit dem jeweiligen Schiedsverfahren. Deshalb dürfe der *lex loci arbitri* keine besondere Bedeutung zukommen. Dieser Argumentation liegt die Theorie eines "transnationalen" Schiedsverfahrensrechts zugrunde.[32] Sehr vereinfacht und auf das Wesentliche reduziert besagt diese These, daß die internationale Schiedsgerichtsbarkeit losgelöst von nationalen Rechtssystemen und Gerichten verfahren solle.[33]

---

27 Mustill/Boyd, S. 1.

28 Für einen internationalen Vergleich siehe Esplugues, R.Gen. 1988, 81; vgl. auch Herrmann, in: Sarcevic (Hrsg.), 6 ("*Generally speaking, frustration tends to result from the fact that the law of the venue is not fully compatible with the agreement of the parties or otherwise not suitable for their case.*"); Lionnet, J.Int'l Arb. 1991, 5; vgl. auch Sandrock, in: Storme/de Ly (Hrsg.), S. 89 ff.

29 Redfern, Int'l Constr.L.Rev. 259; vgl. auch Park, in: Carbonneau (Hrsg.), Recent Developments, S. 80 ff; Hirsch, Arb.J. 1979, 43.

30 Vgl. etwa Paulsson, I.C.L.Q. 1981, 358; ders., I.C.L.Q. 1983, 53; kritisch Mustill, C.L.P. 1984, 133.

31 Paulsson, *ibid.*

32 Vgl. hierzu ausführlich Park, Arb.Int'l 1989, 231.

33 Mustill, C.L.P. 1984, 133.

Die Idee eines von der *lex locus arbitri* losgelösten transnationalen Schiedsverfahrensrechts ist durchaus nachvollziehbar und auch attraktiv.[34] Sie geht jedoch an den Anforderungen der tatsächlichen Gegebenheiten vorbei.[35] Denn nur in dem Umfang, in dem internationale Übereinkommen Anwendung finden, ist wirklich die Anwendung internationalen Rechts gewährleistet. Ansonsten ist das für ein Schiedsverfahren maßgebende Verfahrensrecht immer nationales Recht und unterscheidet sich damit im Regelfall von anderen nationalen Rechten.[36] Dies wird etwa deutlich für den Fall, daß die Parteien die Durchführung eines Schiedsverfahrens beispielsweise in Frankreich vereinbart haben und nun eine der Parteien (abredewidrig) ein Verfahren vor den englischen Gerichten anstrengt.[37] Hier ist es unweigerlich das staatliche englische Schiedsverfahrensrecht, das über die Frage der Verweisung auf das Schiedsverfahren bzw. die Erklärung der eigenen Unzuständigkeit entscheidet. Offensichtlich relevant ist die *lex locus arbitri* etwa auch im Zusammenhang mit der Anerkennung und Vollstreckung von Schiedssprüchen.[38] Auch hier ist es notwendigerweise das Recht des Vollstreckungsstaates, das als maßgeblich zugrundegelegt wird.[39] Mit den deutlichen Worten von Mann: [40]

"No private person has the right or the power to act on any level other than that of municipal law. Every right or power a private person enjoys is inexorably conferred by or derived from a system of municipal law [...] No act of the parties can have any legal effect except as the result of the sanction given to it by a legal system [...] Arbitrators are inevitably subject to the legislative and judicial authorities of the country in which the tribunal functions. Whatever the intentions of the parties may be, the legislative and judicial authorities of the seat control the tribunal's existence, composition and activities. It is

---

34 Zur Praxisrelevanz transnationalen Rechts vgl. auch Berger (Hrsg.), Transnational Law.

35 Differenzierend Schmitthoff, in: Lew (Hrsg.), Contemporary Problems, S. 230.

36 Goldstajn, in: Voskuil/Wade (Hrsg.), Hague-Zagreb Essays 4, S. 297 f; vgl. auch Sandrock, Internationale Vertragsgestaltung, S. 902 ff.

37 Vgl. auch Mustill, C.L.P. 1984, 142:
"The logic of transnationalism demands that the parties are taken to have renounced all ties with domestic law, not simply those which the parties find constricting. So, if the mechanisms for appointing the tribunal break down, or if there is a casual vacancy, the Court cannot and should not lend its help. Nor if an important witness refuses to attend the hearing. Nor if the loosing party fails to honour the award. In these and many other cases, the aggrieved party is without help."

38 Abromson, Suffolk Transnat'l L.J. 1980, 77; Collins, in: Lew (Hrsg.), Contemporary Problems, S. 133.

39 Für eine ausführliche Stellungnahme unter besonderer Berücksichtigung des englischen Rechts vgl. Parc, in: Carbonneau (Hrsg.), Recent Developments, S. 81.

40 In: Sanders (Hrsg.), International Arbitration S. 160 f; vgl. auch Mustill, C.L.P. 1984, 133.

primarily the law of the seat that decides whether and on what conditions arbitration is permitted at all."

Mögen viele der Ansichten Manns heute auch als unzeitgemäß und schiedsunfreundlich kritisiert werden,[41] an seiner zuvor zitierten Aussage kommt auch heute (kaum)[42] ein Schiedsverfahren vorbei.[43] Noch immer sind es die nationalen Rechtsordnungen, die darüber entscheiden, ob und in welchem Maße Schiedsverfahren unterstützt oder kontrolliert werden.[44]

Die Wahl des richtigen Standortes ist für die Durchführung internationaler Schiedsverfahren somit überragend wichtig.[45] Mit den Worten von Redfern:[46]

"When it becomes necessary to resort to international arbitration, in order to settle a dispute [...], the place in which the arbitration is held may well be a matter of critical significance. This is because the law which will govern the arbitration will be the law of the place of arbitration [...]. It is important to know what degree of support this governing law will give to the arbitral process, if called upon to do so. It is also important to know what price is likely to be exacted in return, by way of control over the arbitral process [...]"

Kapitel 3
Die Balance der Interessen

Welches Schiedsverfahrensrecht aber entspricht am ehesten den Erwartungen der Parteien? Diese Frage läßt sich nicht pauschal beantworten. Sie hängt vor allem davon ab, welche Interessen mit dem jeweiligen Schiedsrecht verfolgt werden. Ist es in erster Linie das Interesse der Schiedsparteien an einer größtmöglichen Au-

41 Editors Note, Arb.Int'l 1992, 241; Redfern, Arb. & Disp. Res.J., 174.

42 Es gibt jedoch einige - vor allem in Frankreich entschiedene Fälle -, in welchen die (französischen) Gerichte anerkannt haben, daß internationale Schiedsverfahren in einem transnationalen verfahrensrechtlichen Raum durchgeführt werden können (vgl. etwa *General National Maritime Transport Co. v. Gotaverken Arendal A.B.* [1980] Droit Int'l (Clunet) 660).

43 Für eine ausführliche und kritische Stellungnahme zur sogen. Doktrin eines "*transnational*" oder "*delocalized*" Schiedsverfahrens vgl. mit weiteren Nachweisen Sandrock, Am.Rev.Int'l Arb. 1992, 43 ff.

44 Siehe auch Boyd, in: Lew (Hrsg.) Contemporary Problems, S.149, unter Hinweis auf *Bank Mellat v. Helleniki Techniki S.A.* [1984] Q.B. 301:
"Despite suggestions to the contrary by some learned writers under other systems, our jurisprudence does not recognise the concept of arbitral procedures floating in the transnational firmament, unconnected with any municipal system of law."

45 Redfern, Int'l Constr.L.Rev. 1958, 262; vgl. auch Gaillard, in: Sanders (Hrsg.), S. 283.

46 Redfern, *ibid*, 259.

tonomie des Schiedsverfahrens, an einer größtmöglichen Zügigkeit und Leichtigkeit des Schiedsverfahrens? Oder ist es das öffentliche Interesse an der Gewährleistung staatlicher Kontrolle über das Schiedsverfahren sowie an einer größtmöglichen Einzelfallgerechtigkeit? Die Interessen sind vielfältig.[47] Sie sind einander teils diametral entgegengesetzt.[48] Und genau hier liegt der Ursprung des Problems, mit dem sich jedes Schiedsverfahrensrecht konfrontiert sieht: Welche Interessen werden geschützt und welche werden vernachlässigt? Der Kern des Streits läßt sich dabei auf folgende Formel bringen: Autonomie des Schiedsverfahrens und Zügigkeit *versus* staatlichen Justizgewährungsanspruch und Einzelfallgerechtigkeit.[49] Mit den Worten von Russel:[50]

> "[T]here is a never-ending war between two irreconcilable principles, the high principle which demands justice though the heavens fall, and the low principle which demands that there shall be an end to litigation."

Erst wenn die Klagbarkeit wirksam beschränkt und die Vollstreckung von Schiedsvereinbarungen und -sprüchen durch die Gerichte gewährleistet wird, gewinnt die Schiedsgerichtsbarkeit überhaupt Bedeutung. Sie muß also zu einem

---

47 Eine gute Darstellung über die vielschichtige Interessenlage gibt Sonnauer, S. 9-17. Auzugsweise sollen hier nur folgende Interessen genannt werden: Mitgestaltung des Verfahrens, Zügigkeit, Kostengünstigkeit, Vertraulichkeit, Verbindlichkeit, (rasche) Durchsetzbarkeit, Beachtung der Parteivereinbarung, Fairness und Schutz vor Willkür, Einzelfallgerechtigkeit, Schutz besonders sensibler Bereiche, Sicherung des Rechtsfriedens.

48 Mit den Worten von Herrmann, in: Lew (Hrsg.), Contemporary Problems, S. 164 f: *"It is well known that the views and reviews of the role of the court which national courts play or should play on the arbitration scene differ widely and, it seems, without there being hope for consensus. At one end of the spectrum you may find the view that arbitration would turn into an unacceptable theatre of the absurd or a tragedy if it is not constantly monitored, protected and assisted by a judicial director, stage-hand or, in case of emergency, deus ex machina (all courtesy of the local court). At the other end you may find the view that arbitration - like any good play - would suffer from outside interference and that the artistic freedom of the cast, ie, parties and arbitrators, must not be impeded by local law barriers or benches."* Vgl. auch Fleischhauer, Arb.J. 1986, 17.

49 Vgl. die nachfolgende Aussage von Goff, zitiert bei Rogers, S. 1: *"The fundamental problem which we face is how to reconcile justice with expedition. Perfect justice requires the most careful scrutiny of every fact and document: endless opportunity for every party to explore the case, to question and answer the other side, to persuade the tribunal. Expedition can therefore be seen as the enemy of perfect justice. But we all know that nothing in this world is perfect. We all know that a balance has to be struck. The question is: where are we to strike that balance?"*

50 Russel on Arbitration, S. 284.

gewissen Grad autonom sein.[51] Auf der anderen Seite ist unbestritten, daß Staaten zumindest ein Minimum an Kontrolle über die Schiedsgerichtsbarkeit aufrechterhalten müssen.[52]

Wie weit aber ist die staatsgerichtliche Kontrolle der Schiedsgerichtsbarkeit noch sachgerecht? Es wurde bereits erwähnt, wie sehr diese Frage die Diskussion um die Schiedsgerichtsbarkeit seit jeher stark beeinflußt hat.[53] Daß deren Beantwortung abhängig vom Zeitgeist mitunter starken Schwankungen unterworfen ist, wird anhand der Darstellung der historischen Entwicklung des englischen Schiedsrechts in Teil II dieser Arbeit deutlich. Zu keinem Zeitpunkt aber wurde diese Diskussion mit einer Intensität geführt wie im Zuge der Beratungen und Verabschiedung des Modellgesetzes.[54] Die Darstellung des Ergebnisses dieser Diskussion ist Teil dieser Arbeit - und zwar sowohl im Hinblick auf das Modellgesetz als auch im Hinblick auf das (neue und alte) englische Recht. Der Vergleich des Modellgesetzes mit dem englischen Schiedsverfahrensrecht in diesem Punkt ist schon deshalb interessant, weil die Engländer zu den größten Kritikern des Modellgesetzes zähl(t)en. Wieder einmal ist es Mann, der die englische Haltung unmißverständlich auf den Punkt bringt:[55]

> "There exists a [...] serious threat to the judicial character of arbitration [...] This stems from the draft Model Law which [...] UNCITRAL has prepared and which is likely to be finalized in the near future. It is as unsatisfactory as much of the work that emanates from the United Nations in general and UNCITRAL in particular [...] [T]he Model Law is unacceptable, primarily because it reduces the function of the court and its supervisory powers to a minimum or, one is tempted to say, to less than a minimum."

Historisch betrachtet ist das englische Schiedsverfahrensrecht - anders als die meisten anderen nationalen Schiedsrechte - vor allem durch einen stetig ansteigenden staatsgerichtlichen Interventionismus gekennzeichnet.[56] Damit einher ging ein Verfall der ehemals hervorragenden Reputation des englischen Schiedsrechts. Dem konnte auch der *Arbitration Act* 1979 keinen wirksamen Riegel vor-

---

51 Street, S. 1; zur Partauotonomie vgl. auch Berger, RIW 1994, 12 ff.

52 Hierzu Mann, Civ.Just.Q. 1985, 259, in der ihm eigenen Direktheit:
"Every practitioner is likely to confirm, only academics and the International Chamber of Commerce living in cloud cuckoo-land are likely to deny the legitimacy of legislation intended to afford parties the protection against abuse they need."
Vgl. allgemein auch Cremades, Arbitration 1978, 83.

53 Vgl. auch Diplock, Arbitration 1978, 107.

54 Siehe auch Mustill, in: Sanders (Hrsg.) 22.

55 Mann, Civ.Just.Q., 265.

56 Dies muß zumindest bis zum Erlaß des *Arbitration Act* 1979 gelten.

schieben.[57] Eine Reform des englischen Schiedsverfahrensrechts war damit eine Frage der Zeit. Sie ist nunmehr - man möchte sagen: endlich - durch den *Arbitration Act* 1996 erfolgt.

Die größte Herausforderung, mit der sich das Reformvorhaben konfrontiert sah, war die Beantwortung einer Frage, die Lord Justice Kerr bereits 1984 in seiner *Alexander Lecture* vor dem *Chartered Institute of Arbitrators* aufgeworfen hatte:[58]

> "Given the fact that the courts are indispensable to the effectiveness of the abitral process, the question is: what should be the limits of their role?"

Es ist bereits deutlich geworden, daß sich die Rolle der Gerichte nicht auf die Vollstreckung von Schiedssprüchen beschränkt. Die verschiedenen nationalen Rechtsordnungen sehen vielmehr ein oft umfangreiches Instrumentarium gerichtlicher Befugnisse vor. Diese können grob in zwei Kategorien unterteilt werden. Zum einen verfügen die staatlichen Gerichte über Befugnisse zur Unterstützung der Schiedsgerichtsbarkeit, wie etwa im Zusammenhang mit der Durchsetzung der Schiedsvereinbarung oder der Bildung des Schiedsgerichts. Zum anderen gibt es die eigentlichen Kontrollbefugnisse der Gerichte, etwa bei der Versagung der Anerkennung und Vollstreckung von Schiedssprüchen oder im Rahmen von Rechtsmitteln, die gegen Schiedssprüche statthaft sind.[59] Die beiden Kategorien können nicht immer eindeutig voneinander getrennt werden.

Wie im weiteren Verlauf dieser Arbeit deutlich werden wird, sieht gerade das englische Recht von jeher ein sehr umfangreiches Instrumentarium gerichtlicher Befugnisse vor.[60] Das ist nicht unproblematisch. Zwar werden englische Autoren nicht müde, die (angeblich) lobenswerte Partnerschaft und Kooperation zwischen

---

57 Wie weit dieser Verfall Mitte der 80er Jahre bereits gediehen war, wird daran deutlich, daß die Vereinbarung eines englischen Schiedsforums von amerikanischen Anwaltskanzleien gar als anwaltlicher Kunstfehler eingestuft wurde (vgl. Hacking, Int'l Bus.Lawy. 1980, 161).

58 Kerr, I.C.L.Q. 1985, 1. Die *Alexander Lecture* von Kerr wurde - zu Recht - auch als "*starting point for any British lawyer*", der sich mit dem UNCITRAL Modellgesetz im allgemeinen und dem Verhältnis von staatlicher und Schiedsgerichtsbarkeit im speziellen auseinandersetzt, bezeichnet (vgl. Evans, Arbitration 1987, 121).

59 Kerr, *ibid*, unterteilt das Spektrum der gerichtlichen Befugnisse in "*powers of assistance, powers of intervention, powers of supervision or control, and powers of recognition and enforcement*".

60 In *Prodexport State Company for Foreign Trade v. E. D. & F. Mann Ltd.* [1973] Q.B. 389 (395) bestätigte Macotta J.:
"It is well known that English law is nearly unique in the degree of interference it permits the courts in the conduct of arbitrations and the settlement of disputes thereby."

den Gerichten und der Schiedsgerichtsbarkeit hervorzuheben.[61] Es ist jedoch eine Tatsache, daß jede staatliche Kontrollbefugnis zwangsläufig auf Kosten der schiedsgerichtlichen Autonomie gehen muß.[62] Fraglich ist somit, wo das Limit der gerichtlichen Befugnisse sinnvollerweise liegen soll.

Das Geschäft mit der internationalen Schiedsgerichtsbarkeit stellt von jeher einen bedeutenden Wirtschaftsfaktor in der Londoner City dar. Entsprechend groß war die Lobby, die auf eine Modernisierung des englischen Schiedsrechts drängte. Ziel war der Schutz des Schiedsstandorts England. Gesetze aber werden auch in England nicht ausschließlich von Lobbyisten gemacht. Im Bereich der Schiedsverfahrensgesetzgebung ist es das Departmental Advisory Committee on Arbitration (nachfolgend: DAC), welches durch seine Vorschläge das spätere Recht ganz wesentlich bestimmt.[63] Eine Schlüsselfunktion kommt dabei dem jeweiligen Vorsitzenden des DAC zu. Diese Funktion wird üblicherweise von einem Lordrichter wahrgenommen. Und wie etwa Lord Mustill als Vorsitzender des DAC zur Empfehlung über die Übernahme des Modellgesetz in das englische Recht auf eindrucksvolle Weise bestätigt hat: Die Justiz mit der Reform der Schiedsgesetzgebung - und damit einhergehend der Beschneidung ihrer eigenen Kompetenzen - zu beauftragen, heißt, sich am eigenen Schopf aus dem Sumpf ziehen zu wollen.[64] Dem liegt das Verständnis der englischen Gerichte als Hüter von Recht und Gerechtigkeit, von *natural justice* zugrunde, wie es nachfolgend durch Kerr auf den Punkt gebracht wird:[65]

"With the exception of the Sovereign and the Judicial Committees of the House of Lords and Privy Council, there is virtually no body, tribunal, authority or individual in England whose acts or decisions give rise to binding legal consequences for others, but who are altogether immune from judicial review in the event of improper conduct, breaches of the principles of natural justice, or decisions which clearly transcend any standard of objective reasonableness. Such islands of immunity as remain are constantly shrinking [...] This system is our bulwark against corruption, arbitrariness, bias, improper conduct and - where necessary - sheer incompetence, in relation to acts and decisions with binding legal effect for others. No one having the power to make legally binding decisions in this country should be altogether outside and immune from this system. No one below the highest tribunals should have unreviewable legal powers over others. Speaking from

---

61 Kerr, I.C.L.Q. 1985, 2; Hunter, in: Lew (Hrsg.), Contemporary Problems, S. 195; Mustill, Arbitration 1986, 163; Steyn, Arb.Int'l 1991, 23.

62 Zum Spannungsverhältnis von Zügigkeit und Gerechtigkeit vgl. Saville, Arb.Int'l 1997, 237; vgl. auch Sandrock, JZ 1986, 370.

63 Zwar werden diese Vorschläge bzw. *reports* vom englischen Parlament in mehreren Lesungen diskutiert. Erfahrungsgemäß werden jedoch kaum ernsthafte Änderungen an seinen Vorschlägen gemacht.

64 Zum *Mustill-Report* vgl. *infra* Teil II, Kapitel 3.

65 Kerr, I.C.L.Q. 1985, 15 f.

experience, I believe this to be as necessary in relation to arbitrations in England and abroad as in all other contexts."

Dies macht deutlich, wie sehr das englische Verständnis eine weitreichende Autonomie der Schiedsgerichtsbarkeit ablehnte; ferner, für wie entscheidend eine starke Rolle der Gerichte in diesem Zusammenhang erachtet wurde.[66] Es war in erster Linie diese Haltung der englischen Justiz, welche die Kritik ausländischer Schiedsparteien am englischen System laut werden ließ.

Ein weiterer Kritikpunkt am englischen Schiedsverfahrensrecht sollte dessen Ansehen zunehmend schaden. So war es neben den ohnehin schon umfangreichen Kontrollbefugnissen der Gerichte nicht absehbar, unter welchen Voraussetzungen die Gerichte von ihnen Gebrauch machen würden. Kerr umschreibt diese Kritik wie folgt:[67]

"The Arbitration Acts lay down the powers of the courts in relation to arbitrations, but provide virtually no information about the circumstances in which these powers are in fact exercised by the courts. Thus, the statutes state that the courts have power to remove arbitrators for "misconduct" or other reasons, to set aside or to remit awards, and to permit recourse to the courts on issues of law in certain cases. But what they do not spell out are the principles which govern the actual exercise of these powers. The reason is obvious: the principles governing the relationship between the courts and arbitrations, i.e. the law of arbitration, can at present only be seen diffusely by ploughing through text-books which give a bewildering array of reported decisions in which the courts have in fact intervened or refused to intervene. From this profusion of more or less authoritative decisions it is difficult to extract any lines of predictable principle, in particular for parties from other countries and their legal advisers who are wondering whether to arbitrate in England."

Die Bedeutung der von Kerr so treffend umschriebenen Problematik sollte nicht unterschätzt werden. Es muß sehr zweifelhaft erscheinen, wie die Parteien auf ein Recht vertrauen können, das selbst bei sorgfältiger Studie der entsprechenden *statutes* kaum erfaßbar ist. Die umfassende Darstellung und Analyse auch des einschlägigen Fallrechts und - soweit überhaupt vorhanden - die Herausarbeitung übergeordneter Prinzipien ist deshalb einer der Schwerpunkte dieser Arbeit.

---

66 Vgl. auch Abromson, Suffolk Transnat'l L.J. 1980, 73; Boyd, in: Lew (Hrsg.), Contemporary Problems, 149; Craig, Arb.Int'l 1988, 174; Jaffe, Arbitration 1989, 184; Mustill, Arkiv for Sjorett 1976-77, 321; Wallace, Arb.Int'l 1990, 253; a.A. Mayer, Arb.Int'l 1991, 311.

67 Kerr, I.C.L.Q. 1985, 9.

Teil II
Die historische Entwicklung der Kontrolle der Schiedsgerichtsbarkeit durch die Gerichte in England

Kapitel 1
Einführung

Der *Arbitration Act* 1996 stellt den vorläufigen Abschluß einer langen, über weite Strecken schleppenden Entwicklung des englischen Schiedsverfahrensrechtes dar.[68] Er ist, anders als etwa das Modellgesetz, nicht das Ergebnis eines konzentrierten Schöpfungsaktes. Seine Ursprünge gehen vielmehr bis auf das frühe Mittelalter zurück.[69] Zu diesem frühen Zeitpunkt war die Handelsschiedsgerichtsbarkeit das gängige Mittel der Streitbeilegung unter Kaufleuten.[70] Die Gründe hierfür waren im wesentlichen identisch mit denen, die auch heute für Kaufleute die Schieds- der staatlichen Gerichtsbarkeit vorzugswürdig erscheinen läßt, allen voran die Zügigkeit und Flexibilität des Verfahrens sowie der Sachverstand der Schiedsgerichte.[71]

Kapitel 2
Von *Vinior's Case* bis zum *Arbitration Act* 1979

A. Vinior's Case: *Widerrufbarkeit von Schiedsvereinbarungen*

Das bis zu diesem Zeitpunkt unkomplizierte Nebeneinander von (königlichen) Gerichten und kaufmännischen Schiedsgerichten sollte erstmals zu Beginn des 17. Jahrhunderts belastet werden. Zu dieser Zeit begannen die Gerichte mit der Entwicklung von Konzepten, mit denen die sich weiter professionalisierende Schiedsgerichtsbarkeit in ihren Kompetenzen beschränkt werden sollte. Der Ursprung dieser Entwicklung lag im sog. *Vinior's Case*.[72] In diesem Fall wurde

---

68 Zur jüngeren Entwicklung vor allem des *common law* vgl. Marriot, Arbitration 1993, 41.

69 Mustill, J.Int'l Arb. 1989, 43.

70 Zur Entwicklung der Schiedsgerichtsbarkeit aus Sicht der Geschäftswelt vgl. Ferguson, Brit.J. Law & Soc. 1980, 141.

71 Parker of Waddington, S. 6; Campbell, S. 274; Ferguson, Brit.J.Law & Soc. 1980, 142.

72 (1610) 8 Co. Rep. 80; vgl. auch Comish, Arbitration 1990, 195.

erstmals entschieden, daß es den Parteien zu einem Schiedsverfahren jederzeit vor Ergehen des Schiedsspruchs möglich sein sollte, dem Schiedsgericht seine Befugnis zur Entscheidung abzuerkennen. Zwar stellte ein solcher Widerruf einen Vertragsbruch dar. Dieser verpflichtete gegebenenfalls auch zum Schadensersatz.[73] Entscheidend aber war, daß das Vorhandensein einer Schiedsvereinbarung von den Gerichten nicht als Verteidigung gegen eine Klage anerkannt wurde. Die Gerichte setzten ihre Verfahren mithin auch nicht zugunsten der Durchführung eines Schiedsverfahrens aus.

B. Kill v. Hollister: Doctrine of ouster

In der Folge von *Vinior's Case* verlagerte sich der Schwerpunkt der Diskussion über das Verhältnis von staatlicher und Schiedsgerichtsbarkeit. Ging es zunächst primär um die Frage der Durchsetzbarkeit von Schiedsvereinbarungen, standen nunmehr die eigentlichen Kontroll- und Eingriffsbefugnisse der Gerichte im Mittelpunkt. Dies führte 1746 in *Kill v. Hollister*[74] zu der Entwicklung der sog. *doctrine of ouster.*[75] Diese wird im allgemeinen im Zusammenhang mit der ungleich bekannteren Entscheidung in *Czarnikow v. Roth, Schmidt & Co.* erwähnt,[76] in welcher Lord Justice Scrutton sein berühmtes *dictum* gab "*that there must be no Alsatia, where the Kings writ does not run*".[77] *Czarnikow* aber bestätigte letztlich nur die Entscheidung in *Kill v. Hollister.* Die Parteien hatten in diesem Fall eine Klausel in ihren Schiedsvertrag aufgenommen, wonach die staatlichen Kontrollbefugnisse ausdrücklich ausgeschlossen wurden. Mit dieser Klausel in einem nachfolgenden gerichtlichen Verfahren konfrontiert, entschied das Gericht gegen deren rechtliche Verbindlichkeit. Es wurden im wesentlichen zwei Gründe hierfür gegeben. Zum einen befürchteten die Gerichte, daß "*in time codes of law would come to be administered in various trades differing substantially from the English mercantile law*".[78] Zum anderen - und ausschlaggebend - lag

73 *Newgate v. Degelder* (1666) 2 Keb 10.

74 (1746) 1 Wils. 129.

75 Zur Entwicklung und Begründung vgl. auch Schmitthoff, in: Sanders (Hrsg.), S. 289.

76 [1922] 2 K.B. 478.

77 Mit *Alsatia* war ein Londoner Stadtteil gemeint, dessen überwiegend kriminelle Bewohner sich weitgehend der königlichen Kontrolle entzogen.

78 *Czarnikow v. Roth, Schmidt & Co.* [1922] 2 K.B. 478. Erst mit dem *Arbitration Act* 1996 verlor diese auch als "*selfish and unworthy*" bezeichnete Begründung ihre Bedeutung (vgl. Mann, Civ.Just.Quart. 1985, 259).

dem Urteil das Selbstverständnis des Gerichts zugrunde, als Hüter von Recht und Gerechtigkeit allzuständig zu sein.[79]

C. Kent v. Elstob: Error of law on face of the award

Zur Mitte des 19. Jahrhunderts hatte sich in England die allgemeine Regel herausgebildet, daß ein Rechts- oder Tatsachenfehler des Schiedsgerichts keinen Grund für die Aufhebung oder Abänderung des Schiedsspruchs durch die Gerichte darstellte.[80] Zu dieser Regel gab es eine wichtige Ausnahme. Diese geht auf den Fall *Kent v. Elstob*[81] aus dem Jahr 1802 zurück.[82] Der Klage ging ein unstreitig rechtsfehlerhafter Schiedsspruch voraus. Vor diesem Hintergrund beantragte die Klägerin die Aufhebung des Schiedsspruches. Die Beklagte verwies darauf, daß solche Fehler nicht zu einer Aufhebung durch das Gericht berechtigten. Das Gericht schloß sich der Auffassung der Beklagten zwar grundsätzlich an. Es machte jedoch eine wichtige Ausnahme. So sollte ein Schiedsspruch dann von den Gerichten kassiert werden können, wenn ein Rechtsfehler *on its face*, also im Tenor, in der Begründung oder in einem weiteren Bestandteil des Schiedsspruchs offen erkennbar war.[83] Eine Beschränkung auf bestimmte Fehler existierte nicht. Insoweit einzige Voraussetzung war, daß der gerügte Fehler direkt aus dem Schiedsspruch (nebst Begründung) hervorging. Soweit das Gericht einen Fehler feststellte, kassierte es gleich den gesamten Schiedsspruch. Eine Modifikation des Schiedsspruchs oder ein Rückverweis an das Schiedsgericht war nicht vorgesehen.[84]

Um diese Rechtsfolge zu vermeiden, gingen die Schiedsgerichte mit der Zeit dazu über, ihre Schiedssprüche überhaupt nicht mehr mit Begründungen zu versehen. Denn wo keine Begründung gegeben wurde, da konnte auch kein Rechts-

---

79 Schmitthoff, Commercial Law, S. 64.

80 Vgl. etwa *Hodgkinson v. Fernie* (1857) 3 C.B.N.S. 202.

81 (1802) 3 East 18; bestätigt durch *Hodgkinson v. Fernie, ibid.*

82 Mit dieser Entscheidung wurde die Schiedsgerichtsbarkeit endgültig dem *common law* unterworfen (Parker of Waddington, J.B.L. 1959, 213).

83 Wilde J. brachte das Regel-Ausnahme-Verhältnis in *Holgate v. Killik* (1861) 7 H & N 418 (422) wie folgt auf den Punkt:
"The principle to be collected from the later cases is very plain, viz., that the Courts will not look at anything for the purpose of reviewing the decisions of an arbitrator upon the matters referred to him, except what appears on the face of the award, or some paper so connected with the award as form part of it."
Vgl. auch die Begründung in *Champsey Bhara & Co. v. Jivraj Balloo Spinning and Weaving Co.* [1923] A.C. 480 (487).

84 Steyn, Arbitration 1980, 147.

fehler in einer solchen auftauchen.[85] Folglich standen die Parteien mit relativ leeren Händen da, weil sie den Schiedsspruch nunmehr oftmals nicht mehr nachvollziehen konnten.[86] Problematisch war zudem, daß die *error on the face*-Methode bald ds Gegenteil dessen erreichte, was sie eigentlich zu erreichen suchte. Denn ohne jegliche Begründung waren oftmals auch schwerwiegendere Rechts- oder Tatsachenfehler nicht zu entdecken. Dieser Umstand führte schließlich dazu, daß die *error on the face*-Methode durch den *Arbitration Act* 1979 abgeschafft wurde.

D. Das special case-*Verfahren*

Wenn das englische Schiedsrecht wegen seiner weitgehenden gerichtlichen Eingriffsbefugnisse kritisiert wird,[87] hat das auch heute noch seine Ursache zu einem Teil in dem sog. *special case*-Verfahren.[88] Es handelte sich hierbei um ein Verfahren, wonach ein unterinstanzliches Gericht einem höherinstanzlichen - freiwillig oder auf dessen Weisung - einen Fall hinsichtlich bestimmter Rechtsfragen zur Stellungnahme vorlegte. Erstmals wurde dieses Verfahren durch *s* 5 *Common Law Procedure Act* 1854 auch auf die Schiedsgerichtsbarkeit angewendet. Konnte nach *s* 5 zunächst nur ein abschließender Schiedsspruch Gegenstand eines *special case* sein, wurde dessen Anwendungsbereich nachfolgend durch *s* 19 *Arbitration Act* 1889 weiter ausgedehnt. Danach konnte ("*may*") oder mußte ("*if so directed*") eine jede fallrelevante Rechtsfrage bereits im Vorfeld der schiedsrichterlichen Entscheidung zur Stellungnahme dem zuständigen Gericht vorgelegt werden. Spätestens seit den 70er Jahren hatte sich das *special case*-Verfahren zur gängigsten Methode gerichtlicher Intervention in Schiedsverfahren entwickelt.[89] Es war zuletzt in *s* 21(1) *Arbitration Act* 1950 geregelt. Darin hieß es:

> "(1) An arbitrator or umpire may, and shall if so directed by the High Court, state-
> (a) any question of law arising in the course of the reference; or
> (b) an award or any part of an award,
> in the form of a special case for the decision of the High Court."

---

85 Für eine ausführliche Stellungnahme hinsichtlich des für und wider von Begründungen vgl. Bingham, Arb.Int'l 1985, 141.

86 Soweit die Parteien dies wünschten konnte eine Begründung in einem gesonderten Dokument erfolgen. Für diesen Fall mußten sie sich jedoch verpflichten, das Dokument nicht für etwaige gerichtliche Schritte gegen den Schiedsspruch zu nutzen.

87 Vgl. Einleitung.

88 Ausführlich zur Entwicklung des *special case*-Verfahrens vgl. Conrick, Queensland Inst.Techn.L.J., 1.

89 Thomas, Lloyd's Mar. & Com.L.Q. 1981, 199.

In seiner praktischen Auswirkung nahm *s* 21 den Schiedsgerichten vollumfänglich die Möglichkeit, abschließend über Rechtsfragen zu entscheiden. Theoretisch stand es zwar im Ermessen des Schiedsrichters, dem Antrag einer Partei zur Vorlage eines *special case* an den High Court nachzukommen ("*may*").[90] Eine ablehnende Entscheidung war jedoch gerichtlich überprüfbar. Der High Court konnte den Schiedsrichter im übrigen auch außerhalb eines Rechtsbehelfsverfahrens zu einer Vorlage zwingen ("*shall*"). Auch konnten die Parteien, sozusagen unter Umgehung des Schiedsrichters, direkt mit einer *special case*-Anfrage vor den High Court gehen.[91] Es war deshalb unwahrscheinlich, daß die Schiedsgerichte eine *special case*-Anfrage ablehnten.

Spätestens seit *The Lysland*,[92] einer auch als "*death knell of arbitrator autonomy*" bezeichneten Entscheidung des Court of Appeal,[93] war die Einstellung der englischen Gerichte im *special case*-Verfahren offensichtlich. Lord Denning führte in der genannten Entscheidung aus:[94]

> "[The arbitrator] should agree to state a case whenever the facts, as proved or omitted before him, give rise to a point of law which fulfils these requisites: The point of law should be real and substantial and such as to be open to serious argument and appropriate for decision by a court of law and of such importance that the resolution of it is necessary for the proper determination of the case [...]"

Dies bedeutete, daß die staatlichen Gerichte immer dann, wenn die vorgenannten Voraussetzungen nicht erfüllt waren, das Schiedsgericht zu einer *special case*-Vorlage zwingen konnten. Die genannten Voraussetzungen stellten aufgrund ihrer Auslegungsfähigkeit und Unbestimmtheit keine wirksame Hürde gegen staatsgerichtliche Eingriffe dar. Ein Eingreifen der Gerichte stand vielmehr im freien Ermessen der Gerichte.[95] Folgerichtig entwickelte sich das *special case*-Verfahren in der Praxis zu einem generellen Revisionsrecht.[96]

Die in *The Lysland* beschriebenen Eingriffsbefugnisse der staatlichen Gerichte wurden durch die Entscheidung des Court of Appeal in *Ismail v. Polish*

---

90 *Orion Compania Espanola de Seguros v. Belfort Maatschappij voor Algemene Verzekgringeen* [1962] 2 Lloyd's Rep. 257.

91 *Glafki Shipping Co. S.A. v. Pinions Shipping Co. No. 1 ("The Maira")* [1982] 1 Lloyd's Rep. 261.

92 *Halfdan Grieg & Co. A/S v. Sterling Coal and Navigation Corpn. ("The Lysland")* [1973] 1 Q.B. 843.

93 Parc, Harvard Int.L.J. 1980, 93.

94 *The Lysland*, 862.

95 Für eine kritische Stellungnahme zu *The Lysland* vgl. Parc, Harvard Int.L.J. 1980, 93.

96 Vgl. Kerr, in: Bos/Brownlie, S. 123

Ocean Lines[97] noch erweitert. Waren die Gerichte bis dahin zumindest noch auf die Beantwortung der von den Schiedsrichtern formulierten Fragen zum *special case* gebunden, entfiel nunmehr auch dieses Erfordernis. Lord Denning:[98]

"And I see no reason why the court should not itself amend the question or formulate it afresh [...] so that the real issues [...] can be decided [...]"

Nunmehr konnten die Gerichte nicht nur "passiv" in ein Verfahren eingreifen, also die ihnen vorgelegten Fragen beantworten; vielmehr war ihnen durch die Möglichkeit zur Abänderung und Erweiterung der gestellten Fragen jetzt auch ein aktives Gestalten des Schiedsverfahrens möglich.

Es waren vor allem zwei Kritikpunkte, die letztlich zur Abschaffung des *special case*-Verfahrens führten. Zum einen war das *special case*-Verfahren sehr zeit- und kostenintensiv. Das Schiedsgericht mußte, noch bevor es selber zu einer Entscheidung gekommen war, dem staatlichen Gericht Rechtsfragen zur Beantwortung vorlegen. Oftmals stellte sich im nachhinein heraus, daß es auf diese Fragen nicht entscheidend ankam. Zwangsläufig zogen sich die Verfahren in die Länge. Die zusätzlich entstehenden Kosten waren mitunter erheblich. Zum anderen lud das *special case*-Verfahren zum Mißbrauch ein. Bereits der Erlaß des Schiedsspruches konnte erheblich verzögert werden. War der Schiedsspruch dann ergangen, konnte er noch immer über alle Instanzen unter Berufung auf einen jeglichen Rechtsfehler angegriffen werden. Mit den Worten von Kerr:[99]

"Special cases used to be the exception, but they are becoming the rule and increasingly frequent as a means of delaying the speedy resolution of commercial disputes for which arbitrations are designed [...] [R]espondents with weak cases use the decision of the Court of Appeal in [The Lysland] merely as a means of gaining time in order to postpone a final award against them. In the result we are in the danger of suffering a loss of reputation in our system of commercial arbitration."

E. Die Arbitration Acts *1889, 1934 und 1950*

Eine wirklich umfassende Regelung hatte die Schiedsgerichtsbarkeit und damit auch das Verhältnis zu den Gerichten erstmals durch den *Arbitration Act* 1889

97 [1976] 1 Q.B. 893

98 *Ibid*, 901.

99 *Granvias Oceanicas Armadora S.A.. v. Jibsen Trading Co. ("The Kavo Peiratis")* [1977] 2 Lloyd's Rep. 349; vgl. auch Diplock, Arbitration 1978, 107; Schmitthoff, J.B.L. 1977, 305.

erfahren. Dieser war im wesentlichen unverändert durch den *Arbitration Act* 1950 ersetzt worden. Der *Arbitration Act* 1934 hatte dagegen kaum eine Bedeutung für das Verhältnis der Schieds- zur staatlichen Gerichtsbarkeit. Durch besagte Gesetze hatten die bis dahin zumeist unabhängig von der ordentlichen Gerichtsbarkeit verfahrende Schiedsgerichtsbarkeit endgültig ihre Unabhängigkeit verloren, und zwar sowohl im positiven als auch im negativen Sinne. Einerseits konnte die Schiedsgerichtsbarkeit als anerkanntes Institut der Streitbeilegung nunmehr erstmals auf gerichtliche Unterstützung zählen, wie etwa in Fragen der Beweiserhebung[100] oder bei der Zusammensetzung des Schiedsgerichts.[101] Diese formale "Einbindung" in das Rechtssystem hatte andererseits aber auch erhebliche Kontroll- und Eingriffsbefugnisse der Gerichte mit sich gebracht. Soweit diese nicht durch den *Arbitration Act* 1979 abgeschafft worden waren,[102] galten sie bis zum Inkrafttreten des *Arbitration Acts* 1996. Zu einem ganz wesentlichen Teil wurden diese Befugnisse darüberhinaus durch den *Arbitration Act* 1996 übernommen. Sie sind damit Gegenstand der Untersuchungen in Teil III.

F. Der Arbitration Act *1979*

Die stetig zunehmenden staatlichen Kontrollbefugnisse hatten spätestens in den 70er Jahren zu einer unüberhörbaren Kritik am englischen Schiedsrecht geführt.[103] Einer der zentralen Gründe war - wie bereits erwähnt - das *special case*-Verfahren, welches zunehmend zur Verschleppung von Schiedsverfahren mißbraucht worden war.[104] Ebenso war auch das *error of law*-Verfahren zunehmend Gegenstand harscher Kritik geworden.

Die Beeinträchtigung des ehemals exzellenten Rufs Englands als Standort für Schiedsverfahren[105] und damit einhergehend die Aussicht, Einbußen im lukrativen Schiedsgeschäft hinnehmen zu müssen, hatte schließlich zur Einsetzung des Commercial Court Committees unter der Leitung von Lord Donaldson (nachfolgend: Donaldson Committee) geführt. In seinem *Report on Arbitration* stellte das Donaldson Committee fest:[106]

---

100 *S* 18 *Arbitration Act* 1889, *s* 12 *Arbitration Act* 1950.

101 *S* 5 *Arbitration Act* 1889, *s* 10 *Arbitration Act* 1950.

102 So das *special case*- und das *error of law*-Verfahren.

103 Shenton/Toland, Law & Pol'y.Int'l.Bus. 1980, 647; Hacking, Int'l Law. 1980, 98; Littman, Int'l Lawy. 1979, 256; Schmitthoff, J.B.L. 1977, 305.

104 Schmitthoff, *ibid.*

105 Clark/Lange, Bus.L. 1980, 1623.

106 Donaldson Report, paras 16-17.

"The value of some right to judicial review [...] has proved itself [useful] over the years [...] Certainty of rights and duties is of cardinal importance in a commercial relationship and the absence of an entrenched right of judicial review leads inevitably to uncertainty [...] The most obvious disadvantage of any such a right is that it conflicts with one of the prime objects of arbitration [...] namely the achievement of a speedy and final decision [...] [J]udicial review [...] inevitably causes some delay."

Auf die Empfehlung des Donaldson Committees wurde schließlich der *Arbitration Act* 1979 erlassen. Dieser reformierte den *Arbitration Act* 1950 in Teilbereichen. Die beiden *Acts* stellten bis Inkrafttreten des *Arbitration Acts* 1996 neben dem *common law* die wichtigste Quelle englischen Schiedsrechts dar.[107] Der *Arbitration Act* 1979 ist damit wie auch der *Arbitration Act* 1950 Gegenstand der ausführlichen Untersuchung in Teil III dieser Arbeit. An dieser Stelle sollen deshalb nur stichwortartig die Änderungen umrissen werden, die der *Act* vorsah:

- Abschaffung des *special case*-Verfahrens
- Abschaffung des *error of law*-Verfahrens
- Ersetzung der zuvor genannten Verfahren durch ein neues (eingeschränktes) *right of appeal* sowie durch ein eingeschränktes Recht der Gerichte zur Entscheidung über Rechtsfragen[108]
- Neuschaffung der Befugnis der Gerichte, die Begründung[109] eines Schiedsspruches anzuordnen
- Möglichkeit des Ausschlusses des *right of appeal* für bestimmte Verfahrensarten[110]

Die eigentliche Bedeutung des *Arbitration Acts* 1979 lag in der Ersetzung des *special case*-Verfahrens durch ein *right of appeal*.[111] Der *Act* wurde deshalb auch als "*a rather half-hearted statute*",[112] "*pragmatic compromise*",[113] "*pleasing but not satisfying*"[114] und "*a typically English compromise*"[115] kritisiert.[116]

---

107 Zur Entwicklung in den Jahren 1979 - 1985 vgl. Hacking, J.Int'l Arb. 1985, 7.
108 Vgl. *infra* Teil III, Kapitel 10.
109 Vgl. *infra* Teil III, Kapitel 10, D.II.2.
110 Vgl. *infra* Teil III, Kapitel 10, D.II.4.
111 Barker, Virg.J.Int'l L. 1983, 442.
112 Smedresman, J. Mar.L. & Com. 1979-80, 319.
113 Staughton, New L.J. 1979, 922.
114 Sanders, Arbitration 1980, 11.
115 Rokison, Arbitration 1980, 88.
116 Für eine ausführlichere Analyse des *Arbitration Acts* 1979 vgl. Schmitthoff, Yearbook 1980, S. 231.

Kapitel 3
Der *Mustill-Report*: Ablehnung des Modellgesetzes

Eine entscheidende Rolle für die Entwicklung - besser: den Stillstand - des englischen Schiedsrechts sollte der *Report on the UNCITRAL Model Law on International Commercial Arbitration* (nachfolgend: *Mustill-Report*) spielen. Im Anschluß an die Verabschiedung des Modellgesetzes durch UNCITRAL im Juni 1985 beauftragte das britische Department of Trade and Industry das DAC unter dem Vorsitz von Lord Justice Mustill mit der Überprüfung des Modellgesetzes vor dem Hintergrund einer möglichen Übernahme in das englische Recht.[117] Der weltweit mit Spannung erwartete *report* kann in seiner Bedeutung für das englische Schiedsrecht nicht überschätzt werden.[118] Nicht nur, daß er gleichermaßen das historisch gewachsene Selbstverständnis der englischen Justiz als Hüter von Recht und Gerechtigkeit artikuliert.[119] Er ist mit seiner Empfehlung, das Modellgesetz nicht in englisches Recht zu übernehmen, letztlich auch verantwortlich für den Stillstand der Entwicklung des Schiedsrechts bis zum *Arbitration Act* 1996.[120]

Zumindest Kenner des englischen Rechts hatten diese Empfehlung erwartet.[121] Einer der Hauptgründe für die Ablehnung des Modellgesetzes war das englische Verständnis von der Rolle der Gerichte in der Schiedsgerichtsbarkeit.[122] Die Kritik am Modellgesetz wurde unter anderem an der Frage nach der

117 Der exakte Auftrag lautete (vgl. *Mustill-Report,* para 2):
"1. To consider the draft Model Law [...] upon whether, and if so to what extent, the provisions of the Model Law should be implemented in England [...] and upon what measures should be taken for that purpose [...]2. To examine the operation of the Arbitration Acts 1950 - 1979 in the light of the Model Law and to recommend to the Secretary of State any legislative or other steps which the Committee considers should be taken to improve the system of arbitration in England and Wales."

118 Wetter, Arb.Int'l 1990, 268.

119 Zu diesem Verständnis vgl. auch Kerr, I.C.L.Q. 1985, 15.

120 Dieser Kritik will Mustill, Int'l Bus.Lawy. 1989, 164, nicht folgen:
"In the first place, I would like to make plain the general attitude of the United Kingdom towards the Model Law. It is important to say this because for reasons of habit or juristic chauvinism the United Kingdom is constantly represented as being a kind of luddite wrecker of every innovation in the field of arbitration. This is nonsense, as is made perfectly plain by the fact the European countries which had been limping along with antique arbitration statutes since the last century, and had been fitfully debating reform for decades, were prodded into life by the enactment of the English Arbitration Act of 1979."

121 Vgl. dazu nur *ibid*, 161; ebenso Steyn, Int'l Bus.Lawy. 1989, 432.

122 Davidson, J.B.L. 1990, 481.

Zulässigkeit eines *right of appeal* festgemacht.[123] Wie nachfolgend darzustellen sein wird, sieht das Modellgesetz - anders als das englische Recht zum damaligen Zeitpunkt - kein solches Recht vor.[124] Das gänzliche Fehlen eines *right of appeal* wurde vom DAC für ebenso inakzeptabel befunden wie eine auch nur teilweise Einschränkung desselben.[125] Diese ablehnende Haltung gilt auch für andere Bereiche, in denen das Modellgesetz eine Beschneidung der gerichtlichen Kompetenzen vorsieht. Besonders deutlich wird dies etwa bei der Stellungnahme des *Mustill-Reports* zu Art. 5 Modellgesetz,[126] welcher eine ausdrückliche Beschränkung der gerichtlichen Eingriffsbefugnisse vorsieht.[127]

Kapitel 4
Der *Arbitration Act* 1996

"In England, things tend to take rather a long time to come to fruition." Diese Aussage eines erfahrenen englischen Schiedsexperten[128] hat sicherlich ihre Berechtigung, soweit es um die Reform des englischen Schiedsverfahrensrechts geht. So basierte das englische Schiedsrecht bis 1997 überwiegend auf dem *Arbitration Act* 1950, welcher seinerseits kaum mehr als eine Neufassung des *Arbitration Acts* 1889 war.[129]

Diese Situation sollte sich erst durch Inkrafttreten des *Arbitration Acts* 1996 am 31. Januar 1997 ändern.[130] Der *Act* konsolidiert zum einen die *Arbitration Acts* 1950, 1975 und 1979 sowie das einschlägige *common law*. Zum anderen re-

---

123 Vgl. zur Kritik auch Semple, Arbitration 1990, 95.

124 Vgl. *infra* Teil III, Kapitel 10, C..

125 *Mustill-Report*, para 80.

126 *Mustill-Report*, Appendix 2, I.

127 Zur Kritik am Modellgesetz vgl. auch Schmitthoff, Arb.Int'l 1988, 68.

128 Rokison, Arb.Int'l 1998, 361. Mit Blick auf die Aufgabe des DAC, konkrete Vorschläge für eine Reform des englischen Schiedsverfahrensrechts zu machen, fährt Rokison fort:
"The members of the [DAC] were guilty at times of letting the grass grow under their feet. This [...] follows an English tradition. The story is told of an American tourist who asked the head gardener in Trinity College, Cambridge, how he managed to get the lawn in Great Court to look so good. 'You just mow it for 500 years', was his somewhat condescending reply."

129 Vgl. *supra* Kapitel 2, E..

130 Eingehend zur "Entwicklungsgeschichte" des *Arbitration Acts* 1996 Miller, Arbitration 1996, 250; vgl. auch Bernstein, Handbook, S. 38 ff; Carbonneau, Tulane Mar.L.J. 1997, 137 f.; Lord/Salzedo, S. 58 ff; Wallace, Int'l Constr. L Rev. 1997, 84 f.

formiert er Teile des bis dahin geltende Rechts.[131] Die Gründe, die zum Erlaß des *Arbitration Acts* 1996 führten, sind im wesentlichen vergleichbar mit denen, die bereits für den Erlaß des *Arbitration Acts* 1979 ursächlich waren. Vor allem das sich weiter verschlechternde Ansehen des englischen Schiedsrechts war ausschlaggebend hierfür. Hatte der *Arbitration Act* 1979 noch für eine kurzfristige - wenngleich recht halbherzige - Modernisierung des englischen Rechts gesorgt, wurde dieses spätestens seit Ablehnung des Modellgesetzes endgültig als "*out of step*" mit den Entwicklungen im Ausland angesehen.[132]

Der *Arbitration Act* 1996 verkörpert die "*most extensive statutory reform of English arbitration law, its scope exceeding any previous English statute on arbitration*".[133] In einer für ein anglo-amerikanisches Gesetz untypischen Weise regelt er in 110 *sections* sehr detailliert das Recht der Schiedsgerichtsbarkeit. Er hat damit mehr als den zweifachen Umfang als jedes bisherige englische Schiedsgesetz. Die weitaus meisten der Vorschriften sind indes nicht neu. Entweder entsprechen sie - mehr oder weniger - den Vorschriften des *Arbitration Acts* 1950, oder sie sind reine *restatements* des *common law*.[134]

Kapitel 5
Zwischenergebnis

Die exemplarische Darstellung der geschichtlichen Entwicklung des englischen Schiedsverfahrensrechts verdeutlicht, daß die gerichtlichen Kontrollbefugnisse zumindest bis 1979 kontinuierlich zugenommen haben.[135] Spätestens mit Erlaß des *Arbitration Acts* 1889 hatte sich in England ein System umfassender Kontroll- und Eingriffsbefugnisse der Gerichte fest etabliert. Parker of Waddington nennt folgende Gründe für diese Entwicklung:[136]

> "*1. The natural desire of the courts to keep all adjudications within their sphere;*
> *2. The fear of the growth of a new system of law;*
> *3. The fact that litigants in arbitrations needed the assistance of the courts who in turn exacted a price for such assistance.*"

131 Merkin, Arbitration Act 1996, S. 1.
132 Lord/Salzedo, S. IX.
133 Veeder, England, S. 2.
134 Samuel, Arb. & Disp.Res.L.J. 1999, 2.
135 Vgl. auch Zweigert/Kötz, S. 412; a.A. Roebuck, Arb.Int'l 1994, 395.
136 Parker of Waddington, S. 13; vgl. auch Neill, Arb.Int'l 1990, 274; Evans, Arb. & Disp.Res.L.J. 1999, 41.

Der *Arbitration Act* 1979 hat zwar das *special case*- und das *error of law*-Verfahren abgeschafft und damit zwei besonders umstrittene Befugnisbereiche der Gerichte entfernt. Wie die weiteren Ausführungen jedoch zeigen werden, stellte der *Act* aber nur einen halbherzigen reformerischen Kompromiß dar. Ob auch der *Arbitration Act* 1996 wieder auf halbem Wege stehen bleibt, wird nachfolgend zu untersuchen sein.

Teil III
Befugnisse der Gerichte: rechtsvergleichende Untersuchung

Kapitel 1
Die Existenz einer allgemeinen Eingriffsbefugnis der staatlichen Gerichte

A. Einführung

Die gerichtlichen Eingriffsbefugnisse in ein Schiedsverfahren würden sich nicht umfassend darstellen lassen, wenn man sich lediglich darauf beschränken würde, die positiven Befugnisse zu untersuchen. Entscheidende Bedeutung kommt darüber hinaus auch der Frage zu, ob und inwieweit die Gerichte *über* diese ausdrücklich geregelten Befugnisse *hinaus* tätig werden dürfen. Von Bedeutung ist diese Frage etwa dann, wenn eine staatliche Intervention überhaupt nicht geregelt, also weder ausdrücklich zugelassen noch ausdrücklich ausgeschlossen ist. Es fragt sich, ob die Gerichte in diesem Fall tätig werden dürfen oder ob die Nichtregelung durch den Gesetzgeber als Aufforderung an die Gerichte zu verstehen ist, diese "Lücke" auszufüllen. Gerade für Staaten des *common law* kommt der Beantwortung dieser Frage eine erhebliche Bedeutung zu. Denn hier obliegt die Rechtsentwicklung und -fortbildung zu einem bedeutenden Teil den Gerichten. Aufgrund des im Vergleich zu Staaten des *civil law* oft fragmentarischen Charakters der Gesetze schöpfen die Gerichte somit zwangsläufig ihre Befugnisse aus "selbstgemachtem" Recht.

B. Art. 5 Modellgesetz

Mit Art. 5 bietet das Modellgesetz eine auf den ersten Blick eindeutige Antwort auf die zuvor aufgeworfenen Fragen. Darin heißt es:

> *"In den von diesem Gesetz geregelten Angelegenheiten darf das Gericht nur tätig werden, soweit dieses Gesetz es vorsieht."*[137]

---

137 Der fünfte Bericht der Arbeitsgruppe zum Modellgesetz (vgl. UN-Doc. A/CN.9/246, paras 183 f) hatte zunächst folgende Formulierung vorgesehen, die jedoch als nicht weitgehend genug verworfen wurde:

So innovativ Art. 5 Modellgesetz im internationalen Vergleich bei seiner Aufnahme in das Modellgesetz war, so umstritten war er auch. Dies ist nur allzu verständlich. Art. 5 zielt direkt auf die Schnittstelle zwischen Schieds- und staatlicher Gerichtsbarkeit ab. Die Vorschrift macht es den Gerichten unmöglich, außerhalb der explizit genannten Eingriffsbefugnisse in ein Schiedsverfahren einzugreifen. Ausnahmen sind nicht vorgesehen.

Art. 5 ist eine der wichtigsten Vorschriften des Modellgesetzes.[138] Die Bedeutung der Vorschrift ist allerdings nicht leicht zu erfassen. Zunächst hat es den Anschein, daß die Beschneidung der Kompetenzen der Gerichte das primäre Ziel ist.[139] Die Vorschrift wurde deshalb auch als "*highly undesirable and an attack on the partnership between bench and arbitrators*" bezeichnet.[140] Hunter bringt die Einstellung einiger Staaten, insbesondere wohl Englands, auf den Punkt, wenn er Art. 5 Modellgesetz ein "*somewhat forbidden anouncement*" nennt.[141]

Um der eigentlichen Bedeutung der Vorschrift gerecht zu werden, empfiehlt es sich deshalb, einen Blick auf die *travaux préparatoire zu werfen.* Darin heißt es:[142]

> *"[The purpose of Art. 5] was to achieve certainty as to the maximum extent of judicial intervention, including assistance [...] by compelling the drafters to list [...] all instances of court intervention."*

Herrmann zufolge nimmt Art. 5 selbst keine Stellung zum Ausmaß einer erwünschten Einmischung durch die staatlichen Gerichte. [143] Vielmehr zwinge er lediglich die Verfasser des Modellgesetzes dazu, die als wünschenswert erachteten Interventionsmöglichkeiten der staatlichen Gerichte allesamt explizit im Mo-

---

"In matters governed by this Law concerning the arbitral proceedings or the composition of the arbitral tribunal, courts may exercise supervisory or assisting functions only if so provided in this Law."

138 Fleischhauer, Arb.J. 1986, 20.

139 Die Hong Kong Law Reform Commission nimmt in ihrem Report auf S. 13 wie folgt Stellung:
"On the face of it, the intention of the provision is plain - it is intended to isolate the operation of the law from court supervision, except when court supervision is expressly permitted. Such a provision would allay the fears of those who regard court intervention in the arbitral process as contrary to the spirit of arbitration. We support the intention of the provision, but [are] concerned at the ambiguity in the way it is expressed."

140 Zitiert bei Herrmann, Arb.Int'l 1985, 14 f; vgl. auch ders., Pace L.Rev. 1983, 550.

141 Hunter, Arbitration 1984, 291 unter Verweis auf UN-Doc. A/CN.9/WG./2/9/CRP1.

142 UN-Doc. A/40/17, para 63.

143 Herrmann, in: Lew (Hrsg.), Contemporary Problems, S. 168; ders., Arb.Int'l 1985, 15; vgl. auch Broches, S. 30 f.

dellgesetz aufzuführen.[144] Das ist wohl nur bedingt richtig. Denn mit Art. 5 verlieren die Gerichte nicht nur jegliche Kompetenzen, die für nicht wünschenswert erachtet wurden. Vielmehr wird den Gerichten zudem von vornherein jede Möglichkeit einer flexiblen Reaktion auf unvorhergesehene Fallumstände genommen.[145]

Art. 5 beansprucht nur "*[i]n den von diesem Gesetz geregelten Angelegenheiten*" Geltung.[146] Durch diese Formulierung soll eine Einschränkung des Anwendungsbereichs der Vorschrift zum Ausdruck gebracht werden.[147] Gegenstand von Art. 5 sind demnach nur solche Angelegenheiten, die auch tatsächlich eine Regelung durch das Modellgesetz erfahren haben. So sollten beispielsweise die Bereiche

- Staatenimmunität,
- Zeitlimit für die Vollstreckung von Schiedssprüchen,
- Kompetenz der Schiedsgerichte zur Anpassung von Verträgen oder
- staatsgerichtliche Durchsetzung einstweiligen Maßnahmen, welche von Schiedsgerichten angeordnet wurden

nicht von Art. 5 erfaßt sein.[148] Der UNCITRAL-Kommission zufolge handelt es sich allerdings nicht um eine abschließende Aufzählung.[149] Im übrigen wurde der Anwendungsbereich von Art. 5 offen gelassen.

Gerade die englische Delegation zu den Beratungen am Modellgesetz übte hieran Kritik.[150] So wurde unter anderem bemängelt, daß das Modellgesetz nicht erkennen lasse, welche Angelegenheiten von diesem geregelt werden und welche nicht.[151] Vor allem in zwei Fallgruppen würden die Gerichte vor erhebliche Probleme gestellt. Die erste Fallgruppe zeichne sich dadurch aus, daß eine bestimmte Situation, obgleich nicht selbst vom Modellgesetz geregelt, generell mit einer solchen - vom Modellgesetz geregelten Situation - vergleichbar sei. Hier stelle sich die Frage, ob das Fehlen einer Regelung für oder wider einer entsprechenden Eingriffsbefugnis der Gerichte ausgelegt werden müsse; zweitens, was in Situationen gelten solle, die von UNCITRAL überhaupt nicht bedacht worden seien.

---

144 *Ibid.*

145 In UN-Doc. A/CN.9/264, para 228 heißt es:
"[The effect of Art. 5] would, thus, be to exclude any general or residual powers given to the courts in a domestic system which are not listed in the model law."

146 Vgl. Wortlaut Art. 5 Modellgesetz.

147 Dore, S. 98 f.

148 UN-Doc. A/CN.9/246, paras 187 f.

149 UN-Doc. A/CN.9/264/Add.2, para 22.

150 An dieser Stelle soll nur eine Kurzfassung derselben wiedergegeben werden. Für eine ausführliche Stellungnahme vgl. UN-Doc. A/CN.9/263/Add.2, paras 19-38; vgl. auch Davidson, Civ.Just.Q. 1993, 386 ff.

151 Siehe auch die Diskussion bei Davidson, *ibid.*

Auf die englische Kritik räumte die UNCITRAL-Kommission zwar ein, daß Art. 5 tatsächlich nicht in allen Fällen eine sichere Beurteilung zulasse, ob ein gerichtliches Eingreifen zulässig sei oder nicht.[152] Die englischen Einwände wurden jedoch als unbedeutend verworfen. Dies geschah unter Hinweis darauf, daß die Gerichte des jeweiligen Modellgesetzstaates die Vorschrift nach wie vor zulässigerweise auslegen durften.[153]

Dem ist nach der hier vertretenen Auffassung zuzustimmen. Art. 5 ist sicherlich keine "wasserdichte" Regelung. Es ist denkbar, daß sie unter bestimmten Voraussetzung Anlaß zu Kompetenzstreitigkeiten bieten wird. Ungeachtet dieser Kritik stellt Art. 5 dennoch eine der wesentlichen positiven Errungenschaften des Modellgesetzes dar. Er schützt die Schiedsparteien weitgehend vor Überraschungen, die durch nicht oder nur schwer vorhersehbare Einmischungen staatlicher Gerichte in das Schiedsverfahren verursacht werden können. Die dadurch gewonnene Rechtssicherheit kommt der redlichen Partei des Schiedsverfahrens zugute.

C. Das englische Recht vor 1997

I. Keine gesetzliche Beschränkung staatlicher Eingriffsbefugnisse

Art. 5 Modellgesetz - vom *Mustill-Report* auch als "*pivot*", also als Dreh- und Angelpunkt des Modellgesetzes bezeichnet[154] - stellte einen der wesentlichen Gründe für die Ablehnung des Modellgesetzes durch England dar. Hunter zufolge liegt in Art. 5 gar die "*main philosophical objection*" gegen das Modellgesetz.[155]

Die englische Haltung zu Art. 5 erklärt sich vor dem Hintergrund eines Vergleichs der englischen Rechtslage vor 1997 mit Art. 5 Modellgesetz.[156] Ein solcher Vergleich muß notwendigerweise kurz ausfallen. Vor 1997 gab es im englischen Recht keine vergleichbare Regelung. Eine solche widersprach ihrem Wesen nach der historisch gewachsenen Überzeugung der englischen Justiz, daß die Gerichte in allen Fällen das letzte Wort behalten sollten. Genau so, wie es für die

---

152 UN-Doc. A/CN.9/SR.309, paras 1-3, 6-9.

153 UN-Doc. A/49/17, para 61.

154 *Mustill-Report*, Appendix 2, I.

155 Hunter, Arbitration 1984, 291, schließt sich dem jedoch selbst nicht an: *"However, I foresee no great difficulty in this regard, and there seems to be no fumdamental imcompatibility with the English ideas of the supportive rôle of the courts and the proposals made in the current draft of the model law."*

156 Vgl. auch Rogers, Arb.Int'l 1990, 350.

Gerichte inakzeptabel war, daß ihre Zuständigkeit durch eine Parteivereinbarung ausgeschlossen werden konnte,[157] war auch eine unwiderrufliche Selbstbeschränkung ihrer Kompetenzen durch eine Art. 5 Modellgesetz entsprechende Vorschrift inakzeptabel.

Daneben standen weitere, eher praktische Überlegungen. So sah die englische Delegation bei den Beratungen zum Modellgesetz offenbar keine Möglichkeit, die Schwierigkeiten um den Anwendungsbereich von Art. 5 Modellgesetz auszuräumen.[158] Eine Modifizierung von Art. 5 für den Fall der Übernahme in englisches Recht wurde unter Hinweis auf das vom Modellgesetz postulierte Ziel einer inernationalen Harmonisierung verworfen.[159] Eine Übernahme von Art. 5 in das englische Recht ohne Modifizierungen kam nach dem *Mustill-Report* unabhängig von den vorgenannten grundsätzlichen Bedenken auch aus einem weiteren Grund nicht in Frage. Soweit nämlich der Anwendungsbereich von Art. 5 Modellgesetz nicht abschließend geklärt sei, sah der *Mustill-Report* die Gefahr der Koexistenz zweier völlig unterschiedlicher Systeme staatsgerichtlicher Interventionsmöglichkeiten: ein System für Angelegenheiten, die von Art. 5 erfaßt seien, und eines für solche, die nicht unter Art. 5 fielen.[160]

II. Inherent Jurisdiction *zum Eingriff in ein Schiedsverfahren*

Von entscheidender Bedeutung für das englische Verhältnis von Schiedsgerichtsbarkeit und staatlichen Gerichten war die Frage, ob den Gerichten eine "*inherent jurisdiction*" zum Eingriff in ein Schiedsverfahren zustand.[161] Der Begriff hat kein Gegenstück in der deutschen Terminologie. Er läßt sich deshalb nur ungenau mit "originärer" oder "sich aus der Rechtsnatur ergebende" Zuständigkeit übersetzen. Gemeint ist die Befugnis der Gerichte, auch außerhalb ausdrücklicher Ermächtigungsgrundlagen in ein Schiedsverfahren eingreifen zu können. Die Bedeutung der *inherent jurisdiction* ergibt sich daraus, daß die Gerichte im Falle ihrer Bejahung in Schiedsverfahren eingreifen konnten, *ohne* auf positiv normierte Eingriffsermächtigungen angewiesen zu sein.

Mangels einer entsprechenden gesetzlichen Regelung läßt sich nur anhand des *common law* beurteilen, ob und inwieweit eine *inherent jurisdiction* der engli-

---

157 Sog. "*ouster of jurisdiction*"; vgl. *supra* Teil II, Kapitel 2, B..

158 *Mustill-Report*, Appendix 2, I.

159 *Ibid.*

160 *Mustill-Report*, *ibid*; vgl. hierzu die kritische Stellungnahme von Herrmann, Arb.Int'l 1988, 62 ff.

161 Allgemein vgl. Dockray, L.Q.Rev. 1997, 120; Manson, Aust.L.J. 1983, 449; Starke, Aust.L.J. 1981, 47.

schen Gerichte zum Eingreifen in Schiedsverfahren bestand. Zu diesem Zweck werden nachfolgend die wichtigsten Fälle kurz dargestellt.

1. Analyse des englischen common law

a) Exormisis Shipping S.A. *v.* Oonsoo, The Democratic Peoples Republic of Korea and The Korean Foreign Transportation Corporation (No 1)[162]

In diesem Fall beantragte eine Schiedspartei beim High Court die Aufhebung eines schiedsgerichtlichen Beschlusses zur Zulässigkeit der Nachreichung eines Schriftsatzes. Zugleich sollte der High Court die Ansetzung eines weiteren Termins zur mündlichen Verhandlung verfügen. In einer Entscheidung aus dem Jahr 1975 wies das Gericht den Antrag mit der Begründung zurück, daß ihm für die Anordnung der beantragten Maßnahmen keine Ermächtigungsgrundlage zur Verfügung stehe. Eine solche Ermächtigungsgrundlage könne nur vom Gesetzgeber geschaffen werden.[163] Eine *inherent jurisdiction* als Grundlage zum Eingreifen in das Schiedsverfahren wurde folglich abgelehnt.

b) Japan Line Ltd. *v.* Aggeliki Charis Compania Maritima S.A. ("The Angelic Grace")[164]

Die vorgenannte Rechtsprechung sollte sich im Jahr 1979 durch ein Urteil des Court of Appeal in *The Angelic Grace* entscheidend ändern. In diesem Fall ging es um Schadensersatzforderungen von Schiffseigentümern gegen die Charterer. In einem Zwischenschiedsspruch gewährte das Schiedsgericht den Klägern zwar einen Teil der beantragten Summe. Es tat dies aber unter der Bedingung der Leistung einer entsprechenden Sicherheit. Die Schiffseigner sahen hierin eine Überschreitung der Kompetenzen durch das Schiedsgericht und klagten auf eine diesbezügliche Feststellung. In dem hierauf ergangenen Urteil stellte der High Court unter anderem fest, daß er eine *inherent jurisdiction* zur Entscheidung über die Klage besitze. Der Court of Appeal bestätigte das Urteil des High Court in diesem Punkt. Lord Denning führte hierzu aus:

> *"In my opinion, the High Court has an inherent jurisdiction to supervise the conduct of arbitrators. It is not confined to the statutory powers. The High Court need not go to the extreme step of removing arbitrators. It can supervise their proceedings so as to ensure that they are not guilty of misconduct [...]"*

---

162 [1975] 1 Lloyd's Rep. 432.
163 *Ibid*, 434.
164 [1980] 1 Lloyd's Rep. 288.

Durch dieses Urteil wurde der gerichtlichen Kontrolle von Schiedsverfahren im Vorfeld[165] des Ergehens des Schiedsspruches "Tür und Tor" geöffnet. War zuvor zumindest sehr fraglich, ob den Gerichten eine *inherent jurisdiction* zustand, räumte das Urteil in *The Angelic Grace* solche Zweifel aus. Den Gerichten stand es danach frei, gleich mit welcher Maßnahme und wann immer sie es für erforderlich hielten, in ein laufendes Schiedsverfahren zu intervenieren.

c) Bremer Vulkan Schiffbau und Maschinenfabrik v. South India Shipping Corpn. Ltd. ("The Bremer Vulkan")[166]

Das wohl wichtigste Urteil im Zusammenhang mit der *inherent jurisdiction* der englischen Gerichte ist dasjenige des House of Lords in *The Bremer Vulkan*. Dem Rechtsstreit lagen Mängelrügen im Zusammenhang mit dem Bau von Schiffen zugrunde. Nachdem eine Einigung zwischen den Parteien endgültig gescheitert war, leitete die *South India Shipping Corp.* 1972 das Schiedsverfahren gegen die Bremer Vulkan-Werft ein. Das Verfahren gestaltete sich äußerst schleppend. Dies war nach Ansicht der Bremer Vulkan-Werft vor allem auf das Verhalten der Schiedsklägerin zurückzuführen. 1977 beantragte die Bremer Vulkan-Werft schließlich beim High Court eine Verfügung, die das Schiedsverfahren wegen einer Verschleppung des Verfahrens durch die *South India Shipping Corpn.* stoppen sollte.[167] Der Antrag wurde damit begründet, daß eine zur ordnungsgemäßen Verteidigung erforderliche Beweisführung wegen Zeitablaufs nicht mehr möglich sei.[168] Der High Court entsprach dem Antrag.[169] Das Urteil wurde in zweiter Instanz vom Court of Appeal bestätigt.[170] Wie auch in *The Angelic Grace* stützten die Gerichte ihr Eingreifen auf eine *inherent jurisdiction*.

Der Fall gelangte schließlich vor das House of Lords. Mit einer Mehrheit von drei zu zwei Stimmen verwarf dieses grundsätzlich eine *inherent jurisdiction* der Gerichte in Schiedsverfahren.[171] Eine Ausnahme wurde allerdings zugelassen: So sollte es den Gerichten möglich sein, auf Grundlage der *general jurisdiction* eine

165 Zu den Befugnissen der Gerichte *nach* Ergehen des Schiedsspruchs vgl. *infra* Kapitel 10.

166 [1981] A.C. 909.

167 Die Möglichkeit der Abweisung einer (ordentlichen) Klage wegen Prozeßverschleppung (sog. *dismissal of action for want of prosecution*) stand den Gerichten unstreitig zu. Neu war, daß diese Möglichkeit nunmehr auf ein *Schieds*verfahren angewendet werden sollte.

168 Zum Problem der Verschleppung von Schiedsverfahren vgl. auch Okekeifere, J.Int'l Arb. 1996, 126 ff.

169 [1979] 3 All E.R. 194.

170 [1980] 1 All E.R. 420.

171 [1981] A.C. 909 (979).

einstweilige Anordnung zur "*protection of some legal or equitable right when it was just and convenient so to do*" anzuordnen.[172] Voraussetzung war insoweit jedoch, daß der (endgültige) Verlust eines solchen Rechts drohte und nicht lediglich eine Beeinträchtigung.[173] So sollten beispielsweise Verschleppungsmanöver für sich genommen keinen ausreichenden Grund zur Gewährung einer einstweiligen Anordnung darstellen.

d) Compagnie Européenne de Céreals S.A. *v.* Tradax Export S.A.[174]

In diesem Fall ging es wieder um den Antrag einer Schiedspartei an den High Court, eine *injunction* zur Verhinderung einer Verletzung der Schiedsabrede zu treffen. Das Gericht gab dem Antrag statt. Ohne seine Eingriffsbefugnis überhaupt zu hinterfragen, führte das Gericht aus:[175]

> *"[A] party [to an arbitration agreement] has a right to apply to the court for a injunction to restrain a breach fo the arbitration contract by the other parties, just as with any other breach of contract."*

2. Zwischenergebnis

Die Analyse der einschlägigen englischen Rechsprechung zur *inherent jurisdiction* ergibt ein uneinheitliches Bild. Der Entscheidung in *The Bremer Vulkan* als insoweit einzigen des House of Lords kommt hierbei die größte Autorität zu. Zwar wurde einer *general inherent jurisdiction*, wie sie vom Court of Appeal erstmals eindeutig in *The Angelic Grace* angenommen wurde, eine Absage erteilt. Diese erscheint jedoch halbherzig. Indem unter bestimmten Voraussetzungen das Rechtsmittel der *injunction* auf Grundlage der *inherent jurisdiction* zugelassen wurde, bestand für die Gerichte nach wie vor eine Möglichkeit, in ein Schiedsverfahren ohne positiv normierte gesetzliche Grundlage einzugreifen.

D. Der Arbitration Act *1996*

Nachdem der *Mustill-Report* Art. 5 Modellgesetz als einen der wesentlichen Gründe für die Ablehnung des Modellgesetzes identifiziert hatte, war mit Spannung erwartet worden, ob der *Arbitration Act* 1996 von dieser Position abwei-

172 [1981] A.C. 909, 979 f.
173 Mustill/Boyd, S. 522.
174 [1986] 2 Lloyd's Rep. 301.
175 *Ibid*, 306.

chen würde. In seinem *1996 Report on the Arbitration Bill* (nachfolgend: 1996-Report) nimmt das DAC unter Vorsitz von Lord Justice Saville wie folgt Stellung zu Art. 5 Modellgesetz und der entsprechenden Kritik des *Mustill-Reports*:

"As was pointed out in the Mustill-Report (pp. 50-52) there would be difficulties in importing this Article as it stands. However, there is no doubt that our law has been subject to international criticism that the Courts intervene more than they should in the arbitral process, thereby tending to frustrate the choice the parties have made to use arbitration rather than litigation as the means for resolving their disputes [...] Nowadays the Courts are much less inclined to intervene in the arbitral process than used to be the case. The limitation on the right of appeal to the Courts from awards brought into effect by the Arbitration Act 1979, and changing attitudes generally, have meant that the Courts nowadays generally only intervene in order to support rather than displace the arbitral process. We are very much in favour of this modern approach and it seems to us that it should be enshrined as a principle in the Bill."

Das Ergebnis dieser Empfehlung ist in *s* 1(c) *Arbitration Act* 1996 ("*General principles*") zu finden. Diese lautet:

"The provisions of this part are founded on the following principles, and shall be construed accordingly- [...]
(c) in matters governed by this Part the court should not intervene except were so provided by this Part."

Auf den ersten Blick scheint *s* 1(c) tatsächlich den revolutionären Charakter, der dem *Arbitration Act* 1996 von vielen[176] zugeschrieben wird, zu rechtfertigen. Die Vorschrift wird deshalb von der überwiegenden Literatur begrüßt.[177] Dabei scheint allerdings der Wunsch Vater des Gedankens gewesen zu sein. Zugegeben, mit *s* 1(c) wurde erstmalig das Prinzip der limitierten Eingriffsbefugnis der Gerichte kodifiziert. Hierin ist in jedem Fall ein Fortschritt gegenüber dem alten Recht zu sehen. Ein revolutionärer Charakter kann der Vorschrift im Gegensatz zu Art. 5 Modellgesetz allerdings nicht zugeschrieben werden. Denn im Gegensatz zur letztgenannten Vorschrift handelt es sich bei *s* 1 (c) lediglich um eine *Soll*vorschrift ("*the court* should *not intervene*"). Diese ist zudem (nur) als "*general principle*" verfaßt worden.[178]

---

176 Vgl. statt anderer Redfern, Arb. & Disp.Res.L.J. 1997, 172.

177 Allen voran Rutherford/Sims, S. 41, die *s* 1(c) auch als "*golden thread*" bezeichnen und ferner annehmen, daß die Parteien nunmehr "*precisely and with confidence the limits of [the courts] power*" einschätzen könnten; vgl. auch Merkin, Arbitration Act 1996, S. 13.

178 Diese Tatsache wurde bei der zweiten Lesung über das Gesetz von Lord Wilberforce kritisiert. Die ganz überwiegende Ansicht sprach sich bei den Beratungen jedoch

Den Gerichten steht damit nach wie vor ein Ermessen hinsichtlich des Gebrauchs oder Nichtgebrauchs ihrer *general powers* oder *inherent jurisdiction* in dem durch *The Bremer Vulkan* festgelegten Umfang zu.[179] Entscheidend wird es jedoch darauf ankommen, wie die englischen Gerichte *s* 1(c) auslegen. Eine entsprechende Auslegung darf schon deshalb mit Spannung erwartet werden, weil das Konzept kodifizierter übergeordneter *general principles* dem englischen Recht bislang fremd war.

E. Zwischenergebnis

Dort, wo die englischen Gerichte auf ihr Recht des letzten Wortes verzichten sollen, verlangen sie Sicherheit darüber und Vorhersehbarkeit dessen, was sich an Konsequenzen hieraus ergeben könnte. Im Zusammenhang mit Art. 5 Modellgesetz hatte der *Mustill-Report* hierzu ausgeführt:[180]

> *"[A]nd if it is considered desirable in principle to enact [Art. 5 of] the Model Law, it may be necessary to work out, and state explicitly its intended scope. Until this is done, it will not be possible to assess with precision the effect which enactment would have on current English arbitration law and practice."*

Eine Vorhersehbarkeit war den englischen Richtern bzw. dem englischen Gesetzgeber vor 1997 nicht möglich. Konsequenterweise sah das englische Recht bis zu diesem Zeitpunkt auch keine dem Art. 5 Modellgesetz entsprechende Regelung vor.

Der *Arbitration Act* 1996 hat gegenüber der alten Rechtslage keine dramatische Änderung gebracht. Indem der englische Gesetzgeber sich mit *s* 1(c) *Arbitration Act* 1996 lediglich zu einer Sollvorschrift hat entschließen können, bleibt der Reformversuch auf halbem Wege stecken. Es ist zu hoffen, daß die englische Rechtsprechung bald strikte Richtlinien entwickeln wird, anhand derer die Vorschrift ausgelegt werden kann. Solange dies aber nicht geschehen ist, kann das mit *s* 1(c) *Arbitration Act* 1996 verfolgte Ziel der Limitierung und Vorhersehbarkeit staatlicher Eingriffe in das Schiedsverfahren bestenfalls als das angesehen werden, was es ist: Eine kosmetische Korrektur des englischen Schiedsrechts.

---

gegen eine weitergehende Beschränkung der staatsgerichtlichen Eingriffsbefugnisse aus (vgl. Merkin, Arbitration Act 1996, S. 13).

179 Kritisch Marriot, Arbitration 1996, 109, der sich für eine weitergehende *inherent jurisdiction* der Gerichte ausspricht.

180 *Mustill-Report*, Appendix 2, I.

Ungeachtet seiner zuvor aufgezeigten Schwächen ist demnach Art. 5 Modellgesetz gegenüber *s* 1(c) *Arbitration Act* 1996 vorzugswürdig. Der verbindliche Charakter von Art. 5 Modellgesetz erreicht ein vorbildliches Maß an Vorhersehbarkeit und Berechenbarkeit der staatsgerichtlichen Eingriffsbefugnisse und entspricht damit ganz dem Interesse der Schiedsparteien. Daß die englische Lösung in s 1(c) *Arbitration Act* 1996 aufgrund der durch sie gewährleisteten Flexibiliät im Einzelfall zu gerechteren Ergebnissen kommen kann, bleibt unbestritten.

Kapitel 2
Durchsetzung der Schiedsvereinbarung

A. Einführung

Voraussetzung für die Durchführung eines jeden Schiedsverfahrens ist das Vorliegen eines gültigen Schiedsvertrages. Der Schiedsvertrag enthält die Vereinbarung der Parteien, Ansprüche nur auf dem Schiedswege zu verfolgen. Regelmäßig werden sich die Parteien an eine solche Vereinbarung halten.[181] Möglich ist auch, daß sich die Parteien auf eine Aufhebung der Schiedsvereinbarung einigen und ihren Streit einem staatlichen Gericht übertragen.[182] In diesen Fällen gibt es keine Zuständigkeitsprobleme. Diese entstehen erst dann, wenn eine Partei den Streit abredewidrig vor ein staatliches Gericht trägt, während die andere Partei an der Schiedsabrede festhält. Es stellt sich dann die Frage, ob und unter welchen Voraussetzungen das Gericht befugt ist, den Streit zu verhandeln.

Die Durchführung eines Schiedsverfahrens würde *ad absurdum* geführt, wenn die Parteien durch die Anstrengung eines Verfahrens vor einem staatlichen Gericht ihre Pflichten aus dem Schiedsvertrag umgehen könnten. Jedenfalls aber besteht die Gefahr des Verschleppens des Schiedsverfahrens, soweit die staatlichen Gerichte umfassende und damit zeitraubende Zuständigkeitsprüfungen anstellen würden. Hierdurch würde das Schiedsverfahren eines seiner entscheidenden Vorteile gegenüber staatsgerichtlichen Verfahren beraubt, der Zügigkeit. Damit wird bereits zum Zeitpunkt des Entstehens, also mit Abschluß der Schiedsvereinbarung deutlich, wie sehr das Ge- oder Mißlingen eines Schiedsverfahrens von der Ausgestaltung und Ausübung staatsgerichtlicher Befugnisse abhängig ist.

---

181 Samuel, Jurisdictional Problems, S. 17. Nach einer Studie der Internationalen Handelskammer erfolgt in über 90 % aller Schiedsverfahren ein reibungsloser Ablauf ohne Einmischung der Gerichte (vgl. ICC, Guide to Arbitration, S. 48; vgl. ferner Commercial Court Committee, Final Report, S. 13).

182 Zu der Frage, ob Nichthandeln der Parteien einer einvernehmlichen Aufhebung der Schiedsvereinbarung gleichzusetzen ist, siehe Schmitthoff, Export Trade, S. 183.

B. Art. 8 Modellgesetz

I. Zwingende Verweisung

Das Modellgesetz regelt die Durchsetzung von Schiedsvereinbarungen in Art. 8 Abs. 1. Die Vorschrift wurde Art. II(3) des New Yorker UN-Übereinkommens nachgebildet. Sie lautet:

> *"Wird vor einem Gericht Klage erhoben, die Gegenstand einer Schiedsvereinbarung ist, so hat das Gericht die Parteien auf das schiedsrichterliche Verfahren zu verweisen, sofern eine Partei dies spätestens bei ihrer ersten Erklärung zur Sache beantragt, es sei denn, das Gericht stellt fest, daß die Schiedsvereinbarung nichtig, unwirksam oder undurchführbar ist."*

Die Vorschrift spricht für sich selbst. Danach haben die Gerichte eine schiedsabredewidrige Klage grundsätzlich zwingend an das schiedsrichterliche Verfahren zu verweisen. Ein Ermessenspielraum steht ihnen nicht zu. Verfahrenstechnische Besonderheiten sind weitgehend ohne Bedeutung und bleiben überdies den Rechtsordnungen des rezipierenden Staates überlassen.[183]

II. Versagungsgründe

Auch die in Art. 8 Abs. 1 Modellgesetz genannten Versagungsgründe sind dem Vorbild des Art. II(3) des New Yorker UN-Übereinkommens nachgebildet. Die gleichwohl diskutierten Änderungen wurden allesamt verworfen. So war etwa vorgeschlagen worden, die Verweisung der Klage an das schiedsrichterliche Verfahren nur in ganz offensichtlich ("*manifestly*") nichtigen, unwirksamen oder nicht erfüllbaren Schiedsvereinbarungen zu versagen.[184] Die Prüfungskompetenz der staatlichen Gerichte wäre damit auf eine *prima facie*-Beweisfindung beschränkt worden.[185] Eine solch weitgehende Beschränkung der Prüfungskompetenz der staatlichen Gerichte ging den Verfassern des Modellgesetzes jedoch zu weit. Auch mit Blick auf die Rechtsfolge der Art. 34 und 36 Modellgesetz[186] mußte die diskutierte Änderung als wenig sinnvoll erscheinen. Denn die Voraussetzungen für die Aufhebung des Schiedsspruchs und für die Versagung seiner Vollstreckung sollte *nicht* auf eine *prima facie*-Beweisfindung beschränkt sein. Die Wahrscheinlichkeit wäre deshalb groß gewesen, daß ein Schiedsspruch

---

183 Nöcker, S. 78 f.

184 UN-Doc. A/CN.9/233, para 77.

185 Holtzmann/Neuhaus, S. 303.

186 Vgl. hierzu *infra* Kapitel 10, B. und Kapitel 11, B..

schließlich doch wegen der gleichen Gründe "gekippt" würde, die schon zu einer Abweisung der Schiedseinrede hätten führen müssen.

Weiterhin war vorgeschlagen worden, auch die Vollstreckbarkeit nach dem Recht des Forumstaates als Kriterium in Art. 8 Modellgesetz aufzunehmen.[187] Dieser Vorschlag wurde jedoch unter dem Hinweis darauf abgelehnt, daß er dem angestrebten Zweck der internationalen Förderung und Harmonisierung der Schiedsgerichtsbarkeit zuwiderliefe.[188] Zudem hätte man damit der obsiegenden Partei die Möglichkeit genommen, die Vollstreckung in einem anderen als dem Forumstaat zu betreiben.[189]

In Art. 8 Abs. 1 Modellgesetz wurden schließlich folgende Tatbestandsmerkmale aufgenommen: Nichtigkeit, Unwirksamkeit und Undurchführbarkeit der Schiedsabrede.[190] Mit Blick auf die Herkunft der Ausnahmetatbestände aus dem New Yorker UN-Übereinkommen führen Holtzmann/Neuhaus aus:[191]

"The legislative history of Article 8 provides no other insights into the intended meaning of the terms "null and void, inoperative or incapable of being performed". In addition, the terms in the New York Convention have rarely been the subject of court decisions,[192] so their precise meaning must be left to future development. "

Von "Undurchführbarkeit" sind vor allem die Fälle der Zweckerreichung und der Unmöglichkeit der Zweckerreichung erfaßt.[193] Aber auch in Fällen der Weigerung des Schiedsgerichts, den Streit zu verhandeln, ist Undurchführbarkeit anzunehmen.[194] Gleiches gilt ferner bei Vorliegen eines Gerichtsurteils oder Schiedsspruchs in der selben Sache oder bei einer entgegenstehenden Einigung der Parteien.[195]

---

187 Holtzmann/Neuhaus, S. 303.
188 UN-Doc. A/CN.9/232, para 51.
189 *Ibid.*
190 Es geht hier also nicht um den Hauptvertrag (vgl. Holtzmann/Neuhaus, S. 305).
191 S. 305.
192 v.d. Berg, S. 154.
193 Schlosser, Schiedsgerichtsbarkeit, S. 411 f; ebenfalls könnten hierunter auch die Schiedsvereinbarungen fallen, die - während der 70er und 80er Jahre geschlossen - die Zuständigkeit der früheren Schiedsgerichte des COMECON vorsahen, die nach dem Zusammenbruch der Sowjetunion dann entfielen und deren Wirksamkeit dann während der 90er Jahre zu prüfen war.
194 v.d. Berg, S. 159 f.
195 *Ibid*, S. 158.

III. Schiedsfähigkeit

Art. 8 Modellgesetz enthält keinen direkten Vorbehalt der Schiedsfähigkeit. Obgleich nicht explizit genannt, ist die Einrede der Schiedsfähigkeit auch im Rahmen von Art. 8 Modellgesetz von Bedeutung. Hierfür sprechen vor allem zwei Erwägungen. Zum einen sind die Gerichte der Modellgesetzstaaten schon grundsätzlich nach Art. 1 Abs. 5 Modellgesetz gehalten, die Einrede der Schiedsfähigkeit von Amts wegen zu beachten.[196] Zum anderen ist die Einrede der Schiedsunfähigkeit eine Untergruppe der Einrede der Nichtigkeit.[197]

IV. Parallelität von Schieds- und staatlichem Verfahren

Bisher wurde vor allem die Frage erörtert, wie die Gerichte zu verfahren haben, wenn vor ihnen schiedsabkommenswidrig ein Verfahren eingeleitet wird. In diesem Zusammenhang stellt sich zugleich die Frage, wie die *Schieds*gerichte für diesen Fall entscheiden müssen. Grundsätzlich bestehen zwei Möglichkeiten. Entweder das Schiedsgericht unterbricht sein Verfahren, solange das staatliche Gericht noch nicht abschließend entschieden hat; oder aber es setzt ungeachtet der Prüfung der Sache durch ein staatliches Gericht sein Verfahren fort. Die Vor- bzw. Nachteile liegen auf der Hand. Unterbricht das Schiedsgericht sein Verfahren für die Dauer der Prüfung der Sache durch das Gericht und erklärt sich dieses dann für unzuständig, tritt eine - möglicherweise erhebliche - zeitliche Verzögerung ein. Führt das Schiedsgericht sein Verfahren hingegen ungeachtet der Prüfung der Sache durch ein staatliches Gericht fort und erklärt sich letzteres dann für zuständig, hat das Schiedsverfahren unnötige Kosten verursacht.

Das Modellgesetz regelt diese Frage in Art. 8 Abs. 2:

> *"Ist eine Klage [in einer Angelegenheit, die Gegenstand einer Schiedsvereinbarung ist,] erhoben worden, so kann ein schiedsrichterliches Verfahren gleichwohl eingeleitet oder fortgesetzt werden und ein Schiedsspruch ergehen, während die Sache bei Gericht anhängig ist".*

Die UNCITRAL-Kommissission hat sich somit für eine Fortsetzung des schiedsgerichtlichen Verfahrens entschieden. Dieser Variante wurde der Vorzug gegeben, um der Gefahr von Verschleppungstaktiken durch die Parteien entge-

---

196 Art. 1 Abs. 5 Modellgesetz lautet:
"Dieses Gesetz berührt nicht andere Gesetze dieses Staates, wonach bestimmte Streitigkeiten einem schiedsrichterlichen Verfahren nicht oder nur nach anderen Bestimmungen als denen dieses Gesetzes unterworfen werden dürfen."

197 Holtzmann/Neuhaus, S. 304.

genzuwirken.[198] Vor allem in Zeiten wirtschaftlicher Rezession und dadurch bedingter Geldknappheit erheben Schiedsparteien vor staatlichen Gerichten mitunter einzig deshalb Klage, um das Schiedsverfahren zu verschleppen. Vor diesem Hintergrund wird Art. 8 Abs. 2 in der Literatur deshalb auch überwiegend positiv beurteilt.[199] Allerdings bleibt damit das Risiko bestehen, daß sich die Durch- bzw. Weiterführung des Schiedsverfahrens rückwirkend als sinnlos herausstellt, weil sich zwischenzeitlich das angerufene staatliche Gericht für zuständig erklärt hat.

V. Territorialer Anwendungsbereich

Gemäß Art. 1 Abs. 2 findet das Modellgesetz nur Anwendung, wenn der Ort des schiedsrichterlichen Verfahrens im Hoheitsgebiet des jeweiligen Modellgesetzstaates liegt. Etwas anderes gilt jedoch für dessen Art. 8.[200] Dies hat zur Folge, daß die Gerichte der Modellgesetzstaaten die Einrede des Schiedsvertrages auch für den Fall zu beachten haben, daß das Schiedsverfahren in einem anderen Staat stattfindet.[201] Dahinter steht das als eines der vier Grundprinzipien des Modellgesetzes beschriebene[202] Prinzip der abgeschwächten Delokalisierung. Ziel ist die internationale Gleichbehandlung von Schiedsverfahren und -sprüchen. Auf diesem Wege soll der Erkenntnis Rechnung getragen werden, daß nur eine international harmonische Anerkennung der Einrede des Schiedsvertrages die Effektivität des Schiedsverfahrens gewährleistet.[203] Dabei nimmt das Modellgesetz bewußt in Kauf, daß in diesem Punkt möglicherweise keine Reziprozität zwischen einem Modellgesetzstaat und einem Nichtmodellgesetzstaat gewährleistet ist.

C. Das Englische Recht vor 1997

I. Unterscheidung nach domestic *und* non-domestic *Verfahren*

Das englische Recht vor 1997 unterschied in der Frage des Aussetzens staatlicher Verfahren zugunsten von Schiedsverfahren zwischen *domestic* und *non-domestic* Verfahren. *S* 1(4) *Arbitration Act* 1975 nannte zwei Kriterien für diese Unter-

---

198 UN-Doc. A/CN.9/233, para 80; Holtzmann/Neuhaus, S. 306.

199 Hüßlein-Stich, S. 50; Sonnauer, S. 104 f; wohl auch Granzow, S. 123 f; a.A. Calavros, S. 53 f; ebenso Samuel, Jurisdictional Problems, S. 222 f.

200 Vgl. auch Artikel 9, 35 und 36 Modellgesetz.

201 Granzow, S. 122 f.

202 Herrmann, in: Lew (Hrsg.), Contemporary Problems, S. 167.

203 Calavros, S. 53.

scheidung. Zum einen sollte ein Schiedsabkommen dann nicht *domestic* sein, wenn die Schiedsvereinbarung einen Schiedsort außerhalb Großbritanniens vorsah. Ebenso war ein Schiedsverfahren nicht *domestic*, wenn auch nur eine der Parteien bestimmte Verbindungen mit einem anderen Staat hatte.[204] Für Schiedsverfahren unter Beteiligung von Unternehmen galt, daß diese ihren Sitz oder ihre Hauptverwaltung in Großbritannien haben mußten, damit ein Schiedsabkommen als *domestic* galt.

II. Domestic *Schiedsverfahren*

1. Aussetzung des Verfahrens nach Ermessen

S 4(1) *Arbitration Act* 1950 regelte die Aussetzung des Verfahrens in *domestic* Schiedsverfahren:[205]

> *"If any party to an arbitration agreement [...] commences any legal proceedings, [...] any party to those legal proceedings may [...] apply to [the] court to stay the proceeding, and that court or a judge thereof, if satisfied that there is no sufficient reason why the matter should not be referred in accordance with the agreement, [...] may make an order staying the proceedings."*

Dem Wortlaut nach eröffnete *s* 4(1) *Arbitration Act* 1950 den Gerichten in *domestic* Verfahren ein nahezu uneingeschränktes Ermessen hinsichlich der Aussetzung der Verfahren. Einzige Voraussetzung war, daß nach Ansicht der Gerichte ein "*sufficient reason*" für eine Nichtaussetzung gegeben war. Zu der Frage, wann hiervon auszugehen war, schwieg die Vorschrift. Es hatte sich zu *s* 4(1) jedoch ein umfangreiches Fallrecht entwickelt. Zwar gibt auch dieses keine klaren Richtlinien vor. Doch lassen sich zumindest prinzipielle Rückschlüsse auf die Spruchpraxis der Gerichte ziehen.

---

204 *S* 1(4) *Arbitration Act* 1975 lautete:
"In this section 'domestic arbitration agreement' means an arbitration agreement which does not provide, expressly or by implication, for arbitration in a State other than the United Kingdom and to which neither-
(a) an individual who is a national of, or habitually resident in, any State other than the United Kingdom; nor
(b) a body corporate which is incorporated in, or whose central management and control is exercised in, any State other than the United Kingdom;
is a party at the time the proceedings are commenced."
Diese Legaldefinition hat in der Literatur einige Kritik erfahren. So wird kritisiert, daß durch die negative Formulierung kaum eine klare Unterscheidung möglich war (vgl. Merkin, Arbitration Law, 6.7).

205 Vgl. auch Nathan, Arbitration 1989, 285.

Die Haltung der englischen Gerichte zur Ausübung ihres Ermessens war grundsätzlich durch die Anerkennung von Schiedsvereinbarungen geprägt. Sogenannte *wrongly brought proceedings*,[206] also schiedsabredewidrige Verfahren, wurden zumeist ausgesetzt.[207] Im Einklang damit stand die Beweislast der schiedsunwilligen Partei hinsichtlich solcher Tatsachen, die eine Nichtaussetzung des staatlichen Verfahrens rechtfertigen sollten.[208]

Damit ist allerdings noch nichts darüber gesagt, nach welcher Maßgabe die englischen Gerichte von ihrem Ermessen Gebrauch machten. Weil klare Vorgabe fehlten, war eine exakte Bestimmung über den Ermessensgebrauch nicht möglich. Entgegen der Ansicht von Mustill/Boyd[209] wäre eine solche Bestimmung für die Parteien äußerst wünschenswert gewesen. Denn wenn auch regelmäßig mit der Aussetzung des staatlichen Verfahrens gerechnet werden konnte, so war das Gegenteil keinesfalls die seltene Ausnahme. Folgende Fallgruppen hatten mit erhöhter Wahrscheinlichkeit eine Nichtaussetzung des staatlichen Verfahrens zur Folge.

2. Fallgruppen

a) Fraud

Die wohl wichtigste Fallgruppe war die des *fraud*.[210] Traditionell sah das englische Schiedsrecht für den Fall eines Betrugsvorwurfs besondere Kontroll- und Eingriffsbefugnisse der Gerichte vor. Dies galt nicht nur im Zusammenhang mit der Durchsetzung der Schiedsvereinbarung, sondern auch mit anderen Eingriffsbefugnissen.[211] Der Tatbestand des *fraud* hatte für das Thema der staatlichen Eingriffsbefugnisse in Schiedsverfahren somit eine besondere Bedeutung.

Die hier zu behandelnde Frage lautet, unter welchen Voraussetzungen die Gerichte in Fällen von *fraud* das Verfahren an sich zogen. Voraussetzung für die Beantwortung dieser Frage war zunächst eine Definition des Begriffs. Hier liegt bereits eine der Hauptschwierigkeiten. Denn weder existierte eine Legaldefinition noch war der Begriff durch die Rechsprechung exakt umrissen. Unproblematisch gehörte in diesen Bereich der sogenannte *legal* oder *common law fraud*, also der

---

206 Zum Terminus vgl. Mustill/Boyd, S. 459 f.

207 *Wickham v. Harding* (1859) 28 L.J.Ex 215; vgl. auch Russel on Arbitration, S. 181 basierend auf *Willesford v. Watson* (1873) 8 Ch.App. 480.

208 *Heyman v. Darwins Ltd.* [1942] 1 All E.R. 337.

209 Mustill/Boyd, S. 476.

210 Untechnisch übersetzt etwa "Betrug".

211 Vgl. *infra* Kapitel 4, B.II., Kapitel 10, C.III.4. und D.II.2.c)gg).

vorsätzliche Betrug im rechtstechnischen Sinn.[212] *Fraud* konnte darüber hinaus jedoch auch in allen Fällen persönlicher Unehrlichkeit angenommen werden.[213] Die Rechtsprechung verwendete den Begriff mitunter auch im Zusammenhang mit "*dishonesty*".[214]

Die Gerichte legten den Begriff somit extensiv aus. Dies hatte im Rahmen von *s* 4(1) *Arbitration Act* 1950 zur Folge, daß in allen Fällen konkreter Vorwürfe gegen die persönliche Integrität der Gegenpartei mit einer Nichtaussetzung des gerichtlichen Verfahrens gerechnet werden mußte.[215] Zur Begründung führen Mustill/Boyd aus:[216]

> *"[I]t has always been clear that the existence of an allegation of fraud is sufficient ground for refusing a stay: partly because it is only fair that a party against whom a serious charge is made should have the opportunity of an investigation in open court, and partly because of a feeling that the judge is better capable of dealing with such an issue than an arbitrator."*

Schiedsgerichten wurde also schlicht die Befähigung abgesprochen, über Rechtsstreitigkeiten zu entscheiden, die möglicherweise auch einen Betrug beinhalteten. Mit den Worten von Thomas:[217]

> *"The basic justification [...] must ultimately be traced to a perception of arbitral tribunals as unsuitable or unable to determine disputes involving allegations of fraud."*

Einer kritischen Hinterfragung kann diese Begründung kaum standhalten. Bei der Professionalität und Institutionalisierung, welche die Schiedsgerichtsbarkeit gerade in England erreicht hatte, gab es keinen überzeugenden Grund für die besonderen Eingriffsbefugnisse der Gerichte in Betrugsangelegenheiten.[218]

b) Komplexes Rechtsproblem

Für eine erhöhte Wahrscheinlichkeit der Nichtaussetzung der gerichtlichen Verfahren sprach auch das Vorliegen eines komplexen Rechtsproblems. Zwar wurde in jüngerer Zeit oft das (angeblich) von gegenseitigem Respekt geprägte Verhält-

---

212 *Derry v. Peek* (1889) 14 App.Cas. 337; *Green v. Howell* [1910] 1 Ch. 495.
213 Vgl. etwa *Cook v. Catchpole* (1864) 11 L.T. 264. Für eine eingehendere Analyse vgl. Thomas, Civ.Just.Q. 1990, 393.
214 *Radford v. Hair and Others* [1971] 1 Ch. 758.
215 Vgl. auch *Wallis v. Hirsh* (1856) 1 C.B. 316; *Russel v. Russel* (1880) 14 Ch.D. 471.
216 S. 479.
217 Thomas, Civ.Just.Q. 1990, 402.
218 Vgl. Thomas, Civ.Just.Q. 1990, 402.

nis von Schieds- und staatlicher Gerichtsbarkeit gelobt.[219] Die englischen Gerichte konnten sich jedoch nie ganz von der tief verwurzelten Überzeugung freimachen, daß in erster Linie sie selbst zur Beurteilung schwieriger Rechtsfragen berufen seien.

Die englischen Gerichte machten bei Vorliegen komplexer Rechtsprobleme auch regelmäßig von ihrer *non-stay*-Befugnis Gebrauch.[220] Allerdings muß diese Regelmäßigkeit im Zusammenhang mit der Rechtslage in England vor 1979 gewürdigt werden. Wie bereits dargelegt, hatten die englischen Gerichte bis zum *Arbitration Act* 1979 aufgrund des *special case*-Verfahrens weitgehende Interventionsmöglichkeiten in Rechtsfragen.[221] Es entsprach somit vor 1979 ohnehin der gängigen Praxis der staatlichen Gerichte, verbindliche Stellungnahmen zu Rechtsfragen in Schiedsverfahren zu geben. Nach Abschaffung des *special case*-Verfahrens durch den *Arbitration Act* 1979 nahm diese Bereitschaft jedoch auch mit Blick auf die Nichtaussetzung gerichtlicher Verfahren ab.

c) Mehrheit von Verfahren

Schließlich sprach für das Gebrauchmachen der *non-stay*-Befugnis auch das Vorliegen einer Vielzahl von Streitpunkten zwischen den Parteien, von denen nur einzelne unter die Schiedsabrede fielen. Insbesondere in der älteren Rechtsprechung läßt sich die Bereitschaft der Gerichte erkennen, aus Praktikabilitätserwägungen alle verbundenen Streitigkeiten zwischen den Parteien zu verhandeln.[222] Dabei spielte es dann keine Rolle, wenn einige dieser Streitigkeiten unter eine Schiedsabrede fielen. Diese Fallgruppe hatte jedoch zunehmend an Bedeutung verloren.[223]

3. Scott v. Avery-*Klausel*

Die Parteien zu einem *domestic* Schiedsabkommen konnten also keineswegs mit letzter Sicherheit darauf vertrauen, daß tatsächlich ein Schiedsgericht und nicht ein staatliches Gericht ihren Fall verhandeln würde. Das weitgehende gerichtliche

---

219 Kerr, I.C.L.Q. 1985, 2; Bentil, J.Int'l Arb. 1988, 51.

220 *Clough v. County Livestock Insurance Association Ltd.* (1916) 85 L.J.K.B. 1185; *Navarino Salvors Ltd. v. Narino Recovery Ltd.* (1925) 23 Ll.L.R. 36; *Green Star Shipping Co. v. London Assurance* (1928) 31 Ll.L.R. 4.

221 Vgl. *supra* Teil II, Kapitel 2, D..

222 *Pickethall v. Merhyr Tydvil Local Board* (1886) 2 TLR 805; *Freeman & Sons Ltd. v. Chester RDC* [1911] 1 K.B. 783.

223 *Bulk Oil (Zug) AG v. Trans-Asiatic Oil Ltd. S.A.* [1973] 1 Lloyd's Rep. 129.

Ermessen in der Frage der Aussetzung des Verfahrens stand einem solchen Vertrauen entgegen.

Es war den Parteien jedoch möglich, durch die Aufnahme einer sogenannte *Scott v. Avery*-Klausel in den Schiedsvertrag die Wahrscheinlichkeit staatlicher Intervention durch Nichtaussetzung zu minimieren. In dem gleichnamigen Fall[224] hatte eine Versicherungsgesellschaft in ihre Vertragspolice eine besondere Klausel aufgenommen. Danach waren die Vertragsparteien nicht berechtigt, mit irgendeiner Angelegenheit aus dem Vertragsverhältnis die staatlichen Gerichte anzurufen, soweit nicht *zuvor* ein schiedsrichterliches Urteil hierzu ergangen war.[225] Das Schiedsurteil wurde somit zu einer Voraussetzung für eine gerichtliche Überprüfung gemacht (sog. *condition precedent*).[226] Das House of Lords hatte letztinstanzlich zu der Frage Stellung zu nehmen, ob in einer solchen Klausel nicht eine unzulässige Umgehung des Rechtsweges zu sehen sei (*ouster of jurisdiction*[227]). Die Richter des obersten englischen Gerichts bestätigten in einem ungewöhnlich schiedsfreundlichen Urteil die Zulässigkeit solcher Klauseln.[228] Damit wurde auch den Parteien zu *domestic* Schiedsvereinbarungen ein Mittel in die Hand gegeben, die Möglichkeit einer schiedsabredewidrigen Eröffnung eines Verfahrens vor staatlichen Gerichten - zumindest zeitweise - entgegenzuwirken.

Scott v. Avery-Klauseln waren allerdings kein "Allheilmittel". Sowohl das *common law* als auch der *Arbitration Act* 1950 sahen Fälle der Unwirksamkeit der Klausel vor. Das *common law* ordnete die Unwirksamkeit der Klausel vor allem für zwei Fälle an: Erstens dann, wenn der Beklagte durch sein Verhalten zu erkennen gab, daß er sich nicht auf die Klausel als Verteidigungsmittel stützte;[229] zweitens dann, wenn er selbst mit seinem Verhalten darauf hingewirkt hatte, daß die Schiedsvereinbarung nicht effektiv umgesetzt werden konnte.[230] Eine weitere

---

224 *Scott v. Avery* (1856) 5 H.L.Cas. 811.

225 Vgl. auch *Caledonian Insurance Co. v. Gilmour* [1893] A.C. 85; *Spurrier v. La Cloche* [1902] A.C. 446.

226 Vgl. auch Russel on Arbitration, S. 199 ff.

227 Vgl. *Czarnikow v. Roth, Schmidt & Co.* [1922] 2 K.B. 478; vgl. auch *supra* Teil II, Kapitel 2, B..

228 *Scott v. Avery* (1856) 5 H.L.Cas. 852 f, Lord Campbell:
"[W]hat pretence can there be for saying that there is anything contrary to public policy in allowing parties to contract that they shall not be liable to any action until their liability has been ascertined by a domestic and private tribunal, upon which they themselves agree! [...] I can see not the slightest ill consequences can flow from such an agreement, and I see great advantage that may arise from it."

229 *Toronto Rly Co. v. National British and Irish Millers Insurance Co. Ltd.* (1914) 20 Com Cas 1; *Hardwick Game Farm v. Suffolk Agricultural and Poultry Producers Association* [1964] 2 Lloyd's Rep. 227.

230 *Woodall v. Pearl Assurance Co. Ltd.* [1919] 1 K.B. 593.

Annulierungsmöglichkeit sah der *Arbitration Act* 1950 in *s* 25(4) vor. Diese betraf den Fall, daß ein staatliches Gericht wegen Entfernung eines Schiedsrichters aus seinem Amt oder Betrugs einer Partei die Aufhebung der Schiedsvereinbarung verfügte.[231]

III. Non-domestic *Schiedsverfahren*

1. Zwingende Aussetzung des Verfahrens

S 1 *Arbitration Act* 1975 regelte die Aussetzung staatlicher Verfahren in Fällen von *non-domestic* Schiedsvereinbarungen. Die Vorschrift lautete:

> *"[...] and the court, unless satisfied that the arbitration agreement is null and void, inoperative or incapable of being performed or that there is not in fact any dispute between the parties with regard to the matter agreed to be referred, shall make an order staying the proceedings."*

Die augenscheinliche Ähnlichkeit zwischen *s* 1 *Arbitration Act* 1975 und Art. 8 Modellgesetz folgt daraus, daß sich *s* 1 ebenso wie Art. 8 Modellgesetz an Art. II(3) des New Yorker UN-Übereinkommens orientierte.[232] Anders als Art. 8 Modellgesetz sah *s* 1 jedoch noch für den weiteren Fall, "*that there is in fact no dispute*", eine *non-stay*-Befugnis vor. Nachfolgend soll kurz dargestellt werden, wie die englischen Gerichte die einzelnen *non-stay*-Fallgruppen auslegten.

Anders als *s* 4 *Arbitration Act* 1950 räumte *s* 1 *Arbitration Act* 1975 den Gerichten kein Ermessen hinsichtlich der Aussetzung des Verfahrens ein. Lagen die genannten Ausnahmetatbestände nicht vor, war die Aussetzung des staatlichen Verfahrens somit als zwingende Rechtsfolge vorgesehen ("shall *make an order*").

---

231 *S* 25(4) *Arbitration Act* 1950 lautete:
"Where it is provided [...] that an award under an arbitration agreement shall be a condition precedent to the bringing of an action with respect to any matter to which the agreement applies, the High Court or the Court of Appeal, if it orders [...] that the agreement shall cease to have effect as regards any particular dispute, may further order that the provision making an award a condition precedent to the bringing of an action shall also cease to have effect as regards that dispute."
Zur Aufhebung der Schiedsvereinbarung vgl. *infra* Kapitel 4.

232 *S* 1 *Arbitration Act* 1975 inkorporierte Art. II(3) des New Yorker UN-Übereinkommen weitgehend in englisches Recht.

2. *Versagungsgründe*

a) Null and void, inoperative or incapable of being performed

Die Gerichte hatten ihre Verfahren nicht auszusetzen, wenn eine Schiedsvereinbarung nichtig („*null and void*“) war.[233] Dann nämlich lag im rechtlichen Sinne gar keine Schiedsvereinbarung vor, und es konnte nicht zu einer konkurrierenden Zuständigkeit von staatlichen Gerichten und Schiedsgerichten kommen. Die Beweislast für die Nichtigkeit der Schiedsvereinbarung lag beim Antragsteller.[234]

Im Gegensatz zur nichtigen zeichnete sich die unwirksame („*inoperative*“) Schiedsvereinbarung dadurch aus, daß sie erst später ihre Gültigkeit verlor. Dies konnte sowohl durch Parteivereinbarung als auch durch Gerichtsbeschluß geschehen.[235] Ebenso konnte sich die Unwirksamkeit aus Prinzipien des *common laws* ergeben.[236] Besonderheiten bei der Beurteilung unwirksamer Schiedsvereinbarungen ergaben sich nicht.[237]

Undurchführbare („*incapable of being performed*“) Schiedsvereinbarungen spielten nur eine untergeordnete Rolle. Hierher gehörte etwa die wirtschaftliche Unmöglichkeit oder der Untergang des Vertragsgegenstandes.[238] Nicht unter die von *s* 1 erfaßten Ausnahmen fielen allerdings die Fallgruppen der Erfüllungsverweigerung ("*repudiation*"), der Unmöglichkeit der Erfüllung einer Vertragspflicht („*impossibility*“), des Wegfalls der Geschäftsgrundlage ("*frustration*")[239] und der Sittenwidrigkeit des Hauptvertrages.[240]

233 Nichtigkeit bedeutet in diesem Zusammenhang Nichtigkeit von Anfang an. Nicht erfaßt ist die nur vernichtbare Schiedsvereinbarung (Halsbury's, S. 349); vgl. auch *Hersent v. United Towing Co. Ltd.* (*"The Tradesman"*) [1961] 2 Lloyd's Rep. 183.

234 *Overseas Union Insurance Ltd. v. AA Mutual International Insurance Co. Ltd.* [1988] 2 Lloyd's Rep. 70.

235 Vgl. *infra* Kapitel 4.

236 Z.B. Vereitelung des Vertragszwecks, Wegfall der Geschäftsgrundlage, etc..

237 Für eine weitere Differenzierung vgl. *Radio Publicity (Universal) Ltd. v. Compagnie Luxembourgeoise de Radiodifusion* [1936] 2 All E.R. 721.

238 Für den Fall des Untergangs einer vertragsmäßig herzustellenden, extrem kostenintensiven Maschine vgl. *Northern Regional Health Authority v. Derek Crouch Construction Co. Ltd.* [1984] 26 Build.L.R. 1.

239 *Heyman v. Darwins Ltd.* [1942] 1 All E.R. 337; vgl. auch Sheridan, Arb. & Disp.Res.L.J. 1997, 216 f.

240 *Harbour Assurance Co. (UK) Ltd. v. Kansa General International Assurance Co. Ltd.* [1993] 3 All E.R. 897; *The Rena K* [1979] 1 All E.R. 407.

b) Not in fact any dispute between the parties

Die englischen Gerichte setzten ihre Verfahren weiterhin dann nicht aus, wenn sie zu der Überzeugung gelangt waren, daß tatsächlich überhaupt kein Streit vorlag.[241] Diese Fallgruppe fand keine Entsprechung im New Yorker UN-Übereinkommen. Sie war nur unter zwei Umständen denkbar.

Zum einen gab es diejenigen Fälle, in denen der Beklagte entweder den Anspruch anerkannt hatte, ohne jedoch zu leisten, oder in denen er sich nicht verteidigte.[242] Hier ging die englische Rechtsprechung ohne weiteres davon aus, daß überhaupt kein Streit vorlag. Mithin konnte auch kein solcher an das Schiedsgericht verwiesen werden.

Zum anderen gab es die in der Praxis relevanteren Fälle, in denen der Kläger darlegen konnte, daß der Beklagte keinerlei Verteidigungsmöglichkeiten besaß. Dabei wurde nicht danach unterschieden, ob sich die mangelnde Verteidigungsmöglichkeit unter rechtlichen oder tatsächlichen Gesichspunkten ergab.[243] Praktisch gingen die Gerichte so vor, daß sie sowohl die Klage als auch die Klageerwiderung (materiellrechtlich) prüften. Die Schiedseinrede des Beklagten führte hier also nicht zu einer automatischen Aussetzung des staatlichen Verfahrens. Je nachdem, wie die Prüfung ausfiel, setzten die Gerichte ihr Verfahren aus oder entschieden den Fall. In eindeutigen Fällen geschah dies häufig durch ein sog. *summary judgment*, ein abgekürztes Urteilsverfahren ohne mündliche Verhandlung für eindeutige Fälle.

In der ganz überwiegenden Mehrheit der in Betracht kommenden Verfahren war jedoch keine eindeutige Bestimmung über das Vorliegen eines *dispute* möglich.[244] Ursächlich hierfür war, daß der Beklagte zwar offensichtlich nur äußerst schwache Verteidigungsmittel besaß, gleichwohl aber bei einer kursorischen Prüfung nicht sicher auszuschließen war, daß diese im Verlauf des Verfahrens Relevanz erlangen konnten. In diesen Fällen war aus Sicht der Gerichte sowohl die Aussetzung des Verfahrens als auch die Durchführung desselben vertretbar. Dieser Beurteilungsspielraum kam im Ergebnis einem Ermessen der Gerichte hinsichtlich der Aussetzung des Verfahrens gleich. Ein Ermessensspielraum sollte den Gerichten nach dem eindeutigen Wortlaut von *s* 1 *Arbitration Act* 1979 ("*shall*") aber gerade *nicht* zustehen. Entsprechend unbefriedigend fielen zumeist auch die Begründungen der Gerichte für die Fälle der Nichtaussetzung aus. Da hieß es dann oft, der Beklagte habe keine "*genuine defence*" oder es läge "*not in*

---

241 Thomas, Lloyd's Mar. & Com.L.Q. 1981, 26.

242 *London and North Western Rly Co. v. Jones* [1915] 2 K.B. 35; *London and North Western and Great-Western Joint Rly Companies v. Billington* [1899] A.C. 79.

243 Mustill/Boyd, S. 493, dort FN 3.

244 Rawlings, Arb.Int'l 1997, 422.

reality" ein Streit zwischen den Parteien vor.[245] Zu Recht kritisiert Chitty deshalb auch, daß die Entscheidung über eine Nichtaussetzung des Verfahrens "*on somewhat shaky foundations*" ruhte.[246]

IV. Parallelität von Schieds- und staatlichem Verfahren

Während nach dem Modellgesetz die Schiedsgerichte ihre Verfahren nicht für den Zeitraum der Prüfung der Klage durch ein Gericht aussetzen müssen,[247] fehlte eine entsprechende Regelung im englischen Recht. Die überwiegende Literatur ging aber mit einer gewissen Selbstverständlichkeit davon aus, daß das Schiedsgericht keiner Pflicht unterlag, sein Verfahren für die Dauer der Prüfung der Sache durch ein staatliches Gericht auszusetzen.[248] Hierin wurde ganz überwiegend kein *disrespect to the courts* gesehen.[249]

Im übrigen blieb es den englischen Gerichten unbenommen, unter bestimmten Voraussetzungen das Schiedsverfahren einstweilig auszusetzen. Hiervon machten die Gerichte etwa dann Gebrauch, wenn die parallele Durchführung des Schiedsverfahrens das staatliche Verfahren in irgendeiner Weise behinderte.[250]

D. Der Arbitration Act 1996

I. Wegfall der Unterscheidung zwischen domestic *und* non-domestic

S 9 *Arbitration Act* 1996 ("*stay of legal proceedings*") ersetzt nunmehr *s* 4 *Arbitration Act* 1950 und *s* 1 *Arbitration Act* 1975. Auch der *Arbitration Act* 1996 unterscheidet - wie bereits zuvor der *Arbitration Act* 1950 - zwischen *domestic* und *non-domestic* bzw. *international* Schiedsverfahren. Die entsprechende Vor-

---

245 *Ibid.*

246 Chitty on Contracts, S. 732; vgl. auch Mustill/Boyd, S. 123.

247 Vgl. *supra* Kapitel 2, B.IV..

248 Bernstein, Handbook, 2. Aufl., S. 16 f. Andere Stimmen in der Literatur lehnen eine Weiterführung des Verfahrens vor den Schiedsgerichten generell ab, wenn vor einem staatlichen Gericht die Unzuständigkeit des Schiedsgerichts geltend gemacht wird. Dies geschieht vor allem unter Hinweis auf das Kostenrisiko (vgl. Mustill/Boyd, S. 514 f; Samuel, Jurisdictional Problems, 222 f).

249 Bernstein, *ibid.*

250 *Northern Regional Health Authority v. Derek Crouch Construction Co.* [1984] 26 Build.L.R. 1.

schrift, *s* 86,[251] wurde jedoch wegen eines möglichen Verstoßes gegen EG-Recht nicht in Kraft gesetzt.[252]

Ausschlaggebend hierfür war eine Entscheidung des Court of Appeal in *Phillip Alexander Securities and Futures Ltd v. Bamberger.*[253] In diesem Fall hatten deutsche Kunden eines englischen Dienstleisters diesen ungeachtet einer Schiedsklausel vor deutschen Gerichten verklagt und obsiegende Urteile erwirkt. Der englische Dienstleister klagte nun seinerseits vor dem englischen High Court auf Feststellung, daß die (deutschen) Urteile in England nicht vollstreckbar seien. Nach *s* 1 des einschlägigen *Consumer Arbitration Agreement Act* 1988 hätte die ersuchte Feststellung ergehen müssen, wenn die Parteien Engländer bzw. in England wohnhaft gewesen wären. Gemäß *s* 2 des selben *Acts* sollte dies jedoch nicht für internationale Verfahren unter Beteiligung ausländischer Parteien gelten. Der englische Kläger sah hierin einen Verstoß gegen das Diskriminierungsverbot nach dem EG-Vertrag. Das House of Lords gab ihm Recht. Lord Justice Legatt führte in seiner Urteilsbegründung aus:[254]

"A rule which disadvantages recipients of services in another Member State inevitably restricts the freedom of the service provider to provide services on equal terms to everyone in the Community and is inimical to the objective of the Treaty [...] of achiving an internal market characterised by the abolition of obstacles to the free movement of services. As the Court has made clear, whether the restriction is placed on the provider of the services or the recipient, the effect is the same, and it is inconsistent with the purpose of the Treaty. Nationals in Germany, Spain or Finland may be less inclined to avail themselves of the services of [the plaintiff] because English law does not afford them the same treatment as that which is available to English nationals and in our judgment this is clearly discriminatory and impermissible pursuant to articles 6 and 59 of the Treaty."

Die vorstehende Argumentation wurde mit der bereits genannten Folge der Nichtinkraftsetzung der *ss* 85 - 88 *Arbitration Act* 1996 vom DAC aufgegriffen.[255] Das Ergebnis ist bemerkenswert. Erstmalig unterscheidet das englische Recht in der Frage der *wrongly brought proceedings* nicht mehr zwischen *domestic* und *non-domestic / international* Verfahren. Ebenso bemerkenswert sind die Gründe, die hierzu führten. Nicht grundsätzliche Überlegungen zum Verhältnis

---

251 *S* 86(1) *Arbitration Act* 1996 lautet:
"In section 9 (stay of legal proceedings), subsection 4 (stay unless the arbitration is null and void, inoperative or incapable ob being performed) does not apply to a domestic arbitration agreement."

252 Saville, Lloyd's Mar. & Com.L.Q. 1997, 509; ders., Arb. & Disp.Res.L.J. 1997,155.

253 Urteil vom 12. Juli 1996, auszugsweise veröffentlicht in der *Times* vom 22. Juli 1996.

254 Vgl. Zitat bei Hill, I.C.L.Q. 1997, 278.

255 Vgl. auch Consultation Document on Commencement of the Arbitration Act 1996.

von Schieds- und staatlicher Gerichtsbarkeit,[256] sondern die Zwänge des Gemeinschaftsrechts sind letztlich verantwortlich für diese Reform des englischen Schiedsverfahrensrechts.

II. Antragsberechtigung

S 9(1) stellt klar, daß - gleich ob im Klage- oder im Widerklageverfahren - nur die jeweils (wider)beklagte Partei antragsberechtigt nach *s* 9 ist.[257] Dies stellt insoweit eine Änderung zum Recht vor 1997 dar, als danach "*any party to the proceedings*"[258] antragsberechtigt war. Es erscheint zumindest nicht eindeutig, ob damit auch der (Wider)Kläger gemeint war.[259] *S* 9(1) *Arbitration Act* 1996 beseitigt diese Unklarheit. Der Kläger hat somit nach dem neuen Recht keine Möglichkeit mehr, die Sache vor das Schiedsgericht zu bringen.[260]

III. Andere alternative Streitbeilegungsmechanismen

Eine weitere Neuerung sieht *s* 9(2) vor.[261] Danach kann die Aussetzung des Verfahrens ungeachtet einer Parteivereinbarung erst nach Ausschöpfung *anderer* außergerichtlicher Streitbeilegungsmechanismen[262] vor ein Schiedsgericht zu gehen, beantragt werden. *S* 9(2) hat lediglich deklaratorischen Charakter. Die Vorschrift übernimmt letztlich nur ein *dictum* aus *Channel Tunnel Group Ltd. v. Balfour Beatty Construction Ltd.* [263] in *statute law*. Sie beinhaltet damit keine Änderung zur alten Rechtslage.[264]

---

256 Für eine solche Kritik vgl. Uff/Keating, Arb.Int'l 1994, 180.

257 *S* 9(1) *Arbitration Act* 1996 lautet:
"A party to an arbitration agreement against whom legal proceedings are brought [...] may [...] apply to the court [...] to stay the proceedings [...]"

258 Vgl. *s* 4(1) *Arbitration Act* 1950 und *s* 1(1) *Arbitration Act* 1975.

259 Dies mußte zumindest bis zur Entscheidung des Court of Appeal in *Etri Fans Ltd. v. NMB (UK) Ltd.* [1987] 2 All E.R. 763 gelten. *S* 9(1) folgt letztlich dieser Entscheidung.

260 Harris/Planterose/Tecks, S. 71.

261 *S* 9(2) *Arbitration Act* 1996 lautet:
"An application may be made notwithstanding that the matter is to be referred to arbitration only after the exhaustion of other dispute resolution procedures."

262 Z.B. Expertenkommission oder *mediation*.

263 [1993] A.C. 334.

264 DAC, 1996-Report, para 53; vgl. auch Merkin, Arbitration Act 1996, S. 25.

IV. Aussetzung des Verfahrens

1. Wegfall des Ermessens in domestic *Verfahren*

Als Folge des Wegfalls der Unterscheidung zwischen *domestic* und *non-domestic* schreibt *s* 9(4) *Arbitration Act* 1996 unter Anlehnung an *s* 1 *Arbitration Act* 1979 nunmehr die Pflicht der Gerichte fest, *wrongly brought proceedings* grundsätzlich[265] in *allen*, also auch in den *domestic* Verfahren auszusetzen. Hierin liegt eine der ganz wesentlichen Änderungen gegenüber dem alten Recht, wonach die Aussetzung in *domestic* Verfahren im Ermessen der Gerichte stand.[266]

2. Ausnahmen

Wie bereits *s* 1 *Arbitration Act* 1975 sieht s 9(4) *Arbitration Act* 1996 Ausnahmen zur Aussetzungspflicht für diejenigen Fälle vor, in denen die Schiedsvereinbarung für "*null and void, inoperative or incapable of being performed*" befunden wird. Unterschiede zur alten Rechtslage bestehen nicht. Es wird auf die entsprechenden Ausführungen zu *s* 1 *Arbitration Act* 1975 verwiesen.[267]

Eine wesentliche Änderung zum Recht vor 1997 ist jedoch das Wegfallen des noch in *s* 1 *Arbitration Act* 1975 enthaltenen Tatbestandmerkmals des "*not in fact any dispute between the parties*".[268] Auch für diesen Fall waren die Gerichte nach altem Recht nicht zur Aussetzung des Verfahrens verpflichtet. Ausschlaggebend für eine Reform des englischen Rechts in diesem Punkt war die Entscheidung in *Hayter v. Nelson.*[269] Lord Justice Saville hinterfragte in seiner Urteilsbegründung kritisch die Berechtigung des Ausnahmetatbestandes. Ursprünglich stand dahinter die Überlegung, den Parteien in eindeutig gelagerten Fällen schnell zu einer Entscheidung zu verhelfen. Das sollte durch ein sog. *summary judgment* der Gerichte erreicht werden. Saville zufolge gab es keinen Grund, warum nicht auch ein Schiedsgericht ebenso effizient und schnell wie ein Gericht durch ein dem *summary judgment* ähnliches Verfahren entscheiden könne.[270]

Unter Bezugnahme auf *Hayter v. Nelson* befürwortete auch das DAC die Abschaffung des umstrittenen Tatbestandsmerkmals.[271] Damit korrespondierend wurden die *ss* 33 und 34 *Arbitration Act* 1996 entwickelt. Diese berechtigen das

---

265 Zu den Ausnahmen vgl. nachfolgend in diesem Kapitel, D.IV.2..

266 Vgl. *supra* in diesem Kapitel 2, C.II..

267 Vgl. *supra* Kapitel 2, C.III.2.a).

268 Vgl. Saville, Lloyd's Mar. & Com.L.Q. 1997, 510.

269 [1990] 2 Lloyd's Rep. 265.

270 *Hayter v. Nelson, ibid.*

271 DAC, 1996-Report, para 55.

Schiedsgericht - freilich unter Beachtung etwaiger Parteivereinbarungen -, eine angemessene Verfahrensweise zu wählen.[272] Hiervon betroffen ist auch das Recht zur Wahl einer dem vereinfachten Urteilsverfahren entsprechenden Verfahrensweise.[273]

Der Court of Appeal hatte sich erstmalig in *The Halki*[274] mit *s* 9 *Arbitration Act* 1996 zu befassen. In diesem Fall versuchten die Kläger, ein gerichtliches *summary judgment* für einen Anspruch aus einem Chartervertrag zu erreichen, der Gegenstand eines Schiedsabkommens war.[275] Die Beklagten hatten eine *arguable defence* - wenn überhaupt - nur hinsichtlich eines geringen Teils des Anspruchs. Sie beantragten unter Berufung auf die Schiedsabrede gleichwohl eine Aussetzung des Verfahrens gemäß *s* 9 *Arbitration Act* 1996. In diesem Zusammenhang stellte sich dem Gericht unter anderem die Frage, ob es die Aussetzung des Verfahrens auch wegen anderer als der in *s* 9(4) ausdrücklich genannten Fällen versagen durfte. Der Court of Appeal entschied, daß auch bei Ansprüchen "*to which there is no arguable defence*" nicht mehr durch ein *summary judgement* des High Courts entschieden werden könne.[276] Auf den ersten Blick scheint damit klar zu sein, daß die englischen Gerichte gewillt sind, *s* 9 *Arbitration Act* 1996 konsequent anzuwenden.

V. Wegfall der Scott v. Avery-*Einrede*

Nach dem alten englischen Recht konnten die Parteien durch Aufnahme einer sog. *Scott v. Avery*-Klausel in den Schiedsvertrag ein gerichtliches Verfahren in der Regel bis zum Abschluß des Schiedsverfahrens verhindern.[277] *S* 9(5) *Arbitration Act* 1996 ordnet nunmehr an, daß solche Klauseln keine Gültigkeit mehr besitzen sollen. Die Vorschrift lautet:

> *"If the court refuses to stay the legal proceedings, any provision that an award is a condition precedent to the bringing of legal proceedings in respect of any matter is of no effect in relation to those proceedings."*

---

272 *S* 33 (1)(b) *Arbitration Act* 1996 lautet:
"The tribunal shall [...] adopt procedures suitable to the circumstances of the particular case avoiding unnecessary delay or expense, so as to provide a fair means for the resolution of the matters falling to be determined."

273 Rawlings, Arb.Int'l 1997, 424.

274 *Halki Shipping Corp. v. Sopex Oils Ltd.* [1998] 2 All E.R. 23.

275 Ausführlich Whiteley, Lloyd's Mar. & Com.L.Q. 1998, 164.

276 *Ibid*; vgl. auch Jones, Arbitration 1999, 35; kritisch Whiteley, *ibid.*

277 Vgl. *supra* in diesem Kapitel, C.II.3..

Zur Begründung führt das DAC aus:[278]

"This avoids a situation where the arbitration clause is unworkable, yet no legal proceedings can be successfully brought [...] [I]t appears to be a matter of basic justice that a situation in which a party can neither arbitrate nor litigate must be avoided."

Die Begründung ist nachvollziehbar. Aufgrund des Wegfalls des gerichtlichen Ermessens, wie es vormals in *s* 4 *Arbitration Act* 1950 vorgesehen war, verliert die *Scott v. Avery*-Einrede ihre Bedeutung und Berechtigung. Denn nunmehr sind die Gerichte ohnehin grundsätzlich verpflichtet, ihre Verfahren auszusetzen. In den einzig vorgesehenen Ausnahmen der Nichtigkeit, Ungültigkeit oder Undurchführbarkeit der Schiedsvereinbarung würde die *Scott v. Avery*-Einrede lediglich eine zeitliche Verzögerung und keinerlei Vorteile bewirken. Sie war somit überflüssig geworden.

E. Zwischenergebnis

Der *Arbitration Act* 1996 erreicht eine gelungene Modernisierung des englischen Rechts zur Durchsetzung von Schiedsvereinbarungen. An erster Stelle ist in diesem Zusammenhang der Wegfall der Unterscheidung zwischen *domestic* und *non-domestic* zu nennen. Die erreichte Harmonisierung stellt schon für sich eine positive Errungenschaft dar. Vor allem aber der Wegfall der weitgehenden Ermessensbefugnisse der englischen Gerichte in *domestic* Verfahren überzeugt. Hierdurch wurde einer gewichtigen Kritik am alten englischen Recht Rechnung getragen. Ebenfalls bedeutsam ist der Wegfall der Einrede des "*in fact no dispute*". Er trägt dem Prinzip der Parteiautonomie verstärkt Rechnung, indem nunmehr die Schiedsgerichte ermächtigt sind, in geeigneter Weise auf entsprechende Fallkonstellationen zu reagieren.

Die Regelungen des *Arbitration Acts* 1996 und des Modellgesetzes hinsichtlich der Durchsetzung von Schiedsvereinbarungen sind vergleichbar. Grundlegende Vor- oder Nachteile der jeweiligen Regelungen sind nicht zu erkennen. Vielmehr sind die Gerichte nach beiden Regelungen grundsätzlich zur Aussetzung des Verfahrens verpflichtet, ohne hierüber nach Ermessen befinden zu können. Die zulässigen Ausnahmen sind zudem identisch. Da sie eng gefaßt wurden, ist nicht mit einer Aushebelung der grundsätzlichen Regelungen zu rechnen.

278 1996-Report, para 57; vgl. auch Merkin, Arbitration Act 1996, S. 26.

Kapitel 3
Verlängerung der Frist für die Einleitung des Schiedsverfahrens

A. Einführung

Im unmittelbaren Zusammenhang mit der Durchsetzung von Schiedsvereinbarungen sah und sieht das englische Recht gegenüber dem Modellgesetz die Besonderheit der Befugnis der Gerichte vor, eine von den Parteien vereinbarte Frist für den Beginn eines Schiedsverfahrens nach eigenem Ermessen zu verlängern. Eine entsprechende Regelung fehlt im Modellgesetz.

Einer der wesentlichen Vorteile von Schieds- gegenüber staatsgerichtlichen Verfahren ist die relative Zügigkeit, mit der erstere zum Abschluß gebracht werden können. Dem trägt eine Vielzahl von Schiedsvereinbarungen auch dadurch Rechnung, daß Fristen für bestimmte Verfahrensschritte vereinbart werden. Eine in diesem Zusammenhang übliche Klausel sieht die Einleitung des Schiedsverfahrens innerhalb eines bestimmten Zeitraums vor (sog. *time and bar*-Klausel).[279] Wird diese Frist nicht eingehalten, verliert der Kläger das Recht, seine Ansprüche auf dem Schiedswege geltend zu machen. Da der Gang vor die staatlichen Gerichte ausgeschlossen ist, hat er im Regelfall keinerlei Möglichkeit, seine Ansprüche zu verfolgen. Das führt mitunter zu harten Rechtsfolgen. Dies muß vor allem dann gelten, wenn die Frist ohne Verschulden versäumt wurde.

B. Das englische Recht vor 1997

Diese Problematik wurde bereits frühzeitig von der englischen Rechtsprechung aufgegriffen. Mit dem von ihr entwickelten Grundsatz des sog. *contra proferentum* wurde versucht, die teils unerwünschten, weil sehr weitreichenden Folgen der Fristenvereinbarung abzumildern. Danach wurde die entsprechende Klausel im Zweifel gegen die für ihre Aufnahme in die Schiedsvereinbarung verantwort-

---

279 Ein typisches Beispiel für eine solche Klausel stellt die nachfolgende "Centrocon"-Klausel dar:
"[...] Any claim must be made in writing and claimants' arbitrator apointed within three months of final discharge, and where this provision is not complied with the claim shall be deemed to be waived and absolutely barred [...]."
Die hier gewählte Frist von drei Monaten ist willkürlich. Auch erheblich kürzere Fristen wurden für zulässig befunden (vgl. etwa *Agro Company of Canada Ltd. v. Richmond Shipping Ltd. ("The Simonburn")* [1972] 2 Lloyd's Rep. 355).

liche Partei ausgelegt. Diese konnte sich also mitunter nicht auf die Klausel als Verteidigungsmittel berufen.[280]

Das *common law* wurde in diesem Punkt jedoch als unzureichend empfunden. Hierzu Lord Justice Salmon in *The Pegasus*: [281]

> *"[T]he commercial community [...] and those who practised and administered commercial law [...] were shackled by [...] this type of arbitration clause. It put it out of the power of the Court to grant any relief to a claimant who had allowed perhaps a day or two to run beyond the period [...] specified in the clause, even although the delay could have caused no conceivable harm to the other side."*

Mit *s* 27 *Arbitration Act* 1950 wurde deshalb eine gesetzliche Regelung der so erkannten "Gefahr" erlassen. Darin heißt es:

> *"Where the terms of an agreement to refer future disputes to arbitration provide that any claims to which the agreement applies shall be barred unless [...] some [...] step to commence arbitration proceedings is taken within a time fixed by the agreement, and a dispute arises to which the agreement applies, the High Court, if it is of the opinion that in the circumstances of the case undue hardship would otherwise be caused [...] may [...] extend the time for such period as it thinks proper."*

Die Vorschrift räumte den Gerichten ein nahezu uneingeschränktes Ermessen zur Zeitverlängerung ein. Inhaltlich wurde *s* 27 *Arbitration Act* 1950 vor allem durch das Tatbestandsmerkmal der "*undue hardship*"[282] charakterisiert. Die Rechtsprechung hat dieses großzügig ausgelegt. In *The Pegasus* interpretierte Lord Denning *undue hardship* wie folgt:[283]

> *"'Undue' there simply means excessive. That is, greater hardship than the circumstances warrant. Even though a claimant has been at fault himself, it is undue hardship on him if the consequences are out of proportion to his fault."*

Diese recht weite Auslegung wurde durch das Urteil in *The Jocelyne*[284] ein wenig mehr konkretisiert. Danach sollten bei der Bestimmung von *undue hardship* Kriterien wie Ausmaß der Verspätung, Streitwert, Verschulden des Klägers, Ausmaß des Verschuldens oder Irreführung durch die andere Partei Anwendung

280 *Minister of Materials v. Steel Bros. & Co. Ltd.* [1952] W.N. 114.

281 *Liberian Shipping Corp. v. A. King & Sons Ltd. ("The Pegasus")* [1967] 1 Lloyd's Rep. 302 (309).

282 Übersetzt etwa "unbillige Härte".

283 *The Pegasus* [1967] 1 Lloyd's Rep. 302 (307).

284 *Moscow V/O Exportkhleb v. Helmville Ltd. ("The Jocelyne")* [1977] 2 Lloyd's Rep. 121.

finden.[285] Richtlinienfunktion kam diesen Kriterien indes nicht zu.[286] Die Gerichte entschieden vielmehr jeden Fall ganz individuell, ohne irgendeine Kategorisierung erkennen zu lassen.[287]

Spätestens seit *The Pegasus* war klar, daß die Gerichte *s* 27 *Arbitration Act* 1950 umfassend anwendeten. Das Drohen eines im weitesten Sinne ungerechten Schadens stellte eine ausreichende Anwendungsvoraussetzung dar. Als zwingendes Recht konnte *s* 27 auch nicht durch Parteivereinbarung ausgeschlossen werden.

Weniger eindeutig war die Rechtslage jedoch dann, wenn die betreffende Schiedsvereinbarung dem *Schieds*gericht die Befugnisse aus *s* 27 übertrug, dieses also in Fällen von *undue hardship* die Frist verlängern konnte.[288] Dann war nicht einzusehen, warum es noch einer staatsgerichtlichen Kontrollbefugnis in diesem Punkt bedurfte. So kann davon ausgegangen werden, daß ein qualifiziertes Schiedsgericht ebenso wie der High Court in der Lage gewesen sein sollte, eine "gerechte" Lösung in den von *s* 27 *Arbitration Act* 1950 umschriebenen Fällen zu finden. Im vorgenannten Sinne urteilte auch ein Teil der Rechtsprechung.[289] Andere Urteile kamen zu dem Ergebnis, daß *s* 27 *Arbitration Act* 1950 auch neben einer vergleichbaren Schiedsklausel noch Bestand habe.[290] Eines aber war unstreitig: soweit das Schiedsgericht selbst über eine mögliche Verlängerung der Frist befand, mußte es sich an die in *s* 27 *Arbitration Act* 1950 festgelegten Grundsätze und Ermessensrichtlinien halten. Es bestand ansonsten die Möglichkeit, daß der Schiedsspruch später wegen *misconduct* durch die staatlichen Gerichte aufgehoben wurde.[291]

---

285 *Ibid.*

286 Mustill/Boyd, S. 214.

287 Vgl. auch *Consolidated Investment and Contracting Co. v. Saponaria Shipping Co. Ltd. ("The Virgo")* [1978] 2 Lloyd's Rep. 167; *Libra Shipping & Trading Corpn. Ltd. v. Northern Sales Ltd. ("The Aspen Trader")* [1981] 1 Lloyd's Rep 273.

288 Thomas, Lloyd's Mar. & Com.L.Q. 1981, 535.

289 Vgl. etwa *Timmerman's Graan-En Maal Handel En Maalderij B.V. v. Sachs* [1980] 1 Lloyd's Rep. 194.

290 *Ets. Soules & Cie v. International Trade Development Co. Ltd.* [1979] 2 Lloyd's Rep. 122.

291 Vgl. *infra* Kapitel 10, C.III.4.

C. Der Arbitration Act *1996*

Die Regelung der *s* 27 *Arbitration Act* 1950 findet sich nunmehr in leicht modifizierter Form in *s* 12 *Arbitration Act* 1996 wieder. Der zwingende Charakter der Vorschrift wurde beibehalten.[292]

I. Andere alternative Streitbeilegungsmechanismen

S 12(1)(b) *Arbitration Act* 1996 erweitert den Anwendungsbereich der bisherigen Befugnisse der Gerichte, eine Fristenverlängerung zu gewähren. Diese gelten nunmehr auch in den Fällen, in denen die Parteien der Aufnahme eines Schiedsverfahrens eine andere alternative Form der Streitbeilegung zeitlich vorgeschaltet haben (z.B. Expertengutachten).[293] Die Verfasser des *Arbitration Acts* 1996 reagierten damit auf die wachsende Bedeutung alternativer Streitbeilegungsmechanismen im Vorfeld von Schiedsverfahren.[294]

II. Ausschöpfung aller Möglichkeiten im Schiedsverfahren

Gegenüber dem alten Recht stellt *s* 12(2) *Arbitration Act* 1996 nunmehr klar, daß zunächst alle Möglichkeiten der Fristenverlängerung durch das Schiedsgericht ausgeschöpft sein müssen, bevor die staatlichen Gerichte eine solche Verlängerung gewähren.[295] Die Vorschrift ist ihrem Ihnalt nach nicht neu. In *Comdel Communications v. Siporex Trade*[296] hatte das House of Lords bereits festgestellt, daß der High Court von seiner Befugnis aus *s* 27 *Arbitration Act* 1950 "*in practice*" nur für diesen Fall Gebrauch machen werde. Verbindlich war dies jedoch nicht.

---

292 Merkin, Arbitration Act 1996, S. 29.

293 *S* 12(1) *Arbitration Act* 1996 lautet:
"Where an arbitration agreement to refer future disputes to arbitration provides that a claim shall be barred, or the claimant's right extinguished, unless the claimant takes within a time fixed by the agreement some step-
(a) to begin arbitral proceedings, or
(b) to begin other dispute resolution procedures which must be exhausted before arbitral proceedings can be begun,
the court may by order extend the time for taking that step [...]"

294 Harris/Planterose/Tecks, S. 80.

295 *S* 12(2) *Arbitration Act* 1996 lautet:
"Any party to the arbitration agreement may apply for such an order (upon notice to the other parties), but only after a claim has arisen and after exhausting any available arbitral process for obtaining an extension of time."

296 [1991] 1 A.C. 148.

S 12(3) enthält die bedeutsamste Änderung gegenüber dem alten Recht. Danach wird das Tatbestandsmerkmal der *undue hardship* nunmehr von zwei alternativen Voraussetzungen abgelöst. Die Vorschrift lautet:

> *" The court shall make an order only if satisfied-*
> *(a) that the circumstances are such as were outside the reasonable contemplation of the parties when they agreed the provision in question, and that it would be just to extend the time, or*
> *(b) that the conduct of one party makes it unjust to hold the other party to the strict terms of the provision in question [...]"*

Zur Verlängerung des Zeitlimits sollen die Gerichte jetzt also einerseits berechtigt sein, wenn "*the circumstances are such as were outside the reasonable contemplation of the parties*"; andererseits dann, wenn das Ergebnis der Verfristung ansonsten "*unjust*" wäre.

Die Bedeutung dieser Änderungen gegenüber dem alten Recht ist mangels einschlägiger Rechtsprechung nicht leicht zu erfassen. Die erstgenannte Alternative läßt einen nunmehr erweiterten Anwendungsbereich von *s* 12 *Arbitration Act* 1996 vermuten.[297] Denn eine entsprechende Regelung fehlte in der alten *s* 27 *Arbitration Act* 1950. Wann allerdings vom Vorliegen des Tatbestandsmerkmals ausgegangen werden kann, ist fraglich.

Problematisch ist in erster Linie *s* 12(3)(b) *Arbitration Act* 1996. Anstatt des durch die Rechtsprechung mittlerweile gut ausgefüllten Tatbestandmerkmals der *undue hardship* wird nunmehr dasjenige der *injustice* verwendet. Es darf vermutet werden, daß diese Wortwahl nicht rein zufällig getroffen wurde. Die Rechtsprechung zum Tatbestandsmerkmal der *undue hardship* scheint damit hinfällig zu sein. Damit ist zumindest theoretisch der Weg frei für eine restriktive Auslegung des Begriffs der *injustice*. Ob die Gerichte von dieser Möglichkeit Gebrauch machen werden, bleibt abzuwarten. Soweit bereits Rechtsprechung zu *s* 12 *Arbitration Act* 1996 vorliegt, gibt sie wenig zur Auslegung des Tatbestandsmerkmals *injustice* her.[298] Eine verläßliche Begriffsbestimmung ist zum jetzigen Zeitpunkt daher nicht möglich.

---

297 A.A. Merkin, Arbitration Act 1996, S. 30.

298 Vgl. etwa *Vosnoc Ltd. v. Transglobal Projects Ltd.* [1998] 1 W.L.R. 101; vgl. auch Sleightholme, Business L.R. 1997, 160.

D. Zwischenergebnis

Der Vergleich zeigt, daß *s* 12 *Arbitration Act* 1996 gegenüber dem alten Recht keine dramatischen Veränderungen gebracht hat. Abgesehen von Änderungen eher technischer Natur oder solchen ohne große Relevanz enthält *s* 12 *Arbitration Act* 1996 nur eine einzige bedeutende Änderung. Dies ist die Ersetzung des Tatbestandsmerkmals der *undue hardship* durch dasjenige der *injustice*. Da jedoch versäumt wurde, letzteres zu definieren, ist die Änderung wenig gewinnbringend. Im Gegenteil, die Ungewißheit hinsichtlich der Auslegung von *injustice* dürfte zu Lasten der Schiedsparteien gehen.

Eine Angleichung des englischen Rechts in diesem Punkt an das Modellgesetz - mithin die Abschaffung der genannten Befugnis - wäre eine sinnvolle Alternative gewesen. Diese Möglichkeit ist nicht genutzt worden. Es bleibt zu hoffen, daß die Gerichte nur ausnahmsweise von ihren Befugnissen aus *s* 12 *Arbitration Act* 1996 Gebrauch machen werden. Das Gegenteil ginge zu Lasten der Parteiautonomie bezüglich der Vereinbarung von Fristen und damit letztlich auch zu Lasten der Zügigkeit von Schiedsverfahren insgesamt. Das Modellgesetz vermeidet diese Gefahr, indem es kein entsprechendes Instrument zur Fristenverlängerung vorsieht. Dies mag im Einzelfall zu harten Ergebnissen führen. Die kompromißlose Einhaltung von Fristen ist jedoch eine wesentliche Voraussetzung für einen reibungslosen Geschäftsablauf. Das Modellgesetz stellt die Einhaltung solcher Fristen sicher.

Kapitel 4
Erklärung der Ungültigkeit der Schiedsvereinbarung

A. Einführung

In diesem Kapitel wird die Befugnis der Gerichte zur Erklärung der Unwirksamkeit von Schiedsvereinbarungen behandelt. Aus Sicht der Parteien ist die praktische Rechtsfolge mit der einer Nichtaussetzung von *wrongly brought proceedings* vergleichbar: Das Schiedsgericht kann den Streit nicht mehr verbindlich entscheiden. Allerdings stellt die Erklärung der Ungültigkeit einer Schiedsvereinbarung schon deshalb einen besonders intensiven Eingriff in ein Schiedsverfahren dar, weil in diesen Fällen das Schiedsverfahren in seinem anfänglichen Bestand zielgerichtet angegriffen wird. Anders als beispielsweise bei der Nichtaussetzung staatlicher Verfahren stellt hier das Erliegen des Verfahrens somit nicht lediglich eine Begleiterscheinung des staatlichen Eingriffs dar.

Die nachfolgenden Ausführungen beziehen sich erneut ausschließlich auf das englische Recht. Das Modellgesetz sieht keine entsprechenden Befugnisse der Gerichte vor. Auch die *Feststellung* der Ungültigkeit einer Schiedsvereinbarung kann nach dem Modellgesetz lediglich inzidenter im Rahmen der Prüfung einer Aufhebungsklage nach Art. 34 Modellgesetz oder einer Vollstreckungsgegenklage nach Art. 36 Modellgesetz erfolgen.[299]

B. Das englische Recht vor 1997

Der *Arbitration Act* 1950 ermächtigte die Gerichte in zwei Fällen zur Erklärung der Ungültigkeit.

I. Abberufung von Schiedsrichtern oder Erklärung der Unzuständigkeit

Die erste Möglichkeit der Ungültigkeitserklärung einer Schiedsvereinbarung bestand im Zusammenhang mit den Befugnissen der englischen Gerichte, Schiedsrichter zu ernennen bzw. abzuberufen. Dieser Themenkomplex wird in einem nachfolgenden Kapitel gesondert abgehandelt.[300] *S* 25(2)(b) *Arbitration Act* 1950 ermächtigte den High Court zur Erklärung der Ungültigkeit einer Schiedsvereinbarung, wenn er zuvor die Beauftragung eines Schiedsrichters widerrufen bzw. ihn abberufen hatte. *S* 25(2)(b) *Arbitration Act* 1950 lautete:

> *"Where the authority of an arbitrator [...] is revoked [...] or where [...] the arbitrators are removed [...] the High Court may, on the application of any party to the arbitration agreement, [...] order that the arbitration agreement shall cease to have effect with respect to the dispute referred."*

Wichtig ist in diesem Zusammenhang zunächst die Feststellung, daß es sich bei der Entfernung eines Schiedsrichters aus dem Amt und der Erklärung der Ungültigkeit der Schiedsklausel um zwei voneinander zu trennende Eingriffsbefugnisse der Gerichte handelte.[301] Zwar ist insoweit die erstgenannte Maßnahme Voraussetzung für die Anordnung der zweiten. Sie müssen jedoch keinesfalls immer kumulativ ergehen ("*may*").[302]

---

299 Vgl. hierzu *infra* Kapitel Kapitel 10, B.II.1. und Kapitel 11, B.IV.2.a).

300 Vgl. *infra* Kapitel 5.

301 Mustill/Boyd, S. 498, dort FN 2.

302 *Re Smith and Service and Nelson & Sons* (1890) 25 Q.B.D. 545 (553); Mustill/Boyd, S. 500, dort FN 6 führen aus:
"The policy underlying s 25(2)(b) is difficult to fathom. The shape of the section indicates that revocation and removal are regarded as the primary remedies. Yet the

S 25(2)(b) *Arbitration Act* 1950 stellte einen außerordentlich bedenklichen, weil sehr weitreichenden Eingriff in das Schiedsverfahren dar. Während beispielsweise die Abberufung eines Schiedsrichters die Schiedsfähigkeit des Streits unberührt ließ - die ersatzweise Neubenennung eines neuen Schiedsrichters stellte die Wirksamkeitsvoraussetzungen des Verfahrens wieder her - zielte *s* 25(2)(b) *Arbitration Act* 1950 auf das Beendigung des Schiedsverfahrens insgesamt ab. Nur für den Fall, daß das Schiedsverfahren zu einem irreparablen Stillstand gekommen war, erschien deshalb die Konsequenz aus *s* 25(2)(b) *Arbitration Act* 1950 angemessen.[303] Eine Beschränkung auf solche gravierenden Fälle sah das englische Recht indes nicht vor. So stand es dem High Court frei, in jedem Fall der Abberufung eines Schiedsrichters die Schiedsvereinbarung für ungültig zu erklären und damit das gesamte Verfahren beenden. Da gemäß s 1 *Arbitration Act* 1950 die Abberufung eines Schiedsrichters ihrerseits an keine (gesetzlichen) Voraussetzungen geknüpft war,[304] konnten die Gerichte nach *s* 25(2)(b) theoretisch jede Schiedsvereinbarung nach freiem Ermessen außer Kraft setzen.

Nach dem Wortlaut von *s* 25(2)(b) *Arbitration Act* 1950 ergab sich zudem, daß nur die *gesamte* Schiedsvereinbarung für ungültig erklärt werden konnte. Die Möglichkeit einer teilweisen Ungültigkeitserklärung wurde offenbar nicht gesehen.

II. Fraud

Es ist bereits deutlich geworden, daß das englische Recht den Gerichten in Fällen von Betrugsvorwurf besonders weitgehende Kontrollbefugnisse einräumte.[305] Entsprechend sah auch *s* 24(2) *Arbitration Act* 1950 die Befugnis des High Courts vor, die Schiedsvereinbarung in solchen Fällen für ungültig zu erklären. *S* 24(2) *Arbitration Act* 1950 lautete:

> *"Where an agreement between any parties provides that disputes which may arise in the future between them shall be referred to arbitration, and a dispute which so arises involves the question whether any such party has been guilty of fraud, the High Court shall, so far as may be necessary to enable that question to be determined by the High Court, have power to order that the agreement shall cease to have effect [...]"*

---

consequential remedy of an order that the agreement shall cease to have effect is more far-reaching, since it strikes at the arbitrability of the dispute, and not merely at the tribunal. Moreover, once the remedy is exercised, removal and revocation are unnecessary, since the jurisdiction of the tribunal must fall with the agreement."

303 Vgl. *Pratt v. Swanmore Builders Ltd. and Baker* [1980] 2 Lloyd's Rep. 504.

304 Vgl. *infra* Kapitel 5, C.III.1..

305 Vgl. *supra* die Ausführungen zu Kapitel 2, C.II.2.a).

Hinsichtlich des Eingriffscharakters dieser Vorschrift gelten grundsätzlich die gleichen Bedenken wie zu *s* 25(2)(b) *Arbitration Act* 1950. Sie bedürfen hier deshalb keiner nochmaligen Ausführung.[306] Auch im Rahmen von *s* 24(2) *Arbitration Act* 1950 kam es entscheidend auf die Auslegung des Tatbestandmerkmals *fraud* an. Es war bereits dargestellt worden, daß die englische Rechtsprechung diesen Begriff extensiv auslegte. Alle Fälle persönlicher Unehrlichkeit konnten hierunter subsumiert werden. Das Gericht befand nach freiem Ermessen über das Vorliegen des Tatbestandes und darüber, ob es bei dessen Vorliegen die vorgesehene Rechtsfolge anordnen solle.[307]

C. Der Arbitration Act *1996*

Die Befugnisse des High Courts nach den *ss* 24(2) und 25(2)(b) *Arbitration Act* 1950 sind im *Arbitration Act* 1996 ersatzlos weggefallen. Der *Act* sieht auch keine vergleichbaren Regelungen vor. Eine Begründung ist dem 1996-Report nicht zu entnehmen. Ebenso schweigt sich auch die einschlägige Literatur hierzu aus. Es darf jedoch davon ausgegangen werden, daß besagte Eingriffskompetenzen vor dem Hintergrund der oben deutlich gewordenen Kritik gestrichen wurden.

D. Zwischenergebnis

Die Befugnis, eine Schiedsvereinbarung nach dem alten englischen Recht für ungültig zu erklären, stand außer jedem Verhältnis zu dem damit verfolgten Zweck. Die vorgesehene Rechtsfolge war in den meisten Fällen nicht einmal erforderlich. Ging es den Gerichten in erster Linie um die Abberufung bestimmter Schiedsrichter, wäre die Neubenennung von Schiedsrichtern das angemessene Mittel gewesen. Die Nichtigerklärung der Schiedsvereinbarung muß in diesem Zusammenhang als unverhältnismäßig und im übrigen auch nicht parteiengerecht empfunden werden. Ähnlich unangebracht war die Nichtigerklärung der Schiedsvereinbarung für den Fall eines Betrugsvorwurfes. Die Ansicht, daß solche Fälle nur von Gerichten, nicht aber von Schiedsgerichten entschieden werden können, war grundsätzlich schwer nachzuvollziehen.

Indem der *Arbitration Act* 1996 die *ss* 24(2) und 25(2)(b) *Arbitration Act* 1950 ersatzlos streicht, nimmt er diese Kritik auf und reformiert das bisher gel-

306 Vgl. aber die Ausführungen zu Kapitel 4, B.I..
307 *Ashville Investments Ltd. v. Elmer Contractors Ltd.* [1988] 2 All E.R. 577.

tende Recht in einer Frage von zwar nicht großer praktischer, aber zumindest grundsätzlicher Bedeutung.

Im Ergebnis ist das neue englische Recht in der Frage der Anordnung der Ungültigkeit mit dem Modellgesetz identisch. Den Gerichten ist die Erklärung der Ungültigkeit der Schiedsklausel nicht mehr möglich.

Kapitel 5
Bestellung und Abberufung von Schiedsrichtern

A. Einführung

Die Befugnisse der Gerichte zur Bestellung und Abberufung von Schiedsrichtern ist ein kaum kontrovers diskutierter Bereich.[308] Das mag daran liegen, daß dieser Bereich nicht besonders "spannend" ist. Zumindest das diesbezügliche englische Recht wirkt aufgrund seiner Fülle von Detailregelungen bisweilen ermüdend. In ihrer Bedeutung sollten die Befugnisse zur Bestellung und Abberufung deshalb aber nicht unterschätzt werden. So können Fehler bei der Bestellung des Schiedsgerichts das Verfahren erheblich behindern. Sie können im übrigen auch zur Grundlage einer Aufhebungs- oder Vollstreckungsgegenklage werden.[309] Während das Modellgesetz hier eine geringe Regelungsdichte aufweist, erweist sich zumindest das alte englische Recht in diesem Punkt als "*both complex and detailed*"[310].

Jedenfalls bei der Bestellung von Schiedsrichtern durch die Gerichte - dies gilt eingeschränkt wohl auch bezüglich deren Abberufung - handelt es sich um einen klassischen Bereich der Unterstützung der Schieds- durch die staatlichen Gerichte und weniger um einen solchen der Kontrolle.[311] Die gesetzlichen Regelungen wollen vor allem zwei Ziele erreichen. Einerseits soll sichergestellt werden, daß in jedem Fall ein ordungsgemäß besetztes Schiedsgericht berufen wird. Andererseits soll die einmal hergestellte Funktionstüchtigkeit eines Schiedsgerichts gewahrt bleiben. Zu diesem Zweck wird den Gerichten die Abbe-

---

308 Allgemein zur Bedeutung und Problematik der Ernennung von Schiedsrichtern durch staatliche Gerichte vgl. Varady, Emory J.Int.Disp.Res. 1988, 311; Goldstajn, in: Voskuil/Wade (Hrsg.), Hague-Zagreb Essays 4, S. 297; Trappe, Arbitration 1978, 69.

309 Vgl. *infra* Kapitel 10, B.II.4 und Kapitel 11, B.IV.2.c).

310 Hunter, in: Lew (Hrsg.), Contemporary Problems, S. 198.

311 Vgl. allgemein Voskuil/Freedberg-Swartzburg, in : Sarcevic (Hrsg.), S. 64.

rufung von Schiedsrichtern ermöglicht, wenn diese selbst zur Störungsursache geworden sind.[312]

B. Art. 11 Modellgesetz

I. Bestellung

Die Bestellung von Schiedsrichtern durch die Gerichte ist in Art. 11 Modellgesetz geregelt. Danach sind die Parteien zunächst gehalten, sich auf eine Methode der Schiedsrichterbestimmung zu einigen.[313] Haben sie das nicht getan, bestimmt bei einem mehrköpfigen Schiedsgericht jede Partei eine gleiche Anzahl an Schiedsrichtern. Diese einigen sich dann auf einen weiteren Schiedsrichter. Gelingt keine solche Einigung auf einen weiteren Schiedsrichter, bestimmt diesen auf Antrag der Parteien das Gericht.[314] Können sich die Parteien nicht auf einen Einzelschiedsrichter einigen, wird auch dieser auf Antrag der Parteien vom Gericht bestimmt.[315]

Haben sich die Parteien zwar auf ein Verfahren zur Schiedrichterbestellung geeinigt, kommt es aber dennoch bei der Abwicklung des vereinbarten Verfahrens zu Schwierigkeiten, greift Art. 11 Abs. 4 Modellgesetz ein. Danach kann jede Partei bei dem zuständigen Gericht "*die Anordnung der erforderlichen Maßnahme beantragen*".

So wird sichergestellt, daß in jedem Fall ein entscheidungsfähiges Schiedsgericht zusammengestellt werden kann. Von nicht unerheblicher praktischer Relevanz mit Blick auf die Anerkennung und Durchsetzbarkeit des Schiedsspruchs ist Art. 11(5) Modellgesetz:

> *"Gegen die Entscheidung in einer Angelegenheit, die nach Absatz 3 oder 4 dem [zuständigen] Gericht [...] übertragen wird, ist kein Rechtsmittel zulässig. Das Gericht [...] hat bei der Bestellung eines Schiedsrichters alle nach der Parteivereinbarung für den Schiedsrichter vorgeschriebenen Voraussetzungen angemessen zu berücksichtigen und allen Gesichtspunkten Rechnung zu tragen, die die Bestellung eines unabhängigen und unparteiischen Schiedsrichters sicherstellen [...]"*

Auch in diesem Punkt erweist sich das Modellgesetz als "wasserdicht" gegen Verschleppungsversuche durch schiedsunwillige Parteien. Denn durch die Versa-

---

312 Hunter, in: Lew (Hrsg.), Contemporary Problems, S. 198.
313 Art. 11(2) Modellgesetz.
314 Art. 11(3)(a) Modellgesetz.
315 Art. 11(3)(b) Modellgesetz.

gung von Rechtsmitteln ist es unmöglich, die Ernennung von Schiedsrichtern zum Gegenstand langwieriger Rechtsmittelverfahren zu machen. Die Qualifikation der durch das Gericht zu ernennenden Schiedsrichter wird gleichwohl sichergestellt. Zum einen hat das Gericht die etwaige Parteivereinbarung zu berücksichtigen. Zum anderen haben die Parteien nach Art. 14 Modellgesetz immer noch die Möglichkeit, den Schiedsrichter abzuberufen (bzw. durch das Gericht abberufen zu lassen), wenn der Schiedsrichter sich außerstande zeigen sollte, seine Aufgaben zu erfüllen.[316]

II. Ablehnung und Abberufung

1. Ablehnung

Art. 13 Modellgesetz sieht ein Verfahren zur Ablehnung von Schiedsrichtern vor, welche bestimmten Mindestanforderungen oder anderen vereinbarten Kriterien[317] nicht genügen. Bei der Ablehnung eines Schiedsrichters geht es darum, daß ein Schiedsrichter möglichst überhaupt erst nicht seine Funktion aufnimmt. Entsprechend dem Grundmuster des Modellgesetes richtet sich das Ablehungsverfahren primär nach dem von den Parteien frei zu vereinbarenden Verfahren[318] und hilfsweise nach einem vom Modellgesetz selbst vorgegebenen System.[319] Nur soweit auch dieses Verfahren erfolglos bleibt, kann das zuständige Gericht auf Antrag der ablehnenden Partei intervenieren.[320]

Wie nahezu alle Eingriffsvorschriften des Modellgesetzes war auch Art. 13 Abs. 3 Gegenstand heftig geführter Kontroversen.[321] Nach einer Ansicht sollte es den staatlichen Gerichten gänzlich versagt sein, in ein Ablehnungsverfahren zu intervenieren.[322] Danach sollten die Parteien auf die Aufhebungs- bzw. Vollstreckungsgegenklage angewiesen sein, soweit die Ablehnung erfolglos geblieben war.[323] Auf der anderen Seite gab es die Befürworter möglichst frühzeitiger

---

316 Vgl. *infra* in diesem Kapitel B.II.2..

317 Vgl. Art. 12 Abs. 2 Modellgesetz:
"Ein Schiedsrichter kann nur abgelehnt werden, wenn Umstände vorliegen, die berechtigte Zweifel an seiner Unparteilichkeit oder Unabhängigkeit aufkommen lassen, oder wenn er die zwischen den Parteien vereinbarten Voraussetzungen nicht erfüllt [...]"
Zu den Begriffen der Unparteilichkeit und Unabhängigkeit vgl. Calavros, S. 67 ff.

318 Vgl. Art. 13 Abs. 1 Modellgesetz.

319 Vgl. Art. 13 Abs. 2 Modellgesetz.

320 Vgl. Art. 13 Abs. 3 Modellgesetz.

321 Holtzmann/Neuhaus, S. 407.

322 UN-Doc. A/CN.9/245, para 209.

323 *Ibid.*

staatsgerichtlicher Kontrolle, die zudem ein Aussetzen des schiedsgerichtlichen Verfahrens bis zu einer Entscheidung des Gerichts forderten.[324] Artikel 13 Abs. 3 Modellgesetz ist ein Kompromiß zwischen den zuvorgenannten Ansichten. Darin heißt es:

> "Bleibt die Ablehnung nach dem von den Parteien vereinbarten Verfahren oder nach dem in Absatz 2 vorgesehenen Verfahren erfolglos, so kann die ablehnende Partei binnen dreißig Tagen, nachdem sie von der Entscheidung, mit der die Ablehnung verweigert wurde, Kenntnis erlangt hat, bei dem [zuständigen] Gericht [...] eine Entscheidung über die Ablehnung beantragen; gegen diese Entscheidung ist kein Rechtsmittel zulässig. Während ein solcher Antrag anhängig ist, kann das Schiedsgericht einschließlich des abgelehnten Schiedsrichters das schiedsrichterliche Verfahren fortsetzen und einen Schiedsspruch fällen."

Grundsätzlich hat sich das Modellgesetz damit zwar für die Möglichkeit einer frühzeitigen gerichtlichen Kontrolle entschieden. Es sind jedoch keine Rechtsmittel gegen eine Entscheidung des Gerichts vorgesehen; wichtiger noch, das Schiedsgericht kann nach eigenem Ermessen das Verfahren trotz eines laufenden Gerichtsverfahrens fortsetzen. Die Gefahr von Verschleppungsmanövern ist somit minimiert.[325]

Die Möglichkeit, Schiedsrichter gerichtlich abzulehnen, wirft Fragen nach dem Verhältnis von Art. 13 Abs. 3 Modellgesetz zu den Art. 34 und 36 Modellgesetz auf. So ist fraglich, ob ein nach Art. 13 Abs. 3 Modellgesetz - erfolglos - durchgeführtes Verfahren oder dessen Nichtdurchführung die Aufhebungs- oder Vollstreckungsgegenklage wegen fehlerhafter Bildung des Schiedsgerichts ausschließt. Holtzmann/Neuhaus beantworten diese Frage wie folgt:[326]

> *"The Commission did not address or adopt a written proposal that would have explicitly barred a party from raising such a challenge both during the arbitral proceedings and subsequent court proceedings pursuant to Art. 34 and 36. With respect to the use of the challenge procedure per se, this result is clearly implied in Articles 12 and 13. Those Articles provide a right to challenge an arbitrator only under certain conditions, and those conditions include a requirement that the challenge be brought within the time limit stated therein. Thus, a party who fails to raise a timely challenge should presumably be barred from using that mechanism to raise his objections."*

Die Nichtdurchführung eines Verfahrens nach Art. 13 Abs. 3 Modellgesetz schloß somit ein erneutes Vorgehen gegen den Schiedsspruch gemäß Art. 34 und 36 Modellgesetz wegen des gleichen Grundes aus. Es folgt, daß bei einer erfolg-

---

324 UN-Doc. A/CN.9/245, para 210.

325 Holtzmann/Neuhaus, S. 407.

326 Holtzmann/Neuhaus, S. 408.

losen Durchführung des Verfahrens nach Art. 13 Abs. 3 ebenfalls nicht entsprechend den Art. 34 und 36 vorgegangen werden konnte.

2. *Abberufung*

Anders als bei der Ab*lehnung* geht es bei der Ab*berufung* darum, daß ein Schiedsrichter, der bereits bestellt worden war, sein Amt niederlegt, oder aus ihm entfernt wird. Das Modellgesetz sieht eine entsprechende Regelung in Art. 14 Abs. 1 vor:

> "Ist ein Schiedsrichter rechtlich oder tatsächlich außerstande, seine Aufgabe zu erfüllen, oder kommt er aus anderen Gründen seinen Aufgaben in angemessener Frist nicht nach, so endet sein Mandat, wenn er von seinem Amt zurücktritt oder wenn die Parteien die Beendigung seines Mandats vereinbaren. Bei Meinungsverschiedenheiten über einen dieser Gründe kann jede Partei bei dem [zuständigen] Gericht [...] eine Entscheidung über die Beendigung des Mandats beantragen; gegen diese Entscheidung ist kein Rechtsmittel zulässig."

In der Literatur wird Art. 14 Abs. 1 Modellgesetz - auch im Gegensatz zu Art. 13 Abs. 3 Modellgesetz - geradezu "stiefmütterlich" behandelt.[327] Mit Blick auf den Umfang der staatlichen Eingriffsbefugnisse wird dies der Bedeutung der Vorschrift kaum gerecht. Dazu muß man sich folgendes vergegenwärtigen: Immer dann, wenn ein Schiedsrichter "seinen Aufgaben in angemessener Frist nicht nach[kommt]", kann er auf Antrag einer Partei vom zuständigen Gericht aus seinem Amt entfernt werden. Zwar dürfte unstreitig sein, daß den Gerichten die Möglichkeit verbleiben muß, einen unfähigen Schiedsrichter unter bestimmten Voraussetzungen aus seinem Amt zu entfernen. Doch hätte unter dem Aspekt der Intensität des Eingriffs ein entsprechendes Ermessen der Gerichte klar eingegrenzt werden müssen. Das aber tut Art. 14 Abs. 1 gerade nicht.

C. *Das englische Recht vor 1997*

I. *Einführung*

Das englische Recht der Bestellung von Schiedsrichtern vor 1997 erscheint aufgrund seiner Komplexität und Detailliertheit auf den ersten Blick verwirrend.[328] Das hat seine Ursache u.a. darin, daß nach fünf verschiedenartig besetzten

327 Vgl. etwa die Ausführungen bei Nöcker, S. 102.
328 Vgl. auch die Einführung zu diesem Kapitel.

Schiedsgerichten unterschieden wurde.[329] Nach dem gesetzlichen Leitbild war das typische Schiedsgericht mit nur einem Schiedsrichter besetzt. Jedoch waren auch in England die Drei-Mann-Schiedsgerichte üblich.[330] Die nachfolgenden Ausführungen orientieren sich überwiegend am gesetzlichen Leitbild bzw. am Drei-Mann-Schiedsgericht.

Anders als das Modellgesetz sah das englische Recht kein (gesondertes) Ab*lehnungs*verfahren vor. Zwar stand es den Parteien frei, ein solches zu vereinbaren. Taten sie dies jedoch nicht und war dann eine Partei unzufrieden mit der Wahl der anderen Partei, blieb nur die Möglichkeit der Abberufung des so Ernannten durch die Gerichte. Es wird daher nachfolgend nicht zwischen Ablehnung und Abberufung unterschieden.

---

329 Folgende Zusammensetzungen eines Schiedsgerichts sah das englische Recht vor (vgl. Mustill/Boyd, S. 171):
- bestehend aus einem Schiedsrichter
- bestehend aus zwei Schiedsrichtern, mit einem *umpire* in Reserve
- bestehend aus drei Schiedsrichtern
- bestehend aus mehr als drei Schiedsrichtern
- bestehend aus einem *umpire*.

Der *umpire* ist eine Besonderheit des englischen Rechts und darf nicht mit dem *chairman* verwechselt werden. *S* 20 und *s* 21 *Arbitration Act* 1996 definieren die Begriffe, wie sie im wesentlichen auch schon vor 1997 verstanden wurden. Da die Unterscheidung - insbesondere im amerikanischen Rechtskreis (vgl. auch DAC, 1996-Report, para 80) - immer wieder für Verwirrung sorgt, sollen die genannten Vorschriften zum besseren Verständis nachfolgend wiedergegeben werden:
S 20(1)(4) (*Chairman*):
"(1) Where the parties have agreed that there is to be a chairman, they are free to agree what functions [he shall have] [...]
(4) [Otherwise] [t]he view of the chairman shall prevail in relation to a decision, order or award in respect of which there is neither unanimity nor a majority [...]"
S 21 (*Umpire*):
"(1) Where the parties have agreed that there is to be an umpire, they are free to agree what the functions of the umpire are to be, and in particular -
(a) whether he is to attend the proceedings, and
(b) when he is to replace the other arbitrators as the tribunal with power to make decisions, orders and awards.
(2) If or to the extend that there is no such agreement, the following provisions apply.
(3) The umpire shall attend the proceedings and be supplied with the same documents and other materials as are supplied to the other arbitrators.
(4) Decisions, orders and awards shall be made by the other arbitrators unless and until they cannot agree on a matter relating to the arbitration. In that event [...] the umpire shall replace them as the tribunal with power to make decisions, orders and awards as if he were sole arbitrator."

330 Mustill/Boyd, S. 171.

Das englische Recht unterschied jedoch zwischen *removal of arbitrator* und *revocation of authority*. Hierbei handelte es sich um eine Eigenart des englischen Rechts, die nicht ohne weiteres verständlich ist. Die Rechtsfolge war zumindest aus Sicht des Schiedsrichters die selbe: Er verlor jegliche Kompetenzen, eine verbindliche Streitentscheidung herbeizuführen.[331] Die Unterschiede lagen in den Tatbestandsvoraussetzungen.

II. Bestellung

S 10(1)(a) *Arbitration Act* 1950 regelte die Bestellung des Schiedsrichters eines Ein-Mann-Schiedsgerichts durch die Gerichte:

> *"[W]here an arbitration agreement provides that the reference shall be to a single arbitrator, and all the parties do not [...] concur in the appointment of an arbitrator [...] the High Court or a judge thereof may, on application [...] appoint an arbitrator [...] who shall have the like powers to act in the reference and make an award as if he had been appointed by consent of all parties."*

Wie dem Wortlaut entnommen werden kann ("*may*"), stand es im Ermessen des Gerichts, ob es einen Schiedsrichter ernannte oder nicht.[332] Darin lag einer der Unterschiede zum Modellgesetz. Zwar übte der High Court sein Ermessen regelmäßig dahin aus, daß er einen Schiedsrichter ernannte.[333] Entgegen der Ansicht von Merkin[334] konnte es jedoch keinesfalls als "*settled*" gelten, daß dies auch in jedem Fall so geschehen würde. Vielmehr konnte der High Court, ein Schiedsverfahren faktisch zum Erliegen zu bringen, indem er seine Unterstützung bei der Ernennung des Schiedsrichters verweigerte.

Gemäß *s* 10(1)(b) *Arbitration Act* 1950 galt dies entsprechend für den Fall, daß der Schiedsrichter seine Funktion nicht (mehr) wahrnehmen konnte und eine Neubesetzung durch den High Court im übrigen dem Parteiinteresse entsprach.[335]

---

331 Russel on Arbitration, S. 141 ("*Revocation of the arbitrator's authority is exactly equivalent to his removal.*").

332 Vgl. auch *Tritonia Shipping Inc. v. South Nelson Forest Products Corpn.* [1966] 1 Lloyd's Rep 114.

333 Mustill/Boyd, S. 179.

334 Merkin, Arbitration Law, 9.12.

335 *S* 10(1)(b) *Arbitration Act* 1950:
"[I]f an appointed arbitrator refuses to act, or is incapable of acting, or dies, and the arbitration agreement does not show that it was intended that the vancancy should not be supplied and the parties do not supply the vancancy [...] the High Court [...] may appoint an arbitrator [...]"

Für den Fall der Entfernung des Schiedsrichters aus seinem Amt durch das Gericht sah *s* 25(1)(2) *Arbitration Act* 1950 vor, daß dieses auf Antrag einer Partei einen Ersatzschiedsrichter benennen konnte.[336]

Im Gegensatz zu der entsprechenden Regelung nach dem Modellgesetz konnten gegen die Entscheidung des High Courts bezüglich der Ernennung von Schiedsrichtern Rechtsmittel eingelegt werden.[337]

III. Abberufung

1. Revocation of Authority

S 1 *Arbitration Act* 1950 lautete:

> *"The authority of an arbitrator or umpire appointed by virtue of an arbitration agreement shall, unless a contrary intention is expressed in the agreement, be irrevocable except by leave of the High Court or a judge thereof."*

Die Vorschrift enthielt zwei Aussagen. Erstens sollte es den Parteien im Regelfall nicht mehr möglich sein, einen bereits ernannten Schiedsrichter wieder aus seinem Amt zu entfernen. Wichtiger war jedoch die zweite, versteckte Aussage der Vorschrift. So konnte der High Court auf Anfrage jederzeit und nach eigenem Ermessen die *revocation of authority* des Schiedsrichters verfügen. Mustill/Boyd zufolge soll zwar "*immediately apparent*" gewesen sein, daß die eigentliche Intention von *s* 1 die Erschwerung der Abberufung von Schiedsrichtern durch die Parteien war.[338] Auch sollen die Gerichte zurückhaltend von ihrer Befugnis aus *s* 1 *Arbitration Act* 1950 Gebrauch gemacht haben.[339] Das ändert aber nichts an

---

336 *S* 25(1)(2)(a) *Arbitration Act* 1950:
"(1) Where an arbitrator (not being a sole arbitrator), or two or more arbitrators (not being all the arbitrators) or an umpire who has not entered on the reference is or are removed by the High Court or the Court of Appeal, the High Court may, on the application of any party to the arbitration agreement, appoint a person or persons to act as arbitrator or arbitrators or umpire in place of the person or persons so removed.
"(2) Where [...] a sole arbitrator [...] is removed [...] the High Court may, on the application of any party to the arbitration agreement [...]
(a) appoint a person to act as sole arbitrator in place of the person [...] or persons removed [...]"

337 Merkin, Arbitration Law, 9.4.

338 Mustill/Boyd, S. 526.

339 Thomas, Arbitration 1982, 142 unter Verweis auf *Succula and Pomona Shipping Co. Ltd. v. Harland and Wolff Ltd.* [1980] 2 Lloyd's Rep. 381.

der Tatsache, daß den Gerichten die jederzeitige Abberufung eines Schiedsrichters möglich war.

Hierbei waren die Gerichte an keinerlei gesetzliche Beschränkungen oder Ermessensrichtlinien gebunden. Auch die Rechtsprechung hat hierzu keine klaren Schranken entwickelt.[340] Zu den Kategorien, bei deren Vorliegen die Gerichte ohne weiteres von ihrer vorgenannten Befugnis Gebrauch machten, gehörten vor allem diejenige des *misconducts*[341] und des Verstoßes gegen das Gebot von *natural justice*[342]. So ließ die Rechtsprechung etwa für den Fall von Verfahrensfehlern eine *revocation of authority* zu.[343]

Die Tragweite von *s* 1 *Arbitration Act* 1950 in Verbindung mit *s* 25(2)(b) *Arbitration Act* 1950 wurde bereits in einem vorhergehenden Kapitel erläutert.[344]

Das Ergebnis ist überraschend. Die Gerichte konnten auf Antrag einer Partei nach freiem Ermessen einen Schiedsrichter aus seinem Amt entfernen.

2. Removal

Anders als bei der *revocation of authority* unterlag die *removal* eines Schiedsrichters bestimmten Schranken. Der *Arbitration Act* 1950 sah die Rechtsfolge der *removal* in zwei getrennt geregelten Fällen vor.

a) Misconduct

Gemäß *s* 23(1) *Arbitration Act* 1950 konnte ein Schiedsrichter aus seinem Amt entfernt werden, "*where [he] has misconducted himself or the proceedings*". Mustill/Boyd geben folgende Definition von *misconduct*, soweit er in diesem Zusammenhang relevant ist:[345]

> *"[Misconduct] undoubtedly covers all instances of what would ordinarily be understood as misconduct in the course of the reference. But it also embraces situations in which, although the arbitrator has not necessarily acted unfairly, he has allowed himself*

340 Vgl. aber die grobe Kategorisierung bei Russel on Arbitration, S. 141 ff.

341 *City Centre Properties (ITC Pensions) Ltd. v. Matthew Hall & Co. Ltd.*[1969] 1 W.L.R. 772 (779); ausführlich zum Begriff *misconduct* vgl. *infra* in diesem Kapitel C.III.2. sowie Kapitel 10, C.III.4..

342 *Stockport Metropolitan Borough Council v. O'Reilly* [1983] 2 Lloyd's Rep. 70 (78 f); kritisch Marshall, J.B.L. 1984, 46 f; vgl. auch Scott, Constr.L.J. 1989, 185.

343 *East and West India Dock Co. v. Kirk and Randall* (1887) 12 App.Cas. 738.

344 Vgl. *supra* Kapitel 4, B.I..

345 S. 530; vgl. auch *Veritas Shipping Corpn. v. Anglo-Canadian Cement Ltd.* [1966] 1 Lloyd's Rep. 76; für weitere Ausführungen zum Begriff *misconduct* vgl. *infra* Kapitel 10, C.III.4..

to get into a position where unfairness might reasonably be suspected or foreseen. The arbitrator must not only show no bias, but must also appear to be in a position to act judicially and without any bias."

Diese Definition geht unter anderem zurück auf das Urteil des Court of Appeal in *Modern Engineering (Bristol) Ltd. v. C. Miskin and Sons Ltd.*[346] In diesem Fall stritten die Parteien im Rahmen einer Vorfrage zu dem eigentlichen Verfahren darüber, ob dem Schiedsgericht die Überprüfung eines technischen Zertifikates erlaubt war oder ob dieses auch für das Schiedsgericht als verbindlich gelten mußte. Ohne der (späteren) Klägerin Gelegenheit zu einer Anhörung zu geben, entschied das Schiedsgericht in einer Vorabentscheidung im Sinne der Überprüfbarkeit des Zertifikats. Die unterlegene Partei beantragte daraufhin beim High Court die *removal* des Schiedsrichters nach *s* 23(1) *Arbitration Act* 1950 wegen *misconducts*. Nachdem der High Court den Antrag abgelehnt hatte, ließ der Court of Appeal ihn zu.

Der Court of Appeal stellte fest, daß die Unterlassung der Anhörung aller Parteien schon grundsätzlich einen Fall von *misconduct* konstituiere. Weiter begründete das Gericht seine Entscheidung wie folgt:[347]

> *"The question is whether the way [the arbitrator] conducted himself in the case was such that the parties can no longer have confidence in him. It seems to me that if this arbitrator is allowed to continue with the arbitration one at least of the parties will have no confidence in him."*

Somit sollte es also entscheidend auch darauf ankommen, ob die Parteien ihr Vertrauen in das Schiedsgericht verloren hatten.[348] Im Ergebnis enthielt das Tatbestandsmerkmal *misconduct* damit ein objektives und ein subjektives Element.[349]

Erwähnung verdient in diesem Zusammenhang noch eine weitere Aussage des Court of Appeal in *Modern Engineering (Bristol) v. C. Miskin & Sons Ltd.*. Diese läßt Rückschlüsse auf die grundsätzliche Haltung der englischen Justiz zum Ver-

---

346 [1981] 1 Lloyd's Rep. 135; vgl. auch *Annie Fox and Others v. P. G. Wellfair Ltd.* [1981] 2 Lloyd's Rep. 514.

347 *Modern Engineering (Bristol) Ltd. v. C. Miskin and Sons Ltd.*, *ibid*, 138.

348 Differenzierend *Hagop Ardahalian v. Unifert International S.A.* ("*The Ellissar*") [1984] 2 Lloyd's Rep. 84.

349 Das objektive Element wird noch deutlicher in *Pratt v. Swanmore Builders Ltd. and Baker* [1980] 2 Lloyd's Rep. 504 (509):
"While it would not be right to remove the arbitrator simply for the mistakes he has undoubtly made, I have to look at these mistakes and ask myself whether, by reason of them, the arbitration has been reduced to such confusion that there is no reasonable prospect for justice being done, if it is permitted to continue."

hältnis von Schieds- und staatlicher Gerichtsbarkeit zu. Lord Denning führte aus:[350]

"Arbitration is now one of the most important spheres of activity in the system of administering justice in this land. The courts, I feel, must show an example and see that arbitrations are properly conducted so as to earn and deserve the confidence of those who appear before them."

Man wird im Ergebnis nicht ganz falsch liegen, in diesem Zusammenhang "*to show an example*" frei mit "ein Exempel statuieren" zu übersetzen. Scheinbar ging es dem Court of Appeal mit der von ihm angeordneten Rechtsfolge des *removals* eben nicht nur um die Herstellung von Einzelfallgerechtigkeit. Vielmehr läßt die zuvor genannte Aussage Lord Dennings vermuten, daß mit diesem Urteil ein deutliches Signal an die Zunft der Schiedsrichter insgesamt gegeben werden sollte: "Beachtet die Gebote von *natural justice* oder Ihr werdet Eures Amtes enthoben!"[351]

b) Failure to use all reasonable dispatch

Gemäß *s* 13(3) *Arbitration Act* 1950 konnten die Gerichte eine *removal* ferner dann vornehmen, wenn der Schiedsrichter das Verfahren nicht mit der gebotenen Zügigkeit betrieb. Die Vorschrift lautete:

"The High Court may, on the application of any party to a reference, remove an arbitrator or umpire who fails to use all reasonable dispatch in entering on and proceeding with the reference and making an award [...]"

Zunächst zum Verhältnis von *s* 13(3) *Arbitration Act* 1950 zu *s* 23(1) *Arbitration Act* 1950. *S* 13(3) war spezieller. Die Vorschrift war nur anwendbar, soweit sich die eingetretene Verzögerung direkt aus einem Mangel an Zügigkeit und Eile der Verfahrensgestaltung durch den Schiedsrichter ergab. *S* 23(1) erfaßte dagegen diejenigen Fälle, in denen sich die Verzögerung aus einem *misconduct* des Schiedsrichters ergab.[352]

S 13(3) betraf den klassischen Fall des *mismanagements* eines Schiedsrichters. Erforderlich war also nicht, daß dieser bestimmte Fehler machte. Um den Tatbestand von *s* 13(3) zu erfüllen, reichte es vielmehr aus, daß der Schiedsrichter das Verfahren nicht mit der erforderlichen Zügigkeit betrieb. Was noch als

---

350 *Modern Engineering (Bristol) Ltd. v. C. Miskin and Sons Ltd.* [1981] 1 Lloyd's Rep. 135 (138).

351 In diesem Sinne auch Scott, Constr.L.J. 1989, 188.

352 *Pratt v. Swanmore Builders Ltd. and Baker* [1980] 2 Lloyd's Rep. 504 (512).

"*reasonable*" zügig anzusehen war, stand im freien Ermessen der Gerichte. Das *common law* zeigte diesbezüglich keine erkennbaren Schranken auf. Jedoch mußte der Schiedsrichter - abgesehen von Fällen von Krankheit oder ähnlichen Hindernissen - die Verzögerung schuldhaft herbeigeführt haben; schließlich verlor er im Falle einer *removal* nicht nur sein Amt, sondern auch seine Vergütungsansprüche.[353]

D. Der Arbitration Act *1996*

Die Befugnisse der Gerichte zur Bestellung und Abberufung von Schiedsrichtern werden in den *ss* 15 - 27 des *Arbitration Acts* 1996 größtenteils neu geregelt. Im Unterschied zu den entsprechenden Regelungen des alten Rechts fällt auf, daß die einschlägigen Regelungen im neuen *Act* übersichtlich zusammengefaßt worden sind. Inhaltlich orientiert sich das neue Recht teils am Modellgesetz,[354] teils an den bisherigen Regelungen des englischen Rechts.

I. Ernennung

1. Failure of appointment procedure

S 18 ist die Kernvorschrift der insgesamt fünf Vorschriften, welche die Ernennung von Schiedsrichtern durch die Gerichte betreffen.[355] Wie auch nach dem Modellgesetz können die Parteien gemäß *s* 18(1) *Arbitration Act* 1996 grundsätzlich frei vereinbaren, wie sie ein Versagen der ursprünglich vorgesehenen Ernennungsmethode beheben wollen.[356] Indem die Vorschrift von einem "*failure of proceeding*" spricht, verdeutlicht sie, daß die Befugnisse nicht nur für den Fall des Versagens der Parteien vorgesehen sind. Vielmehr sind auch diejenigen Fälle erfaßt, in denen ein Schiedsrichter - etwa wegen Krankheit - sein Amt nicht aus-

---

353 *S* 13(3) 2. Halbsatz *Arbitration Act* 1950 lautete:
"[...] and an arbitrator who is removed by the High Court under this subsection shall not be entitled to receive any remuneration in respect of his services."
Vgl. zur Begründung auch *Succula Ltd. and Pomona Shipping Co. Ltd. v. Harland and Wolff Ltd.* [1980] 2 Lloyd's Rep. 381 (384).

354 Vgl. DAC, 1996-Report, para 80.

355 Vgl. *ss* 16(7), 17(3)(4), 18, 19, 21(5)(6) *Arbitration Act* 1996.

356 Die Vorschrift lautet:
"The parties are free to agree what is to happen in the event of a failure of the procedure for the appointment of the arbitral tribunal [...]"

üben kann oder in denen eine dritte mit der Ernennung beauftragte Person oder Institution dieser Pflicht nicht nachkommt.[357]

S 18(2) *Arbitration Act* 1996 bestimmt, daß hilfsweise dem Gericht entsprechende Befugnisse zukommen. Eine Auflistung enthält *s* 18(3) *Arbitration Act* 1996. Die Vorschrift lautet:

"Those powers are -
(a) to give directions as to the making of any necessary appointments;
(b) to direct that the tribunal shall be constituted by such appointments (or any one or more of them) as have been made;
(c) to revoke any appointment already made;
(d) to make any necessary appointments itself."

Wie im übrigen auch nach Art. 11 Abs. 4 Modellgesetz sind die Gerichte nach *s* 18(3) *Arbitration Act* 1996 nicht auf die Ernennung von Schiedsrichtern beschränkt. Vielmehr wird ihnen mit *s* 18(3)(a)-(c) *Arbitration Act* 1996 darüberhinaus die Möglichkeit gegeben, auf andere Art und Weise auf Probleme bei der Bestellung des Schiedsgerichts zu reagieren. Dahinter steht die Intention des Gesetzgebers, den Gerichten die Möglichkeit einer flexiblen Reaktion auf verschiedenartige Fallkonstellationen zu eröffnen.[358]

a) Power to give directions

Zunächst können die Gerichte nunmehr nach *s* 18(3)(a) *Arbitration Act* 1996 Anweisungen hinsichtlich der Ernennung geben. Der Umfang dieser Befugnis ist nur schwer einzuschätzen. Anders als Art. 11 Abs. 4 Modellgesetz fällt aber eine direkte Ernennung von Schiedsrichtern wohl nicht unter diese Vorschrift. Dieser Fall ist gesondert in *s* 18(3)(c) *Arbitration Act* 1996 geregelt.

Vorstehend wurde bereits erwähnt, daß *s* 18 *Arbitration Act* 1996 auch im Falle des Versagens Dritter gelten sollte, wenn also beispielsweise eine beauftrage Schiedsinstitution mit der Bestellung des Schiedsgerichts beauftragt worden war. Inwieweit auch diese Dritten vom Gericht direkt angewiesen werden können, erscheint fraglich. Harris/Planterose/Tecks dazu aus:[359]

"The court could not direct an appointing person or body to make an appointment which it had failed to make, because that person or body would not be before the court."

---

357 Davidson, J. B. L. 1997, 108.
358 Rutherford/Sims, S. 81.
359 S. 95.

Diese Ansicht kann jedoch nicht geteilt werden. Bereits der Wortlaut von *s* 18(1) *Arbitration Act* 1996 läßt darauf schließen, daß die Befugnisse der Gerichte eben nicht nur hinsichtlich eines Versagens der Parteien gelten sollten. Folgerichtig muß es den Gerichten auch möglich sein, ihre Befugnisse überall dort, wo sie "gebraucht" werden, einzusetzen. Wenn beispielsweise eine dritte Institution bei der Ernennung der Schiedsrichter versagt - und zwar gleich aus welchem Grund - dann kann auch davon ausgegangen werden, daß die Gerichte direkt an dieser Stelle ansetzen werden, also diesen Dritten Anweisungen geben, die Ernennung vorzunehmen. Dies wird in einigen Fällen auch erforderlich sein. Denn es wird den Parteien, etwa aufgrund einer entsprechenden Vereinbarung, gegebenenfalls nicht mehr möglich sein, dem beauftragten Dritten nach dessen Benennung noch konkrete Weisungen zu erteilen.

b) Power to direct the tribunal

Nach *s* 18(3)(b) *Arbitration Act* 1996 kann das Gericht anweisen, daß sich das Schiedsgericht in der von den Parteien beschlossenen Weise konstituiert. Unglücklicherweise lassen sich dem 1996-Report keine Aussagen zum beabsichtigten Anwendungsbereich der Vorschrift entnehmen. Dieser scheint jedoch begrenzt zu sein. Er betrifft in erster Linie wohl die Situation, daß sich die von den Schiedsparteien bestimmten Schiedsrichter nicht wie vorgesehen auf einen weiteren (vorsitzenden) Schiedsrichter einigen können. Denkbar ist weiterhin der Fall, daß zwar alle Schiedsrichter ordentlich benannt worden sind, sich diese jedoch aus irgendeinem Grund nicht wie vorgesehen zu einem Schiedsgericht konstituieren.

c) Power to revoke appointments

Nach *s* 18(3)(c) *Arbitration Act* 1996 haben die Gerichte die Befugnis, bereits vorgenommene Ernennungen wieder rückgängig zu machen. Systematisch paßt diese Vorschrift eigentlich nicht unter *s* 18(3) *Arbitration Act* 1996. Hier geht es ja um die Ernennung und nicht um die Abberufung von Schiedsrichtern. Der 1996-Report führt zur Begründung aus:[360]

> *"It will be noted that we have given the Court power to revoke any appointments already made. This is to cover the case where unless the Court took this step it might be suggested thereafter that the parties had not been fairly treated, since one had his own choice [of an] arbitrator while the other had an arbitrator imposed on him by the Court in circumstances that were not fault of his own."*

---

360 Para 88.

S 18(3)(c) geht auf den Fall *BKMI Industrieanlagen v. Dutco*[361] zurück. Nach der Schiedsvereinbarung sollte hier jede Partei einen Schiedsrichter benennen dürfen. Eine Partei hatte die Ausübung dieses Rechts ohne Verschulden versäumt. Dies hatte die ersatzweise Benennung eines entsprechenden Schiedsrichters durch eine Schiedsorganisation zur Folge. Der Schiedsspruch wurde später wegen Ungleichbehandlung der Parteien aufgehoben.[362] Um so bedingte Aufhebungen zukünftig vermeiden zu können, soll es dem Gericht nunmehr möglich sein, die Ursache des vermeintlichen Übels gleich beim Entstehen zu beseitigen.

Die Ausübung des Rechts nach *s* 18(3)(c) *Arbitration Act* 1996 scheint danach in den folgenden Situationen in Betracht zu kommen: Erstens, das Gericht macht die ersatzweise Benennung eines Schiedsrichters durch eine dritte Person oder Institution rückgängig und benennt entweder selbst einen Ersatzschiedsrichter bzw. ordnet an, daß nunmehr die jeweilige Partei eine solche Benennung nachholen könne; zweitens, das Gericht widerruft die Ernennung auch des anderen Schiedsrichters, also desjenigen, der ordnungsgemäß von der anderen Partei benannt worden war und ernennt selbst ersatzweise einen Schiedsrichter für diese Partei. Auch so wäre die Ungleichbehandlung wettgemacht.

d) Power to make necessary appointments

In *s* 18(3)(d) ist schließlich das mit Art. 11 Abs. 4 Modellgesetz korrespondierende Recht des Gerichts geregelt, erforderlichenfalls selbst einen Ersatzschiedsrichter zu benennen. Sinnvollerweise wird auch nach *s* 18(3)(d) die bisherige Praxis[363] beibehalten, dem ersuchten Gericht Vorschläge zur Person des ersatzweise durch das Gericht zu benennenden Schiedsrichters zu machen.

2. Power in case of default to appoint sole arbitrator

S 17 *Arbitration Act* 1996 regelt eigens den Fall, daß eine von zwei Parteien ihrer Pflicht bzw. ihrem Recht zur Benennung eines Schiedsrichters nicht rechtzeitig nachkommt. Für diesen Fall bestimmt *s* 17, daß die Partei, die "ihren" Schiedsrichter benannt hat, diesen zum alleinigen Schiedsrichter erklären kann. In *s* 17(4) wird der "*party in default*", also derjenigen, welche die Benennung eines eigenen Schiedsrichters versäumt hat, über die Anrufung der Gerichte eine Möglichkeit eröffnet, den eingetretenen „Schaden" wieder zu beseitigen. Danach soll den Gerichten auf Antrag die Befugnis zustehen, die Benennung des von der

---

361 [1994] A.D.R.L.J. 36.

362 Vgl. Rutherford/Sims, S. 81; Harris/Planterose/Tecks, S. 96.

363 Vgl. Harris/Planterose/Tecks, S. 97.

gegnerischen Partei benannten Schiedsrichters zum Einzelschiedsrichter wieder rückgängig zu machen. Richtlinien zur Ausübung des gerichtlichen Ermessens sind nicht vorgesehen. Nach Ansicht des DAC[364] ist die Ermessensausübung "*best left for the Courts to develop, given the specific circumstances of each case, and in the light of the overall philosophy of the [Act].*"

3. Procedure for appointment of arbitrators

S 16 *Arbitration Act* 1996 regelt das der eigentlichen Ernennung der Schiedsrichter vorgelagerte Verfahren der Bestimmung des Ernennungsverfahrens. Primär soll die Verfahrensbestimmung durch Parteivereinbarung erfolgen. Anders als das Modellgesetz unterscheidet *s* 16 *Arbitration Act* 1996 hierbei nach einer Mehrzahl von verschiedenartig besetzten Schiedsgerichten.[365]

Wie auch nach dem Modellgesetz kommt den Gerichten bei der Bestimmung der Verfahrensweise lediglich eine Auffangfunktion zu. *S* 16(7) *Arbitration Act* 1996[366] verweist diesbezüglich auf *s* 18 *Arbitration Act* 1996. Können sich also die Parteien nicht einigen und greift auch keine der gesetzlichen Hilfsregelungen in *s* 16 *Arbitration Act* 1996, kommen den Gerichten durch diesen Verweis die selben Befugnisse zu wie bei der Ernennung der Schiedsrichter gemäß *s* 18 *Arbitration Act* 1996.

4. Ermessen

Das Gericht unterliegt bei der Ausübung seiner Befugnisse nach den *ss* 16-18 keinen Ermessensbeschränkungen im engeren Sinn. *S* 19 sieht allerdings vor, "*[that] the court shall have due regard to any agreement of the parties as to the qualifications required of the arbitrators*".

---

364 *1996-Report*, para 85.

365 Es wird nach folgender Besetzung des Schiedsgerichts unterschieden:
- mit einem Schiedsrichter,
- mit zwei Schiedsrichtern,
- mit zwei Schiedsrichtern und einem *chairman* und schließlich
- mit zwei Schiedsrichtern und einem *umpire* (zu den Begriffen des *chairman* und *umpire* vgl. in diesem Kapitel, C.I.).

366 *S* 16(7) *Arbitration Act* 1996 lautet:
"In any other case (in particular, if there are more than two parties) section 18 applies as in the case of a failure of the agreed appointment procedure."

5. Appeal

Anders als nach dem Modellgesetz ist gegen eine gerichtliche Entscheidung nach den *ss* 16-18 ein *appeal* zulässig. Hierzu das DAC:[367]

> *"The Model Law stipulates that there shall be no appeal from a decision of the Court. We have not gone as far as this since there may well be questions of important general principle which would benefit from authoritative appelate guidance."*

Das bringt zwar die Gefahr einer Verschleppung mit sich. Diese wird jedoch dadurch minimiert, daß der *appeal* zunächst durch das erstinstanzliche Gericht zugelassen werden muß ("*leave of the court*").

II. Abberufung

1. Revocation of authority

Die Unterscheidung nach *revocation of authority* und *removal of arbitrator* wird auch im *Arbitration Act* 1996 beibehalten. Auch nach dem neuen Recht ist keine inhaltliche Unterscheidung hinsichtlich der Rechtsfolge beabsichtigt.[368]

S 23 *Arbitration Act* 1996 ersetzt *s* 1 *Arbitration Act* 1950. Die Vorschrift bedingt eine einschneidende Änderung des alten Rechts. Denn die Gerichte verlieren grundsätzlich jegliche Befugnisse, einen Schiedsrichter abzuberufen. Die umstrittenen, weil unbegrenzten Ermessensbefugnisse der Gerichte zur Abberufung von Schiedsrichtern nach *s* 1 *Arbitration Act* 1950 entfallen somit.

Von diesem Grundsatz macht *s* 23(5) zwei Ausnahmen. So sollen einerseits die Befugnisse des Gerichts nach *s* 18(3)(c) *Arbitration Act* 1996[369] ("*power to revoke appointments*") unberührt bleiben; ansonsten ist eine Abberufung nunmehr nur noch gemäß *s* 24 *Arbitration Act* 1996 ("*removal of arbitrator*") möglich.[370]

Die Bedeutung von *s* 23 liegt somit vor allem in der Feststellung, daß ein Schiedsrichter - abgesehen von dem seltenen Ausnahmefall der *s* 18(3)(c) - durch die Gerichte einzig nach *s* 24 abberufen werden kann. Anders formuliert, eine *re-*

---

367 *1996-Report*, para 98.

368 Der *1996-Report*, para 98, führt dazu aus, daß die verschiedenen Begriffe "*have been adopted simply as a matter of correct English usage. The difference in terms is not intended to be of any legal significance.*"

369 Vgl. *supra* in diesem Kapitel D.I.1.c).

370 Vgl. *infra* in diesem Kapitel D.II.2..

vocation of authority ist ausschließlich einer entsprechenden Parteivereinbarung vorbehalten, während ein *removal of arbitrator* Sache des Gerichts ist.[371]

Weiterhin ist es den Parteien nunmehr erstmalig ohne Zulassung des Gerichts möglich, einen Schiedsrichter gegen dessen Willen abzuberufen. Nach dem alten Recht war für die Abberufung eines Schiedsrichters entweder die Zustimmung des Schiedsrichters oder die des Gerichts erforderlich.[372]

2. Removal of arbitrator

S 24 stellt nunmehr die zentrale Vorschrift für die Abberufung von Schiedsrichtern dar. Die Vorschrift ersetzt die *ss* 13(3) und 23(1) *Arbitration Act* 1950. Erstmalig sieht das neue englische Recht mit *s* 24(1) eine abschließende Aufzählung der Gründe vor, welche die Gerichte zur Entfernung von Schiedsrichtern aus deren Amt berechtigen.[373] Die Vorschrift lautet:

"A party to arbitral proceedings may [...] apply to the court to remove an arbitrator on any of the following grounds-
(a) that circumstances exist that give rise to justifiable doubts as to his impartiality;
(b) that he does not possess the qualifications required by the arbitration agreement;
(c) that he is physically or mentally incapable of conducting the proceedings or there are justifiable doubts as to his capacity to do so;
(d) that he has refused or failed-
(i) properly to conduct the proceedings, or
(ii) to use all reasonable dispatch in conducting the proceedings or making an award,
and that substantial injustice has been or will be caused to the applicant."

a) Justifiable doubts as to impartiality

S 24(1)(a) orientiert sich an Art. 12 Modellgesetz. Im Unterschied zu Art. 12 nennt *s* 24(1)(a) jedoch lediglich die *impartiality*, nicht aber einen Zweifel an der Unabhängigkeit (*lack of independence*) als Grund für die Abberufung. Es wurde befürchtet, daß ansonsten langwierige und überflüssige Diskussionen hinsichtlich des Umfangs der Unabhängigkeit zu erwarten seien.[374] Weiter wurde die Möglichkeit gesehen, daß die Parteien unter Umständen daran gehindert sein könnten, Schiedsrichter mit besonderen Verbindungen auf dem entsprechenden Fachgebiet

---

371 Merkin, Arbitration Act 1996, S. 43.
372 Vgl. *K/S Norjarl A/S v. Hyundai Heavy Industries Co. Ltd.* [1991] 3 All E.R. 211; Rutherford/Sims, S. 89.
373 Vgl. Zekos, J.Int'l Arb. 1998, 67 f.
374 Merkin, Arbitration Act 1996, S. 44.

zu benennen. Denn diese könnten stets als Mangel an Unabhängigkeit ausgelegt werden. Im übrigen wurde die explizite Nennung des Unabhängigkeitserfordernisses auch als überflüssig angesehen.[375] Soweit dieses in nennenswertem Umfang nicht mehr gewährleistet sei, so die Überlegung, liege jedenfalls ein Zweifel an der Unparteilichkeit des Schiedsrichters vor.[376]

b) Lack of qualifications

Ein Schiedsrichter kann gemäß *s* 24(1)(b) ferner dann aus seinem Amt entfernt werden, wenn er nicht die nach dem Schiedsvertrag verlangten Qualifikationen besitzt. Gemeint sind danach zunächst unstreitig solche, die explizit im Schiedsvertrag genannt sind. Unter *s* 24(1)(b) fallen zudem unstreitig solche Qualifikationen, die zwar nicht explizit im Schiedsvertrag festgelegt sind, von dessen Vorliegen die Parteien vor dem Hintergrund des konkreten Streits aber als selbstverständlich ausgehen dürfen.

c) Incapacity

Die Gerichte können einen Schiedsrichter weiter dann aus seinem Amt entfernen, wenn zumindest berechtigte Zweifel an seinem körperlichen oder geistigen Zustand bestehen. Die praktische Bedeutung dieser Regelung ist als gering einzustufen.

d) Failure of proper conduct

S 24(1)(d)(i) *Arbitration Act* 1950 enthält schließlich den bedeutsamsten Grund für die *removal*. Verstößt danach ein Schiedsrichter gegen die Pflicht zur ordnungsgemäßen Verfahrensführung ("*proper conduct*") und resultiert hieraus gegenwärtig oder zukünftig eine erhebliche Ungerechtigkeit ("*substantial injustice*"), kann der Schiedsrichter aus seinem Amt entfernt werden. Merkin bringt es auf den Punkt, wenn er diese Norm eine "*catch-all provision*" nennt.[377] Letztlich ist *s* 24(1)(d)(i) nichts anderes als eine Wiederholung von *s* 23(1) *Arbitration Act* 1950 ("*misconduct*").[378] Das in Literatur wie Rechtsprechung so ungeliebte, weil uferlose Tatbestandsmerkmal des *misconducts* wurde durch dasjenige des *inproper conduct* ersetzt. Welches Ziel der englische Gesetzgeber hiermit letzt-

375 *Ibid.*
376 DAC, 1996-Report, para 101.
377 Arbitration Act 1996, S. 45.
378 Vgl. *supra* in diesem Kapitel, C.III.2.a).

lich erreichen wollte, ist unklar. Denn die Ersetzung eines unbestimmten Rechtsbegriffs durch einen ebenso unbestimmten Rechtsbegriff bringt keine erkennbaren Vorteile mit sich. Dieses Dilemma scheint das DAC auch erkannt zu haben. So heißt es in seinem 1996-Report:[379]

> *"We trust that the Courts will not allow [this] matter to be abused by those intent on disrupting the arbitral process [...] We have every confidence that the Courts will carry through the intent of this part of the Bill, which is that it should only be available where the conduct to the arbitrator is such as to go so beyond anything that could reasonably be defendend that substantial injustice has resulted or will result."*

Ohne hier unterstellen zu wollen, daß das so geäußerte Vertrauen des DAC notwendigerweise enttäuscht werden muß, bleibt doch folgendes festzuhalten: Es besteht - wie bereits nach dem *Arbitration Act* 1950 - weiterhin die *Möglichkeit* einer Entfernung von Schiedsrichtern durch die Gerichte, ohne daß letztere klaren Schranken unterworfen wären. Es ist Aufgabe der Gerichte, den Terminus *inproper conduct* einzugrenzen. Da diesen eine solche Eingrenzung jedoch auch beim Begriff *misconduct* nicht gelungen ist, ist in diesem Punkt keine wesentliche Änderung zu erwarten.

e) Reasonable dispatch

S 24(1)(d)(ii) übernimmt schließlich die Regelung aus *s* 13(3) *Arbitration Act* 1950, wonach ein Schiedsrichter, der nicht mit der gebotenen Zügigkeit auf einen Abschluß des Verfahrens hinarbeitet, seiner Funktion entbunden werden kann. Mit der Ausnahme, daß auch ein Verstoß hiergegen nur in Fällen von "*substantial injustice*" auszugehen ist, enthält die Vorschrift gegenüber *s* 13(3) *Arbitration Act* 1950 keine grundlegenden Änderungen.

E. Zwischenergebnis

Ein Vergleich des alten und neuen englischen Rechts zur Bestellung und Abberufung von Schiedsrichtern ergibt ein uneinheitliches Bild. Bei der Ernennung von Schiedsrichtern durch die Gerichte haben sich keine dramatischen Änderungen ergeben. Die Befugnisse der Gerichte sind jedoch erweitert worden. Vor allem die Möglichkeit der Gerichte, neben der eigentlichen Ernennung von Schiedsrichtern auch entsprechende Anweisungen zu erteilen, ist neu. Dadurch wird den Gerichten eine flexiblere Reaktion auf die jeweilige Problematik im Einzelfall

---

379 Para 105.

ermöglicht. Diese Änderungen sind deshalb grundsätzlich zu begrüßen. Es ist zudem nicht ersichtlich, wie dadurch die Unabhängigkeit des Schiedsverfahrens gefährdet werden könnte. Denn zum einen stellen die neu hinzugekommenen Befugnisse ein Minus im Vergleich zu der auch vormals vorgesehenen Ernennung von Schiedsrichtern dar. Zum anderen ist ihnen gemein, daß sie allesamt lediglich der Unterstützung des Schiedsverfahrens dienen und nicht der Kontrolle.

Nicht ganz so positiv fällt der Vergleich hinsichtlich der Abberufung von Schiedsrichtern aus. Zu begrüßen ist hier zunächst die Abschaffung der Befugnisse aus *s* 1 *Arbitration Act* 1950, wonach die Gerichte sozusagen freie Hand zur *revocation of authority* hatten. Dieses Recht stellte eine der intensivsten Eingriffsbefugnisse in das Schiedsverfahren überhaupt dar. Die Reform blieb jedoch auf halbem Weg stecken. So wurde insbesondere versäumt, das weite Tatbestandsmerkmal des *misconducts* in *s* 23(1) *Arbitration Act* 1950 wirklich abzuschaffen. In der Gestalt des *inproper conduct* wurde es vielmehr in *s* 24(1)(d)(i) *Arbitration Act* 1996 Bestandteil auch des neuen englischen Rechts. Ebenso unverändert blieb schließlich das vormals in *s* 13(3) vorgesehene Recht, einen "langsamen" Schiedsrichter seines Amtes zu entheben.

Im Ergebnis bleibt festzuhalten, daß der *Arbitration Act* 1996 das Recht der Abberufung von Schiedsrichtern nicht zur vollen Überzeugung reformiert hat.

Einen Vergleich mit den entsprechenden Regelungen des Modellgesetzes braucht der *Arbitration Act* 1996 dennoch nicht zu scheuen. Der Grund liegt darin, daß auch das Modellgesetz in einer ganz untypischen Weise den Gerichten in Art. 14 einen nahezu unbegrenzten Ermessensspielraum zur Abberufung von Schiedsrichtern einräumt.

Kapitel 6
Die Befugnis des Schiedsgerichts zur Entscheidung über die eigene Zuständigkeit

A. Einführung

Die wichtigste Voraussetzung dafür, daß ein Schiedsgericht einen Fall verhandeln und verbindlich entscheiden kann, ist seine Zuständigkeit. Sie läßt sich aufgrund entsprechender Parteivereinbarungen zumeist unproblematisch feststellen. In Grenzbereichen der zu entscheidenden Streitigkeit kann mitunter unklar sein, was noch und was nicht mehr von der Schiedsvereinbarung der Parteien gedeckt ist. In diesem Zusammenhang stellt sich die Frage, ob das Schiedsgericht selbst über die eigene Zuständigkeit entscheiden kann und, falls ja, welche rechtliche Verbindlichkeit einer solchen Entscheidung zukommt.

Die Bedeutung einer solchen Befugnis ergibt sich aus der Uberlegung, daß der Angriff auf die Zuständigkeit des Schiedsgerichts zu den gängigsten Mitteln schiedsunwilliger Parteien gehört, das Schiedsverfahren zu verschleppen bzw. zum Erliegen zu bringen.[380] Nur indem den Schiedsgerichten die Kompetenz zur Entscheidung über die eigene Zuständigkeit eingeräumt wird und diese auch nur in begrenztem Umfang durch die staatlichen Gerichte überprüfbar ist, kann diesem Mißbrauch begegnet werden.[381]

Daß den staatlichen Gerichten eine *abschließende* Prüfungskompetenz zur Zuständigkeit zukommt - im Regelfall im Rahmen eines Aufhebungs- oder Vollstreckungsverfahrens - wird einhellig angenommen.[382] Weitaus uneinheitlicher ist der Meinungsstand jedoch hinsichtlich des Zeitpunktes, zu dem die gerichtliche Kontrolle erfolgen sollte. Während in England traditionell die Auffassung vertreten wurde, daß die Gerichte bereits *vor* Ergehen eines Schiedsspruchs über die Zuständigkeit des Schiedsgerichts entscheiden konnten, sieht etwa das Modellgesetz eine solche Befugnis erst nach Ergehen des Schiedsspruchs vor.[383] Der Streit konzentriert sich im wesentlichen also auf die Frage, ob dem Schiedsgericht die anfängliche und abschließende Kompetenz zur Entscheidung über die eigene Zuständigkeit zusteht oder nicht.[384]

Die Kompetenz der Schiedsgerichte zur abschließenden Entscheidung über die eigene Zuständigkeit und die unabhängige Gültigkeit der Schiedsklausel vom Hauptvertrag sind zwei zwingend miteinander verbundene Themen.[385] Denn damit das Schiedsgericht darüber entscheiden kann, muß die Unabhängigkeit der Schiedsklausel vom Hauptvertrag gewährleistet sein. Deutlich wird das insbesondere, wenn dem Schiedsgericht die Entscheidung über Abwicklungsstreitigkeiten wegen Ungültigkeit, Nichtigkeit oder Beendigung des Hauptvertrages übertragen wurde. Wäre in diesem Fall die Schiedsklausel nicht unabhängig vom Hauptver-

---

380 Lew, in: ders. (Hrsg.) Contemporary Problems, S. 75.

381 Vgl. auch Wetter, Arb.Int'l 1987, 329.

382 Metzger, in: Commercial Arbitration, S. 317 f; Sanders, in: Eisenmann, S. 32; für eine eingeschränkte abschließende Prüfungsbefugnis der Gerichte dagegen Schmitthoff, in: Schultsz/v.d. Berg, S. 293.

383 Allerdings besteht nach Art. 16 Abs. 3 Modellgesetz die Möglichkeit, daß das Schiedsgericht einen Zwischenschiedsspruch zur Gültigkeit der Schiedsvereinbarung erläßt. Dieser kann dann immer noch zum Gegenstand einer Anfechungsklage wegen Unzuständigkeit gemacht werden. Ob das Schiedsgericht hingegen einen solchen Zwischenschiedsspruch erläßt, liegt in seinem Ermessen.

384 Samuel, Jurisdictional Problems, S. 177.

385 Allgemein Hill, Lloyd's Mar. & Com.L.Q. 1992, 306; Rosen, Fordham Int'l.L.J. 1994, 599; Delaume, in: Carbonneau (Hrsg.), S. 204.

trag gültig, könnte das Schiedsgericht weder über seine Zuständigkeit noch über die Streitigkeit selbst mangels gültiger Schiedsklausel entscheiden.[386]

B. Unabhängigkeit der Schiedsklausel

I. Art. 16 Abs. 1 Modellgesetz

Das Modellgesetz regelt die Selbständigkeit der Schiedsklausel in Art. 16 Abs. 1:

> *"[Zum Zweck der Entscheidung über die eigene Zuständigkeit] ist eine Schiedsklausel, die Bestandteil eines Vertrags ist, als eine von den übrigen Bestimmungen des Vertrags unabhängige Vereinbarung zu behandeln."*

In Art. 16 Abs. 1 Modellgesetz kommt die zuvor angesprochene enge Verzahnung der Selbständigkeit der Schiedsklausel und der Kompetenz zur verbindlichen Entscheidung über die eigene Zuständigkeit deutlich zum Ausdruck. Dank der eindeutigen Regelung in Art. 16 Abs. 1 bestehen bezüglich der Selbständigkeit der Schiedsklausel nach dem Modellgesetz keine Zweifel. Sie ist gewährleistet.

II. Das englische Recht vor 1997

Die Selbständigkeit der Schiedsklausel hatte im englischen Recht bis zum *Arbitration Act* 1996 keine gesetzliche Regelung erfahren.[387] Bis zu diesem Zeitpunkt war sie lediglich durch das *common law* geregelt. Dessen Darstellung ist deshalb problematisch, weil die einschlägigen Urteile teilweise widersprüchlich sind. So führt etwa Lord Megaw in *Dalmatia Dairy Industries Ltd. v National Bank of Pakistan* aus:[388]

> *"[I]n English law, no arbitrator can have jurisdiction, however wide the wording of the arbitration clause which the parties or alleged parties insert into their contract, to decide a dispute as to the initial existence or validity of the alleged contract in which the arbitration clause appears."*

Ganz anders liest sich dagegen folgende Stellungnahme Lord Diplocks in *The Bremer Vulkan*:[389]

---

386 Calavros, S. 44; ebenso Schwebel, S. 18.
387 Svernlöv, J.Int'l Arb. 1992, 115; ders., J.Int'l Arb. 1991, 37
388 [1978] 2 Lloyd's Rep. 223 (286).
389 *The Bremer Vulkan* [1981] A.C. 909 (980).

"The arbitration clause constitutes a self-contained contract collateral[390] *or ancillary*[391] *to the [...] agreement itself."*

Scheinbar hat sich das *common law* in der Zeit zwischen dem *Dalmatia*-Fall (1978) und dem *Bremer Vulkan*-Fall (1981) bezüglich der Selbständigkeit der Schiedsklausel also grundlegend geändert.[392] Dies aber ist nicht ganz richtig.[393] So war zumindest bis 1993[394] bei Vorliegen folgender (vorgeblicher) Nichtigkeitsgründe die Selbständigkeit der Schiedsklausel nicht anerkannt: Rechtswidrigkeit des Hauptvertrages oder Verstoß gegen den *ordre public,*[395] Nichteintritt einer aufschiebenden Bedingung des Hauptvertrages[396] sowie Einigungsmangel und mangelnde Geschäftsfähigkeit[397].

Besondere Erwähnung verdient hier die Fallgruppe, in der eine Partei durch Irrtum, Betrug, *misrepresentation*[398] oder Nötigung zum Vertragsschluß bewegt worden war. Es wurde bereits festgestellt, daß das englische Recht die Schiedsgerichtsbarkeit insbesondere bei Betrugsvorwürfen besonderer staatlicher Kontrolle unterstellte.[399] Dies galt grundsätzlich auch für den Bereich der Selbständigkeit der Schiedsklausel. In *Heyman v. Darwins* wurde es als überaus wichtig bezeichnet, daß der Schiedsrichter in diesen Fällen keine Zuständigkeit haben dürfe.[400] Den Schiedsgerichten wurde in diesen Kategorien die Kompetenz abgesprochen, ein faires und korrektes Verfahren zu garantieren.

Bewegung kam in das *common law* zur *separability* durch das Urteil des Court of Appeal im Jahr 1993 in *Harbour Assurance Co. (UK) Ltd. v. Kansa General International Insurance Co. Ltd. and Others*.[401] Hier hatte ein Versicherungsunternehmen auf Feststellung der Nichtigkeit eines mit der Beklagten geschlossenen Rückversicherungsvertrages geklagt. Die Klage wurde damit begründet, daß die Beklagte nicht die erforderliche Lizenz besäße, Versicherungsgeschäfte in England zu tätigen. Der Vertrag enthielt eine Schiedsklausel. Nach

---

390 Im Sinne von „zusätzlich".
391 *Ibid.*
392 Vgl. auch Boyd/Veeder, Revue Arbitrage 1991, 221 ff.
393 Samuel, J.Int'l Arb. 1986, 95.
394 Vgl. *infra* die Ausführungen zum *Harbour Assurance*-Fall.
395 *Joe Lee Ltd. v. Lord Dalmeny* [1927] 1 Ch. 300; *Overseas Union v. AA Mutual International Co. Ltd.* [1988] 2 Lloyd's Rep. 63 (71).
396 *Payne & Routh v. Hugh Baird & Sons* (1921) 9 Ll.L.Rep. 167.
397 *Slade v. Metrodent Ltd.* [1953] Q.B. 112.
398 Zur *misrepresentation* beim Kauf einer englischen *Private Limited Company* vgl. Dierksmeier, S. 98 ff.
399 Vgl. *supra* Kapitel 4, B.II..
400 *Heyman v. Darwins Ltd.* [1942] 1 All E.R. 337.
401 [1993] 1 Lloyd's Rep. 455.

Ansicht der Klägerin war durch die Nichtigkeit des Hauptvertrages notwendigerweise auch die Schiedsklausel betroffen. Die Beklagte vertrat die gegenteilige Auffassung. Der Court of Appeal folgte - auf den ersten Blick - der Argumentation der Beklagten. Das Urteil wird in der einschlägigen Literatur deshalb auch als endgültige Anerkennung der *separability* gefeiert.[402] Eine nähere Analyse der Urteilsbegründung ergibt jedoch, daß auch der *Harbour Assurance*-Fall keine undifferenzierte und damit endgültige Anerkennung der *separability* gebracht hat.[403] Zum einen ist feststzustellen, daß dieses Urteil des Court of Appeals nicht die zuvor genannten Urteile des House of Lords kassieren konnte, also auch nicht das in *Heyman v. Darwins*. Entscheidend aber ist, daß auch im *Harbour Assurance*-Fall die selbständige Gültigkeit der Schiedsklausel keinesfalls immer automatisch angenommen wurde, wenn der Hauptvertrag ansonsten nichtig oder ungültig war. So heißt es in der Urteilsbegründung etwa:[404]

> *"In every case the logical question was not whether the issue of illegality went to the validity of the contract but whether it went to the validity of the arbitration clause.* In this *case*[405] *illegality did not affect the validity of the arbitration clause, which on its proper construction was wide enough to cover a dispute as to the initial illegality of the contract."*

Deutlicher noch heißt es in dem Urteil:[406]

> *"Saying arbitration clauses, because separable, are never affected by the illegality of the principal contract is as much a case of false logic as saying they must be [...] The most common example of cases in which the ground of invalidity of the substantive obligations of the contract also necessarily entails the invalidity of the arbitration clause are cases of initial invalidity, such as the absence of consensus in idem, non est factum, mistake as to person, and so forth."*

Anders formuliert: Die *separability* der Schiedsklausel ist keineswegs zwangsläufig der Fall; vielmehr bedarf es hierzu immer einer Prüfung des Einzelfalles vor allem mit Blick auf den genauen Wortlaut der Klausel.

Im Ergebnis bleibt damit festzuhalten, daß das englische Recht die Selbständigkeit der Schiedsklausel bis 1997 nicht voll anerkannt hatte.[407] Seit dem *Harbour Assurance*-Fall kann zwar von einer liberalen Einstellung der englischen

---

402 Vgl. etwa Merkin, Arbitration Act 1996, S. 22; Veeder, England, S. 23; Rutherford/Sims, S. 56; vgl. auch DAC, 1996-Report, para 43.
403 Vgl. auch Kaplan, Arb.Int'l 1992, 228 f.
404 [1993] 1 Lloyd's Rep. 455 (469).
405 Betonung vom Verfasser hervorgehoben.
406 [1993] 1 Lloyd's Rep. 455 (469).
407 Differenzierend Chatterjee, Arb. & Disp.Res.L.J. 1996, 297 ff.

Gerichte ausgegangen werden. Voraussetzung für die Anerkennung war jedoch immer eine Prüfung im Einzelfall.

Eines darf dabei allerdings nicht übersehen werden. Auch nach dem früheren englischen Recht konnten die Parteien eine Unselbständigkeit der Schiedsklausel vermeiden, wenn sie statt einer Schiedsklausel einen vom Hauptvertrag getrennten separaten Schiedsvertrag vereinbarten. Auch nach englischem Recht stand die Selbständigkeit eines solchen separaten Schiedsvertrages außer Frage.

III. Der Arbitration Act *1996*

Mit *s* 7 *Arbitration Act* 1996 sieht nunmehr erstmalig englisches *statutory law* die Unabhängigkeit der Schiedsklausel vor.[408] Anders als Art. 16 Modellgesetz regelt *s* 7 *Arbitration Act* 1996 die Selbständigkeit der Schiedsklausel und die Frage der Kompetenz-Kompetenz allerdings nicht in direktem Zusammenhang.[409] Dahinter stehen jedoch rein akademische Überlegungen, die für die Schiedspraxis keine Bedeutung haben.[410] *S* 7 lautet:

> *"Unless otherwise agreed by the parties, an arbitration agreement which forms or was intended to form part of another agreement (whether or not in writing) shall not be regarded as invalid, non-existent or ineffective because that other agreement is invalid, or did not come into existence or has become ineffective, and it shall for that purpose be treated as a distinct agreement."*

Im Unterschied zu Art. 16 Abs. 1 Modellgesetz fällt auf, daß die Selbständigkeit der Schiedsklausel nicht als übergeordnetes Prinzip verankert wurde.[411] Ihr Anwendungsbereich ist vielmehr genau definiert. Dadurch sollte jedoch vor allem eine Klarstellung erreicht werden. Eine inhaltliche Unterscheidung zu der entsprechenden Regelung des Modellgesetzes war nicht beabsichtigt.[412]

---

408 Vgl. auch Gross, Arb.Int'l 1995, 85.
409 DAC, 1996-Report, para 43.
410 Vgl. zur Begründung etwa Davidson, J.B.L. 1997, 117.
411 DAC, 1996-Report, para 44.
412 *Ibid.*

C. Kompetenz-Kompetenz

I. Einführung

Schiedsgerichte leiten ihre Befugnis zur Entscheidung von Streitigkeiten ausschließlich aus entsprechenden Parteivereinbarungen ab.[413] Eine andere Quelle schiedsgerichtlicher Zuständigkeit existiert nicht. Schiedsgerichte müssen sich folglich streng in dem durch die Parteivereinbarung gesteckten Rahmen halten. Diese Verpflichtung führt immer dann zu Konflikten, wenn die Zuständigkeit des Schiedsgerichts gerügt wird. So setzt einerseits eine Untersuchung der eigenen Zuständigkeit diese bereits voraus. Andererseits käme jedes Schiedsverfahren durch eine Zuständigkeitsrüge zu einem plötzlichen Ende, wäre dem Schiedsgericht nicht die Untersuchung der eigenen Kompetenz möglich.

Vor diesem Hintergrund stellen sich zwei Fragen von grundsätzlicher Bedeutung. Erstens, inwieweit darf ungeachtet der logischen bzw. konzeptionellen Problematik ein Schiedsgericht über seine eigene Zuständigkeit entscheiden? Zweitens, in welchem Umfang ist eine dahingende Entscheidung für die Parteien verbindlich?[414]

Diese Fragen werden heute ganz überwiegend unter dem Begriff "Kompetenz-Kompetenz" abgehandelt.[415] Sinnvollerweise ist hier zunächst mit der Auslegung des Begriffs zu beginnen. Wie ein internationaler Vergleich zeigt, wird dieser nicht immer mit der gleichen Bedeutung verwendet.[416] So wird heute zumindest im kontinentaleuropäischen Raum der Begriff Kompetenz-Kompetenz überwiegend gebraucht, um die Befugnis des Schiedsgerichts zu einer bis zum Ergehen des Schiedsspruchs *verbindlichen* Entscheidung über die eigene Zuständigkeit zu beschreiben.[417] In Anlehnung an Sonnauer bietet es sich an, hier von einer "echten" Kompetenz-Kompetenz zu sprechen.[418] Von einer unechten oder vorläufigen[419] Kompetenz-Kompetenz wird man dagegen bei der Verwendung

---

413 Redfern/Hunter, S. 271 f.

414 Zum Streit- und Meinungsstand vgl. etwa Habscheid, in: FS Baur, S. 425; ders., SJZ 1982, 321; Schmitthoff, in: Schultsz/v.d. Berg (Hrsg.), S. 285; Sanders, in: Eisenmann, S. 31.

415 Zur Herkunft des Begriffes vgl. Schlosser, Arb.Int'l 1992, 199 f.

416 Habscheid, SJZ 1982, 321.

417 Vgl. Sanders, Revue Arbitrage 1980, 243.

418 Sonnauer, Jurisdictional Problems, S. 58. Soweit nachfolgend der Begriff der Kompetenz-Kompetenz ohne Zusatz verwendet wird, ist die echte Kompetenz-Kompetenz gemeint.

419 Vgl. Schlosser, Schiedsgerichtsbarkeit, Rn. 486.

des Begriffs durch die englische Justiz oder Jurisprudenz sprechen müssen.[420] Zur kontinentaleuropäischen Verwendung des Begriffs besteht ein wesentlicher Unterschied. Kompetenz-Kompetenz bedeutet hier nicht, daß die schiedgerichtliche Entscheidung bis zum Ergehen des Schiedsspruchs auch der staatsgerichtlichen Kontrolle entzogen sein muß.

II. Art. 16 Modellgesetz

Das Modellgesetz regelt die Kompetenz-Kompetenz in Art. 16. Darin heißt es:

> "1. Das Schiedsgericht kann über die eigene Kompetenz einschließlich aller Einreden bezüglich des Bestehens oder der Gültigkeit der Schiedsvereinbarung entscheiden [...]
> 3. Das Schiedsgericht kann über eine Einrede nach Absatz 2 als Vorfrage oder in einem Schiedsspruch zur Sache entscheiden. Bejaht das Schiedsgericht seine Zuständigkeit als Vorfrage, so kann jede Partei binnen dreißig Tagen, nachdem sie von dem Beschluß Kenntnis erlangt hat, bei dem in Artikel 6 bezeichneten Gericht eine Entscheidung beantragen; gegen die Entscheidung ist kein Rechtsmitel zulässig. Während ein solcher Antrag anhängig ist, kann das Schiedsgericht das schiedsrichterliche Verfahren fortsetzen und einen Schiedsspruch fällen."

Die Formulierung von Art. 16 ist das Ergebnis kontrovers geführter Debatten. Während etwa die englische Delegation für die Zulässigkeit möglichst frühzeitiger staatsgerichtlicher Kontrolle in diesem Punkt argumentierte,[421] vertraten andere Delegationen[422] die Position, eine solche Kontrolle dürfe erst nach dem Ergehen des Schiedsspruchs erfolgen. Den verschiedenen Positionen lagen konzeptionell grundsätzlich unterschiedliche Überlegungen zugrunde. Überwiegend wurde in der Möglichkeit frühzeitiger staatsgerichtlicher Kontrolle in Fragen der Kompetenz-Kompetenz die Gefahr des Mißbrauchs durch Verzögerungstaktiken und der Behinderung des Schiedsgerichts durch die Parteien gesehen.[423] Anders sah dies die englische Delegation, welche die Vorteile - insbesondere den der Zeit- und Geldersparnis - einer möglichst frühzeitigen gerichtlichen Überprüfbarkeit der schiedsgerichtlichen Zuständigkeit betonte.[424] Wenn schon eine staatsgerichtliche Kontrolle in Fragen der Zuständigkeit des Schiedsgerichts erforderlich sei, so die Überlegung, dann doch besser zu einem möglichst frühen Zeitpunkt.

---

420 Dies muß zumindest bis 1997 gelten. Durch eine entsprechende Änderung des betreffenden Rechts durch den *Arbitration Act* 1996 hat der Begriff nunmehr auch in England eine andere Bedeutung erfahren (vgl. *infra* in diesem Kapitel, IV.).

421 UN-Doc. A/CN.9/SR. 316, para 5.

422 So etwa die Position der französischen oder niederländischen Delegation (vgl. UN-Doc. A/CN. 9/245, para 13).

423 Melis, in: Sanders (Hrsg.), UNCITRAL's Project, S. 96.

424 UN-Doc. A/CN.9/SR. 316, para 5.

Nur so ließe sich wirksam der Gefahr begegnen, Zeit und Geld dadurch zu verlieren, daß ein Schiedsspruch wegen Zuständigkeitsmängeln nicht anerkannt oder vollstreckt werden könne.[425]

Art. 16 Modellgesetz in seiner endgültigen Fassung stellt einen Kompromiß zwischen den unterschiedlichen Ansichten dar. Art. 16 Abs. 1 Satz 1 Modellgesetz verankert das Prinzip, daß vor Ergehen des Schiedsspruches grundsätzlich keine gerichtliche Überprüfung der schiedsgerichtlichen Zuständigkeit erfolgen darf.

Einzige Ausnahme hierzu stellt Art. 16 Abs. 3 Modellgesetz dar. Danach können die Gerichte ein Zwischenfeststellungsurteil des Schiedsgerichts zur Zuständigkeit überprüfen. Hierfür ist eine Frist von 30 Tagen vorgesehen. Das Schiedsgericht kann für diesen Fall nach eigenem Ermessen sein Verfahren aussetzen oder weiterführen, solange die Sache vor dem staatlichen Gericht verhandelt wird.

Befindet das Schiedsgericht dagegen erst in seinem Schiedsspruch zur Sache über seine Zuständigkeit (vgl. Art. 16 Abs. 3 Satz 1 2. Alt. Modellgesetz), steht nur die Aufhebungsklage nach Art. 34 Modellgesetz und der Vollstreckungsversagungsantrag nach Art. 36 Modellgesetz zur Verfügung.

III. Das englische Recht vor 1997

Die englische Haltung in Sachen Kompetenz-Kompetenz wurde bereits im vorhergehenden Kapitel bei der Darstellung der Diskussion um Art. 16 Modellgesetz deutlich.[426] Lord Wilberforce brachte diese Haltung nochmals mit aller Deutlichkeit zum Ausdruck, als er das Prinzip der Kompetenz-Kompetenz als "*totally unacceptable*" bezeichnete.[427] Er begründete seine Ablehnung unter anderem damit, daß Schiedsrichter durch eine Kompetenz-Kompetenz zu einer leichtfertigen Bejahung ihrer Zuständigkeit verleitet würden.[428]

Diese Ablehnung geht auf eine Rechtsprechung zurück, die ihren Ursprung in *Christopher Brown Ltd. v. Genossenschaft Österreichischer Waldbesitzer Holzwirtschaftsbetriebe Registrierte Genossenschaft mbH*[429] hat. In diesem Fall hatte der Kläger ein Schiedsverfahren eingeleitet, in dem er Ansprüche auf Schadensersatz wegen Nichtlieferung geltend machte. Die beklagte Schiedspartei rügte die

---

425 *Ibid.*

426 Zu den Befugnissen der Schiedsrichter nach altem englischen Recht vgl. auch Rokison, in: Lew (Hrsg.), Contemporary Problems, S. 86.

427 UN-Doc. A/CN.9/SR.316, para 5.

428 *Ibid.*

429 [1954] 1 Q.B. 8; vgl. auch *Dalmia Dairy Industries Ltd. v. National Bank of Pakistan* [1978] 2 Lloyd's Rep. 223 (284).

Zuständigkeit des Schiedsgerichts. Ihrer Ansicht nach war der Hauptvertrag nichtig, woraus sich zwangsläufig auch die Nichtigkeit der Schiedsklausel ergeben sollte. Das Schiedsgericht befand den Hauptvertrag jedoch für gültig. Es erklärte sich für zuständig und entschied den Fall im Sinne des Klägers. In der sich anschließenden Klage auf Vollstreckung führte das Gericht zunächst aus:[430]

"It is not the law that arbitrators, if their jurisdiction is challenged or questioned, are bound immediately to refuse to act until their jurisdiction has been determined by some court which has power to determine it finally. Nor is it the law that they are bound to go on without investigating the merits of the challenge and to determine the matter in dispute, leaving the question of their jurisdiction to be held over until it is determined by some court which has the power to determine it."

Insoweit scheint es also, daß das Prinzip der Kompetenz-Kompetenz grundsätzlich anerkannt wurde. Dann heißt es jedoch weiter:[431]

"They are entitled to inquire into the merits of the issue whether they have jurisdiction or not, not for the purpose of reaching any conclusion which will be binding upon the parties - because that they cannot do - but for the purpose of satisfying themselves as a preliminary matter whether they ought to go on with the arbitration or not [...] They are entitled, in short, to make their own inquiries in order to determine their own course of action, and the result of that inquiry has no effect whatsoever upon the rights of the parties."

Der Entscheidung des Schiedsgerichts über die eigene Kompetenz wurde also jegliche rechtliche Wirkung abgesprochen.[432] Das House of Lords ging in seiner Entscheidung in *Willcock v. Pickfords*[433] noch einen Schritt weiter. Der Entscheidung lag die Frage zugrunde, ob die Schiedsvereinbarung als Teil der allgemeinen Geschäftsbedingungen als wirksam zwischen den Parteien vereinbart galt. Lord Justice Roskill:[434]

"One thing is clear in this branch of the law [...] An arbitrator cannot decide his own jurisdiction. Therefore whenever a question arises whether or not there has been a submission to arbitration, an arbitrator cannot in English law decide that issue. The only tribunal to decide it is the Court."

---

430 [1954] 1 Q.B. 12.
431 *Ibid*, 13.
432 Siehe auch Menzies, Arb. & Disp.Res.L.J. 1997, 198.
433 [1979] 1 Lloyd's Rep. 244.
434 [1979] 1 Lloyd's Rep. 244 (245).

Dies warf die Frage auf, ob, anders als etwa noch in *Christopher Brown v. Genossenschaft Österreichischer Waldbesitzer*, die Schiedsgerichte überhaupt noch zu einer - auch unverbindlichen - Entscheidung über die eigene Zuständigkeit befugt waren. Insoweit bejahend jedoch das Urteil des Court of Appeal in *Harbour v. Kansa.*[435]

Den englischen Gerichten war es somit jederzeit, vor allem aber auch *vor* Ergehen des Schiedsspruchs möglich, abschließend über die Frage der Zuständigkeit des Schiedsgerichts zu entscheiden. Das Prinzip der Kompetenz-Kompetenz hatte vor 1997 somit keine volle Gültigkeit in England.

IV. Der Arbitration Act *1996*

Dies sollte sich mit Erlaß des *Arbitration Acts* 1996 ändern. Durch die *ss* 30 - 33 hat das Prinzip der Kompetenz-Kompetenz in England erstmalig eine Kodifizierung und weitgehende Anerkennung erfahren.[436] Die inhaltlich detaillierte Neuregelung gleicht in wesentlichen Teilen Art. 16 Modellgesetz, an der sich die *ss* 30 - 33 orientieren.[437]

1. Grundsatz der Anerkennung

S 30(1) *Arbitration Act* 1996 kodifiziert das *common law* hinsichtlich der grundsätzlichen Befugnis der Schiedsgerichte zur Entscheidung über die eigene Zuständigkeit so, wie es bereits in *Harbour v. Kansa* formuliert worden war.[438] Die Vorschrift enthält für sich genommen damit keine Änderung zum alten Recht. Sie lautet:

> *"Unless otherwise agreed by the parties, the arbitral tribunal may rule on its own substantive jurisdiction, that is, as to:*
> *(a) whether there is a valid arbitration agreement;*
> *(b) whether the tribunal is properly constituted; and*
> *(c) what matters have been submitted to arbitration in accordance with the arbitration agreement."*

Im Unterschied zu Art. 16 Modellgesetz beläßt *s* 30 *Arbitration Act* 1996 den Parteien die Entscheidung darüber, ob sie das Schiedsgericht mit einer Kompe-

---

435 *Harbour Assurance Co. (UK) Ltd. v. Kansa General International Assurance Co. Ltd.* [1993] 3 All E.R. 897; vgl. auch die Ausführungen *supra* in diesem Kapitel B.II..

436 Für eine kurze Übersicht vgl. Sleightholme, B.L.R. 1997, 162.

437 Vgl. DAC, 1996-Report, para 137.

438 Merkin, Arbitration Act 1996, S. 52.

tenz-Kompetenz ausstatten. Wollen sie dies nicht, können sie eine entsprechende Ausschlußvereinbarung treffen. Hieran wird sich schwerlich Kritik üben lassen. Der Grundsatz der Parteiautonomie ist einer der tragenden Grundsätze des modernen Schiedsverfahrensrechts.[439] Für den nach Menzies eher unwahrscheinlichen Fall, daß die Parteien dem Schiedsgericht die Kompetenz-Kompetenz versagen, bleibt das bisherige Recht anwendbar.[440] Relevant wird das vor allem mit Blick auf die Rechtsfolgen von *s* 31 und *s* 32 *Arbitration Act* 1996.[441]

Weiter fällt auf, daß *s* 30(1) *Arbitration Act* 1996 im Unterschied zu Art. 16 Modellgesetz das Tatbestandsmerkmal der "*substantive jurisdiction*" definiert.[442] Relevante Unterschiede hinsichtlich des Umfangs der Kompetenz-Kompetenz ergeben sich hieraus aber nicht.[443] Die Kategorisierung in den *subsections* (a)-(c) hat vielmehr klarstellenden Charakter. So stellt *subsection* (c) etwa klar, daß auch eine *teilweise* Verneinung (bzw. Bejahung) der Kompetenz durch das Schiedsgericht zulässig ist.[444]

2. *Voraussetzung und Verfahren*

S 31 *Arbitration Act* 1996 regelt - wiederum in Anlehnung an Art. 16 (Abs. 2) Modellgesetz - die Voraussetzungen und das Verfahren bei Einwänden gegen die Zuständigkeit des Schiedsgericht.[445] Gemäß *s* 31(1)(2) *Arbitration Act* 1996 sind die Parteien verpflichtet, entsprechende Einwände zum frühstmöglichen Zeitpunkt vorzubringen ("*not later than the time he takes the first step in the proceedings*" bzw. "*as soon as possible*"). Danach sind sie mit dem Einwand der Unzuständigkeit grundsätzlich ausgeschlossen.

Ausnahmsweise kann das Schiedsgericht nach *s* 31(3) Einwände entgegen den *subsections* (1) und (2) dann zulassen, wenn es dies für gerechtfertigt hält. Da-

---

439 Herrmann nennt diesen Grundsatz "*the most fundamental principle*" (vgl. ders., in: Lew (Hrsg.), Contemporary Problems, S. 166).
440 Menzies, Arb. & Disp. Res.L.J. 1997, 198.
441 Vgl. *infra* in diesem Kapitel, C.III.2. u. 3..
442 Vgl. die *subsections* (a)-(c).
443 Davidson, J.B.L. 1997, 113.
444 Rutherford/Sims, S. 102.
445 *S* 31(1)(2) lautet:
"(1) An objection that the arbitral tribunal lacks substantive jurisdiction at the outset of the proceedings must be raised by a party not later than the time he takes the first step in the proceedings to contest the merits of any matter in relation to which he challenges the tribunal's jurisdiction [...]
(2) Any objection during the course of the arbitral proceedings that the arbitral tribunal is exceeding its substantive jurisdiction must be made as soon as possible after the matter alleged to be beyond its jurisdiction is raised."

durch soll sichergestellt werden, daß die harten Rechtsfolgen von *s* 31(1)(2) *Arbitration Act* 1996 nicht in ganz unbegründeten Fällen eintreten.

Hat eine Partei rechtzeitig die mangelnde Zuständigkeit des Schiedsgerichts gerügt, stehen dem Schiedsgericht drei Möglichkeiten zur weiteren Verfahrensweise zur Verfügung. Es kann einerseits per Zwischenfeststellungsschiedsspruch isoliert die Frage der Zuständigkeit entscheiden.[446] Ferner kann das Schiedsgericht zusammen mit der Sachentscheidung im eigentlichen Schiedsspruch über die Zuständigkeit befinden.[447] In diesen beiden Fällen kann eine gerichtliche Überprüfung der Zuständigkeit dann im Rahmen des Aufhebungs- bzw. Vollstreckungsverfahrens stattfinden.[448] Schließlich bleibt es dem Schiedsgericht unbenommen, sein Verfahren auszusetzen und die Frage der Zuständigkeit einem staatlichen Gericht zur Entscheidung vorzulegen.[449]

3. Umfang staatlicher Kontrollbefugnisse

Das eigentliche Kernstück der Reform der Kompetenz-Kompetenz findet sich in *s* 32 *Arbitration Act* 1996. Die Vorschrift regelt die Frage, ob und unter welchen Voraussetzungen die Gerichte bereits während des laufenden Verfahrens, also vor Ergehen des Zwischenfeststellungs- bzw. (Schluß-)Schiedsspruchs über die Zuständigkeit des Schiedsgerichts entscheiden können. *S* 32 *Arbitration Act* 1996 lautet:

> *"(1) The court may, on the application of a party to arbitral proceedings [...] determine any questions as to the substantive jurisdiction of the tribunal [...]*
> *(2) An application under this section shall not be considered unless-*
> *(a) it is made with the agreement in writing of all the other parties to the proceedings, or*
> *(b) it is made with the permission of the tribunal and the court is satisfied-*
> *(i) that the determination of the question is likely to produce substantial savings in costs,*
> *(ii) that the application was made without delay, and*
> *(iii) that there is good reason why the matter should be decided by the court [...]"*

Folgt man der Erwartung des DAC wird ein gerichtliches Eingreifen in ein laufendes Schiedsverfahren in Zuständigkeitsangelegenheiten nunmehr die selte-

446 *S* 31(4)(a) *Arbitration Act* 1996.
447 *Ibid.*
448 Vgl. *infra* Kapitel 10 u. 11.
449 *S* 31(5) *Arbitration Act* 1996 lautet:
"The tribunal may in any case, and shall if the parties so agree, stay proceedings whilst an application is made to the court under section 32 (determination of prelimininary point of jurisdiction)."

ne Ausnahme sein.[450] Bei näherer Betrachtung der zuvor zitierten Vorschrift ist dieser Erwartung zuzustimmen.[451] Zwar können die Gerichte gemäß *s* 32(1) *Arbitration Act* 1996 auch weiterhin grundsätzlich bereits vor Ergehen des Schiedsspruchs die Zuständigkeit der Schiedsgerichte überprüfen. Hierzu müssen jedoch entweder alle Parteien dem Schiedsverfahren zustimmen, oder das Schiedsgericht muß seine Zustimmung geben. Im letztgenannten Fall müssen kumulativ noch die unter den *subsections* (2)(b)(i)-(iii) genannten Voraussetzungen vorliegen.[452]

Die einzelne Partei hat somit keine Möglichkeit der Herbeiführung einer gerichtlichen Zuständigkeitsentscheidung vor Ergehen des Schiedsspruchs mehr.

D. Zwischenergebnis

Das englische Recht zur Kontrolle der Schiedsgerichtsbarkeit bei der Bestimmung der eigenen Zuständigkeit hat durch den *Arbitration Act* 1996 eine einschneidende Reform erfahren.

Das alte englische Recht hatte die *doctrine of separability* bis 1993 nicht vollständig anerkannt. Das sollte sich durch die Entscheidung des Court of Appeal in *Harbour Assurance v. Kansa* weitgehend ändern. Allerdings wurde die *separability* auch nach diesem Urteil nicht undifferenziert anerkannt.

Der *Arbitration Act* 1996 kodifiziert erstmalig das Prinzip der Selbständigkeit der Schiedsvereinbarung und macht es damit wirklich "wasserfest". Der *Act* erkennt die *separability* nunmehr endgültig an. Er zieht damit einen Schlußstrich unter die bis dahin zähflüssige und graduelle Entwicklung des *common law* in dieser Frage. Im Ergebnis ist das neue englische Recht zur Regelung der Unabhängigkeit von Schiedsvereinbarungen nunmehr weitgehend mit dem Modellgesetz vergleichbar.

Gleiches gilt hinsichtlich der Anerkennung der Kompetenz-Kompetenz. Mit den *ss* 30 - 32 *Arbitration Act* 1996 sieht das englische Recht erstmalig eine abschließende Regelung der Kompetenz-Kompetenz vor. Bei dieser Regelung handelt es sich um mehr als eine Kodifizierung existierenden *common laws*. Denn wenngleich die Rechtsprechung es vor 1997 mit steigender Tendenz vermied, Entscheidungen von Schiedsgerichten über die eigene Zuständigkeit zu kassieren,

---

450 1996-Report, para 141.

451 Ebenso Harris/Planterose/Tecks, S. 138.

452 Vgl. auch Carbonneau, Tulane Mar.L.J. 1997, 145; Zekos, J.Int'l Arb. 1998, 63, kritisiert, daß es aufgrund des den Gerichten in *s* 30(2)(b)(i)-(iii) eingeräumten Ermessens wieder einmal an ihnen liegt, in welchen Fällen es zu einer staatsgerichtlichen Kontrolle kommt. Dabei übersieht er allerdings, daß es sich bei den genannten Ermessensvorschriften lediglich um *zusätzliche* Hürden handelt.

war sie hieran keinesfalls verbindlich gehindert. Dies aber ist nunmehr grundsätzlich der Fall. Denn nur unter den alternativen Voraussetzungen, daß entweder alle Parteien oder das Schiedsgericht eine entsprechende Entscheidung des Gerichts beantragt, kann dieses im Vorfeld der Entscheidung eingreifen.

Die *ss* 30 - 32 *Arbitration Act* 1996 tragen den Prinzipien der Unabhängigkeit und Effektivität des Schiedsverfahrens damit ebenso Rechnung wie dem der Parteiautonomie. Sie verkörpern eine gelungene Reform des alten englischen Rechts.

Auch den Vergleich mit Art. 16 Modellgesetz brauchen die *ss* 30 - 32 nicht zu scheuen. Die Regelungen sind ihrem wesentlichen Inhalt nach grundsätzlich vergleichbar. Im Gegensatz zu Art. 16 Modellgesetz ist *s* 30 *Arbitration Act* 1996 zwar abdingbar. Aus den oben genannten Gründen liegt hierin jedoch kein Nachteil.

Kapitel 7
Unterstützung bei der Beweiserhebung

A. Art. 27 Modellgesetz

Schiedsgerichte sind nicht zur Anordnung staatlicher Zwangsmaßnahmen befugt.[453] Bei der Beweisaufnahme sind sie deshalb mitunter auf staatliche Unterstützung angewiesen. Bei den Beratungen zum Entwurf des Modellgesetzes herrschte Einigkeit darüber, eine entsprechende Regelung in das Modellgesetz aufzunehmen. Umfang und Art der Pflicht zur Unterstützung waren dagegen äußerst streitig.[454] Streitig war vor allem, ob und inwieweit ein durch die staatlichen Gerichte unterstütztes schiedsgerichtliches Beweisverfahren von dem "klassischen" staatlichen Beweisverfahren abweichen dürfe. Das Ergebnis der Beratungen findet sich in Art. 27 Modellgesetz. Darin heißt es:

> *"Das Schiedsgericht oder eine Partei mit Bewilligung des Schiedsgerichts kann das zuständige Gericht dieses Staates um Unterstützung bei der Beweisaufnahme ersuchen. Das Gericht kann das Ersuchen im Rahmen seiner Zuständigkeit und nach seinen für die Beweisaufnahme geltenden Verfahrensvorschriften erledigen."*

Die Verfasser des Modellgesetzes konnten sich mithin nicht dazu durchringen, ein staatliches Tätigwerden in Beweisfragen an bestimmte Richtlinien zu binden oder diese gar zu einem Tätigwerden zu verpflichten. So liegt bereits das

453 Vgl. Calavros, S. 119 ff.
454 Holtzmann/Neuhaus, S. 734.

"ob" des Tätigwerdens einzig im Ermessen des Gerichts. Mit Blick auf die Funktionalität des Schiedsverfahrens hätte es sich möglicherweise angeboten, die Gerichte in begrenztem Umfang zur Unterstützung bei der Beweiserhebung zu verpflichten. In Bereichen des staatlichen Gewaltmonopols, wie etwa bei der Beweiserhebung, ist die Unterstützung durch die Gerichte mitunter unabdingbare Voraussetzung für das Funktionieren eines Schiedsverfahrens. Es hätte deshalb nahegelegen, die Gerichte zumindest in gewissem Umfang zur Hilfestellung zu verpflichten. Dies ist nicht geschehen. Den Gerichten steht es somit frei, durch die Verweigerung ihrer Hilfe ein Schiedsverfahren "totlaufen" zu lassen.

Ferner wäre zu überlegen gewesen, die Gerichte mit der Befugnis auszustatten, das Schiedsgericht mit der Durchführung entsprechender Beweiserhebungsmaßnahmen zu beauftragen. Auch hierzu konnten sich die Verfasser des Modellgesetzes nicht durchringen.

B. Das englische Recht vor 1997

Das englische Recht der Unterstützung der Schiedsgerichte durch die staatlichen Gerichte in Verfahrensangelegenheiten[455] ist mitunter auch als "*highly developed legal framework*" bezeichnet worden.[456] Dem kann beigepflichtet werden. Anders als das Modellgesetz wies das englische Recht in diesem Punkt eine hohe Regelungsdichte auf. Die Befugnisse der staatlichen Gerichte waren detailliert geregelt. Das brachte jedoch auch einen hohen Grad an Komplexität mit sich.

Abgesehen von der höheren Regelungsdichte, unterschied sich das englische Recht in Beweisfragen inhaltlich nicht entscheidend von Art. 27 Modellgesetz. So sah *s* 12(4) *Arbitration Act* 1950 vor:

> *"Any party to a reference under an arbitration agreement may sue out a writ of subpoena ad testificandum or a writ of subpoena duces tecum, but no person shall be compelled under any such writ to produce any document which he could not be compelled to produce on the trial of an action, and the High Court or a judge therof may order that a writ of subpoena ad testificandum or of subpoena duces tecum shall issue to compel the attendance before an arbitrator or umpire of a witness wherever he may be within the United Kingdom."*

Auch nach dem englischen Recht gab es also kein "Beweiserhebungssonderrecht" der Schiedsgerichte. Die Anordnung und Durchsetzung von Zwangsmaß-

455 Einen Überblick über die Unterstützung der Schiedsgerichte durch die englischen Gerichte in Beweiserhebungsfragen geben Loble/Mendelblatt, in: National Report, S. 113.

456 Hunter, in: Lew (Hrsg.), Contemporary Problems, S. 201.

nahmen war den staatlichen Gerichten vorbehalten. Zwar konnten die Parteien solche Maßnahmen nach dem geltenden Verfahrensrecht erwirken ("*sue out*"); auch hatten sie nach der Maßgabe des geltenden Verfahrensrechts einen Anspruch gegen den High Court auf Anordnung der entsprechenden Maßnahme.[457] Den so geladenen Zeugen stand es allerdings frei, vor dem High Court eine Aufhebung der Anordnung zu beantragen.

S 12 *Arbitration Act* 1950 bezog sich gemäß dem ausdrücklichen Verweis in *subsection* (4) zudem nicht auf internationale Beweisverfahren. Soweit etwa Zeugenaussagen außerhalb Großbritanniens eingeholt werden mußten, standen den Parteien oder dem Schiedsgericht keinerlei Rechte oder Befugnisse zu.

C. Der Arbitration Act *1996*

Der *Arbitration Act* 1996 regelt das Beweiserhebungsverfahren nunmehr in *s* 43. Die Vorschrift basiert teils auf *s* 12(4) *Arbitration Act* 1950, teils auf Art. 27 Modellgesetz.[458] Sie lautet:

> *"(1) A party to arbitral proceedings may use the same court procedures as are available in relation to legal proceedings to secure the attendance before the tribunal of a witness in order to give oral testimony or to produce documents or other material evidence.*
>
> *(2) This may only be done with the permission of the tribunal or the agreement of the other parties.*
>
> *(3) The court procedures may only be used if-*
>
> *(a) the witness is in the United Kingdom, and*
>
> *(b) the arbitral proceedings are being conducted in England and Wales or, as the case may be, Northern Ireland.*
>
> *(4) A person shall not be compelled by virtue of this section to produce any document or other material evidence which he could not be compelled to produce in legal proceedings."*

Wie bereits *s* 12(4) *Arbitration Act* 1950 sieht auch *s* 43(1) *Arbitration Act* 1996 das Recht der Parteien vor, die Gerichte um ihre Unterstützung bei der Beweiserhebung zu ersuchen. Im übrigen bleibt es den Schiedsgerichten verwehrt, selbst entsprechende Zwangsmaßnahmen anzuordnen. Die wesentlichen Befugnisse sowohl der Gerichte wie auch der Schiedsgerichte bleiben somit unverändert.

457 Mustill/Boyd, S. 350.
458 DAC, 1996-Report, para 213.

Neu ist dagegen die an Art. 27 Modellgesetz angelehnte *s* 43(2) *Arbitration Act* 1996. Danach bedarf ein entsprechender Antrag an die Gerichte entweder der vorherigen Genehmigung der Gerichte oder der Zustimmung der Parteien. Der *1996-Report* begründet diese Änderung damit, daß es den Parteien nicht mehr möglich sein soll, von einem zuvor durch das Schiedsgericht festgelegten Verfahren abzuweichen.[459] Als Beispiel sei hier nur die Vereinbarung eines *document-only*-Verfahrens genannt. War die einzelne Partei nach dem alten Recht nicht gehindert, auch in einem solchen Fall die Gerichte in Beweisfragen anzurufen, kann sie dies nunmehr nur noch mit Zustimmung des Schiedsgerichts (bzw. der Zustimmung auch der anderen Parteien). Auf diese Weise wird die Einhaltung der Parteivereinbarung sichergestellt.

S 43(3) *Arbitration Act* 1996 beschränkt das in *s* 43(1) *Arbitration Act* 1996 genannte Recht zum einen auf die Ladung etc. von Zeugen, die sich in Großbritannien aufhalten;[460] zum anderen muß das Schiedsverfahren in England, Wales oder Nordirland durchgeführt werden ("*arbitral proceedings [...] being* conducted *in* [...]"). Nach *s* 2(3) *Arbitration Act* 1996 soll *s* 43 jedoch unabhängig vom *Sitz* des Schiedsgerichts Anwendung finden. Es wird also zwischen Sitz und Durchführung des Schiedsverfahrens unterschieden.[461] Denkbar ist beispielsweise der Fall, daß nur ein Teil des Verfahrens - etwa zu Zwecken einer Beweisaufnahme vor Ort - nach England ausgelagert wird.[462]

Gemäß *s* 43(4) *Arbitration Act* 1996 bleibt es dabei, daß Zeugen vor einem Schiedsgericht den gleichen Aussageverweigerungsschutz genießen wie vor den staatlichen Gerichten.[463]

---

459 *Ibid.*

460 Soweit diese sich außerhalb Großbritanniens aufhalten, ist das Verfahren nach *s* 44(2)(a) *Arbitration Act* 1996 einschlägig. Danach kann das Gericht auf Antrag der Parteien ein entsprechendes Rechtshilfegesuche an ein ausländisches Gericht stellen (Veeder, England, S. 39).

461 Vgl. hierzu die kritischen Anmerkungen von Maxwell, Arb.Int'l 1997, 431.

462 Merkin, Arbitration Act 1996, S. 70.

463 Rutherford/Sims, S. 150. Erstmalig stellt der *Arbitration Act* 1996 in *s* 34(1)(2)(f) jedoch klar, daß die Schiedsgerichte ansonsten nicht an die für die Gerichte geltenden Beweisregeln gebunden. Die Vorschrift lautet:
"(1) It shall be for the tribunal to decide all procedural and evidential matters, subject to the right for the parties to agree any matter.
(2) Procedural and evidential matters include- [...]
(f) whether to apply strict rules of evidence (or any other rules) as to the admissibility, relevance or weight of any material (oral, written or other) sought to be tendered on any matters of fact or opinion, and the time, manner and form in which such material should be exchanged and pretended;"

D. *Zwischenergebnis*

Das englische Recht der Beweiserhebung in Schiedsverfahren hat sich durch den *Arbitration Act* 1996 nur unwesentlich geändert. Nach wie vor stehen den Schiedsgerichten keinerlei Befugnisse zu, Zwangsmaßnahmen eigenständig anzuordnen. Die Gerichte sind weiterhin an das entsprechende Prozeßrecht gebunden. Neu ist in *s* 43 *Arbitration Act* 1996 gegenüber *s* 12(4) *Arbitration Act* 1950 lediglich, daß ein Tätigwerden der staatlichen Gerichte grundsätzlich von der Zustimmung der Schiedsgerichte abhängen soll. Die einzelne Partei kann mithin Beweiserhebungsmaßnahmen der Gerichte nicht mehr beantragen.

Der Vergleich von *s* 43 *Arbitration Act* 1996 mit Art. 27 Modellgesetz läßt eine weitgehende Ähnlichkeit erkennen. Beide Normen orientieren sich an dem Grundsatz, daß Zwangsmaßnahmen im Beweisverfahren den Gerichten vorbehalten bleiben. Dabei haben die Schiedsparteien zumindest nach dem englischen Recht einen Anspruch auf die Unterstützung durch die Gerichte, soweit sie dieses Recht auch als Partei eines ordentlichen Verfahrens hätten.

Kapitel 8
Anordnungen im einstweiligen Rechtschutz

A. *Einführung*

Ungeachtet ihrer steigenden Popularität hat die Schiedsgerichtsbarkeit einige entscheidende Nachteile gegenüber der staatlichen Gerichtsbarkeit. Eine der Hauptursachen liegt darin, daß den Schiedsgerichten keine Befugnis zur Anordnung von Zwangsmaßnahmen zusteht. Hierin liegt auch der Grund, warum die Schiedsgerichtsbarkeit auf die staatliche Unterstützung angewiesen ist, wenn sie verbindliche und durchsetzbare Resultate erzielen will.[464] Zu den Bereichen, in denen die Schiedsgerichte traditionell auf die Unterstützung der staatlichen Gerichte angewiesen sind, gehört der des einstweiligen Rechtsschutzes.[465] Dabei kann es durchaus vorkommen, daß die Schiedsgerichte Anordnungen gleichen Inhalts wie die staatlichen Gerichte treffen können. Der Unterschied besteht darin, daß im Regelfall nur die gerichtlichen Anordnungen durchsetzbar sind.[466]

---

464 Redfern/Hunter, S. 308 f.

465 Stalev, in: Sanders (Hrsg.), ICCA Congress Series No. 6, S. 103.

466 Zum Verhältnis von schieds- und staatsgerichtlich angeordneten einstweiligen Maßnahmen vgl. auch Wagoner, Arbitration 1996, 131.

B. Art. 9 Modellgesetz

Das Modellgesetz regelt die Anordnung von einstweiligen Maßnahmen in Art. 9:

> "Mit einer Schiedsvereinbarung ist es nicht unvereinbar, wenn eine Partei vor oder während des schiedsrichterlichen Verfahrens bei einem Gericht eine vorläufige oder sichernde Maßnahme beantragt und das Gericht eine solche Maßnahme anordnet."

Die Vorschrift ist im Zusammenhang mit Art. 8 Abs. 1 Modellgesetz zu lesen.[467] Danach dürfen die staatlichen Gerichte bei Vorliegen einer wirksamen Schiedsvereinbarung grundsätzlich nicht tätig werden. Art. 9 stellt somit eine Durchbrechung von Art. 8 Abs. 1 Modellgesetz dar, soweit es um die Anordnung vorläufiger Maßnahmen geht.

Diese Durchbrechung liegt im Interesse der Parteien. Der Grund liegt darin, daß eine einstweilige gerichtliche Maßnahme mitunter zur Durchführung eines Schiedsverfahrens erforderlich sein kann. Calavros stellt in diesem Zusammenhang die kritische Frage, warum das eigentlich so sei.[468] Seiner Ansicht nach wäre es nicht nur denkbar, sondern auch wünschenswert, daß die entsprechenden Maßnahmen durch das Schiedsgericht erfolgen können.[469]

Dagegen wird jedoch angeführt, daß die entsprechende Befugnis der Gerichte gewährleiste, daß die Parteien auch im Zeitraum *vor* der Konstituierung des Schiedsgerichts nicht schutzlos sind. Das Schiedsgericht kann zumindest zu diesem Zeitpunkt keine Maßnahmen anordnen.

Weniger zwingend einleuchtend ist dagegen, warum die Unterstützung der Gerichte auch *nach* Konstituierung des Schiedsgerichts noch erforderlich sein soll. So ist gemäß Art. 17 Modellgesetz auch das Schiedsgericht zur Anordnung vorläufiger Maßnahmen befugt.[470] Es fragt sich deshalb, ob - und falls ja - warum es hier noch eine konkurrierende Zuständigkeit der Gerichte gibt.[471] Art. 9 Modellgesetz ist nach seinem Wortlaut weiter gefaßt. Die Gerichte können danach "alle vorläufigen oder sichernden Maßnahmen" anordnen. Einschränkungen wer-

---

467 Vgl. Semple, Arb. & Disp.R.L.J. 1994, 273; vgl. auch Sandrock/Nöcker, S. 74 ff.

468 S. 55.

469 *Ibid.*

470 Art. 17 Modellgesetz lautet:
"Haben die Parteien nichts anderes vereinbart, so kann das Schiedsgericht, wenn eine Partei es beantragt, jeder Partei auferlegen, alle vorläufigen oder sichernden Maßnahmen zu ergreifen, die das Schiedsgericht in bezug auf den Gegenstand des Streites für notwendig erachtet. Das Schiedsgericht kann von jeder Partei im Zusammenhang mit einer solchen Maßnahme angemessene Sicherheit verlangen."

471 Ausführlich hierzu Nöcker, S. 111 ff.

den nicht gemacht. Holtzmann/Neuhaus führen zum Anwendungsbereich von Art. 9 Modellgesetz aus:[472]

"Article 9 is not limited to any particular kind of interim measures. Thus it applies to measures to conserve the subject matter of the dispute; measures to protect trade secrets and proprietary information; measures to preserve evidence; pre-award attachments to secure an eventual award and similar seizures of assets; measures required from third parties; and enforcement of any interim measures ordered."

Im Unterschied zu Art. 9 bezieht sich Art. 17 Modellgesetz dagegen lediglich auf Maßnahmen, "die das Schiedsgericht in bezug auf den Gegenstand des Streites für notwendig erachtet". Ein Anwendungsvorrang von Art. 17 etwa wegen Spezialität läßt sich daraus aber nicht ableiten.[473] Die Durchsetzbarkeit einstweiliger Maßnahmen erfordert die Anwendbarkeit von Art. 9 neben Art. 17. Beide Vorschriften sind nebeneinander anwendbar und es steht den Parteien frei, ob sie vorläufige Maßnahmen beim Schieds- oder beim staatlichen Gericht beantragen. Kommt es dagegen ersichtlich auf die (zügige) zwangsweise Durchsetzung einer vorläufigen Sicherung an, sind die Parteien vor dem Hintergrund eines möglichst effektiven Rechtsschutzes gut beraten, direkt vor die staatlichen Gerichte zu gehen.[474]

Abschließend sei hier noch eine Anmerkungen zum Recht der staatlichen, respektive der Schiedsgerichte zur Befugnis der Anordnung von Sicherheitsleistungen gemacht.[475] Artikel 17 Satz 2 Modellgesetz lautet:

"Das Schiedsgericht kann von jeder Partei im Zusammenhang mit einer [vorläufigen oder sichernden Maßnahme, die das Schiedsgericht in bezug auf den Gegenstand des Streites für notwendig erachtet] angemessene Sicherheit verlangen."

Der Anwendungsbereich von Artikel 17 Satz 2 ist begrenzt. Das Recht des Schiedsgerichts, Sicherheiten zu verlangen, besteht nur im Zusammenhang mit der Anordnung einstweiliger Maßnahmen. Nicht erfaßt ist dagegen das Recht, Sicherheitsleistungen auch für die gesamten Verfahrenskosten oder für die den Parteien entstehenden Rechtverfolgungskosten anzuordnen. Den staatlichen Gerichten steht kein entsprechendes Recht zu.

---

472 S. 333 unter Verweis auf UN-Doc. A/CN.9/245, para 188.

473 Anders wohl Thieffry, in: Antaki/Prujiner (Hrsg.), S. 381.

474 Nöcker, S. 114.

475 Wie *infra* in diesem Kapitel, C.II. deutlich wird, hat dieser Themenbereich in England eine äußerst kontroverse Diskussion um die Eingriffsbefugnisse der staatlichen Gerichte in Schiedsverfahren ausgelöst.

C. *Das englische Recht vor 1997*

I. *Umfassende Befugnisse*

Das Recht der einstweiligen Maßnahmen nahm einen relativ breiten Raum im alten englischen Schiedsverfahrensrecht ein. Dem lag das englische Verständnis zugrunde, wonach die Unterstützung durch die staatlichen Gerichte wesentliche Voraussetzung für ein effektives Schiedsverfahren war.[476] Dies galt insbesondere auch für einstweilige Anordnungen durch die Gerichte.[477]

Die wesentlichen Befugnisse der Gerichte waren in *s* 12(6) *Arbitration Act* 1950 geregelt.[478] *S* 12(6)(h) gab den Gerichten das Recht "*of making orders in respect of [...] interim injunctions*". Dieses Recht wurde von den Gerichten weit ausgelegt. Es stand den Gerichten beispielweise selbst dann zu, wenn sie ihr Verfahren ausgesetzt hatten.[479] Ebenso waren die englischen Gerichte zur Anordnung von einstweiligen Verfügungen nach *s* 12(6)(h) befugt, wenn die Parteien ein anderes als das englische Recht vereinbart hatten.[480] Voraussetzung war in diesem Fall allerdings, daß das Schiedsverfahren in England stattfand.[481]

II. *Anordnung von Sicherheiten: die* Ken-Ren-*Fälle*

Gemäß *s* 12(6)(a) *Arbitration Act* 1950 konnte der High Court die Parteien zur Leistung von Sicherheiten für die entstehenden (bzw. erwarteten) Verfahrensko-

---

476 Redfern/Hunter, S. 308 ff.
477 Hill, Lloyd's Mar. & Com.L.Q. 1992, 310.
478 *S* 12(6) *Arbitration Act* 1950 lautete:
"The High Court shall have, for the purpose of and in relation to a reference, the [...] power of making orders in respect of - [...]
(a) security for costs;
(b) discovery of documents and interrogatories;
(c) the giving of evidence by affidavit;
(d) examination on oath of any witness [...];
(e) the preservation, interim custody of sale of any goods which are the subject matter of the reference;
(f) securing the amount in dispute in the reference;
(g) the detention, preservation or inspection of any property [...]; and
(h) interim injunctions or the appointment of a receiver;
as it has for the purpose of and in relation to an action or matter in the High Court [...]"
479 *The Rena K* [1979] 1 All E.R. 397.
480 *Channel Tunnel Group Ltd. & France Manche S.A. v. Balfour Beatty Construction Ltd.* [1992] 2 W.L.R. 741 (757).
481 *Ibid.*

sten verpflichten. Dieses Recht sollte in jüngerer Zeit für ein weiteres "*Highlight*" in der Diskussion um die Befugnisse der englischen Gerichte im Verhältnis zur Schiedsgerichtsbarkeit führen.[482] Auslöser waren die sog. *Ken-Ren*-Fälle, die 1994 ihren Weg bis vor das House of Lords machten.[483] Aufgrund der Beachtung, die die *Ken-Ren*-Fälle in der internationalen Literatur gefunden haben,[484] sowie der Bedeutung der durch sie aufgeworfenen Fragen, sollen sie nachfolgend gesondert behandelt werden.

Dem lag folgender Sachverhalt zugrunde: Coppée-Lavalin, ein belgischer Anlagenbauer, hatte von der kenianischen Ken-Ren den Auftrag zur Erstellung einer chemischen Fabrik erhalten. Nach dem Vertrag sollten etwaige Streitigkeiten gemäß den ICC-Schiedsverfahrensregeln entschieden werden. Sitz des Schiedsgerichts sollte London sein. Es kam zum Streit. Umgehend nach Aufnahme des Schiedsverfahrens beantragte Coppée-Lavalin nach *s* 12(6)(a) *Arbitration Act* 1950 beim englischen High Court, Ken-Ren zur Leistung einer Sicherheit für die voraussichtlich entstehenden Rechtsverfolgungskosten zu verpflichten. Hintergrund war, daß man im Falle eines Obsiegens damit rechnete, diese Kosten nicht ersetzt zu bekommen. Ken-Ren befand sich zum Zeitpunkt des Verfahrens bereits in Liquidation.

Ken-Ren beantragte unter Verweis auf die Entscheidung des Court of Appeal in *Bank Mellat v. Helliniki Techniki S.A.*[485] die Abweisung des Antrags. In diesem Fall war entschieden worden, daß in internationalen Schiedsverfahren, die nach den ICC-Schiedsverfahrensregeln durchgeführt wurden, von *s* 12(6)(a) *Arbitration Act* 1950 regelmäßig kein Gebrauch zu machen war. Zur Begründung war unter anderem darauf abgestellt worden, daß *s* 12(6)(a) *Arbitration Act* 1950 im Wesentlichen als unvereinbar mit den ICC-Schiedsverfahrensregeln anzuse-

---

482 Zur Frage der Prozeßkostensicherheit in internationalen Schiedsverfahren vgl. auch Sandrock, in: FS Gaul, S. 607 ff.

483 Es handelte sich hierbei die Fälle *Coppée-Lavalin S.A./ N.V. v. Ken-Ren Chemicals and Fertilisers Limited* und *Voest-Alpine Aktiengesellschaft v. Ken-Ren Chemicals and Fertilisers Limited* (beide) [1994] 2 All E.R. 449. Die Fälle waren hinsichtlich ihrer in diesem Zusammenhang relevanten Fakten und Rechtsfindungen gleichgelagert. Die nachfolgenden Ausführungen zu den Fakten beziehen sich auf den erstgenannten Fall.

484 Schon im Vorfeld der Entscheidung des House of Lords war den Fällen eine ganz außergewöhnliche Bedeutung beigemessen worden. Bei Scott, Legal Business 1994, 64 heißt es etwa:
"*In fact, when the House of Lords delivers its judgment, the world will be watching. Their Lordships, claim several leading practitioners, have in their hands nothing less than the future of international commercial arbitration in this country.*"
Für eine ausführliche Abhandlung der Thematik vgl. vor allem Barrington, Am.Rev.Int.Arb. 1995, 65.

485 [1984] Q.B. 291.

hen sei. Denn diese, so die *ratio*, stellten eine abschließende Verfahrensordnung dar. Und wenn danach kein Recht auf Anordnung von Sicherheitsleistungen für die den Parteien entstehenden Rechtsverfolgungskosten vorgesehen sei, dann müsse es damit sein Bewenden haben. Schließlich hätten sich die Parteien bewußt für diese Schiedsverfahrensregeln entschieden.[486]

Das "Dilemma" in den *Ken-Ren*-Fällen war folgendes: Unter Berücksichtung der besonderen Umstände des Einzelfalles erschien die Anordnung von Sicherheiten durchaus geeignet und sogar erforderlich, um ein gerechtes Ergebnis zu erzielen. Denn es war unter den besonderen Fallumständen absehbar, daß Ken-Ren im Falle eines ihr ungünstigen Schiedsspruches nicht zur Aufbringung der gegnerischen Rechtsverfolgungskosten in der Lage sein würde.

Auf der anderen Seite galt es zu berücksichtigen, daß sich die Parteien bewußt für ein ICC-Schiedsverfahren und damit eben gegen die staatliche Gerichtsbarkeit entschieden hatten. Es stellte sich dem Gericht die Frage, ob die Parteien mit dieser Entscheidung nun also "*for better or worse*" leben mußten? Lord Justice Mustill als einer der zur Entscheidung hierüber berufenen Lordrichter brachte das Problem folgendermaßen auf den Punkt:[487]

> *"The fact remains however that an uncorrectable miscarriage of justice is something which parties risk by agreeing to entrust their disputes to a private dispute-resolution system which has very few internal resources to deal with someone who will not play fair. The parties choose arbitration for better or for worse. They relish the better features, of which there are many. When things take a turn for the worse there are limits beyond which they cannot be allowed, consistently with their arbitration agreement, to run to the courts for help. In the end, and with much hesitation, I have come to the conclusion that an order for security for costs does not conform with the type of procedure which the parties have impliedly chosen, and that an order for security should be refused notwithstanding that on a narrower view it appears to answer the justice in the case."*

Diese Ansicht Mustills entsprach allerdings nicht der Mehrheit der Richter. Es folgt, daß das House of Lords in den Ken-Ren-Fällen für die Ausübung des gerichtlichen Ermessens zugunsten einer Anordnung im Sinne von *s* 12(6)(a) votierte. Diese Entscheidung wurde überwiegend[488] als ein Rückschritt des engli-

---

486 Barrington, Am.Rev.Int.Arb. 1995, 69.

487 *Coppée Lavalin S.A./N.V. v. Ken-Ren Chemicals and Fertilisers Limited*, [1994] 2 All E.R. 449 (470 f).

488 Nicht alle Stimmen in der Literatur waren so kritisch. Davenport, Arb.Int'l 1994, 310, etwa schreibt:
"Those who want complete independence of arbitrators from any order by a state court, will clearly regret the decision [...] [It can, however, not be seen] to be a cause for anyone to think that the end of the world is at hand for international arbitration in England. The decision is like many decisions of the higher courts, one

schen Schiedsverfahrensrecht hin zur verstärkten Kontrolle von Schiedsverfahren eingestuft und dementsprechend kritisiert.[489]

III. Mareva injunction

Besondere Erwähnung im Zusammenhang mit den Maßnahmen im einstweiligen Rechtschutz verdient noch die *Mareva injunction.*[490] Anders als die Befugnisse des High Court unter *s* 12(6) *Arbitration Act* 1950 ermöglichte die *Mareva injunction* es den Gerichten, über die Befugnisse von *s* 12(6) hinaus das gesamte Vermögen des Antragsgegners einzufrieren bzw. zu sichern.[491] Die Besonderheit für das englische Recht lag darin, daß es bis zur Entwicklung der *Mareva injunction* unmöglich war, einen Antragsgegner daran zu hindern, sein Vermögen außer Landes zu schaffen, bevor nicht zuvor durch ein staatliches Urteil seine Zahlungsverpflichtung festgestellt worden war.[492] Die *Mareva injunction* stand allen Klägern bzw. Antragsstellern eines Schiedsverfahrens zur Verfügung, welche die Sicherung eines ihnen günstigen Schiedsspruchs erstrebten, und zwar bereits vor Einleitung des Schiedsverfahrens. Voraussetzung war insoweit lediglich die Glaubhaftmachung der Gefahr einer Vermögensverbringung.[493]

---

in which the views of the extremists, (in this case those prepared to die at the barricades for the cause of total arbitral independence) were not accepted."

489 Vgl. etwa Branson, Arb.Int'l 1994, 314:
"[I]t is utterly inexplicable why [the court] refused even to deal with the submission by Ken-Ren that arbitrators, not courts, should make such [security] decisions [...] In many respects, the Ken-Ren decision is more troublesome than the 'case stated' procedure that previously caused so much criticism of arbitration practice in London before 1979 [...] Now, Ken-Ren has created a similar risk in choosing London as a venue. Now, there can be litigation in the English courts that will be uncertain, expensive and time consuming and [...] could stop the arbitration permanently."

490 Benannt nach dem Fall *Mareva Compania Naviera S.A. v. International Bulk Carriers Limited* [1975] 2 Loyd's Rep. 509. Auf Fälle der Schiedsgerichtsbarkeit wurde das Instrument der *Mareva Injunction* erstmalig in *The Rena K* [1979] 1 All E.R. 397 angewendet. Eingehend Nöcker, 81 ff; vgl. weiter Michell, Osgoode Hall L.J. 1996, 741; Willoughby/Connal, E.I.P.R.1997, 479; Rogers, Lloyd's Mar. & Com.L.Q. 1991, 231; Hoyle, Business L.R. 1988, 251.

491 Shenton, Int'l Bus.Lawy. 1984, 103.

492 Zicherman, Univ. of Pittsburgh L.Rev. 1989, 669.

493 *J.T. Stratford & Sons Ltd. v. Lindley* [1967] Loyd's Rep. 133; *Ninemia Maritime Corp. v. Trave Schiffahrtsgesellschaft m.b.H und Co. KG ("The Niedersachsen")* [1983] 2 Lloyd's Rep. 600 (605).

Die Befugnisse der Gerichte in Angelegenheiten des einstweiligen Rechtsschutzes finden sich nunmehr in *s* 44 *Arbitration Act* 1996.[494] Sie haben im Vergleich zum alten Recht erhebliche Änderungen erfahren. Diese gehen unter anderem darauf zurück, daß der neue *Act* viele der vormals den Gerichten zustehenden Befugnisse nunmehr ganz bzw. primär den Schiedsgerichten zuweist.[495] Die Schiedsgerichte haben nach dem neuen *Act* etwa die Befugnisse, Zeugen unter Eid zu vernehmen,[496] bestimmte beweissichernde Maßnahmen[497] oder Untersuchungen des Verfahrensgegenstandes anzuordnen.[498]

S 44 kommt damit in erster Linie eine Auffangfunktion zu.[499] Die danach den Gerichten zugewiesenen Befugnisse sind zwar teils deckungsgleich mit den vorgenannten Befugnissen der Schiedsgerichte. Sie sind im allgemeinen jedoch weiter gefaßt und erlauben die Anordnung von Maßnahmen auch in besonders sensiblen Bereichen, in denen die Schiedsgerichte nicht tätig werden dürfen. Ein Beispiel bildet der Eingriff in die Rechte Dritter oder die Anordnung bestimmter Zwangsmaßnahmen.[500] *S* 44(1)(2) lautet:

> *"(1) Unless otherwise agreed by the parties, the court has for the purposes of and in relation to arbitral proceedings the same power of making orders about the matters listed below as it has for the purposes of and in relation to legal proceedings.*
>
> *(2) Those matters are-*
>
> *(a) the taking of evidence of witnesses;*
>
> *(b) the preservation of evidence;*
>
> *(c) making orders relating to property which is the subject of the proceedings or as to which any question arises in the proceedings [...];*
>
> *(d) the sale of any goods the subject of the proceedings;*
>
> *(e) the granting of an interim injunction or the appointment of a receiver."*

Die Liste der Befugnisse ist weitgehend identisch mit der nach *s* 12(6) *Arbitration Act* 1950. Die bedeutendste Änderung ist die Aussparung des Rechts, Sicherheitsleistungen für Schiedsverfahrenskosten anzuordnen. Dieses Recht wird

---

494 Vgl. Landau, J.Int'l Arb. 1996, 125 f.

495 Merkin, Arbitration Act 1996, S. 71; zum grundsätzlichen Verhältnis von Schieds- und staatlicher Gerichtsbarkeit in Fragen des einstweiligen Rechtschutzes Mustill, in: ICCA, S. 119; vgl. auch Redfern, Tex.Int'l L.J. 1995, 71.

496 Vgl. *s* 38(5) *Arbitration Act* 1996.

497 Vgl. *s* 38(6) *Arbitration Act* 1996.

498 Vgl. *s* 38(4) *Arbitration Act* 1996.

499 Landau, J.Int'l Arb. 1996, 126, weist auf die wichtige Frage der Vollstreckbarkeit entsprechender Maßnahmen hin.

500 Harris/Planterose/Tecks, S. 179.

als Reaktion auf die Kritik an den *Ken-Ren*-Fällen nunmehr ausschließlich den Schiedsgerichten eingeräumt.[501] Wie sich auch aus *s* 44 *Arbitration Act* 1996 sowie aus *s* 70(6)[502] *Arbitration Act* 1996 ergibt, ist den Gerichten somit das Recht aus *s* 12(6)(a) *Arbitration Act* 1950 gänzlich entzogen worden.

Mit Ausnahme der Befugnis zum Verkauf von Sachen,[503] der Anordnung von einstweiligen Verfügungen ("*interim injunctions*")[504] und der Ernennung eines Zwangsverwalters[505] können die in *s* 44(2) *Arbitration Act* 1996 genannten Befugnisse ebenso von den Schiedsgerichten ausgeübt werden. Wichtig ist in diesem Zusammenhang *s* 44(5) *Arbitration Act* 1996:

"In any case the court shall act only if or to the extent that the arbitral tribunal, and any arbitral or other institution or person vested by the parties with power in that regard, has no power or is unable for the time being to act effectively."

Hierdurch wird die primäre Zuständigkeit der Schiedsgerichte in den ihnen eingeräumten Befugnissen sichergestellt. Den Gerichten obliegt diesbezüglich kein Ermessensspielraum ("*shall*"). Sie bleiben danach für den Zeitraum vor Handlungsfähigkeit des Schiedsgerichts zuständig oder aber für den Fall, daß die Parteien das Schiedsgericht nicht mit den entsprechenden Befugnissen ausgestattet haben.[506]

Für eine weitere Beschränkung der gerichtlichen Befugnisse sorgt *s* 44(3)(4) *Arbitration Act* 1996. Danach dürfen die Gerichte Anordnungen zur Sicherstellung von Beweisen und Vermögensgegenständen nur in Fällen von Dringlichkeit treffen. Soweit diese nicht gegeben ist, muß das Schiedsgericht solchen gerichtlichen Anordnungen zustimmen. Von dieser Vorschrift betroffen sind in erster Linie *Mareva injunctions*[507] und die sog. *Anton Pillar Orders*, wonach geschäftlicher wie auch privater Besitz zur Auffindung von Beweisen bei Verdunkelungs-

---

501 *S* 38(3) *Arbitration Act* 1996 lautet:
"The tribunal may order a claimant to provide security for the costs of the arbitration. This power shall not be exercised on the ground that the claimant is-
(a) an individual ordinarily resident outside the United Kingdom, or
(b) a corporation or association incorporated or formed under the law of a country outside the United Kingdom, or whose central management and control is exercised outside the United Kingdom."

502 Gem. *s* 70(6) *Arbitration Act* 1996 dürfen die Gerichte Sicherheiten ausschließlich für gerichtliche *appeal*-Verfahren anordnen.

503 Vgl. *s* 44 (2)(d) *Arbitration Act* 1996.

504 Vgl. s 44 (2)(e) *Arbitration Act* 1996.

505 Vgl. s 44 (2)(e) *Arbitration Act* 1996.

506 Die entsprechende *s* 38 *Arbitration Act* 1996 ist abdingbares Recht.

507 Vgl. *supra* in diesem Kapitel B.III..

gefahr durchsucht werden darf.[508] Diese Vorschriften dienen laut DAC der Verhinderung der Gefahr "*that the Court might be used to interfere with or usurp the arbitral process*".[509]

S 44(6) *Arbitration Act* 1996 sieht schließlich noch einen weiteren Mechanismus vor, die Priorität schiedsgerichtlicher gegenüber gerichtlichen Anordnungen sicherzustellen. Die Vorschrift lautet:

> *"If the court so orders, an order made by it under this section shall cease to have effect in whole or in part on the order of the tribunal [...] in relation to the subject matter of the order."*

Die Gerichte können also anordnen, daß eine zuvor von ihnen gemäß *s* 44 *Arbitration Act* 1996 getroffene Anordnung ganz oder teilweise ihre Wirkung verliert, soweit das zuständige Schiedsgericht zwischenzeitlich seinerseits eine Anweisung über den gleichen Gegenstand getroffen hat. Diese Befugnis wurde von Teilen der Literatur auch als radikale Veränderung des Verhältnisses der staatlichen zu den Schiedsgerichten gepriesen.[510] Sicherlich, das Konzept mag neu sein. Dabei darf jedoch nicht übersehen werden, daß es noch immer die staatlichen Gerichte sind, die darüber entscheiden, ob ihre Anordnungen durch ein Schiedsgericht aufgehoben werden können oder nicht. Ebenso gut hätte die Vorschrift vorsehen können, daß die Gerichte auf Anfrage eines Schiedsgerichts ihre zuvor getroffene Anordnung aufheben.

D. Zwischenergebnis

Wie der Vergleich des alten und neuen englischen Rechts zur Anordnung einstweiliger Maßnahmen zeigt, gehen die Schiedsgerichte gestärkt aus der Reform hervor. Ihnen werden viele derjenigen Befugnisse zugesprochen, die zuvor ausschließlich den Gerichten zustanden. Zwangsmaßnahmen können sie allerdings auch nach dem neuen Recht nicht anordnen. Hier verbleibt es bei der Alleinzuständigkeit der staatlichen Gerichte. Diese haben im übrigen ungeachtet der Stärkung der Schiedsgerichte nur in einem Bereich wirklich an Befugnissen verloren. Sie dürfen jetzt keine Sicherheitsleistungen für die Schiedsverfahrenskosten mehr anordnen.

---

508 Zum einschlägigen Verfahren siehe die *High Court Practice Direction for Anton Pillar Orders and Mareva injunctions,* veröffentlicht in [1994] All E.R. 52.

509 1996-Report, para 215.

510 Vgl. etwa Rutherford/Sims, S. 152.

Im Vergleich des neuen englischen Rechts mit dem Modellgesetz fällt vor allem auf, daß das englische Recht detaillierter und umfangreicher geregelt ist. Das Modellgesetz weist mit Art. 9 eine generalklauselartige Ermächtigungsnorm auf, die keinerlei Schranken vorsieht. Das ist bedenklich. Die Grenze zwischen noch unterstützender und schon restriktivem Eingriff in ein Schiedsverfahren ist auch bei einstweiligen Anordnungen fließend. Es wäre deshalb wünschenswert gewesen, die entsprechenden Befugnisse der Gerichte zu konkretisieren.

Kapitel 9
Entscheidung über einen *preliminary point of law*

A. Keine Regelung nach dem Modellgesetz

Das Modellgesetz sieht an keiner Stelle das Recht der Gerichte vor, bereits vor Ergehen des Schiedsspruchs verbindlich über eine Rechtsfrage zu entscheiden. Wie bereits mehrfach im Verlauf dieser Arbeit deutlich geworden ist, entspricht es bereits der Philosophie des Modellgesetzes, staatsgerichtliche Kontrollbefugnisse auf ein Minimum zu reduzieren.[511] Insbesondere im Vorfeld der schiedsrichterlichen Entscheidung läßt das Modellgesetz daher kaum staatsgerichtliche Eingriffe zu.[512]

B. Das englische Recht vor 1997

Nach dem alten englischen Recht konnten die englischen Gerichte auch vor Ergehen des Schiedsspruchs zu Rechtsfragen Stellung nehmen bzw. diese entscheiden.

Einerseits bestand die Möglichkeit, einen Zwischenschiedsspruch zum Gegenstand eines *appeal*-Verfahren zu machen. Der Zwischenschiedsspruch wurde zum Zweck der Überprüfung wie ein Schiedsspruch behandelt. Es bestanden somit keinerlei Besonderheiten gegenüber dem "regulären" *appeal*-Verfahren.

Zum anderen sah *s 2 Arbitration Act* 1979 ein besonderes Verfahren vor, welches dem High Court eine Entscheidung[513] über ihm vorgelegte Rechtsfragen

511 Vgl. etwa die Ausführungen *supra* Kapitel 1, B..

512 Vgl. hier auch die Diskussion über den günstigsten Zeitpunkt staatlicher Kontrolle im Zusammenhang mit der Kompetenz-Kompetenz, *supra* Kapitel 6.

513 Der Terminus "Entscheidung" wird hier im untechnischen Sinne gebraucht. Dazu, inwieweit die "Entscheidung" des High Court tatsächlich verbindlichen Charakter hatte, vgl. *infra* in diesem Kapitel.

ermöglichte. Danach war es unter bestimmten Voraussetzungen möglich, dem High Court eine Rechtsfrage aus dem laufenden Schiedsverfahren zur Entscheidung vorzulegen *("determination of preliminary point of law")*, ohne daß hierfür der „Umweg" über einen Zwischenschiedsspruch gegangen werden mußte.

Die *determination of preliminary point of law* war ihrem Wesen nach dem 1979 abgeschafften *special case*-Verfahren sehr ähnlich.[514] Wie zuvor nach dem *special case*-Verfahren sollte es auch nach 1979 - wenngleich unter wesentlichen Einschränkungen - möglich sein, eine für das Schiedsverfahren entscheidungsrelevante Rechtsfrage dem zuständigen staatlichen Gericht vorzulegen.

Es sind vor allem zwei Fallkonstellationen, in denen sich die *determination of preliminary point of law* anbot. Die erste zeichnete sich dadurch aus, daß von der Entscheidung einer bestimmten, möglicherweise umstrittenen Rechtsfrage das Ergebnis des ganzen Verfahrens abhing. Hier sollte die Entscheidung des Gerichts für Klarheit und Verbindlichkeit sorgen. Weniger praxisrelevant war die zweite Fallgruppe. Hier hing von einem zentralen, beispielsweise politischen Ereignis die Entscheidung gleich einer Vielzahl von Schiedsverfahren ab.[515]

S 2(1)(2) *Arbitration Act* 1979 lautete:

> *"(1) Subject to subsection (2) [...], on an application to the High Court made by any of the parties to a reference-*
>
> *(a) with the consent of an arbitrator who has entered on the reference or, if an umpire has entered on the reference, with his consent, or*
>
> *(b) with the consent of all the other parties,*
>
> *the High Court shall have jurisdiction to determine any question of law arising in the course of the reference.*
>
> *(2) The High Court shall not entertain an application under subsection (1)(a) above with respect to any question of law unless it is satisfied that-*
>
> *(a) the determination of the application might produce substantial savings in costs to the parties; and*
>
> *(b) the question of law is one in respect of which leave to appeal would be likely to be given under section 1(3)(b) above."*

Es bestand nach *s* 2 *Arbitration Act* 1979 also zwar grundsätzlich die Möglichkeit, eine Rechsfrage noch *vor* Ergehen des Schiedsspruches durch die Gerichte entscheiden zu lassen. Der einzelnen Partei war es jedoch nicht mehr möglich, eine solche Entscheidung des Gerichts herbeizuführen. Denn Voraussetzung war entweder die Zustimmung aller Parteien oder diejenige des Schiedsrichters.

---

514 Zum *special case*-Verfahren vgl. *supra* Teil II, Kapitel 2, D..

515 Harris/Planterose/Tecks, S. 183. Der DAC-1996-Report, para 218, nennt als Beispiele für solche zentrale Ereignisse die Schließung des Suez-Kanals oder das U.S. Sojabohnen Export-Embargo.

S 2 *Arbitration Act* 1979 konnte somit nur sehr bedingt als Instrument zur Verschleppung des Schiedsverfahrens benutzt werden. Vielmehr eröffnete die Vorschrift den Parteien die Möglichkeit, bereits zu einem frühen Zeitpunkt eine Rechtsfrage zu klären, die sonst möglicherweise später Gegenstand eines *appeals* geworden wäre.

In diesem Zusammenhang stellt sich die praxisrelevante Frage, inwieweit die *determination* des High Courts verbindlich war. Hiervon hing einerseits ab, ob das Schiedsgericht an die Rechtsfindung des Gerichts gebunden war. Zum anderen war bedeutsam, ob der Schiedsspruch im *appeal*-Verfahren erneut auf der gleichen Grundlage angegriffen werden konnte.

Die Wahl des Terminus "*determine*" anstatt etwa der Termini "*order*" oder "*judge*" sprach gegen das Erwachsen der Entscheidung in Rechtskraft.[516] Die gleiche Frage konnte deshalb erneut im Rahmen eines *appeals* nach *s* 1 *Arbitration Act* 1979 Gegenstand einer gerichtlichen Prüfung sein. Auch das Schiedsgericht war nicht verpflichtet, die *determination* des High Courts seinem Schiedsspruch zugrundezulegen.

Vor dem Hintergrund der Unverbindlichkeit einer *determination* stellt sich die Frage nach deren Sinn. Mit den Worten von Lord Donaldson:[517]

> *"[T]he parties nip down the road to pick the brains of one of Her Majesty's Judges and, thus enlightened, resume the arbitration."*

Ganz so unkompliziert war das Verfahren nach *s* 2 *Arbitration Act* 1979 allerdings nicht. Zunächst mußten sich alle Parteien auf einen entsprechenden Antrag einigen. War dies nicht möglich, mußte die Zustimmung des Schiedsrichters eingeholt werden. Dann entschied der High Court zunächst über seine Zuständigkeit, um in einem weiteren Schritt sein Ermessen auszuüben, ob er auch tätig werden wolle. Erst dann konnte eine Entscheidung in der Sache, also eine Beantwortung der aufgeworfenen Rechtsfrage erfolgen.

In der Praxis scheint das Verfahren nach *s* 2 *Arbitration Act* 1979 keine besonderen Schwierigkeiten bereitet zu haben.[518] Zumindest theoretisch aber boten sowohl die Zuständigkeitskriterien nach *s* 2(2) *Arbitration Act* 1979 als auch das generelle Zulassungsermessen hinreichend Problemstoff. So war nicht klar, wann nach *s* 2(2)(a) "*substantial savings in cost*" für die Parteien erreicht werden

516 *Babanaft International Co. S.A. v. Avant Petroleum Inc. ("The Oltenia")* [1982] 2 Lloyd's Rep. 99.

517 *Ibid,* 106.

518 Weder Rechtsprechung noch Literatur haben sich intensiver mit der Vorschrift auseinandergesetzt.

konnten.[519] Hierzu hätte es einer Vorhersehbarkeit über den weiteren Verlauf des Verfahrens bedurft, die es nicht geben konnte.[520]

Ebenso unklar war auch, woran der High Court sein Ermessen nach *s* 2(1) *Arbitration Act* 1979 zu orientieren hatte.[521] Hier kann vermutet werden, daß Faktoren wie etwa 1) die Bedeutung der zu klärenden Rechtsfrage, 2) die Einigkeit aller Parteien hinsichtlich ihrer Klärung oder auch 3) die von den Parteien verfolgte Absicht eine Rolle gespielt haben werden.

C. Der Arbitration Act *1996*

Das Recht der Gerichte zur Entscheidung über einen *preliminary point of law* bleibt nach dem *Arbitration Act* 1996 im wesentlichen unverändert. Es wurden allerdings einige Änderungen vorgenommen, die das gerichtliche Tätigwerden an weitere Voraussetzungen knüpfen.

So steht es den Parteien gemäß *s* 45(1) *Arbitration Act* 1996 frei, einen Ausschluß des entsprechenden Rechts zu vereinbaren.[522] *S* 45(1) macht ein Eingreifen der Gerichte weiter ausdrücklich davon abhängig, daß die zu entscheidende Rechtsfrage die Rechte mindestens einer Partei "*substantially*" zu beinträchtigen in der Lage gewesen sein muß.[523] Ganz so neu wie diese Einschränkung auf den ersten Blick wirkt, ist sie nicht. Letztlich versteckt sich dahinter nichts anderes als eine Umformulierung der vormals - durch Verweis auf *s* 1(3)(b) *Arbitration Act* 1979 - in *s* 2(2)(b) *Arbitration Act* 1979 genannten Bedingung. Danach mußte die Rechtsfrage die Voraussetzungen für eine Zulassung zum *appeal* er-

519 Vgl. *Vasso (owners) v. Vasso (cargo owners)* (*"The Vasso"*) [1983] 2 Lloyd's Rep. 346.

520 *D/S A/S Idaho v. Peninsular and Oriental Steam Navigation Co.* ("*The Strathnewton*") [1982] 2 Lloyd's Rep. 296 (348). Zu der noch ungleich schwierigeren Voraussetzung nach *s* 2(2)(b) vgl. *infra* die Ausführungen in Kapitel 10, C.II.1.b).

521 Daß ein solches Ermessen bestand, ergab sich zwar nicht unmittelbar aus dem Wortlaut von *s* 2(1), dafür aber aus *s* 2 (2A) ("... *from a decision of the High Court to entertain or not to entertain an application under subsection (1)(a) above.*"); vgl. auch "*The Oltenia*" [1982] 2 Lloyd's Rep. 99 (103).

522 *S* 45(1) *Arbitration Act* 1996 lautet:
"Unless otherwise agreed *by the parties, the court may on the application of a party to arbitral proceedings [...] determine any question of law arising in the course of the proceedings which the court is satisfied substantially affects the rights of one or more of the parties.*" (Betonung vom Verfasser hervorgehoben)

523 *Ibid.*

füllen.[524] *S* 45(1) bewirkt daher in erster Linie eine Klarstellung der bisherigen Rechtslage.[525]

Neu hinzugekommen ist das in *s* 45(2)(b)(ii) *Arbitration Act* 1996 genannte Erfordernis einer prompten Antragstellung ("*without delay*"). Hierbei ist auf den frühstmöglichen Termin abzustellen, an dem die Parteien die Relevanz der besagten Rechtsfrage erkennen konnten.[526]

Gegen die Entscheidung des Gerichts, eine Rechtsfrage zur Entscheidung anzunehmen, ist ein Rechtsmittel nur mit vorheriger Zulassung des Gerichts gegeben.[527] Das gleiche soll für die eigentliche, materielle Entscheidung des Gerichts gelten. Hier sieht *s* 45(5) *Arbitration Act* 1996 weiter vor, daß die Zulassung nicht erfolgen soll „*unless the court considers that the question is one of general importance, or is one which for some other special reason should be considered by the* Court of Appeal." Die Erfahrung mit dem alten Recht zeigt, daß die Gerichte Rechtsmittel aller Voraussicht nach nur ausnahmsweise zulassen werden.[528]

D. Zwischenergebnis

Wie bereits eingangs des Kapitels festgestellt wurde, ändert der *Arbitration Act* 1996 die Befugnisse der Gerichte zur *determination of preliminary point of law* nur unwesentlich. Die gleichwohl erfolgten Änderungen erfolgten sämtlich unter dem Aspekt, den Parteien noch größere Zurückhaltung beim Gebrauch dieses Rechtsmittels aufzuerlegen. In diesem Sinne ist es als die vielleicht bemerkenswerteste Änderung anzusehen, daß ohne ausdrückliche Zulassung durch das Gericht kein Rechtsmittel gegen dessen Entscheidung eingereicht werden kann. Der Gefahr einer mißbräuchlichen Verschleppung des Verfahrens scheint damit wirksam begegnet zu sein. Ganz auszuschließen ist diese trotzdem nicht. Zwar schreibt *s* 45(4) *Arbitration Act* 1996 ausdrücklich vor, daß das Schiedsgericht sein Verfahren ungeachtet eines Verfahrens nach *s* 45(1) *Arbitration Act* 1996 fortsetzen kann. Von dieser Möglichkeit wird das Schiedsgericht mit Blick auf ein mögliches *appeal*-Verfahren nach *s* 69 *Arbitration Act* 1996 aber nur dann Gebrauch machen, wenn es mit hoher Wahrscheinlichkeit das Ergebnis der rich-

524 Vgl. *infra* Kapitel 10, C.II.1.b).
525 Merkin, Arbitration Act 1996, S. 74.
526 Harris/Planterose/Tecks, S. 185.
527 Vgl. *s* 45(5) *Arbitration Act* 1996.
528 Merkin, Arbitration Act 1996, S. 75, dort FN 9 unter Hinweis auf *The Oltenia* [1982] 2 Lloyd's Rep. 99.

terlichen Meinungsfindung vorhersagen kann. Hiervon ist regelmäßig nicht auszugehen.

Das Modellgesetz enthält keine der *s* 45 *Arbitration Act* 1996 entsprechende Vorschrift. Welche Lösung vorzugswürdig ist, läßt sich nicht eindeutig beantworten. So sind beispielsweise Fallkonstellationen denkbar, in denen die Möglichkeit des "Ausleihens" des juristischen Sachverstandes der Gerichte durchaus sinnvoll erscheinen kann. Dieser Vorteil muß jedoch auf diejenigen Fälle beschränkt bleiben, in denen das zuständige Schiedsgericht nicht selbst auch in der Lage wäre, den Sachverhalt juristisch ebenso sachverständig zu bearbeiten. Entscheidend ist letztlich aber der folgende Gesichtspunkt: Es ist der einzelnen Partei auch nach *s* 45 *Arbitration Act* 1996 nicht möglich, gegen den Willen der anderen Partei(en) oder den des Schiedsgerichts eine *determination* der Gerichte zu erwirken. So wird sichergestellt, daß die Autonomie des Schiedsverfahrens nicht in Frage gestellt wird.

Kapitel 10
Aufhebung und Abänderung des Schiedsspruchs

A. Einführung

Das Herz der Debatte hinsichtlich des Umfangs zulässiger staatlicher Kontroll- und Eingriffsbefugnisse waren schon immer die entsprechenden Befugnisse in der *post award stage*, also nach Ergehen des Schiedsspruchs. In diesem Kapitel werden die gerichtlichen Befugnisse zur Aufhebung und Abänderung von Schiedssprüchen durch die Gerichte behandelt. Anders als der im nachfolgenden Kapitel behandelte Bereich von Anerkennung und Vollstreckung war derjenige der Aufhebung von Schiedssprüchen nach englischem Recht sehr umstritten. Er war zudem von höchster praktischer Bedeutung.[529] Anerkennung und Vollstreckung von Schiedssprüchen haben durch das New Yorker UN-Übereinkommen über die Anerkennung und Vollstreckung von ausländischen Schiedssprüchen eine international harmonische und zufriedenstellende Regelung gefunden. Anders die Aufhebung oder Anfechtung von Schiedssprüchen. Traditionell sahen nationale Rechtsordnungen hier stets eigene Regelungen vor. Das englische Recht stellt ein Beispiel dafür dar, wie sehr sich die meisten Staaten bis vor nicht allzu langer Zeit einer Harmonisierung in diesem Bereich widersetzt haben. Das Modellgesetz ist der erste Versuch, auch in diesem Bereich internationale Konformität zu erreichen. Inwieweit sich das englische Recht hinsichtlich dieses Be-

529 Berger, International Economic Arbitration, S. 647.

reichs durch den *Arbitration Act* 1996 entwickelt hat, wird von entscheidender Bedeutung für dessen weltweite Akzeptanz sein.

B. Aufhebung des Schiedsspruchs nach dem Modellgesetz

I. Aufhebungsklage

Das Modellgesetz regelt die Angreifbarkeit des Schiedsspruchs in Art. 34. Die danach vorgesehene Aufhebungsklage stellt die einzige Möglichkeit dar, aktiv[530] gegen den Schiedsspruch vorzugehen. Entsprechend intensiv und kontrovers verliefen die Beratungen zu Art. 34 Modellgesetz.[531] Die staatsgerichtlichen Kontrollbefugnisse hinsichtlich des Schiedsspruchs haben schon immer den Kern der Debatte über den Umfang zulässiger staatlicher Eingriffe ausgemacht. Richtigerweise erachtete die UNCITRAL-Kommission die Ausgestaltung von Art. 34 Modellgesetz deshalb auch als entscheidend für den Gesamterfolg, den das Modellgesetz haben würde.[532] Bereits anfangs der Beratungen war deutlich geworden, welch ehrgeiziges Ziel verfolgt wurde: Die Aufhebungskontrolle durch die staatliche Gerichtsbarkeit sollte auf ein absolutes Minimum reduziert werden.[533] Dieses Ziel sollte durch eine abschließende und restriktive Auflistung aller Aufhebungsgründe erreicht werden.[534]

Das Ergebnis der zahlreichen Debatten zu Art. 34 Modellgesetz folgt in einem ganz wesentlichen Punkt der Philosophie der UNCITRAL-Kommission, staatliche Kontrolle vorhersehbar und überschaubar zu machen und sie ansonsten auszuschließen. So heißt es in Absatz 1:

> "Gegen den Schiedsspruch kann beim Gericht nur Aufhebungsklage nach den Absätzen 2 und 3 erhoben werden."

Dadurch erreicht das Modellgesetz gleich eine zweifache Einschränkung der staatlichen Eingriffs- und Kontrollbefugnisse. Einerseits ist die Aufhebungsklage nach Art. 34 der einzige Rechtsbehelf gegen den Schiedsspruch. Das Modellgesetz hat sich damit bewußt gegen jede Möglichkeit der inhaltlich-

530 Zur eher "passiven" Vollstreckungsgegenklage vgl. *infra* Kapitel 11, B..
531 Holtzmann/Neuhaus, S. 911.
532 UN-Doc. A/CN. 9/207, para 107.
533 UN-Doc. A/CN. 9/207, para 103.
534 UN-Doc. A/CN. 9/207, para 109.

materiellrechtlichen Überprüfung des Schiedsspruchs entschieden.[535] Es sind - vielleicht einmal abgesehen von dem *ordre public*-Vorbehalt - ausschließlich schwere Verfahrensverstöße, die zu einer Aufhebung des Schiedsspruchs führen können. Diesen Punkt gilt es bei einem Vergleich mit dem englischen Recht im Auge zu behalten.

Zum anderen ist durch Art. 34 Abs. 1 Modellgesetz gewährleistet, daß nur in den in Absatz 2 enumerativ aufgeführten Fällen eine Aufhebung des Schiedsspruchs erfolgen kann. Mit Blick auf die Art. 4 und 16 Abs. 2 Modellgesetz sind die einzelnen Aufhebungsgründe zudem restriktiv auszulegen. So ist es den Parteien etwa verwehrt, gegen den Schiedsspruch solche Einwände zu erheben, mit denen sie wegen Verfristung bereits vor Erlaß desselben ausgeschlossen waren.[536] Nachfolgend sollen nunmehr die einzelnen Aufhebungsgründe analysiert werden.

II. Die einzelnen Aufhebungsgründe

1. Subjektive Schiedsunfähigkeit und Ungültigkeit des Schiedsvertrages

In Art. 34 Abs. 2(a)(i) Modellgesetz heißt es:

> "Ein Schiedsspruch kann [...] nur aufgehoben werden, [...] wenn die klagende Partei Beweis erbringt, [...] daß eine der Parteien, die eine Schiedsvereinbarung im Sinne des Art. 7 geschlossen haben, in irgendeiner Hinsicht hierzu nicht fähig war, oder daß die Schiedsvereinbarung nach dem Recht, dem die Parteien sie unterstellt haben, oder, falls die Parteien hierüber nichts bestimmt haben, nach dem Recht dieses Staates ungültig ist [...]"

Die Vorschrift wurde in Anlehnung an Art. 5 I a des New Yorker UN-Übereinkommens entworfen. Anders als dieser verzichtet Art. 34 Abs. 2(a)(i) Modellgesetz jedoch auf eine Bezugnahme auf das kollisionsrechtliche Statut der subjektiven Schiedsfähigkeit.[537] Maßgeblich hierfür war die Auffassung der Kommission, das Statut der subjektiven Schiedsfähigkeit sei nicht bestimmbar genug.[538] Wann von einer Unfähigkeit im vorgenannten Sinne auszugehen ist,

---

535 Calavros führt auf S. 147 aus, daß die staatlichen Gerichte den Schiedsspruch nur auf seine "externe Legalität" hin überprüfen dürfen.

536 Herrmann, in: Lew (Hrsg.), Contemporary Problems, S. 172.

537 In Art. 5 I a des New Yorker Abkommens wird auf "*the law applicable to [the parties]*" Bezug genommen; vgl. auch Schlosser, Schiedsgerichtsbarkeit, Rn. 354.

538 Bei Holtzmann/Neuhaus, S. 916, heißt es hierzu:
"The Commission eliminated the clause from the text of Article 34, explaining that the term was 'either incomplete or misleading', since it could be taken to refer to

bleibt somit weitestgehend dem nationalen Kollisionsrecht des jeweiligen Modellgesetstaates vorbehalten.

2. *Verletzung des rechtlichen Gehörs*

Gemäß Art. 34 Abs. 2 (a)(ii) Modellgesetz kann ein Schiedsspruch ferner dann aufgehoben werden, wenn die klagende Partei Beweis erbringt,

> "[...], daß sie von der Bestellung des Schiedsrichters oder von dem schiedsrichterlichen Verfahren nicht gehörig in Kenntnis gesetzt worden ist, oder daß sie aus einem anderen Grund ihre Angriffs- oder Verteidigungsmittel nicht hat geltend machen können [...]".

Eine ausführliche Stellungnahme zu Art. 34 Abs. 2 (a)(ii) erübrigt sich. Die Vorschrift ist Art. 5 I b des New Yorker UN-Übereinkommens nachempfunden. Besonderheiten des Modellgesetzes ergeben sich nicht.

3. *Überschreitung der Entscheidungskompetenz*

Nach Art. 34 Abs. 2 (a)(iii) Modellgesetz kann das Gericht einen Schiedsspruch weiter dann aufheben, wenn

> "[...] der Schiedsspruch eine Streitigkeit betrifft, die in der Schiedsabrede nicht erwähnt ist oder nicht unter die Bestimmungen der Schiedsklausel fällt, oder [wenn] er Entscheidungen enthält, welche die Grenzen der Schiedsabrede oder der Schiedsklausel überschreiten; kann jedoch der Teil des Schiedsspruchs, der sich auf Streitpunkte bezieht, die dem schiedsrichterlichen Verfahren unterworfen waren, von dem Teil, der Streitpunkte betrifft, die ihm nicht unterworfen waren, getrennt werden, so kann nur der erstgenannte Teil des Schiedsspruchs aufgehoben werden [...]".

Art. 34 Abs. 2 (a)(iii) Modellgesetz ist Art. 5 I c des New Yorker UN-Übereinkommens nachempfunden. Calavros zufolge ist die praktische Bedeutung der Vorschrift eher gering.[539] Dies sei überwiegend darauf zurückzuführen, daß

---

any of a number of different bodies of substantive law: the law of nationality, of domicile, or of residence of the parties."
Eingehender zu der in Art. 34 Abs. 2(a)(i) enthaltenen Kollisionsproblematik: Calavros, S. 150 ff, der hier das Personalstatut anwenden will; a.A. Nöcker, S. 157 f, nach dessen Ansicht auf das Statut des Forums zurückgegriffen werden müsse; vgl. weiter v.d. Berg, S. 277.

539 Calavros, S. 155.

die erfahrenen internationalen Schiedsgerichte eine sehr genaue Überprüfung ihrer Zuständigkeit vornähmen.[540]

Im Zusammenhang mit Art. 34 Abs. 2 (a)(iii) Modellgesetz ist auf Art. 16 Abs. 2 Modellgesetz hinzuweisen. Danach ist die Einrede der Unzuständigkeit des Schiedsgerichts spätestens mit der Klagebeerwiderung vorzubringen. Konsequenterweise müßte eine Partei auch im Rahmen des Verfahrens nach Art. 34 Modellgesetz mit ihrer Einrede der Unzuständigkeit präkludiert sein, soweit sie nicht Art. 16 Abs. 2 Modellgesetz beachtet hat. Dessen ungeachtet heißt es jedoch in einer Stellungnahme UNCITRALs zu diesem Punkt:[541]

> *"[I]t was recognised that the failure to raise such a plea could not have the effect of a waiver in all circumstances, especially where the plea [...] was that the dispute was non-arbitrable or that the award was in conflict with public policy."*

Es wurde allerdings davon Abstand genommen, festzulegen, unter welchen Umständen Ausnahmen zu Art. 16 Abs. 2 zulässig seien. Eine solche Festlegung wurde den jeweiligen Modellgesetzstaaten überlassen.[542] Art. 16 Abs. 2 findet aber jedenfalls dann keine Anwendung, wenn sich die Zuständigkeitsüberschreitung erst im Schiedsspruch manifestiert.[543]

4. *Verstoß gegen die Vorschriften oder gegen die Schiedsabrede über die Bildung des Schiedsgerichts und die Durchführung des Schiedsverfahren*

Gem. Art. 34 Abs. 2 (a)(iv) Modellgesetz kann ein Schiedsspruch aufgehoben werden, wenn

> "[...] die Bildung des Schiedsgerichts oder das schiedsrichterliche Verfahren der Vereinbarung der Parteien nicht entsprochen hat, es sei denn, daß die Vereinbarung ihrerseits einer Bestimmung dieses Gesetzes, von der die Parteien nicht abweichen können, widersprochen hat oder, sofern eine Vereinbarung nicht getroffen wurde, die Bildung des Schiedsgerichts oder das schiedsrichterliche Verfahren diesem Gesetz widersprochen hat [...]".

Anders als Art. 34 Abs. 2 (a)(i)-(iii) Modellgesetz weicht Art. 34 Abs. 2 (a)(iv) deutlich von seinem "Vorbild" - Art. 5 I d New Yorker UN-Übereinkommen - ab. Auf diese Weise begegneten die Verfasser des Modellgesetzes einem Mißstand, der aus dem Wortlaut von Art. 5 I d des New Yorker Ab-

---

540 *Ibid.*
541 UN-Doc. A/40/17, para 288.
542 UN-Doc. A/40/17, para 289.
543 Nöcker, S. 161.

kommens herrührte. Danach wurde auch in dem Verstoß gegen eine zwingende Bestimmung des anwendbaren nationalen Rechts kein Hinderungsgrund für die Vollstreckung des Schiedsspruches gesehen, solange dies nur der Parteivereinbarung entsprach.

Fraglich ist, ob auch Bagatellverstöße und solche, welche die Schiedsspruchfindung in keiner Weise beeinflußt haben, immer zu einer Aufhebung des Schiedsspruches führen müssen. Anders formuliert: Steht den Gerichten ein Ermessen darüber zu, Bagatellverstöße von der Rechtsfolge des Art. 34 auszunehmen? Die Debatte hierüber wurde kontrovers geführt.[544] Ein klares Ergebnis hat sie nicht erbracht. Insbesondere wurde davon abgesehen, Art. 34 Abs. 2 Modellgesetz um eine diesebezügliche Klarstellung zu erweitern. In den *travaux préparatoires* heißt es abschließend zu diesem Thema *"[that] it was understood that an award might be set aside on any of the grounds listed in paragraph (2) irrespective of whether such ground had materially affected the award."*[545] Ins Auge fällt hier die Formulierung "*might*". Eine wörtliche Auslegung der vorgenannten Stellungnahme spricht für einen Ermessensspielraum der staatlichen Gerichte. Allerdings läßt sich der Diskussion entnehmen, daß die staatlichen Gerichte zu einer zurückhaltenden Ausübung ihres Ermessens angehalten sind.

5. *Objektive Schiedsfähigkeit*

Nach Art. 34 Abs. 2 (b)(i) Modellgesetz kann ein Schiedsspruch aufgehoben werden,

> "[...] wenn das Gericht feststellt, daß der Gegenstand des Streits nach dem Recht dieses Staates nicht auf schiedsrichterlichem Weg geregelt werden kann [...]".

Die Vorschrift ist Art. 5 II (a) des New Yorker UN-Übereinkommens nachempfunden. Vor allem um das zur Bestimmung der objektiven Schiedsfähigkeit anwendbare Recht drehten sich die Beratungen.[546] Letztlich wurde aus Gründen

---

544 Jugolawien etwa plädierte dafür, den staatlichen Gerichten ein generelles Ermessen darüber einzuräumen, welche Verstöße zu einer Aufhebung führen sollten (vgl. UN-Doc. A/CN. 9/263, addendum 1, Art. 34, para 5), während Schweden den Anwendungsbereich von Art. 34 Abs. 2 nur eröffnet sehen wollte, soweit die schiedsrichterliche Entscheidungsfindung durch den Verstoß nachweislich beinflußt worden sei (vgl. UN-Doc. A/CN. 9/263, Art. 34, para 8).

545 UN-Doc. A/40/17, para 303.

546 Die Frage nach der kollisionsrechtlichen Anknüpfung soll, da nicht unmittelbar Gegenstand dieser Arbeit, an dieser Stelle nicht eingehender untersucht werden; vgl. hierzu aber Nöcker, S. 162 ff; Calavros, S. 155 f; Hüßlein-Stich, S. 181 f; Ungar, Colum.J.Transnat'l.Law 1987, 717; Holtzmann/Neuhaus, S. 918 f.

der "*predictability and certainty*" hinsichtlich möglicher Verstöße gegen die objektive Schiedsfähigkeit das Recht des Schiedsortes favorisiert.[547]

Im Unterschied zu den unter Art. 34 Abs. 2 (a) Modellgesetz genannten Fällen - hier ist die klagende Partei beweislastig - hebt das Gericht nach Art. 34 Abs. 2 (b) Modellgesetz den Schiedsspruch auf, wenn es einen Verstoß "feststellt". Die *travaux preparatoires* lassen keinen sicheren Schluß darauf zu, wie die Befugnisse bzw. Pflichten der Gerichte hinsichtlich ihres Tätigwerdens unter Art. 34 Abs. 2 (b) Modellgesetz gegenüber denen unter Art. 34 Abs. 2 (a) Modellgesetz abzugrenzen sind. Insbesondere wird nicht deutlich, ob die Gerichte nach der erstgenannten Vorschrift etwa einer Ermittlungspflicht unterliegen; ebensowenig wird deutlich, ob sie einer Amtspflicht zum Tätigwerden unterliegen, soweit sie Kenntnis von einem Verstoß gegen die objektive Schiedsfähigkeit erlangt haben. Bei wörtlicher Auslegung der Vorschrift ist hiervon allerdings nicht auszugehen.[548]

6. *Verstoß gegen den* ordre public

Schließlich kann der Schiedsspruch nach Art. 34 Abs. 2 (b)(ii) aufgehoben werden,

> "[...] wenn das Gericht feststellt, daß der Schiedsspruch der öffentlichen Ordnung dieses Staates widerspricht."

Wie auch jedes nationale Schiedsverfahrensrecht kennt das Modellgesetz einen *ordre public*-Vorbehalt. Für den Umfang staatlicher Eingriffs- und Kontrollmöglichkeiten kommt diesem - genauer gesagt: dessen Auslegung - wesentliche Bedeutung zu.[549] Entscheidend ist, was bereits einen solchen Verstoß konstituiert. In diesem Zusammenhang hat der *ordre public*-Vorbehalt im Wesentlichen eine Auffangfunktion. Es sollen eben auch jene für schwerwiegend erachteten Verfahrens- und materiellrechtlichen Verstöße noch sanktioniert werden können, die nicht bereits ausdrücklich geregelt sind. Es läßt sich darüber streiten, inwieweit dem *ordre public*-Vorbehalt des Modellgesetzes eine selbständige oder nur

547 UN-Doc. A/40/17, paras 292 f.

548 Vgl. auch UN-Doc. A/CN. 9/SR. 318, paras 7 - 8, wonach den staatlichen Gerichten ein Ermessensspielraum verbleiben soll; anders Calavros, S. 155, für den kein Zweifel an einer Amtspflicht besteht, ohne daß er jedoch auf die Ermessensproblematik eingeht.

549 Allgemein vgl. Buchanan, Am.Bus.L.J. 1988/89, 511.

subsidiäre Bedeutung zukommt.[550] Der Streit ist jedoch ohne praktische Relevanz. Denn worauf es ankommt, ist die gleichwie geartete *Möglichkeit* der Gerichte zu einem Eingreifen in das Schiedsverfahren. Der *ordre public*-Vorbehalt bietet diese Möglichkeit.

Eine Definition des *ordre public*-Vorbehalts des Modellgesetzes ist nicht möglich. Es gibt keinen solchen des Modellgesetzes, sondern nur einen des jeweiligen Modellgesetzstaates. Notwendigerweise muß deshalb ein Vergleich des Modellgesetzes mit der englischen Rechtslage in diesem Punkt scheitern. Die *trauveaux preparatoires* geben einen Hinweis auf eine inhaltliche Begrenzung des *ordre public*-Vorbehaltes im weitesten Sinne. So wurde die Frage diskutiert, ob das Modellgesetz anstatt eines "einfachen" einen *ordre public international*[551] vorsehen sollte. Letzterer unterscheidet sich vom erstgenannten dadurch, daß nur noch ganz wesentliche Verfahrens- oder materiellrechtliche Verstöße ein staatliches Eingreifen rechtfertigen. Sanders führt hierzu aus:[552]

> *"The notion of the latter is more restricted than the former. International public policy, according to a generally accepted doctrine, is confined to violation of really fundamental conceptions of the legal order in the country concerned."*

Im Ergebnis wurde die Beschränkung auf einen *droit public international* unter Hinweis auf die mangelnde Präzision des Begriffes aber abgelehnt.[553]

III. Aufhebungsverfahren

1. Zuständiges Gericht, Rechtsmittel

Gemäß Art. 34 Abs. 2 Modellgesetz ist das in Art. 6 Modellgesetz bezeichnete Gericht (ausschließlich) zuständig. Die Frage, ob über die Aufhebungsklage in einem ordentlichen oder in einem besonderen Verfahren zu befinden ist, richtet sich nach dem Prozeßrecht des rezipierenden Staates.[554] Gegen das Urteil stehen den Parteien sämtliche nach der nationalen Rechtsordnung vorgesehene Rechts-

---

550 Vgl. Calavros, S. 160, der die Relevanz des *ordre public* nur noch bei "inhaltlichen Mißgriffe[n] des Schiedsspruchs" sieht, oder Hüßlein-Stich, S. 186, die auf die selbständige Bedeutung hinweist.

551 Vgl. allgemein zum Begriff Bartos, S. 29 ff; Gottwald, in: FS Nagel, S. 66 ff; Kornblum, in: FS Nagel, S. 140 ff; Schlosser, Schiedsgerichtsbarkeit, Rn. 734 ff.

552 Sanders, in: Académie de Droit International (Hrsg.), S. 224; vgl. auch Craig, Arb.Int'l 1988, S. 197.

553 UN-Doc. A/CN.9/233, para 22.

554 Calavros, S. 162.

mittel zur Verfügung. Das Modellgesetz macht diesbezüglich keine Einschränkungen.

2. *Aussetzung des Aufhebungsverfahrens*

Art. 34 Abs. 4 Modellgesetz sieht eine für das Modellgesetz einmalige verfahrenstechnische Möglichkeit des zuständigen staatlichen Gerichts vor. Darin heißt es:

> "Ist die Aufhebungsklage erhoben worden, so kann das Gericht in geeigneten Fällen auf Antrag einer Partei das Aufhebungsverfahren für einen vom Gericht zu bestimmenden Zeitraum aussetzen und dadurch dem Schiedsgericht Gelegenheit geben, das schiedsrichterliche Verfahren wiederaufzunehmen oder andere Maßnahmen zu treffen, die nach Auffassung des Schiedsgerichts die Gründe für die Aufhebung beseitigen."

Das Rechtsinstitut der Aussetzung des Verfahrens ist ebenso wie das der Rückverweisung an das Schiedsgericht dem Recht der *common law*-Staaten gut bekannt. Gegenteiliges gilt allerdings für Staaten des *civil law*. Die beabsichtigte Übernahme dieses Rechtsinstitut in das Modellgesetz begegnete bei den Beratungen deshalb anfangs erheblichen Irritationen. Befürchtet wurde vor allem ein "Hin und Her" zwischen Schiedsgericht und Gericht, welches dem Wesen der Schiedsgerichtsbarkeit als ein in sich geschlossenes Mittel zur Rechtsfindung widerspreche.[555] Die Kommission hat den so vorgetragenen Bedenken jedoch eine Absage erteilt - dies wohl zurecht, handelt es sich bei der Möglichkeit der Aussetzenung des Verfahrens doch um eine sinnvolle Alternative zur Aufhebung des Schiedsspruchs durch das angerufene Gericht. Den Gerichten steht mit Ausnahme der beschränkten Möglichkeiten nach Art. 33 Modellgesetz keine Möglichkeit zur Verfügung, einen fehlerhaften Schiedsspruch abzuändern bzw. eine solche Abänderung zu verfügen. Rechtsfolge der Fehlerhaftigkeit im Sinne von Art. 34 Modellgesetz wäre also immer die Aufhebung des Schiedsspruchs. Dies erscheint zumindest dann, wenn der Fehler noch behebbar ist, nicht im Interesse der Parteien an einem zügigen und kostengünstigen Ergebnis. Dem Schiedsgericht wird durch die Aussetzung des staatlichen Verfahrens die Möglichkeit eröffnet, durch eine Korrektur seiner Fehler den Parteien die bisherigen "Früchte" des Verfahrens zu erhalten.

Art. 34 Abs. 4 Modellgesetz darf auch nicht dahingehend mißverstanden werden, daß das Schiedsgericht bei einer Rückverweisung des Schiedsspruchs vom Gericht zu einer Wiederaufnahme des Verfahrens oder zur Einleitung bestimmter Maßnahmen verpflichtet wäre. So spricht die Vorschrift schon nicht von einer

555 UN-Doc. A/CN. 9/SR. 318, para 78.

"Rückverweisung" im technischen Sinn.[556] Vielmehr kann das Gericht die Klage "aussetzen, und dadurch dem Schiedsgericht Gelegenheit geben"[557], die Gründe für die Aufhebungsklage zu beseitigen. Damit lebt zwar die Entscheidungsbefugnis des Schiedsgerichts wieder auf.[558] Es ist jedoch nicht davon auszugehen, daß das Schiedsgericht von Amts wegen das Verfahren wieder aufzunehmen und die geeigneten Maßnahmen zu treffen hat. Der Wortlaut des Art. 34 Abs. 4 Modellgesetz ("Gelegenheit") spricht vielmehr dafür, daß das Schiedsgericht in keiner Weise verpflichtet ist, überhaupt tätig zu werden.

Wichtig ist weiter die Frage, ob das Gericht dem Schiedsgericht irgendwelche Vorgaben oder Auflagen bezüglich der gerügten Mängel machen kann. Die Frage ist zu verneinen.[559] Wiederum spricht der Wortlaut des Art. 34 Abs. 4 Modellgesetz ("Maßnahmen [...] nach Auffassung des *Schieds*gerichts") gegen irgendwelche Befugnisse der Gerichte hinsichtlich der verbindlichen Anordnung durchzuführender Maßnahmen. Damit folgt auch Art. 34 dem grundlegenden Prinzip des Modellgesetzes, wonach Anweisungen und Auflagen seitens des staatlichen Gerichts gegenüber dem Schiedsgericht nicht vorgesehen sind.[560]

Damit bleibt festzuhalten, daß nach Art. 34 Abs. 4 Modellgesetz dem Schiedsgericht zwar die Möglichkeit der Heilung der in Art. 34 Abs. 2 Modellgestz genannten Mängel ermöglicht wird. Eine damit einhergehende Befugnis der Gerichte zur verbindlichen Anordnung von Maßnahmen ist jedoch nicht vorgesehen.[561]

3. *Frist*

Das Modellgesetz sieht in Art. 34 Abs. 3 eine Frist von drei Monaten für die Einlegung der Aufhebungsklage vor. Diese vergleichsweise kurze Frist gewährleistet ein Höchstmaß an Rechtssicherheit mit Blick auf den unanfechtbaren Be-

---

556 Insoweit unzutreffend die Ausführungen von Hüßlein-Stich, S. 188 f, oder von Calavros, S. 163 ff.

557 Vgl. Art. 34 Abs. 4 Modellgesetz.

558 Vgl. Nöcker, S. 166, m. w. N..

559 So auch Nöcker, S. 166 und Calavros, S. 165.

560 Vgl. UN-Doc. 19 A/CN. 9/245, para 154; bei Holtzmann/Neuhaus, S. 920, heißt es dazu:
"[I]nstructions would be inappropriate; [...] it may be guessed that it was thought that providing for such instructions would tend to make the arbitral tribunal an organ of the court rather than a party-structured dispute resolution mechanism."

561 Unverbindliche Vorschläge des Gerichts stellen dagegen eine durchaus sinnvolle und auch zulässige Alternative dar. Hier bietet sich eine konkrete Möglichkeit zu einer fruchtbaren Zusammenarbeit von Gericht und Schiedsgericht.

stand des Schiedsspruchs.[562] Art. 34 Abs. 3 Modellgesetz ist zwingendes Recht.[563]

4. *Schicksal der Schiedsvereinbarung*

Art. 34 Modellgesetz regelt primär nur die Gültigkeit des Schiedsspruchs. Das Schicksal der Schiedsvereinbarung ist dort hingegen nicht geregelt. Soll also das Schiedsgericht auch nach erfolgreicher Aufhebungsklage noch zur Streitentscheidung berufen sein? Dies wird man mit Sicherheit nur verneinen können, soweit der Grund für die Aufhebung in der Ungültigkeit der Schiedsklausel liegt. Gleiches gilt, wenn die Parteien die Schiedsvereinbarung einvernehmlich aufheben. Ansonsten aber wird nicht klar, welche Auswirkungen die Aufhebung des Schiedsspruchs auf die Gültigkeit der Schiedsvereinbarung hat. In der Literatur wird zum Teil die Ansicht vertreten, daß rein logisch die Aufhebung des Schiedsspruches das Schiedsverfahren in den Stand zurückversetzen müßte, den dieses kurz vor der Verkündung des Schiedsspruches hatte.[564]

Die *trauvaux preparatoires* lassen keinen sicheren Schluß auf das Schicksal der Schiedsvereinbarung zu. Zwar wurde die Frage in den Beratungen erörtert. So war zunächst vorgesehen, den Parteien eine dreimonatige Frist einzuräumen, innerhalb derer sie die Wiedereinsetzung des Schiedsgerichts hätten verlangen können.[565] Die entsprechende Klausel wurde jedoch ohne weitere Begründung wieder verworfen.

IV. Zwischenergebnis

Das Modellgesetz beschränkt die gerichtlichen Eingriffsbefugnisse gegen einen Schiedsspruch auf ein Minimum. Überprüfungen von Schiedssprüchen auf inhaltliche Fehler sind - sieht man einmal vom *ordre public*-Vorbehalt ab - generell ausgeschlossen. Solche wegen verfahrensrechtlicher Mängel werden enumerativ in Art. 34 Modellgesetz genannt. Sie sind begrenzt auf schwere Verfahrensverstöße. Eine entsprechende Auslegung hat zudem restriktiv zu erfolgen.

Das Modellgesetz erreicht dadurch eine weitgehende Unabhängigkeit des Schiedsverfahrens von den staatlichen Gerichten. Dies ist grundsätzlich zu begrüßen. Gleichwohl birgt ein so konsequenter Ausschluß staatlicher Kontrollbefugnisse auch das Risiko, daß den Parteien keine Handhabe gegen im weitesten

562 UN.-Doc A/CN. 9/264, para 1.
563 Zur Begründung vgl. UN-Doc. A/40/17, para 304.
564 Mustill/Boyd, S. 565.
565 UN-Doc. A/CN. 9/WG. II/WP. 42. Art. 41(4). Voraussetzung sollte auch hier sein, daß Grund für die Aufhebung nicht die Ungültigkeit des Schiedsspruchs war.

Sinne "ungerechte" Schiedssprüche zusteht. Die Verfasser des Modellgesetzes haben die Schiedsgerichte diesbezüglich mit einem großen Vertrauensvorschuß ausgestattet.

C. Das englische Recht vor 1997

I. Einführung

Eines der Ziele des *Arbitration Acts* 1979 war eine Neudefinition des Verhältnisses zwischen Schieds- und staatlichen Gerichten auf der Basis reduzierter staatlicher Eingriffs- und Kontrollbefugnisse.[566] Das Ergebnis der Reform war ein eingeschränktes Rechtsmittelsystem in *s* 1 *Arbitration Act* 1979.[567] Für sich genommen bereits kompliziert erreichte dieses System durch entsprechende Auslegung der Gerichte einen Grad an Komplexität, der von ausländischen Rechtsanwendern kaum noch zu durchschauen war.

Von Kritikern oft übersehen, fußte die Angreifbarkeit von Schiedssprüchen nach dem alten englischen Recht neben *s* 1 *Arbitration Act* 1979 noch auf einem zweiten Standbein. Dies waren die Befugnisse der Gerichte zur Aufhebung eines Schiedsspruchs und zur Rückverweisung an das Schiedsgericht nach den *ss* 22 und 23 *Arbitration Act* 1950.[568]

II. Kontrolle nach dem Arbitration Act *1979*

1. Appeal

a) Questions of law

S 1(2) *Arbitration Act* 1979[569] beschränkte die Möglichkeit eines *appeals* ausdrücklich auf *questions of law*. Tatsachenfragen waren damit ausdrücklich ausgeschlossen.[570] Die Unterscheidung nach Rechts- und Tatsachenfragen war somit relevant für die Kontrollbefugnisse der Gerichte nach dem *Arbitration Act* 1979.[571] Eine Definition der *question of law* sah *s* 1 *Arbitration Act* 1979 allerdings nicht vor. Auch der einschlägigen Rechtsprechung lassen sich hierzu weder

---

566 Kerr, J.B.L. 1980, 178 f.
567 Vgl. *infra* in diesem Kapitel, C.II..
568 Vgl. *infra* in diesem Kapitel, C.III..
569 Ausführlich zu dieser Vorschrift Gibson-Jarvie/Hawker, S. 17 ff.
570 Zu der Rechtslage vor 1979 vgl. Goodhart, Law Quar.Rev. 1955, 402.
571 Schmitthoff, Export Trade, S. 647 ff.

klare Richtlinien[572] noch ein Trend entnehmen.[573] In der verbleibenden Unsicherheit lag eine der Schwachstellen des *Arbitration Acts* 1979. Es war naheliegend, daß die unterlegene Partei Tatsachenfragen als Rechtsfragen zu tarnen versuchte, um so die Restriktionen von *s* 1 *Arbitration Act* 1979 zu umgehen.[574] Schwerer aber wog, daß den Gerichten mangels klarer gesetzlicher Abgrenzungskriterien faktisch ein Beurteilungsspielraum darüber eingeräumt war, was noch bzw. was nicht mehr als Rechtsfrage einzuordnen war. Es war nicht auszuschließen, daß bei der Beurteilung hierüber sachfremde Kriterien wie etwa das Gerechtigkeitsempfinden des berufenen Richters eine Rolle spielten. Zumindest in Grenzfällen verblieb somit eine Restunsicherheit hinsichtlich der Unterscheidung zwischen Tatsachen- und Rechtsfragen.

b) Leave of the court

aa) Einführung

Ein nach *s* 1 *Arbitration Act* 1979 erfolgreicher *appeal* mußte zwei Hürden nehmen. Zunächst einmal mußte er überhaupt durch den High Court zur Verhandlung zugelassen werden. Erst nachdem diese Zulassung (*leave*) erfolgt war, entschied das Gericht in der eigentlichen Sache. Der eindeutige Schwerpunkt der Diskussion um das englische *system of appeal* lag in der Zulassung. Der *Arbitration Act* 1979 unterschied in *s* 1(3) nach zwei alternativen Voraussetzungen für die Zulassung eines *appeals*. Die Vorschrift lautete:

> *"An appeal under this section may be brought by any of the parties to the reference-*
> *(a) with the consent of all the other parties to the reference; or*
> *(b) subject to section 3*[575] *below, with leave of the High Court."*

Nach *s* 1(3)(a) *Arbitration Act* 1979 konnte ein *appeal* also entsprechend einer Parteivereinbarung erfolgen. Dieser Fall war unproblematisch. Zum einen entfiel aufgrund der Parteiautonomie im Falle eines Konsenses jegliches Span-

---

572 Staughton, New L.J. 1979, 920. Grob verallgemeinernd wurden Fragen betreffs des Umfangs oder der Bedeutung eines Vertrages als Rechtsfragen (vgl. etwa *Islamic Republic of Iran Shipping Lines v. Royal Bank of Scotland* [1987] 1 Lloyd's Rep. 266) und solche, die das Verhalten der Parteien betrafen, als Tatsachenfragen (vgl. etwa *Moran v. Lloyd's* [1983] 2 All.E.R. 200) eingestuft.

573 Vgl. aber *Geogas S.A. v. Trammo Gas Ltd.* [1993] Lloyd's Rep. 215 (231).

574 Diplock, Arbitration 1978, 109 *„never ceased to wonder at what an ingenious advocate can dress up as constituting an arguable point of law."*

575 Gemäß *s* 3 *Arbitration Act* 1979 können die Parteien ihr Recht nach *s* 1(3) *Arbitration Act* 1979 ausschließen (vgl. *infra* in diesem Kapitel, B.II.4.).

nungsverhältnis zwischen Schieds- und staatlicher Gerichtsbarkeit. Zum anderen war die Rechtslage nach *s* 1(3)(a) *Arbitration Act* 1979 auch eindeutig: in diesem Falle war zwingend eine Überprüfung des Schiedsspruches durch den High Court vorzunehmen. Es bestanden keine diesbezüglichen Ermessensbefugnisse. *S* 1(3)(a) *Arbitration Act* 1979 hatte kaum praktische Bedeutung. Die Zustimmung der obsiegenden Partei zum *appeal* war regelmäßig nicht zu erlangen.

Von zentraler Bedeutung für den *Arbitration Act* 1979 und damit für das Verhältnis von Schieds- und staatlicher Gerichtsbarkeit überhaupt war deshalb *s* 1(3)(b) *Arbitration Act* 1979. Denn nur dann, wenn ein *appeal* zugelassen wurde, konnte überhaupt eine Kontrolle des Schiedsspruches stattfinden.[576] Wurde die Zulassung verweigert, war der Schiedsspruch nunmehr weitgehend unangreifbar.[577] *S* 1(3)(b) *Arbitration Act* 1979 war somit das "Nadelöhr", welches jeder *appeal* passieren mußte, soweit nicht ausnahmsweise *s* 1(3)(a) *Arbitration Act* 1979 zum Tragen kam.

Die inhaltliche Ausgestaltung der Vorschrift wurde ihrer zentralen Bedeutung allerdings nicht gerecht.[578] Die Vorschrift enthielt lediglich *ein* Tatbestandsmerkmal, welches das gerichtliche Ermessen einschränkte. So mußte die zu klärende Rechtsfrage die Rechte zumindestens einer Partei "*substantially*"[579] berühren können. Zu der entscheidenden Frage nach der Ausübung des gerichtlichen Ermessens nahm *s* 1 *Arbitration Act* 1979 nicht mit einem Wort Stellung. Samuel meint dazu:[580]

> *"The draftsmen of the Act, it appears, either never considered how the leave requirement was going to work, or simply could not think of any satisfactory criteria for it [...] To be fair, it is probably beyond the wit of man to work out satisfactory criteria for distinguishing which types of legal questions should be appealable and which should not. The mistake was in thinking either that no such criteria were needed, or that such could ever be found."*

576 Zur Unterscheidung von *leave to appeal* und *appeal* vgl. auch Charles, Arbitrator 1988, 106; vgl. auch Meisel, Cahiers de Droit 1984, 670 ff.

577 "Weitgehend" deshalb, weil nach *s* 1(6) *Arbitration Act* 1979 eine ablehnende Entscheidung des High Court unter bestimmten Voraussetzungen vom Court of Appeal überprüft werden konnte (vgl. *infra* in diesem Kapitel, C.II.3.).

578 Vgl. auch die Kritik von Donaldson, C.L.P. 1983, 6.

579 Vgl. *s* 1(4) *Arbitration Act* 1979.

580 J.Int'l Arb. 1985, 53 f.

bb) Substantial affection of rights

Eine nur unwesentliche Einschränkung der nach *s* 1(3)(b) *Arbitration Act* 1979 freien Ermessensbefugnisse stellte das Erfordernis der *substantial affection* in *s* 1(4) *Arbitration Act* 1979 dar. Die Vorschrift lautete:

> *"The High Court shall not grant leave under subsection (3)(b) [...] unless it considers, having regard to all the circumstances, the determination of the question of law concerned could substantially affect the rights of one or more of the parties to the arbitration agreement [...]"*

Bei der Zulassung eines *appeals* kam es somit wesentlich auf den Begriff der *substantiality* an. Eine Legaldefinition sah der *Arbitration Act* 1979 nicht vor. Ebensowenig läßt sich der einschlägigen Rechtsprechung eine einheitliche Definition des Begriffs entnehmen. Die praktische Bedeutung von *s* 1(4) *Arbitration Act* 1979 war offenbar gering. Es wurden keine strenge Anforderungen an das Vorliegen von *substantiality* gestellt.[581] Ausreichend schien gewesen zu sein, daß das fragliche Recht den Ausgang des Verfahrens in irgendeiner Weise beeinflussen konnte. An *s* 1(4) scheiterten deshalb lediglich rein akademische Fragen.[582]

Als Zwischenergebnis bleibt damit festzuhalten, daß - abgesehen von der geringen Hürde in *s* 1(4) *Arbitration Act* 1979 - ein Schiedsspruch grundsätzlich in allen Rechtsfragen angreifbar war. Den Gerichten stand hinsichtlich der Zulassung eines *appeals* also ein nahezu uneingeschränktes Ermessen zu.

cc) Ausübung des Ermessens: die Nema-/ Antaios-*Richtlinien*

(1) The Nema

Was der Gesetzgeber versäumt hatte, mußten die Gerichte nachholen. So kam schon kurze Zeit nach Verabschiedung des *Arbitration Acts* 1979 die Frage nach der Ermessensausübung unter *s* 1(3)(b) *Arbitration Act* 1979 vor die Gerichte und wurde schließlich vom House of Lords in oberster Instanz entschieden. In

---

581 *Bulk Oil (Zug) A.G. v. Sun International and Sun Oil Trading Co.* [1984] 1 Lloyd's Rep. 655 (657).

582 Mit den Worten von Donaldson M.R. in *Aden Refinery Co. Ltd. v. Ugland Management Co. Ltd. ("The Ugland Obo One")* [1987] Q.B. 650 (656):
"This subsection is, as is apparent, intended to prevent appeals on academic questions of law, which were a feature of the old special case procedure."
Vgl. auch *Stinnes Interoil GmbH v. Halcoussis & Co ("The Yanxilas")* [1982] 2 Lloyd's Rep. 445; *President of India v. Jadranska Slobodna Plovidba* [1992] 2 Lloyd's Rep. 274.

seinem Urteil zu dem Fall *BTP Tioxide Ltd. v. Pioneer Shipping Ltd. and Armada Marine S.A.* ("*The Nema*")[583] entwickelte das House of Lords Richtlinien, welche die Ausübung des Ermessens nach *s* 1(3)(b) *Arbitration Act* 1979 regeln sollten. Der Fall hatte eine herausragende Bedeutung für das englische Schiedsverfahrensrecht. Er wird nachfolgend kurz dargestellt.[584]

The Nema befaßte sich mit der Charter eines Seefrachtschiffes. Nach dem Chartervertrag sollte das Schiff im Zeitraum April bis Dezember 1979 insgesamt sieben Fahrten von Europa nach Kanada und zurück unternehmen. Aufgrund eines Streiks der Dockarbeiter konnte das Schiff bereits bei seiner zweiten Fahrt nicht nach Zeitplan beladen werden. Durch die eintretende Verzögerung wurde die Durchführung der geplanten sieben Fahrten im vorgesehenen Zeitraum unmöglich gemacht. Der Chartervertrag regelte zwar die Rechte und Pflichten der Parteien für den Fall eines Streiks unter bestimmten Voraussetzungen. Auch wurden zwei Zusätze zu dem Vertrag vereinbart, welche die eingetretene Situation regeln sollten. Die Sache wurde jedoch schließlich vor ein Schiedsgericht gebracht. Im wesentlichen ging es hier um die Fragen, ob Chartervertrag und Zusätze rechtlich untrennbare Bestandteile eines Vertrages waren und ob der Chartervertrag aufgrund des Streiks seine rechtliche Verbindlichkeit verloren hatte.

Das Schiedsgericht befand Vertrag und Zusätze für trennbar und entschied, daß der Vertrag zum Erliegen gekommen war (*frustrated*).[585] Auf Antrag der unterlegenen Partei ließ der Commercial Court die Sache gem. *s* 1(3)(b) *Arbitration Act* 1979 zum *appeal* zu. Goff J. zur Begründung:[586]

> *"I cannot find any other circumstances in this case which should persuade me not to exercise my discretion to grant leave to appeal."*[587]

---

583 [1982] A.C. 724.

584 Siehe auch Donaldson, C.L.P. 1983, 6; Lawrence, N.L.J. 1983, 623; Lewis, Lloyd's Mar. & Com.L.Q. 1982, 271; MacFarlane, B.L.R. 1983, 154; Malek, N.L.J. 1981, 1302; Rhodes, H.K.L.J. 1984, 159; Shenoi, Tex.Int'l L.J. 1982, 258.

585 *The Nema* [1980] 1 Lloyd's Rep. 519.

586 *Ibid*, 521.

587 Seine zugrundeliegende Auffassung bringt Goff J. deutlicher noch in dem Fall *Schiffahrtsagentur Hamburg Middle East v. Virtue Shipping Corp.* [1981] 1 Lloyd's Rep. 533 (538) zum Ausdruck:
"I can find nothing in the Act which indicates that in considering whether or not to give leave to appeal from the arbitrator's award, any limit should be placed on the 'question of law' except that it must be such that its determination could substantially affect the rights of one or more of the parties."

Uber den Court of Appeal gelangte die Sache schließlich vor das House of Lords.[588] Dies wies den vom Commercial Court eingeschlagenen Weg zurück. Kritisiert wurde vor allem, daß die Entscheidung über die Zulassung des *appeals* einzig von *s* 1(4) *Arbitration Act* 1979 abhängig gemacht worden war, ohne bei der nach *s* 1(3) gebotenen Ermessensentscheidung weitere Umstände des Falles zu berücksichtigen.[589] Lord Roskill zufolge hatte sich das diesbezügliche Ermessen an der dem *Arbitration Act* 1979 zugrundeliegenden Überzeugung des Gesetzgebers zu orientieren, Schiedsgerichtsbarkeit wieder zu mehr Autonomie zu verhelfen. Staatliche Eingriffe sollten folglich nur noch restriktiv zuzulassen sein.[590] Die Begründung des Commercial Courts, so Lord Roskill weiter, lade dagegen geradezu zu einem Mißbrauch des *appeals* ein.[591]

Das House of Lords entwickelte deshalb in seinem Urteil die sog. Nema-Richtlinien zur Ausübung des gerichtlichen Ermessens nach *s* 1(3) *Arbitration Act* 1979. Diese werden nachfolgend dargestellt. Die Richtlinien unterschieden zunächst einmal nach Auslegung (*construction*) des streitbefangenen Vertrages und nach dessen grundsätzlicher Gültigkeit, wie etwa im Falle des Wegfalls der Geschäftsgrundlage (*frustration*). Innerhalb der Kategorie Auslegung wurde weiter unterschieden nach sog. "*one-off*"-Klauseln auf der einen Seite und nach Standard-Klauseln, wie sie typischerweise in einer Vielzahl von Verträgen einer bestimmten Art enthalten sind, auf der anderen Seite. Schließlich wurde auch innerhalb der Kategorie *frustration* eine Unterscheidung danach gemacht, ob diese nur die Parteien oder aber auch Dritte unmittelbar betraf.

(a) Auslegung

(aa) "One-off"*-Klauseln*

In Fällen von "*one-off*"-Klauseln bzw. -Verträgen sollte im Regelfall das Ermessen nach *s* 1(3) *Arbitration Act* 1979 dahingehend ausgeübt werden, einen *appeal* nicht zuzulassen. Lediglich in Fällen offensichtlicher Fehlentscheidungen des

---

588 *The Nema* [1982] A.C. 724.

589 *Ibid*, 739.

590 *Ibid*, 742; Lord Diplock führt hierzu auf S. 739 f aus:
"[There are] several indications in the Act itself of Parliamentary intention to give effect to the turn of the tide in favour of finality in arbitral awards [...] at any rate where this does not involve exposing arbitrators to a temptation to depart from 'principles of law'."

591 *Ibid*, 745 f.

Schiedsrichters sollten hiervon Ausnahmen gemacht werden. Lord Diplock stellt fest:[592]

"[In this category] leave should not normally be given unless it is apparent to the judge upon a mere perusal of the reasoned award itself without the benefit of adversarial argument, that the meaning ascribed to the clause by the arbitrator is obviously wrong."

Entscheidend sollte es also darauf ankommen, ob die Auslegung der Klausel *"obviously wrong"* war. Wann von Offensichtlichkeit im vorgenannten Sinne auszugehen war, stand im Ermessen des erkennenden Richters. Und selbst wenn dieser die geforderte Offensichtlichkeit nicht erkennen konnte, sollte die Zulassung eines *appeals* doch auch nur "*normally*" - also im Regelfall - verweigert werden. Dem erkennenden Richter stand es somit frei, die Sache auch in Fällen nicht offensichtlicher Fehler zum *appeal* zuzulassen.

Zusammenfassend läßt sich in Fällen von "*one-off*"-Klauseln sagen, daß hier eine starke Voreingenommenheit gegen die Zulassung gerichtlicher Überprüfungen von Schiedssprüchen bestand. Eine endgültige Sicherheit hierüber hatten die Schiedsparteien allerdings nicht. Die Gerichte behielten in allen Fällen das Recht auf das letzte Wort. Es war dem erkennenden Richter überlassen, wann er einen Rechtsfehler des Schiedgerichts für offensichtlich genug hielt, ihn zu einer Kontrolle durch die das Gericht zuzulassen.

(bb) Standard-Klauseln

Mit Blick auf die Auslegung von Standard-Verträgen und Klauseln befand Lord Diplock:[593]

"[R]ather less strict criteria are in my view appropriate where questions of construction of contracts in standard terms are concerned."

Die Gerichte waren anders als in den vorgenannten *one-off*-Klauseln gehalten, nicht nur in Fällen offensichtlicher Unrichtigkeit, sondern auch in anderen Fällen eine Überprüfung von Auslegungsfragen durch die Gerichte zuzulassen.[594] Die Entscheidung des Schiedsgerichts mußte also nicht "*obviously wrong*" sein. Es reichte hier schon, wenn diese "*likely wrong*" oder "*probably wrong*" war.[595]

---

592 *The Nema* [1982] A.C. 724.
593 *The Nema* [1982] A.C. 743.
594 Vgl. hierzu nachfolgend in diesem Kapitel.
595 Vgl. auch Jaffe, Tex.Int'l L.J. 1989, 75.

Diese Unterscheidung basierte auf der Überzeugung, daß gerade Standard-Verträge und -Klauseln einer einheitlichen Rechtsprechung hinsichtlich ihrer Gültigkeit und Auslegung bedurften. Als Grund wurde unter anderem angeführt, daß in der Wirtschaft ein Bedürfnis nach einer einheitlichen Auslegung solcher Standardverträge und Klauseln bestand, diese aber nur durch eine einheitliche Rechtsprechung der Gerichte gewährleistet werden konnte.[596] War somit das angerufene Gericht der Auffassung, daß die Beantwortung der aufgeworfenen Frage "*significantly to the clarity and certainty of English commercial law*"[597] beitragen würde, dann sprach dies für eine Zulassung des *appeals*. Jedoch sollte es auch hier darauf ankommen, daß der Schiedsrichter in erkennbarer Weise falsch entschieden hatte.[598] Entscheidend kam es also darauf an, *wie* erkennbar falsch die Entscheidung des Schiedsrichters gewesen sein mußte. Offensichtlichkeit wie in den *one-off*-Fällen wurde nicht gefordert; ansonsten entfiele bereits der Grund für eine Unterscheidung zu den Standard-Klausel-Fällen. Wenngleich sich dem englischen Fallrecht auch keine annähernd exakte Bestimmung hinsichtlich des geforderten Grades der Erkennbarkeit entnehmen läßt, eines schien doch klar: Solange die umstrittene Frage nur von grundsätzlichem Interesse für das englische *commercial law* war, mußte mit einem Eingreifen der Gerichte gerechnet werden.

(b) Frustration, cases of wider significance

Die Kriterien für Fälle von *frustration* unterschieden sich teils von denen im Zusammenhang mit der Auslegung von Verträgen. Vorstehend wurde bereits deutlich, daß sich die Zulassung eines *appeals* unter anderem an der Bedeutung des jeweiligen Falles orientierte. In diesem Kontext ist es auch zu verstehen, wenn danach unterschieden wurde, ob nur die Parteiinteressen betroffen waren oder aber auch die Interessen Dritter. Fälle von *frustration* wiesen nach Ansicht der Lordrichter bereits *per se* eine höhere Wahrscheinlichkeit auf, daß auch dritte Interessen betroffen sein konnten. Konkret wurde das daran festgemacht, daß eine bestimmte Ursache u.U. die *frustration* gleich einer Vielzahl von Verträgen zur Folge haben konnte. In einem solchen Fall sollte sozusagen durch ein "Mu-

596 Vgl. *Skips A/S Nordheim and Others v. Syrian Petroleum Co. Ltd. and Petrofina S.A. ("The Varenna")* [1983] 2 Lloyd's Rep. 592 (597).

597 *B.V.S. S.A. and Another v. Kerman Shipping Co. S.A. ("The Kerman")* [1982] 1 W.L.R. 166 (171).

598 Vgl. *Aden Refinery Co. Ltd. v. Ugland Management Co. Ltd. ("The Ugland Obo One")*1 Q.B. 650 (651).

sterurteil" der Gerichte Klarheit auch für alle dritten Parteien zu anderen Schiedsvereinbarungen gelten. Hierzu führt Lord Diplock aus:[599]

> *"Where such is the case it is in the interests of legal certainty that there should be some uniformity in the decisions of arbitrators as to the effect [...] of such an event upon similar transactions, in order that other traders may be sufficiently certain where they stand as to be able to close their own transactions without recourse to arbitration. In such a case [...] it might be a proper exercise of the judge's discretion to give leave to appeal in order to express a conclusion as to the frustrating effect of the event that would afford guidance binding upon the arbitrators in other arbitrations arising out of the same event, if the judge thought that in the particular case in which leave to appeal was sought the conclusion reached by the arbitrator, although not deserving to be stigmatised as one which no reasonable person could have reached was, in the judges view, not right."*

Wie sich aus den letzten beiden Halbsätzen des Zitates ergibt, waren an eine Zulassung von Fällen grundlegender Bedeutung deutlich geringere Voraussetzungen zu knüpfen als an einfach gelagerte "*one-off*"-Fälle. Ausreichend war danach, wenn der Richter von der nicht erforderlichenfalls offensichtlichen Unrichtigkeit des Schiedsspruches ausging, ohne daß diese Überzeugung freilich ganz zweifelsfrei die einzig richtige sein mußte ("*not [...] one which no reasonable person could have reached*").[600] Faktisch hatten die Gerichte in solchen Fällen freies Ermessen. Soweit sie der Auffassung waren, daß die aufgeworfene Rechtsfrage Bedeutung über den konkreten Fall hinaus hatte, waren sie geradezu angehalten, den *appeal* zuzulassen.

(2) The Antaios

In dem Fall *Antaios Compania Naviera S.A. v. Salen Rederierna A.B.* ("*The Antaios*")[601] hatte das House of Lords erneut Gelegenheit, zu der nach *s* 1(3)(b) *Arbitration Act* 1979 geforderten Ermessensausübung Stellung zu nehmen.[602] Wieder ging es im Zusammenhang mit der Charter eines Schiffes um die Auslegung einer Vertragsbruchklausel. Das House of Lord bestätigte zunächst die in *The Nema* zu Standard-Klauseln entwickelte Rechtsprechung.[603] Gleichzeitig wurde

---

599 *The Nema* [1982] A.C. 744.

600 Parker J. verstand das Merkmal "*[i]n the judge's view*" folgerichtig auch als "*in the judge's provisional view*" (vgl. *The Kerman* [1982] 1 W.L.R. 173).

601 *Antaios Compania Naviera S.A. v. Salen Rederierna A.B.* [1985] A.C. 191.

602 Zur weiteren Entwicklung des englischen Fallrechts nach der Entscheidung in *The Antaios* vgl. Samuel, J.Int'l Arb. 1988, 9 ff.

603 Ausführlich Thomas, J.B.L. 1985, 200.

diese in einem wesentlichen materiellrechtlichen[604] Punkt erweitert. So sollte ein *appeal* auch dann zugelassen werden, wenn es zu der streitigen Frage uneinheitliche unterinstanzliche Rechtsprechung gab. Zur Begründung wurde angeführt, daß nur auf diese Weise das Ziel der Einheitlichkeit des *commercial laws* erreicht werden konnte.[605]

dd) Zwischenergebnis

Dem *Arbitration Act* 1979 lag das gesetzgeberische Ziel zugrunde, eine Stärkung der schiedsgerichtlichen Autonomie durch die Einschränkung gerichtlicher Kontrolle zu erreichen.[606] Mit Blick auf das Kernstück der Reform, *s* 1(2)-(4) *Arbitration Act* 1979, wurde dieses Ziel jedoch nur sehr bedingt erreicht.

Zunächst ist festzuhalten, daß der *Arbitration Act* 1979 in *s* 1(2) ein genelleres und uneingeschränktes Revisionsrecht vorsah ("*on any question of law*"). *S* 1(3) *Arbitration Act* 1979 sollte die Funktion zufallen, dieses generelle Revisionsrecht zu limitieren. Es ist bezeichnend für das englische Verständnis von der Rolle der Gerichte in der Schiedsgerichtsbarkeit, daß die Limitierung in das Ermessen der Gerichte gestellt wurde. Vorgaben jeglicher Art, wie diese Ermessensausübung stattzufinden hatte, sah der *Act* nicht vor. *S* 1(3) *Arbitration Act* 1979 konnte seiner angedachten Funktion somit nicht gerecht werden.

Auch die *Nema-/Antaios*-Richtlinien waren nur bedingt geeignet, staatliche Eingriffe in das Schiedsverfahren wirksam und im Einzelfall vorhersehbar zu begrenzen.[607] Grundsätzlich darf bereits nicht übersehen werden, daß es sich dabei nicht um zwingendes Recht, sondern vielmehr um Richtlinien ("*guidelines*") handelte. Als solche hatten diese zwar unbestritten argumentativen, jedoch keinen zwingenden Charakter. Lord Denning bringt dies wie folgt auf den Punkt:[608]

> *"[T]he judge has in law a complete discretion. Useful as guidelines often are, nevertheless it must be remembered that they are only guidelines. They are not barriers. You can step over guidelines without causing them any harm. You can move them, if need be, to suit the occasion. So let each case depend on its circumstances."*

---

604 *The Antaios* behandelte auch Verfahrensfragen. So sollte beispielsweise bei der Anhörung zu einem Antrag auf Zulassung der mündliche Vortrag der Parteien nur noch begrenzt auf die "*nature of the question of law*" zulässig sein ([1985] A.C. 207).

605 *The Antaios* [1985] A.C. 204.

606 Commercial Court Committee, Report on Arbitration, S. 1

607 Vgl. auch Shenoi, Tex.Int'l L.J. 1982, 267.

608 *Italmare Shipping Co. v. Ocean Tanker Co. Inc. ("The Rio Sun")* 1 W.L.R. 1982, 158 (162).

Die Bedeutung der Richtlinien mußte aber auch dann zweifelhaft erscheinen, wenn man einmal ihren verbindlichen Charakter unterstellte. Denn es handelte sich bei Ihnen um eine Aufzählung und Kategorisierung bestimmter Faktoren und Umständen, welche bei der Ermessensausübung zu berücksichtigen waren. Diese Aufzählung war jedoch keineswegs vollständig. Sie hat diesen Anspruch auch nie erhoben.[609] Soweit der zu entscheidende Fall nicht durch die Richtlinien geregelt war, hatte der erkennende Richter hinsichtlich seiner Ermessensausübung keinerlei Vorgaben. In der Ausübung seines Ermessens war er folglich ungebunden.

Fiel ein Sachverhalt in den Anwendungsbereich der Richtlinien, stellte sich oftmals das Problem seiner Kategorisierung. So hing der Erfolg eines Zulassungsantrags oftmals von der Einstufung der streitgegenständlichen Klausel als "*one-off*"- oder als Standardklausel ab. Da es sich hierbei jedoch nicht um in jedem Falle klar trennbare Kategorien handelte, hing das Ergebnis oftmals vom Zufall ab.

Innerhalb der "*one-off*"-Klauseln war nie deutlich geworden, wann eine Auslegung durch den Schiedsrichter "*obviously wrong*" war. Schwieriger noch war die Einstufung einer Standard-Klausel als "*likely wrong*" oder "*probably wrong*". In beiden Kategorien galt, daß vor allem in schwierigen Rechtsfragen eine solche Einstufung nicht ohne weiteres im einfachen Anhörungsverfahren getroffen werden konnte. Die Folge mußte sein, daß schwierige Rechtsfragen im Gegensatz zu einfach gelagerten Rechtsfragen eher selten zum *appeal* zugelassen wurden. Denn die Gerichte waren zumeist nicht bereit, bei solch schwierigen Rechtsfragen eine Entscheidung des Schiedsgerichts als "*obviously*" oder "*likely wrong*" einzustufen.

Die Regelung der Zulassung des *appeals* vermochte somit nicht zu überzeugen. Sowohl die Weigerung des englischen Gesetzgebers, das entsprechende Recht zum *appeal* klar zu begrenzen als auch die Auslegung von *s* 1 *Arbitration Act* 1979 durch eine verwirrende und weich kategorisierende Rechtsprechung behinderten die Autonomie des Schiedsverfahrens.

c) Entscheidung des Gerichts

Hatte der *appeal* die Hürde der Zulassung genommen, entschied der High Court nun in der eigentlichen Sache. Während die Zulassung nur unter mehr oder weniger strengen Voraussetzungen erfolgte, erging die Entscheidung in der Sache einzig unter dem Aspekt, ob ein Rechtsfehler vorlag. Dabei wurde nicht nach schwe-

609 *Bulk Oil (Zug) A.G. v. Sun International Ltd. and Sun Oil Trading Co.* [1983] 2 Lloyd's Rep. 587 (589).

ren oder geringen, offensichtlichen oder weniger offensichtlichen Rechtsverstößen unterschieden.[610]

S 1(2) Satz 2 *Arbitration Act* 1979 regelte die Entscheidungsmöglichkeiten des High Court in der Sachentscheidung:

"[A]nd on the determination of such an appeal the High Court may by order-
(a) confirm, vary or set aside the award; or
(b) remit the award to the reconsideration of the arbitrator or umpire together with the court's opinion on the question of law which was the subject of appeal [...]"

aa) Bestätigung des Schiedsspruchs

Soweit der *appeal* abgewiesen wurde, geschah dies zumeist durch ausdrücklichen Beschluß, der gleichzeitig ausdrücklich den Schiedsspruch bestätigte.[611] Enthielt der zurückweisende Beschluß keine solche Bestätigung, konnten die Parteien ihn beantragen. Die Bestätigung bezog sich notwendigerweise nur auf den Tenor des Schiedsspruchs. Sie konnte sich zudem auch auf eine andere als die vom Schiedsgericht gegebene Begründung stützen.[612] Die Bestätigung des High Courts mußte sich auch nicht zwingend auf den gesamten Schiedstenor beziehen. Möglich war auch eine bloße Teilbestätigung und die Zurückverweisung des restlichen Tenors an das Schiedsgericht.[613] Die Bestätigung durch den High Court machte den Schiedsspruch jedoch noch nicht vollstreckbar.[614]

bb) Inhaltliche Abänderung des Schiedsspruchs

Der High Court hatte nach *s* 1(2)(a) 2. Alt. *Arbitration Act* 1979 weiterhin die Möglichkeit, den Schiedsspruch inhaltlich abzuändern ("*vary*"). Diese Vorschrift ermöglichte einen Eingriff in das Schiedsverfahren, wie er intensiver kaum denkbar war. Nicht nur wurde die Entscheidung des Schiedsgerichts in ihrer Gesamtheit oder in Teilen kassiert; vielmehr konnte das Gericht nach der genannten

610 *Vinava Shipping Co. Ltd. v Finelvet A.G. ("The Chrysalis")* [1983] 1 Lloyd's Rep. 503 (506).
611 Vgl. etwa *Richco International Ltd. v. Alfred C. Toepfer International ("The Bonde")* [1991] 1 Lloyd's Rep. 136.
612 Vgl. etwa *Empresa Cubana de Fletes v. Kissavos Shipping Co. S.A. ("The Agathon") (No. 2)* [1984] 1 Lloyd's Rep. 183 (192).
613 Mustill/Boyd, S. 617.
614 Vgl. zu den Vollstreckungsvoraussetzungen *infra* Kapitel 11, C..

Vorschrift die eigentliche Entscheidungsfindung an sich ziehen. Mustill/Boyd führen hierzu aus: [615]

"We suggest that such an order will only be appropriate where the variation [...] follows inevitably from the Court's determination of the question of law. Where this is not the case, it is not for the court to speculate as to what the arbitrators decision would or might have been; the proper course is to remit the award for reconsideration, together with the Court's opinion on the question of law."

Zwar war es durchaus möglich, daß zwingend eine bestimmte Entscheidung aus der Rechtsauffassung durch das Gericht folgen mußte. Auch mag man darüber streiten, ob es in solchen Fällen nicht sinnvoll gewesen sein kann, das Gericht diese Entscheidung gleich treffen zu lassen. Eine Notwendigkeit hierfür bestand indes nicht. Denn es war in jedem Fall möglich, den Schiedsspruch an das Schiedsgericht zurückzuverweisen und dieses entscheiden zu lassen. Vor dem Hintergrund der Intensität des staatlichen Eingriffs sowie auch einer möglichen "Mißbrauchsgefahr" durch die Gerichte stellte die Befugnis zur inhaltlichen Abänderung eines Schiedsspruchs somit einen äußerst bedenklichen Eingriff in die schiedsgerichtliche Autonomie dar.

cc) Aufhebung des Schiedsspruchs

Einen ähnlich schwerwiegenden Eingriff stellte die Möglichkeit der Aufhebung des Schiedspruches dar.[616] Die Aufhebung ist von der Rückverweisung des Schiedsspruches an das Schiedsgericht zu unterscheiden.[617] Anders als bei der Rückverweisung hatte das Schiedsgericht bei der Aufhebung keine Möglichkeit einer Korrektur des Schiedsspruches mehr. Dieser wurde vielmehr für gesamtnichtig erklärt.

Problematisch erscheint in diesem Zusammenhang, welche Auswirkungen die Aufhebung für die Schiedsvereinbarung hatte.[618] Theoretisch mußte die Schieds*vereinbarung* von der Aufhebung unberührt und die Parteien damit auch weiter an diese gebunden gewesen sein. Schließlich wurde lediglich der Schiedsspruch, nicht aber die Schiedsvereinbarung aufgehoben. Das *common law* schien dieser

615 S. 617 unter Verweis auf *River Plates Produkts Netherlands BV v. Etablissement Coargrain* [1982] 1 Lloyd's Rep. 628.

616 Dies ist zwar auch die Rechtsfolge von Art. 34 Modellgesetz. Dabei darf aber nicht übersehen werden, daß das Modellgesetz nur bei schwerwiegenden Verfahrens- und *ordre public* Verstößen überhaupt ein Eingriffsrecht der Gerichte vorsieht, während das englische Recht keine vergleichbare Einschränkung machte.

617 Vgl. *infra* in diesem Kapitel, B.II.i.c)dd).

618 Vgl. auch *supra* in diesem Kapitel, A.III.4..

Logik jedoch nicht folgen zu wollen. Soweit nämlich die Aufhebung des Schiedsspruches nicht mit einer Rückverweisung an das Schiedsgericht verbunden war, wurde gleichzeitig auch das Schiedsgericht seiner Zuständigkeit enthoben.[619]

Eine Analyse des einschlägigen Fallrechts ergibt allerdings, daß nur zurückhaltend und nur bei schwerwiegenden Fehlern von der Aufhebung Gebrauch gemacht wurde. Insoweit unterschied sich das englische Recht praktisch nicht von Art. 34 Modellgesetz. Gleichwohl bleibt festzuhalten, daß die Möglichkeit zur Aufhebung für jeden verfahrens- oder materiellrechtlichen Fehler gleich welcher Schwere und Bedeutung bestand und auch nicht durch das *common law* eingegrenzt war.

dd) Zurückverweisung an das Schiedsgericht

Nach *s* 1(2)(b) *Arbitration Act* 1979 konnte ein Schiedsspruch schließlich mit einer "*opinion*" versehen an das Schiedsgericht zurückverwiesen werden. Der Terminus ist mißverständlich. Tatsächlich ging es nicht um eine (unverbindliche) Meinung des Gerichts. Vielmehr verbarg sich hinter der *opinion* des Gerichts die verbindliche Entscheidung zu der jeweiligen Rechtsfrage.[620] Das Schiedsgericht hatte diese nur noch umzusetzen.

Mustill/Boyd zufolge stellte die Rückverweisung an das Schiedsgericht den *proper course* dar, soweit der High Court einen Rechtsfehler festgestellt hatte.[621] Diese Aussage stand jedoch im Widerspruch zu Teilen der englischen Rechtsprechung. So hieß es etwa in *The Tzelepi*, daß eine Rückverweisung nur dann erfolgen sollte, wenn neben der vom Gericht beantworteten Rechtsfrage noch mindest ein weiterer Punkt der Stellungnahme durch das Schiedsgericht bedurfte.[622] Letztere Ansicht schien eher dafür zu sprechen, daß die Abänderung des Schiedsspruches und nicht die Rückverweisung an das Schiedsgericht der Regelfall war.

2. Anordnung von Begründungen

Anders als nach dem Modellgesetz[623] bedurfte ein Schiedsspruch zu seiner Gültigkeit nach dem englischen Recht keiner Begründung. Da eine Begründung die

---

619 *Stockport Metropolitan Borough Council v. O'Reilly* [1983] 2 Lloyd's Rep. 70.

620 Mustill/Boyd, S. 620 f, erklären den Terminus vor dem Hintergrund seiner historischen Entwicklung.

621 S. 617.

622 *Islamic Republic of Iran Shipping Lines v. Zannis Compania Naviera S.A.* („The Tzelepi") [1991] 2 Lloyd's Rep. 265.

623 Gemäß Art. 31 Abs. 2 Modellgesetz ist der Schiedsspruch mangels einer anderslautenden Parteivereinbarung grundsätzlich zu begründen.

Wahrscheinlichkeit der Angreifbarkeit wegen eines Rechtsfehlers und damit einer möglichen Ungültigkeit des Schiedsspruches eher steigerte, wurde sie deshalb oftmals nicht gegeben. Um aber eine Überprüfung der Schiedssprüche nach *s* 1(2) *Arbitration Act* 1979 zu ermöglichen, bedurfte der High Court einer möglichst umfassenden Begründung. Es ließ sich ja ansonsten nicht feststellen, ob die Entscheidung des Schiedsgerichts rechtsirrig war. Dies zu ermöglichen, war Sinn und Zweck von *s* 1(5)(6) *Arbitration Act* 1979.[624] *S* 1(5) *Arbitration Act* 1979 lautete:

> *"(5) [I]f an award is made and, on an application made by any of the parties to the reference,-*
> *(a) with the consent of all the other parties to the reference, or*
> *(b) subject to section 3 below, with leave of the court,*
> *it appears to the High Court that the award does not or does not sufficiently set out the reasons for the award, the court may order the arbitrator or umpire concerned to state the reasons for his award in sufficient detail to enable the court, should an appeal be brought under this section, to consider any question of law arising out of the award."*

Voraussetzung für eine Auflage nach *s* 1(5) *Arbitration Act* 1979 war entweder ein Antrag aller Parteien oder aber, vorausgesetzt die Parteien hatten keine Ausschlußvereinbarung getroffen, die Zulassung des Antrags durch den High Court. Die Vorschrift folgte in ihrem Aufbau *s* 1(2) *Arbitration Act* 1979. Zu unterscheiden waren also einerseits die Zulassung des Antrags, andererseits die Entscheidung in der Sache selbst. Besondere Zulassungskriterien gab es nicht. In der Praxis wurde nicht zwischen Zulassung und Entscheidung in der Sache unterschieden.[625]

3. On-appeal

Sowohl die Zulassungsentscheidung nach *s* 1(3)(b) *Arbitration Act* 1979 als auch die Entscheidung in der Sache gem. *s* 1(2) *Arbitration Act* 1979 konnten Gegenstand eines weiteren *on-appeals* an den Court of Appeal sein. *S* 1(6A) *Arbitration Act* 1979 erschwerte die Voraussetzungen hierfür jedoch erheblich. So mußte auch der *on-appeal* zunächst zugelassen werden. Erst dann erfolgte die Prüfung in der Sache.

---

624 Staughton, New L.J. 1979, 922.

625 Staughton, *ibid*; *Michael I. Warde v. Feedex International Inc.* [1984] 1 Lloyd's Rep. 310 (311).

4. *Exclusion Agreements*

a) *Einführung*

S 1 *Arbitration Act* 1979 schränkte die Möglichkeit eines *appeals* zwar ein. Wie vorstehend ausgeführt bot sie den Schiedsparteien jedoch keine abschließende Sicherheit hinsichtlich der Endgültigkeit des Schiedsverfahrens.

Dem zu begegnen war die Intention von *s* 3 *Arbitration Act* 1979. Die Vorschrift sollte es den Parteien unter bestimmten Voraussetzungen und Einschränkungen ermöglichen, einen *appeal* gänzlich auszuschließen. Damit hob sie dem Anschein nach den seit *Czarnikow v. Roth, Schmidt & Co.* geltenden Grundsatz auf, *"[that] [t]here shall be no Alsatia where the Kings writ does not run"*,[626] daß also kein Bereich der Zuständigkeit der staatlichen Gerichtsbarkeit gänzlich entzogen werden konnte.[627] Es wird nachfolgend aufzuzeigen sein, ob *s* 3 *Arbitration Act* 1979 tatsächlich einer Umkehrung der *Czarnikow*-Entscheidung gleichkam.

b) *Eingeschränkter Anwendungsbereich*

S 3(1) *Arbitration Act* 1979 enthielt die Zulässigkeitsvoraussetzungen für ein *exclusion agreement*:

> *"Subject to the following provisions of this section and section 4 below-*
> *(a) the High Court shall not, under section 1(3)(b) above, grant leave to appeal with respect to a question of law arising out of an award, and*
> *(b) the High Court shall not, under section 1(5)(b) above, grant leave to make an application with respect to an award, [...]*
> *if the parties to the reference in question have entered into an agreement in writing [...] which excludes the right of appeal under section 1 above in relation to that award [...]"*

Damit nannte *s* 3(1) *Arbitration Act* 1979 eine wichtige Einschränkung der Möglichkeit, staatliche Kontrollrechte auszuschließen. So konnten nur die Kon-

626 [1922] 2 K.B. 478.

627 Mit den Worten von Lord Diplock in *The Nema* [1982] A.C. 740:
"Section 3 gives effect to a reversal of public policy in relation to arbitration as it had been expounded more than half a century before in Czarnikow v. Roth, Schmidt & Co. [...] Exclusion agreements, which oust the statutory jurisdiction of the High Court to supervise the way in which arbitrators apply the law in reaching their decisions in individual cases, are recognised as being no longer contrary to public policy."

trollrechte nach *s* 1 *Arbitration Act* 1979 ausgeschlossen werden. Für alle anderen Kontrollmöglichkeiten, etwa nach dem *Arbitration Act* 1950 oder dem *common law*, behielt die *Czarnikow*-Entscheidung ihre Gültigkeit.[628]

c) Domestic *Schiedsabkommen*

S 3 *Arbitration Act* 1979 unterschied hinsichtlich der Zulässigkeit von *exclusion agreements* nach *domestic* und *international*.[629] Für *domestic* Schiedsabkommen sah *s* 3(6) *Arbitration Act* 1979 folgende Sonderregelung vor:

> *"An exclusion agreement shall be of no effect in relation to an award made on, or a question of law arising in the course of a reference under, an arbitration agreement which is a domestic arbitration agreement unless it is entered into after the commencement of the arbitration in which the award is made or, as the case may be, in which the question of law arises."*

In *domestic* Schiedsabreden konnten die Parteien die staatlichen Kontrollbefugnisse nach *s* 1 *Arbitration Act* 1979 also nicht ausschließen. Hinter dieser Ausnahmevorschrift stand die Befürchtung, daß es im Gegensatz zu den internationalen Schiedsverfahren in den *domestic* Verfahren eher zu einem Ungleichgewicht der Kräfte kommen konnte. Schwächeren Parteien sollte hier nicht der Schutz der staatlichen Gerichte entzogen werden können.

d) Special category disputes

Bedeutender als *s* 3(6) *Arbitration Act* 1979 war als Ausnahmevorschrift zu *s* 3(1) *Arbitration Act* 1979 in der Praxis *s* 4 *Arbitration Act* 1979. Die Vorschrift lautete:

> *"[I]f an arbitration award or a question of law arising in the course of a reference relates, in whole or in part, to-*

---

628 In diesem Zusammenhang waren vor allem *ss* 22(1) und 23(2) *Arbitration Act* 1950 von Bedeutung, wonach ein Schiedsspruch ebenfalls an das Schiedsgericht zurückverwiesen bzw. aufgehoben werden konnte (vgl. *infra* in diesem Kapitel, C.III.).

629 *S* 3(7) *Arbitration Act* 1979 definierte ein *domestic agreement* wie folgt:
"[A]n arbitration agreement which does not provide, expressly or by implication, for arbitration in a State other than the United Kingdom and to which neither-
(a) an individual who is a national of, or habitually resident in, any State other than the United Kingdom, nor
(b) a body corporate which is incorporated in, any State other than the United Kingdom,
is a party at the time the arbitration agreement is entered into."

(a) a question or claim falling within the Admiralty jurisdiction of the High Court, or
(b) a dispute arising out of a contract of insurance, or
(c) a dispute arising out of a commodity contract,
an exclusion agreement shall have no effect in relation to the award or question [...]"

Die drei von *s* 4(1) *Arbitration Act* 1979 genannten Gruppen umfaßten einen Großteil aller in England stattfindenden internationalen Schiedsverfahren. In die "*Admiralty Jurisdiction*" des High Court fielen weitestgehend die Ansprüche im Zusammenhang mit dem Eigentum oder Besitz von Schiffen, deren Betrieb oder sonstigen Nutzung.[630] Ein "*commodity contract*" war nach der Legaldefinition von *s* 4(2)(a) *Arbitration Act* 1979 ein Kaufvertrag über Waren, die auf Waren- oder Rohstoffmärkten gehandelt wurden.

Daß gerade in diesen Fällen keine *exclusion agreements* zulässig waren, minderte die praktische Bedeutung von *s* 3(1) ganz erheblich. Ursächlich für diese Annahme war die Überlegung des englischen Gesetzgebers, daß ein Bedürfnis nach einer einheitlichen Entwicklung des *common laws* zum Handelsrecht bestünde.[631] Diese war seiner Ansicht nur dann zu erreichen, wenn die für die Entwicklung des Handelsrecht als maßgeblich erachteteten Schiedsfälle auch weiterhin staatsgerichtlicher Kontrolle zugänglich waren.[632] Vor diesem Hintergrund wurden diejenigen Kategorien, die möglicherweise am meisten von *s* 3(1) *Arbitration Act* 1979 profitiert hätten, von dessen Anwendungsbereich ausgenommen. Das Einzelfallinteresse der Parteien an einem abschließenden Schiedsverfahren hatte hinter dem Allgemeininteresse an einer einheitlichen Rechtsentwicklung zurückzustehen.

III. Kontrolle nach dem Arbitration Act *1950*

1. Einführung

Neben den Eingriffs- und Kontrollbefugnissen im Rahmen des *appeal*-Verfahrens nach *s* 1 *Arbitration Act* 1979 sah das englische Recht in den *ss* 22(1) und 23(2) *Arbitration Act* 1950 weitere Kontrollbefugnisse der Gerichte vor. Danach konnten die Gerichte unter bestimmten Voraussetzungen einen Schiedsspruch an das Schiedsgericht zurückverweisen oder den Schiedsspruch aufheben.

630 Vgl. *s* 20 *Supreme Court Act* 1981.
631 Vgl. die kritischen Anmerkungen von Mann, Civ.Just.Quart. 1985, 259.
632 *Ibid.*

Die genannten Vorschriften lassen sich in etwa mit Art. 34 Modellgesetz[633] vergleichen. Wie Art. 34 sahen auch *ss* 22(1) und 23(2) *Arbitration Act* 1950 kein generelles Revisionsrecht vor. Die vorgesehenen Rechtsfolgen waren nur für schwere Verfahrensverstöße oder materiellrechtliche Verstöße erheblichen Gewichts vorgesehen.[634] Problematisch war, in welchem Verhältnis die Vorschriften zu *s* 1 *Arbitration Act* 1979 standen. Eine entsprechende Regelung fehlte. Ein bestimmtes Prioritätsverhältnis der Vorschriften zueinander gab es somit nicht. Insbesondere waren die *ss* 22(1) und 23(2) *Arbitration Act* 1950 nicht durch die jüngere *s* 1 *Arbitration Act* 1979 verdrängt worden. Hiergegen sprach die Tatsache, daß die vorgenannten Vorschriften anders als etwa *s* 21 *Arbitration Act* 1950 (*statement of case*) nicht durch den *Arbitration Act* 1979 widerrufen worden waren.

2. *Verfahren*

Wenn auch nicht ausdrücklich genannt, war für ein Einschreiten des High Courts nach *ss* 22(1) und 23(2) *Arbitration Act* 1950 der Antrag einer Schiedspartei erforderlich. Gegen eine Entscheidung des Gerichts war unter der Voraussetzung der Zulassung (*leave of the court*) ein *appeal* an den Court of Appeal möglich.

3. *Abgrenzung zwischen den Rechtsfolgen der Aufhebung und der Rückverweisung*

S 22(1) *Arbitration Act* 1950 lautete:

> *"In all cases of reference to arbitration the High Court or a judge thereof may from time to time remit the matters referred, or any of them, to the reconsideration of the arbitrator or umpire."*

Dem Wortlaut nach anders *s* 23(2):

> *"Where an arbitrator or umpire has misconducted himself or the proceedings, or an arbitration or award has been improperly procured, the High Court may set the award aside."*

Wenngleich *s* 23(2) *Arbitration Act* 1950 anders als *s* 22(1) *Arbitration Act* 1950 ihre Rechtsfolge ausdrücklich an das Vorliegen des Tatbestandsmerkmals

633 Vgl. *supra* in diesem Kapitel, B..
634 Jaffe, Tex.Int'l L.J. 1989, 84 unter Hinweis auf *Re Montgomery Jones & Co. and Liebenthal & Co.* (1898) 78 L.T.R. 406.

"*misconduct*" knüpfte, wurde in der Praxis doch nicht systematisch zwischen den Vorschriften unterschieden.[635] Ob eine Entscheidung des Schiedsgericht aufgehoben oder lediglich zurückverwiesen wurde, beurteilten die Gerichte nach freiem Ermessen, und zwar weniger mit Blick auf die Tatbestandsvoraussetzungen als vielmehr mit Blick auf die Angemessenheit der Rechtsfolge.[636] In Fällen schwerwiegender Verstöße wurde deshalb regelmäßig der Schiedsspruch aufgehoben.[637] Hierbei orientierte sich die Rechtsprechung daran, ob auch ein Urteil unter den gleichen Voraussetzungen aufgehoben worden wäre.[638] Nach Halsbury's wurde ein Schiedsspruch aufgehoben und nicht zurückverwiesen *"[w]here an arbitrator has so conducted himself that a reasonable person would think that there was a real likelihood that the arbitrator could not or would not fairly determine the issues on the basis of the evidence and argument to be adduced before him [or where an award] has been improperly procured, for example by fraud*[639]*."*

4. Misconduct

Die meisten der Fallgruppen, bei deren Vorliegen die Gerichte von der Rechtsfolge der *ss* 22 und 23 *Arbitration Act* 1950 Gebrauch machten, können unter den Oberbegriff *misconduct* subsumiert werden. Andere bildeten eine davon mehr oder weniger getrennte Fallgruppe. Die Grenzen waren fließend. Praktische Bedeutung hatte eine Unterscheidung nicht.

Der Begriff *misconduct* ist bereits an anderer Stelle definiert worden.[640] Anhand der recht allgemeinen Definition ließ sich nicht exakt bestimmen, unter welchen Voraussetzungen die Gerichte *misconduct* im Sinne von *ss* 22 und 23 *Arbitration Act* 1950 annehmen würden. Es haben sich in der englischen Rechtsprechung jedoch bestimmte Fallgruppen herausgebildet, bei deren Vorliegen die Gerichte mit hoher Wahrscheinlichkeit von *misconduct* ausgingen.

a) Bestechlichkeit und Parteilichkeit

In Fällen von Bestechlichkeit oder Parteilichkeit gingen die Gerichte ohne weiteres von *misconduct* aus. Parteilichkeit sollte bereits vorliegen, soweit nur ein ent-

---

635 Mustill/Boyd, S. 547.
636 Halsbury's, S. 401.
637 *Ibid*
638 *Re Fuerst Bros. & Co Ltd. and Stephenson* [1951] 1 Lloyd's Rep. 429; *Modern Engineering (Bristol) Ltd. v. C. Miskin & Son Ltd.* [1981] 1 Lloyd's Rep. 135.
639 Halsbury's, S. 402.
640 Vgl. *supra* Kapitel 5, C.III.2.a).

sprechendes Risiko bestand.[641] In einem solchen Fall bot sich neben der Möglichkeit der Aufhebung des Schiedsspruchs noch die Entfernung des betroffenen Schiedsrichters aus seinem Amt nach *s* 23 (1) *Arbitration Act* 1950 an.[642]

b) Verletzung der Informationspflicht, des rechtlichen Gehörs und des Gleichbehandlungsgrundsatzes

Die englischen Gerichte nahmen ferner *misconduct* an, soweit das Schiedsgericht Informationen, gleich welcher Art (z.B. schriftliche Stellungnahme, Zeugenvernehmung etc.), einer Partei akzeptierte ohne die Gegenpartei davon in Kenntnis zu setzen.[643] Gleiches galt, soweit versäumt worden war, relevante Dokumente zu übersetzen.[644]

c) Verstoß gegen die Gebote von Fairness und natural justice

Misconduct stellte ferner dar, wenn gegen das Gebot von Fairness und das Pinzip von *natural justice* verstoßen wurde. Eine inhaltliche Unterscheidung zwischen beiden Begriffen wurde nicht vorgenommen.[645] Der Begriff der Fairness war nicht ersichtlich weiter gefaßt als der der *natural justice*. Er war allerdings "untechnischer" und wurde somit den besonderen Gegebenheiten eines Schiedsverfahrens eher gerecht. Ein Verstoß gegen das Fairnessgebot konstituierte zumeist auch einen solchen gegen das Prinzip von *natural justice*. Eine abschließende Definition von *natural justice* würde über das Thema dieser Arbeit hinausgehen.[646] Letztlich kumulieren alle grundlegenden Verfahrensprinzipien, wie beispielsweise das des rechtlichen Gehörs, in *natural justice*. Erforderlich ist, daß die Ordnungsmäßigkeit des Verfahrens den Parteien auch zu jedem Zeitpunkt erkennbar ist.

d) Excess of jurisdiction

Hatten die Parteien keine gültige Schiedsvereinbarung getroffen oder hatte das Schiedsgericht seine Kompetenzen überschritten, konnte der Schiedsspruch eben-

---

641 *Bremer Handesgesellschaft m.b.H. v. Ets Soules et Cie and Anthony Scott* [1985] 1 Lloyd's Rep. 160 (164).

642 Vgl. *supra* Kapitel 5, C.III.. Eine Rückverweisung an den belasteten Schiedsrichter war in diesen Fällen zwar theoretisch denkbar, praktisch jedoch ausgeschlossen.

643 *Bache v. Billingham* (1894) 1 Q.B. 107.

644 *Rotheray & Sons Ltd. v. Carlo Bedarida & Co* [1961] 1 Lloyd's Rep 220.

645 Mustill/Boyd, S. 551, bevorzugen den Fairnessbegriff.

646 Vgl. aber Saville, Arb.Int'l 1997, 238; Hepburn, Aust.Bus.L.Rev. 1993, 43.

falls mit der Rechtsfolge der *ss* 22 und 23 *Arbitration Act* 1950 angegriffen werden.

Teils wird ein solcher *excess of jurisdiction* neben, teils als Untergruppe zum *misconduct* genannt. Die systematische Einordnung ist jedoch ohne Bedeutung. Mustill/Boyd kritisieren dabei zutreffend, daß ein Schiedsspruch, der unter Verletzung von Zuständigkeitsvereinbarungen zustandegekommen sei, schon *per se* keinerlei rechtliche Wirkung haben konnte.[647] Deshalb wäre auch das Nichtigkeitsfeststellungsurteil und nicht die Aufhebung die angemessene Rechtsfolge gewesen.[648]

e) *Inkompetenz und schlechte Verfahrensführung*

In *Pratt v. Swanmore Builders Ltd. and Baker* war entschieden worden, daß auch die Inkompetenz eines Schiedsrichters - zumindest im Zusammenhang mit einer *holding out of expertise* - *misconduct* darstellen konnte.[649] Ob und in welchen Fällen eine nicht notwendigerweise offensichtliche Inkompetenz für sich allein bereits *misconduct* begründete, bleibt weitgehend unklar. Das *common law* schweigt zu dieser Frage.

Offensichtliche Inkompetenz stellte dagegen auch für sich genommen *misconduct* dar. Offensiche Inkompetenz lag nach der Rechsprechung jedenfalls dann vor, wenn das Schiedsverfahren so sehr beeinträchtigt worden war "*that there [was] no reasonable prospect of justice being done, if it [was] permitted to continue.*"[650] Mustill/Boyd legten die Meßlatte niedriger. Ihrer Ansicht nach sollte es ausreichen, wenn der Mangel an Fähigkeit, Erfahrung und Sorgfalt des Schiedsrichters oder an souveräner Verfahrensführung ein Ausmaß erreicht hatte, daß die Erwartung der Parteien diesbezüglich nicht mehr erfüllt werden konnte.[651]

In engem Zusammenhang mit dem Vorwurf der Inkompetenz stand derjenige der schlechten Verfahrensführung (*mishandling*). In *Williams v. Wallis and Cox* setzte der High Court *mishandling* dann *misconduct* gleich, wenn "*such a mishandling of the arbitration [...] is likely to amount to some substantial miscar-*

---

647 Mustill/Boyd, S. 554 unter Hinweis auf *Prodexport State Co. for Foreign Trade v. E.D. and F. Man Ltd.* [1972] 2 Lloyd's Rep. 375 (382).

648 *Ibid.*

649 [1980] 2 Lloyd's Rep 504.

650 *Ibid*, 509.

651 *Bremer Handelsgesellschaft mbH v. Ets Soules et Cie and Anthony G Scott* [1985] 1 Lloyd's Rep 160 (164).

riage of justice."[652] Hier wurde also auf die Summe aller Verfahrensfehler unabhängig von ihrer Einzelfallbedeutung abgestellt.

f) Verletzung der schiedsrichterlichen Hinweispflicht

Nach dem englischen *common law* unterlagen die Schiedsgerichte im laufenden Verfahren einer Hinweis- und Informationspflicht hinsichtlich der Beweiswürdigung und vorläufigen Einschätzung der Erfolgsaussichten der Parteien.[653] Den Parteien sollte so ermöglicht werden, durch entsprechende Verfahrenshandlungen auf die aktuelle Entwicklung des Verfahrens zu reagieren. Die englische Rechtsprechung zu der Frage, ob die Verletzung der Informationspflicht *misconduct* begründete, war uneinheitlich. Während Teile der Rechtsprechung einem dahinlautenden Prinzip eine Absage erteilten, nahmen andere *misconduct* unter den geschilderten Voraussetzungen an.[654]

g) Eingestandene Fehler

Der High Court konnte einen Schiedsspruch ferner dann an das Schiedsgericht zurückweisen, wenn, ohne daß ein Fall von *misconduct* vorgelegen hätte, das Schiedsgericht einen Fehler eingestanden und das Gericht um die Möglichkeit der Nachbesserung desselben ersucht hatte.[655] Hierüber befanden die Gerichte dann nach freiem Ermessen. Die Rechtsprechung läßt keine eindeutigen Schlüsse darauf zu, welcher Art der zugestandene Fehler gewesen sein muß. Wesentliche Beschränkungen scheint es nicht gegeben zu haben. Bei der Ausübung des gerichtlichen Ermessens mußten Gerechtigkeitsaspekte gegen den Aspekt der Zügigkeit des Schiedsverfahrens abgewogen werden. Mustill/Boyd führen dazu aus:[656]

> *"A case could be argued for allowing the arbitrator to give effect to second thoughts, at least if the application for remission were made promptly. But we believe this would be a mistake, because it would tend to expose the abitrator to undesirable pressure from the disappointed party to persuade him to think that the Court will give them a second chance. Still less should an arbitrator be allowed to feel that he can or should reopen the reference because the losing party has induced in him a sense of doubt about the correctness of his decision."*

---

652 [1914] 2 K.B. 478 (485).

653 *Faghirzadeh v. Rudolf Wolff (S.A.) (Pty) Ltd.* [1977] 1 Lloyd's Rep. 630 (639).

654 *ICCO International Corn Co NV v. Interbulk Ltd.* [1984] 2 Lloyd's Rep. 66 (75).

655 *MacPherson Train & Co Ltd.. v. J. Milhem & Sons* [1955] 2 Lloyd's Rep 59; *RS Hartley Ltd. v. Provincial Insurance Co Ltd.* [1957] 1 Lloyd's Rep. 121.

656 S. 560, dort FN 19.

Die Praxis der Gerichte sah jedoch anders aus. Deutlich wird dies das durch die folgende Aussage von Lord Donaldson, der zu der gleichen Frage Stellung nimmt:[657]

"[The Court is free to remit an award in] any cases where, notwithstanding that the arbitrators have acted with complete propriety, due to mishap or misunderstanding, some aspect of the dispute which has been the subject of the reference has not been considered and adjudicated upon as fully as or in a manner which the parties were entitled to expect and it would be inequitable to allow any award to take effect without some further consideration by the arbitrator."

h) Neue Beweismittel

Schließlich konnte der High Court einen Schiedsspruch unter bestimmten Voraussetzungen dann zurückverweisen, wenn nach dessen Ergehen neue und möglicherweise relevante Beweismittel gefunden wurden.[658] Wenngleich diese auch keine Fallgruppe von *misconduct* im eigentlichen Sinn darstellt, fällt sie doch in den Anwendungsbereich von *s* 22(1) *Arbitration Act* 1950. Mustill/Boyd legen unter Hinweis auf *The Vimeira (No 2)*[659] folgenden Test zugrunde:[660]

"The evidence must be of weight. It must be such as would probably have a substantial effect, or an important influence on the result of the case having regard, inter alia, to its apparent credibility."

5. Rechtswirkung von Aufhebung und Rückverweis

Wurde der Schiedsspruch zurückverwiesen, erhielt das Schiedsgericht - eigentlich *functus officio* - seine Zuständigkeit und Funktionen zurück. Im Regelfall betraf die Rückverweisung den gesamten Schiedsspruch. Es konnten jedoch auch lediglich Teilbereiche zurückverwiesen werden. Der jeweils zurückverwiesene Teil galt dann zum Zwecke einer erneuten Entscheidungsfindung als aufgehoben. Das Schiedsurteil war nur als Ganzes vollstreckbar.[661] Insoweit war das englische Recht dem Modellgesetz in Art. 34 Abs. 4 vergleichbar.

Das kann dagegen nicht von der Praxis der englischen Gerichte gesagt werden, den Schiedsspruch mitunter auch an ein anderes als das ursprünglich von

---

657 *King v. Thomas Mc Kenna* [1991] 1 All E.R. 653.

658 *Re Keighley, Maxsted & Co. and Durant & Co.* [1893] 1 Q.B. 405.

659 *Aiden Shipping Co. Ltd. v. Interbulk Ltd.. ("The Vimeira (No 2)")* [1985] 2 Lloyd's Rep 377 (400).

660 Mustill/Boyd, S. 561 f.

661 *Johnson v. Latham* (1851) 20 L.J.Q.B. 236.

den Parteien gewählte Schiedsgericht zu verweisen.[662] Diese Praxis verstieß in einem außergewöhlich intensiven Maße gegen das Prinzip der Parteiautonomie. Als Begründung für eine solche Vorgehensweise ist lediglich denkbar, daß sich das ehemalige Schiedsgericht als gänzlich inkompetent erwiesen hatte. Aber auch in diesem Fall war die Aufhebung des Schiedsspruchs das angemessene Mittel, sicher aber nicht die Beauftragung eines fremden Schiedsgerichts.

6. Zwischenergebnis

Wie bereits eingangs des Kapitels erwähnt, waren die Befugnisse des High Court nach den *ss* 22(1) und 23(2) *Arbitration Act* 1950 denen aus Art. 34 Modellgesetz vergleichbar. Dennoch bestanden wesentliche Unterschiede. Grundlegend war folgende Unterscheidung: Während die Aufhebungs- und Rückverweisunggründe nach Art. 34 Exklusivitätscharakter haben, fungierten jene nach *ss* 22(1) und 23(2) *Arbitration Act* 1950 eher als Auffangtatbestand. Sie erweiterten damit noch die Kontrollbefugnisse der englischen Gerichte nach *s* 1 *Arbitration Act* 1979.

Das englische Recht führte im Gegensatz zum Modellgesetz die Gründe für eine Aufhebung nicht einzeln auf. Mit *ss* 22 und 23 *Arbitration Act* 1950 ermöglichte das englische Recht vielmehr eine generalklauselartige Aufhebung und Rückverweisung. Die englische Rechtsprechung zum Begriff des *misconducts* läßt zwar eine vage Kategorisierung erkennen. Dies kann aber nicht darüber hinwegtäuschen, daß es den Gerichten freistand, auch außerhalb dieser Kategorien *misconduct* anzunehmen.

D. Der Arbitration Act *1996*

I. Appeal on a point of law

1. Beibehaltung der alten Rechtsposition

Mit besonderer Spannung war im Vorfeld des *Arbitration Acts* 1996 erwartet worden, ob dieser das bisher in *s* 1 *Arbitration Act* 1979 enthaltene Recht eines *appeal on a point of law* beibehalten oder abschaffen würde.[663] Für die Abschaffung sprach das so nachdrücklich postulierte Ziel der Reform, staatliche Interventionsmöglichkeiten auf ein Minimum zu reduzieren. Wie bereits dargestellt,

---

662 Mustill/ Boyd, S. 567.
663 Harris/Planterose/Tecks, S. 254.

sieht das Modellgesetz keine generelle Möglichkeit zur Anfechtung des Schiedsspruchs auf Grundlage eines Rechtsfehlers vor und entspricht damit dem internationalen Trend der Immunisierung von Schiedsprüchen gegen Angreifbarkeit wegen Rechtsmängeln.[664]

Um das Ergebnis gleich vorwegzunehmen: Wer auf eine radikale Änderung des englischen Rechts in diesem Punkt gesetzt hat, wird enttäuscht. Hier bewahrheitet sich ein weiteres mal die Erkenntnis, daß das englische Recht "*has been slow to acknowledge and respect the autonomy of the parties in this respect*" [gemeint ist der Ausschluß der appeal-Möglichkeiten].[665] *S* 69 *Arbitration Act* 1996 spiegelt, wenngleich mit einer wichtigen Ausnahme,[666] das zuvor nach *s* 1 *Arbitration Act* 1979 und der einschlägigen Rechtsprechung geltende Recht wider. Der Grundsatz bleibt unverändert. So heißt es nunmehr in *s* 69(1) *Arbitration Act* 1996:

> *"Unless otherwise agreed by the parties, a party to arbitral proceedings may [...] appeal to the court on a question of law arising out of an award made in the proceedings [...]"*

Nach wie vor können die Parteien damit grundsätzlich wegen jedes Rechtsfehlers vor die staatlichen Gerichte gehen, um den Schiedsspruch anzugreifen.

2. Leave to appeal

Liegt nicht das Einverständnis aller Parteien zu einem *appeal* vor, bedarf es wie bereits nach der alten Rechtslage der Zulassung der Klage durch das Gericht (*leave*). Anders als nach der alten Rechtslage sind die Zulassungskriterien nunmehr vom *Act* selbst geregelt. *S* 69(3) *Arbitration Act* 1996 lautet:

> *"Leave to appeal shall be given only if the court is satisfied-*
> *(a) that the determination of the question will substantially affect the rights of one or more of the parties,*
> *(b) that the question is one which the tribunal was asked to determine,*
> *(c) that, on the basis of the findings of fact in the award-*
> *(i) the decision of the tribunal on the question is obviously wrong, or*
> *(ii) the question is one of general public importance and the decision of the tribunal is at least open to serious doubt, and*
> *(d) that, despite the agreement of the parties to resolve the matter by arbitration, it is just and proper in all the circumstances for the court to determine the question."*

664 Refern/Hunter, S. 435; Davidson, J.B.L. 1997, 122.
665 Rokison, Arb.Int'l 1998, 363.
666 Vgl. *infra* in diesem Kapitel, D.I.4..

a) Substantial affection

S 69(3)(a) *Arbitration Act* 1996 übernimmt *s* 1(4) *Arbitration Act* 1979 in das neue Recht. Danach sollen Bagatellsachen sowie Rechtsfragen rein akademischer Natur nicht zu einem *appeal* berechtigen. Besondere Abweichungen zum alten Recht bestehen nicht. Es kann deshalb davon ausgegangen werden, daß das Tatbestandsmerkmal der *substantial affection* weiterhin großzügig ausgelegt wird.

b) Gegenstand des Schiedsverfahrens

S 69(3)(b) *Arbitration Act* 1996 enthält keine neue Regelung. Ein *appeal* ist danach nur dann zulässig, wenn die zugrundeliegende Rechtsfrage bereits Gegenstand von Erörterungen vor dem Schiedsgericht war. Unterlegene Schiedsparteien waren offenbar in verstärktem Maße dazu übergegangen, die Begründungen von Schiedssprüchen sorgfältig auf jeden noch so unbedeutenden Rechtsfehler hin zu prüfen, einzig mit dem Ziel, einen "Aufhänger" für ein *appeal*-Verfahren zu finden. Dabei war es ganz gleich, ob der Rechtsfehler einen Punkt betraf, der vorher Gegenstand der Verhandlungen gewesen war.[667] Diesem Mißstand soll nunmehr dadurch begegnet werden, daß nur die Rechtsfragen, die den Parteien erkennbar wichtig gewesen sind, zu einem *appeal* berechtigen.[668] Voraussetzung ist insoweit, daß diese Fragen vor dem Schiedsgericht verhandelt wurden.

S 69(3)(b) *Arbitration Act* 1996 ist ein sinnvoller Versuch, eine ausufernde *appeal*-Praxis einzudämmen.[669] Allerdings besteht die Gefahr, daß die Parteien in den Schiedsverfahren nunmehr möglichst viele - auch scheinbar irrelevante - Punkte ansprechen werden, um sich so zumindest die Möglichkeit für ein späteres *appeal*-Verfahren zu wahren. Dies würde zu einer erheblichen Verzögerung der Schiedsverfahren führen.

c) Übernahme der Nema-/Antaios-Richtlinien

Auch *s 69*(3)(c) *Arbitration Act* 1996 ist auf den ersten Blick neu. Eine vergleichbare Regelung enthielt der *Arbitration Act* 1979 nicht. Bei näherer Betrachtung fällt jedoch auf, daß die genannten Tatbestandsmerkmale weitgehend den Nema-/Antaios-Richtlinien entsprechen. Das ist kein Zufall. Nach dem Wil-

---

667 Rutherford/Sims, S. 212.

668 Vgl. zur alten Rechtlage *Petraco (Bermuda) Ltd. v. Petromed International S.A.* [1988] 2 Lloyd's Rep. 357.

669 Vgl. auch Harris/Planterose/Tecks, S. 256.

len des Gesetzgebers sollten diese Richtlinien, wenngleich in einer extrahierten Form, kodifiziert werden.[670] Dies geschah allerdings nur zum Teil.

Die Richtlinien hatten einerseits nach sog. "*one-off*"-Klauseln und Standard-Klauseln unterschieden, andererseits nach Fragen der Auslegung sowie solchen betreffend die Gültigkeit des Vertrages differenziert.[671] *S* 69(3)(c) *Arbitration Act* 1996 differenziert nur noch nach einfachen Rechtsfragen[672] und solchen "*of general public importance*".[673] Dem erklärten Willen des DAC zufolge ist hierdurch aber keine inhaltliche Unterscheidung zum bisher geltenden *common law*, also insbesondere zu den Nema-/Antaios-Richtlinien beabsichtigt.[674] Vielmehr sind nach dem neuen *Act* Rechtsfragen "*of general public importance*" nichts anderes als Rechtsfragen im Zusammenhang mit Standard-Klauseln.[675] Vormals als "*one-off*"-Klauseln bezeichnete Klauseln sind der neuen Systematik zufolge nunmehr regelmäßig als einfache Rechtsfragen einzustufen.

Es ist nicht klar, mit welcher gesetzgeberischen Intention der Wegfall der Unterscheidung nach Auslegung und Gültigkeit von Verträgen erfolgte. Ein Erklärungsansatz ist, daß aus Gründen der Einfachheit und Übersichtlichkeit auf diese weitere Unterscheidung verzichtet wurde. Da das Recht eines *appeal on a point of law* jedoch insgesamt nicht geändert, sondern eben nur kodifiziert werden sollte, empfiehlt es sich, das *common law* hierzu im Auge zu behalten.[676]

d) Just and proper

Gemäß *s* 69(3)(d) *Arbitration Act* 1996 muß das Gericht zudem davon überzeugt sein, daß die Zulassung des *appeals* als "*just and proper in all the circumstances*" anzusehen ist. Eine entsprechende Vorschrift war im *Arbitration Act* 1979 nicht vorgesehen. *S* 69(3)(d) *Arbitration Act* 1996 soll es den Gerichten ermöglichen, flexibel auf die Einzelumstände eines Falles zu reagieren. Hierzu wird ihnen ein weiter Ermessenspielraum eingeräumt. Diesen zu bestimmen ist in Ermangelung einschlägiger Rechtsprechung nicht möglich.

---

670 Merkin, Arbitration Act 1996, S. 105; vgl. auch Davis, Build. & Constr.L. 1989, 290.

671 Vgl. *supra* in diesem Kapitel C.II.1.b)cc).

672 Vgl. s 69(3)(c)(i) *Arbitration Act* 1996.

673 Vgl. s 69(3)(c)(ii) *Arbitration Act* 1996.

674 1996-Report, paras 286-288.

675 Lord/Salzedo, S. 56, merken jedoch an:
"Nevertheless there will be cases involving standard terms which are not of general public importance and in this regard the new test may be more restrictive as in such cases leave to appeal will only be granted if the arbitrator is plainly wrong."

676 So auch Merkin, Arbitration Act 1996, S. 105.

3. Weitere Voraussetzungen

Weitere Voraussetzungen prozessualer Art für die Zulassung eines *appeals* sieht *s* 70(2)(3) *Arbitration Act* 1996 vor.[677] Danach müssen vor der Zulassung jegliche Möglichkeiten einer Überprüfung bzw. Korrektur des Schiedsspruches innerhalb des Schiedsverfahrens ausgeschöpft sein.[678] Zudem ist eine Antragsfrist von 28 Tagen vorgesehen.[679]

4. Exclusion agreements

Die einzig wirklich bedeutsame Reform des alten *right of appeal* erfolgte im Zusammenhang mit dem entsprechenden Ausschlußrecht der Parteien ("*exclusion agreements*"). Auch nach dem *Arbitration Act* 1979 konnten die Parteien grundsätzlich den Ausschluß des *rights of appeal* vereinbaren.[680] Dieses Recht war jedoch Gegenstand erheblicher Einschränkungen. Besondere Bedeutung kam dabei *s* 4 *Arbitration Act* 1979 zu, wonach für die sog. *special case categories* kein Ausschluß vereinbart werden konnte.[681]

Das Recht der Parteien zum Ausschluß eines *appeals* findet sich nunmehr in *s* 69(1) *Arbitration Act* 1996.[682] Die Vorschrift stellt klar, daß der Verzicht der Parteien auf eine Begründung des Schiedsspruchs dem Auschluß des *rights of*

---

677 Siehe den Verweis in *s* 69(2) *Arbitration Act* 1996.

678 *S* 70(2) *Arbitration Act* 1996:
"An application or appeal may not be brought if the applicant or appellant has not first exhausted-
(a) any available arbitral process of appeal or review, and
(b) any available recourse under section 57 (correction of award or additional award)."

679 *S* 70(3) *Arbitration Act* 1996:
"Any application or appeal must be brought within 28 days of the date of the award or, if there has been any arbitral process of appeal or review, of the date when the applicant or appellant was notified of the result of that process."

680 *S* 3 *Arbitration Act* 1979; vgl. *supra* in diesem Kapitel, B.II.4..

681 Vgl. *supra* in diesem Kapitel, C.II.4.d).

682 *S* 69(1) Satz 1 *Arbitration Act* 1996:
"Unless otherwise agreed *by the parties, a party to arbitral proceedings may (upon notice to the other parties and to the tribunal) appeal to the court on a question of law arising out of an award made in the proceedings."* (Betonung vom Verfasser hervorgehoben)

appeal gleichkommt.[683] Gemäß *s* 5 *Arbitration Act* 1996 muß der Ausschluß des *appeals* schriftlich erfolgen.[684]

Im Unterschied zum alten Recht ist beim Ausschluß von Revisionsrechten nach dem neuen *Act* nicht mehr nach *domestic* und *international* Schiedsvereinbarungen zu unterscheiden. War nach dem alten Recht eine Ausschlußvereinbarung in *domestic* Verfahren nur gültig, soweit sie *nach* Beginn des Schiedsverfahrens getroffen wurde, entfällt diese Einschränkung nunmehr. Zwar hatte der *Arbitration Act* 1996 ursprünglich in *s* 87 die Beibehaltung dieser Unterscheidung vorgesehen.[685] Die *ss* 85 - 87 wurden jedoch nicht in Kraft gesetzt.[686]

Die bedeutendste Änderung im Zusammenhang mit der Neuregelung von *exclusion agreements* durch das neue Recht ist der Wegfall von *s* 4 *Arbitration Act* 1979 und damit der *special categories*.[687] Da ein Großteil der bedeutenden internationalen Verfahren in diese sog. *special categories* fiel, existierte tatsächlich nur ein sehr eingeschränktes Recht zum Ausschluß staatlicher Revisionskontrolle.[688] Durch den Wegfall von *s* 4 entfällt diese Einschränkung. Erstmalig ist es somit den Parteien gleich welcher Art von Schiedsverfahren möglich, staatliche Revisionskontrolle verbindlich auszuschließen.[689]

5. *Entscheidung des Gerichts*

Wie bereits nach dem *Arbitration Act* 1979 unterliegt das Gericht in seiner Entscheidung keinerlei Beschränkungen, soweit der *appeal* zugelassen ist. Auch weiterhin kann das Gericht den Schiedsspruch bestätigen, abändern, zur *reconsideration* an das Schiedsgericht zurückweisen oder aufheben.[690] Neu dabei ist,

---

683 *S* 69(1) Satz 2 *Arbitration Act* 1996:
"An agreement to dispense with reasons for the tribunal's award shall be considered an agreement to exclude the court's jurisdiction under this section."

684 Zur Rechtslage vor 1997 vgl. *Arab African Energy Corporation Ltd. v. Olieprodukten Nederland BV* [1983] 2 Lloyd's Rep. 419.

685 *S* 87(1)(b) *Arbitration Act* 1997:
"[...] [A] domestic arbitration agreement to exclude the jurisdiction of the court under [...] section 69 [...] is not effective unless entered into after the commencement of the arbitral proceedings in which the question arises or the award is made."

686 The Arbitration Act 1996 (Commencement No. 1) Order 1996; vgl. auch Veeder, England, S. 5.

687 Vgl. *supra* in diesem Kapitel, C.4.d).

688 *Ibid.*

689 Beachte aber, daß eine Kontrolle nach *s* 68 (*"serious irregularities"*, vormals *"misconduct"*) nicht ausgeschlossen werden kann.

690 *S* 69(7) *Arbitration Act* 1996 lautet:
"On an appeal under this section the court may by order-
(a) confirm the award,

daß nach dem neuen Recht nunmehr auch die Möglichkeit einer teilweisen Zurückverweisung oder Aufhebung vorgesehen ist. Neu ist ferner die Bestimmung, daß eine (auch teilweise) Aufhebung nur dann erfolgen darf, wenn eine Rückverweisung "*inappropriate*" wäre.

Nicht verändert wurde hingegen das Recht der Gerichte zur Abänderung des Schiedsspruchs. Hier wurde eine dringend gebotene Möglichkeit zur Modernisierung des englischen Schiedsrechts versäumt.

6. On-appeal

Sowohl gegen die Entscheidung des Gerichts über den Zulassungsantrag als auch gegen die Sachentscheidung des Gerichts können die Parteien gemäß *s* 69(8) *Arbitration Act* 1996 einen *appeal* einlegen.[691] Voraussetzung ist in beiden Fällen wiederum die Zulassung durch den High Court. Dabei gilt in letzterem Falle zusätzlich, daß die Sache von "*general importance*" ist oder aus einem sonstigen besonderen Grund vom Court of Appeal behandelt werden sollte.[692]

7. Zwischenergebnis

S 69 *Arbitration Act* 1996 übernimmt im wesentlichen das alte Recht zum *appeal on a point of law*. Die neugeschaffene Möglichkeit eines umfassenden Ausschlußrechts der Parteien ist als einzig wirkliche Reform in diesem Bereich zu begrüßen. Damit gibt *s* 69 *Arbitration Act* 1996 Anlaß zu grundsätzlicher Kritik. Es stellt sich die Frage, ob es nicht sinnvoll gewesen wäre, das entsprechende Recht nach dem Vorbild des Modellgesetzes gänzlich abzuschaffen. Der engli-

---

(b) vary the award,
(c) remit the award to the tribunal, in whole or in part, for reconsideration in the light of the court's determination, or
(d) set aside the award in whole or in part.
The court shall not exercise its power to set aside an award, in whole or in part, unless it is satisfied that it would be inappropriate to remit the matters in question to the tribunal for reconsideration."

691 *S* 69(8) *Arbitration Act* 1996 lautet:
"The decision of the court on an appeal under this section shall be treated as a judgement of the court for the purposes of a further appeal. But no such appeal lies without the leave of the court which shall not be given unless the court considers that the question is one of general importance or is one which for some other special reason should be considered by the Court of Appeal."

692 *Ibid.*

sche Gesetzgeber hat diese Chance versäumt. Rokison führt hierzu in seiner *Freshfield Lecture* aus dem Jahr 1997 aus: [693]

> *"It may seem unfortunate that a statute which has gone so far down the path of recognizing and giving effect to party autonomy has not taken the final step of abolishing judicial review of the merits, whether of fact or of law, especially since it will be some time before further valuable parliamentary time will be allocated to arbitration law reform."*

II. Serious irregularity

1. Wegfall von misconduct

Der *appeal* wegen eines *errors of law* war bereits nach dem alten Recht nicht die einzige Möglichkeit, gegen einen Schiedsspruch vorzugehen. Daneben bestanden nach den *ss* 22(1) und 23(2) *Arbitration Act* 1950 weitere Möglichkeiten, einen Schiedsspruch anzugreifen. Voraussetzung war insofern das Vorliegen von *misconduct.*[694] Der Begriff war jedoch sehr unbestimmt. Auch die Gerichte hatten es nicht vermocht, eine abschließende Definition zu entwickeln. Hinzu kam in den letzten Jahren eine weiter zunehmende Tendenz einer extensiven Auslegung des Begriffs. Die Abschaffung des Begriffs war deshalb vorprogrammiert.[695] Auch mit Blick auf die im Ausland weiter abnehmende Popularität des englischen Handelsschiedsverfahrensrechts erschien die Abschaffung von *misconduct* im englischen Interesse.[696]

Die *ss* 22(1) und 23(2) *Arbitration Act* 1950 werden nunmehr durch *s* 68 *Arbitration Act* 1996 ersetzt.[697] Danach ist zentrale Voraussetzung für ein gerichtliches Eingreifen das Vorliegen einer "*serious irregularity*". So heißt es in *s* 68(1) *Arbitration Act* 1996:

> *"A party to arbitral proceedings may [...] apply to the court challenging an award in the proceedings on the ground of serious irregularity affecting the tribunal, the proceedings or the award.*

Der Begriff der *serious irregularity* ist nicht neu. Bereits im Jahr 1978 war in einem Bericht des DAC vorgeschlagen worden, diesen anstatt von *misconduct* zu

---

693 Rokison, Arb.Int'l 1988, 361.

694 Vgl. *supra* in diesem Kapitel, C.III.4..

695 Bernstein, Handbook, S. 206; Rutherford/Sims, S. 207; Merkin, Arbitration Act 1996, S. 98.

696 Zur Kritik vgl. etwa Rutherford/Sims, S. 208.

697 Wallace, Int'l Constr.L.Rev. 1997, 80, nennt *s* 68 *Arbitration Act* 1996 "*potentially extremely important*".

verwenden.[698] Es fragt sich jedoch, welche Verbesserung der Terminus gegenüber dem des *misconduct* bringt. Denn auch der Begriff der *serious irregularity* bietet für sich genommen keinen hinreichenden Grad an Bestimmtheit. Zekos geht deshalb davon aus, daß die Gerichte auf die Rechtsprechung zum Begriff *misconduct* zurückgreifen werden.[699]

Dies aber hieße im Ergebnis nichts anderes, als die bekannten Schwächen des alten Rechts in das neue zu "importieren". Es darf bezweifelt werden, daß dies der gesetzgeberischen Intention entsprochen hat.[700]

2. Bedeutung und Definition

a) Kumulative Tatbestandsvoraussetzungen

Die eigentliche Bedeutung von *s* 68 *Arbitration Act* 1996 liegt darin, daß die Vorschrift in *subsection* (2) nunmehr eine abschließende Definition von *serious irregularity* vorsieht. Nach dem Vorbild von Art. 34 Modellgesetz enthält *s* 68(2) *Arbitration Act* 1996 eine Liste teils auf bekannten *common law*-Prinzipien basierender Tatbestände. Die Liste ist abschließend. Vor allem dadurch unterscheidet sich *s* 68 *Arbitration Act* 1996 erheblich von den *ss* 22(1) und 23(2) *Arbitration Act* 1950. Die in *s* 68(2) *Arbitration Act* 1996 aufgeführten Anfechtungsgründe sind allesamt prozessualer Art.

Zwei Voraussetzungen müssen kumulativ erfüllt sein, um den Tatbestand der *serious irregularity* zu erfüllen. Zunächst muß zumindest einer der in *subsection* (2)(a)-(i) genannten Anfechtungsgründe gegeben sein. Dieser muß zudem von den Gerichten als so schwerwiegend eingestuft werden, daß dem Anfechtenden "*substantial injustice*" geschieht oder geschehen wird.

b) Substantial injustice

Das Erfordernis der *substantial injustice* ist neu. Die Gerichte sind danach angehalten, ihr Ermessen nur sehr restriktiv auszuüben. Konkrete Vorgaben werden allerdings nicht gemacht. Es ist damit nach wie vor Sache der Gerichte, wie sie ihr Ermessen letztlich ausüben.

---

698 Vgl. Merkin, Arbitration Act 1996, 98.
699 Zekos, J.Int'l Arb. 1998, 70.
700 In diesem Sinne auch Veeder, England, S. 60.

c) *Die einzelnen Anfechtungsgründe*

Gemäß *s* 68(2)(a) - (i) *Arbitration Act* 1996 ist eine *serious irregularity* in folgenden Fällen anzunehmen:

aa) "Failure by the tribunal to comply with section 33 (general duty of tribunal)"

S 68(2)(a) *Arbitration Act* 1996 verweist auf s 33 *Arbitration Act* 1996. Ein Verstoß gegen *s* 33 *Arbitration Act* 1996 konstituiert damit einen Anfechtungsgrund nach *s* 68 *Arbitration Act* 1996. Dieser wurde auch als der vielleicht wichtigste aller in *s* 68 *Arbitration Act* 1996 genannten Anfechtungungsgründe bezeichnet.[701] Mit einer gewissen Wahrscheinlichkeit wird er sich auch als der wohl problematischste erweisen. Denn die in *s* 33 *Arbitration Act* 1996[702] genannten Erfordernisse der fairen und unparteiischen Verhandlungsführung sowie der Pflicht zur Bestimmung einer den Umständen entsprechenden Verfahrensweise kommen wegen ihrer bewußt weiten Fassung zwar dem Schiedsgericht entgegen. Dieses ist weitgehend frei in der Verfahrensführung und nicht an konkrete Vorgaben gebunden. Doch hat es den Anschein, daß durch den Verweis von *s* 68(2)(a) *Arbitration Act* 1996 auf *s* 33 *Arbitration Act* 1996 auch die Gerichte ebenso frei sind in der Bestimmung, was ihrer Ansicht nach eine faire Verfahrensweise darstellt. Hier liegt Konfliktpotential. Es wäre sinnvoll gewesen, die Bezugnahme von *s* 68(2)(a) *Arbitration Act* 1996 auf *s* 33(2)(a) *Arbitration Act* 1996 stärker einzugrenzen.[703] So aber sind die Gerichte faktisch frei in der Annahme eines Fairnessverstoßes. Daraus folgt, daß die Gerichte bei einer entsprechenden Absicht

---

701 Merkin, Arbitration Act 1996, S. 99.

702 *S* 33 *Arbitration Act* 1996 lautet:
"(1) The tribunal shall-
(a) act fairly and impartially as between the parties, giving each party a reasonable opportunity of putting his case and dealing with that of his opponent, and
(b) adopt procedures suitable to the circumstances of the particular case, avoiding unnecessary delay or expense, so as to provide a fair means for the resolution of the matters falling to be determined.
(2) The tribunal shall comply with that general duty in conducting the arbitral proceedings, in its decisions on matters of procedure and evidence and in the exercise of all other powers conferred on it."

703 Offenbar hat das DAC dieses Problem auch gesehen. So heißt es in 1996-Report, para 151:
"It is to be hoped that the Courts will take a dim view of those who try to attack awards because of suggested breaches of this clause which have no real substance. At the same time, it can hardly be suggested that awards should not be open to attack when the tribunal has not acted in accordance with the principles stated."

nahezu ungebunden die Aufhebung eines Schiedsspruches wegen Fairnessverstoßes verfügen können.

bb) "The tribunal exceeding its powers (otherwise than by exceeding its substantive jurisdiction)"

Da sich dieser Grund nicht auf Fälle fehlender *substantive jurisdiction* bezieht,[704] dürfte er in der Praxis keine allzugroße Bedeutung haben. In den Anwendungsbereich der Vorschrift fällt etwa die Anordnung von Zwangsmaßnahmen, zu der die Schiedsgerichte grundsätzlich nicht befugt sind.[705]

cc) "Failure by the tribunal to conduct the proceedings in accordance with the procedure agreed by the parties"

S 68(2)(c) bezieht sich auf *s* 34 *Arbitration Act* 1996, wonach die Parteien die anzuwendenden Verfahrensvorschriften bestimmen können. Probleme sind in diesem Bereich nicht zu erwarten. Ein etwaiger Verstoß ist - auch aufgrund des Schriftformerfordernisses[706] - leicht nachprüfbar.

dd) "Failure by the tribunal to deal with all the issues that were put to it"

S 68(2)(d) übernimmt das *common law*-Prinzip, nach dem ein Schiedsspruch, der nicht umfassend alle Streitpunkte erledigt, an das Schiedsgericht zur Nachbesserung zurückverwiesen werden kann.[707]

ee) "Any arbitral or other institution or person vested by the parties with powers in relation to the proceedings or the award exceeding its powers"

S 68(2)(e) *Arbitration Act* 1996 meint den Fall, daß nicht das Schiedsgericht selbst, sondern eine beauftragte dritte Institution oder Person ihre Befugnisse

---

704 Zur Anfechtung wegen mangelnder *substantive jurisdiction* vgl. *infra* in diesem Kapitel, D.III..

705 Vgl. aber *supra* Kapitel 8.

706 Vgl. *s* 5 *Arbitration Act* 1996.

707 Vgl. *Thomas v. Countryside Council for Wales* [1994] 4 All E.R. 853. Dies gilt nicht, soweit das Schiedsgericht die Sache bei den Beratungen oder der Urteilsfindung berücksichtigt hat, ohne daß dies allerdings einen Niederschlag im Tenor oder in der Begründung gefunden hätte (*Obaseki Bros. v. Reif & Son* [1952] 2 Lloyd's Rep. 264).

überschreitet. Als Beispiel sei hier etwa ein zweitinstanzliches Berufungsschiedsgericht genannt.

ff) "Uncertainty or umbiguity as to the effect of the award"

Dieser Grund kodifiziert das *common law*-Prinzip, daß ein Schiedsspruch frei von Mehrdeutigkeiten und ohne weiteres vollstreckbar sein muß.[708] Wie durch die Worte "*as to the effect*" verdeutlicht, bezieht sich *s* 68(2)(f) *Arbitration Act* 1996 allerdings nur auf den Schiedstenor bzw. auf die für seine Vollstreckung unabdingbaren Bestandteile des jeweiligen Schiedsspruches. Soweit einzig die Begründung des Schiedsspruches nicht diesen Anforderungen genügt, soll dies für sich noch keine *serious irregularity* darstellen.[709]

gg) "The award being obtained by fraud or the award or the way in which it was procued being contrary to public policy"

S 68(2)(g) *Arbitration Act* 1996 kodifiziert den englischen *ordre public*-Vorbehalt. Im Gegensatz zum Modellgesetz müssen hier keine Überlegungen angestellt werden, ob es sich um einen einfachen oder etwa um einen *ordre public international*-Vorbehalt handelt.[710] Da sich der *Arbitration Act* 1996 anders als das Modellgesetz nicht ausschließlich auf internationale Verfahren bezieht, ist von einem "einfachen" und damit strengeren Vorbehalt auszugehen. Die anzuwendenden Maßstäbe sind voraussichtlich die gleichen wie bereits nach der alten Rechtslage.[711]

hh) "Failure to comply with the requirements as to the form of the award"

S 68(2)(h) *Arbitration Act* 1996 bezieht sich auf *s* 52 *Arbitration Act* 1996. Danach gelten bestimmte Mindestanforderungen für die Form eines Schiedsspruches, soweit die Parteien keine anderslautende Vereinbarung getroffen haben.[712]

---

708 *River Plate Products Netherland BV v. Etablissement Coargrain* [1982] 1 Lloyd's Rep. 628.

709 Merkin, Arbitration Act 1996, S. 100.

710 Zur Terminologie und Bedeutung vgl. *supra* in diesem Kapitel, A.II.6..

711 Vgl. Mustill/Boyd, S. 228 f.

712 Für diesen Fall sind als Mindestvoraussetzungen vorgesehen: der Schiedsspruch muß schriftlich ergehen und mit den Unterschriften aller Schiedsrichter versehen werden, er muß eine Begründung enthalten, auf den Sitz des Schiedsgerichts hinweisen, und er muß ein Datum enthalten.

ii) "Any irregularity in the conduct of the proceedings or in the award which is admitted by the tribunal or by any arbitral or other institution or person vested by the parties with powers in relation to the proceedings or the award"

S 68(2)(i) *Arbitration Act* 1996 kodifiziert das bereits nach dem alten *common law* geltende Prinzip, daß das Schiedsgericht durch das Eingeständnis eines Fehlers eine Rückverweisung durch das Gericht erreichen konnte. Die Vorschrift korrespondiert mit *s* 57 *Arbitration Act* 1996. Danach können die Parteien in Ermangelung einer anderslautenden Vereinbarung beim Schiedsgericht beantragen,

"[to] correct an award so as to remove any clerical mistake or error arising from an accidental slip or ommision or clarify or remove any ambiguity in the award [...]"

Das wirft die Frage nach dem Verhältnis von *s* 68(2)(i) *Arbitration Act* 1996 und *s* 57 auf. *S* 68 ist weiter gefaßt. Hier reicht im Gegensatz zu *s* 57 *Arbitration Act* 1996 bereits "*any irregularity*" für einen Rückverweis aus, während *s* 57 *Arbitration Act* 1996 einen "*clerical mistake*" fordert, also einen gravierenden Fehler.[713] Diese Unterscheidung verliert jedoch ihre Bedeutung im Hinblick darauf, daß nach *s* 68(2) *Arbitration Act* 1996 kumulativ auch noch eine "*substantial injustice*" gefordert wird. Im Ergebnis scheint *s* 68(2)(i) *Arbitration Act* 1996 damit nur in den Fällen Bedeutung zuzukommen, in denen sich das Schiedsgericht weigert, dem Antrag einer Partei nach *s* 57 *Arbitration Act* 1996 zu entsprechen.

3. Entscheidung des Gerichts

S 68(3) *Arbitration Act* 1996 eröffnet den Gerichten verschiedene Reaktionsmöglichkeiten auf einen festgestellen Fall von *serious irregularity*.[714] Wie bereits nach dem alten Recht kann der Schiedsspruch zur Korrektur an das Schiedsgericht zurückverwiesen oder aber aufgehoben werden. Neu ist dagegen, daß die Gerichte nunmehr auch die Unverbindlichkeit oder Nichtigkeit eines Schieds-

---

713 Für den Fall einer Mehrdeutigkeit bzw. Unschlüssigkeit verzichtet *s* 57 dagegen auf das Erfordernis besonderer Schwere.

714 *S* 68(3) *Arbitration Act* 1996 lautet:
"If there is shown to be a serious irregularity affecting the tribunal, the proceedings or the award, the court may-
(a) remit the award to the tribunal, in whole or in part, for reconsideration,
(b) set the award aside in whole or in part, or
(c) declare the award to be of no effect, in whole or in part.
The court shall not exercise its power to set aside or to declare an award to be of no effect, in whole or in part, unless it is satisfied that it would be inappropriate to remit the matters in question to the tribunal for reconsideration."

spruches *feststellen* können.[715] Ferner kodifiziert *s* 68(3) *Arbitration Act* 1996 nunmehr ausdrücklich, was bereits nach dem *common law*[716] galt: Die Aufhebung des Schiedsspruchs und die Feststellung von dessen Ungültigkeit darf nur erfolgen, wenn das Gericht eine Rückverweisung an das Schiedsgericht für "*inappropriate*" hält.

III. Substantive jurisdiction

1. *Einleitung*

Schließlich sieht der *Arbitration Act* 1996 in *s* 67 noch eine dritte Möglichkeit des Vorgehens der Gerichte gegen einen Schiedsspruchs vor. Sie betrifft den Fall der mangelnden *substantive jurisdiction*. Die Vorschrift lautet:

> *"A party to arbitral proceedings may [...] apply to the court-*
> *(a) challenging any award of the arbitral tribunal as to its substantive jurisdiction; or*
> *(b) for an order declaring an award made by the tribunal on the merits to be of no effect, in whole or in part, because the tribunal did not have substantive jurisdiction [...]"*

S 67 *Arbitration Act* 1996 muß in Zusammenhang mit *ss* 30 - 32 *Arbitration Act* 1996 gelesen werden. Nach *s* 30 *Arbitration Act* 1996 steht dem Schiedsgericht grundsätzlich die Kompetenz-Kompetenz in Fragen der Zuständigkeit zu.[717] Eine Entscheidung hierüber kann entweder im (Schluß)Schiedsspruch zur Sache oder aber in einem gesonderten Zwischenschiedsspruch ergehen.[718] *S* 67 *Arbitration Act* 1996 ermöglicht den Gerichten eine Überprüfung der Zuständigkeit der Schiedsgerichte auf Grundlage des Schiedsspruchs oder Zwischenschiedsspruchs. Die Vorschrift ist im englischen Recht neu. Zuvor wurden Zuständigkeitsüberschreitungen im Rahmen der Rechtsfolgen der *ss* 22 und 23 *Arbitration Act* 1950 geahndet. Auch war das Vorliegen eines (Zwischen)Schiedsspruch keine Voraussetzung.

2. *Abgrenzung zur* serious irregularity

Es hätte sich möglicherweise angeboten, die Befugnisse der Gerichte aus *s* 67 *Arbitration Act* 1996 zusammen mit denen aus *s* 68 *Arbitration Act* 1996 ("*se-*

---

715 Rutherford/Sims, S. 209; Harris/Planterose/Tecks, S. 251.

716 Vgl. *Miller's Timber Trust Co. Ltd. v. Plywood Factory Julius Potempa Ltd.* (1939) 63 Ll.L.R. 184.

717 Vgl. *supra* Kapitel 6, C.IV..

718 *Ibid.*

rious irregularity") in einer Vorschrift zu regeln - so geschehen etwa in Art. 34 Modellgesetz. Das Ergebnis bleibt jedoch gleich.

Als problematisch könnte sich jedoch die Abgrenzung von *s* 68(2)(b) *Arbitration Act* 1996 ("*tribunal exceeding its powers otherwise than by exceeding its substantive jurisdiction*")[719] und *s* 67 *Arbitration Act* 1996 erweisen. Diese Abgrenzung kann mitunter vor dem Hintergrund von *s* 31 *Arbitration Act* 1996 Bedeutung erlangen. Will danach eine Partei nicht ihr Recht auf eine spätere Anfechtung wegen mangelnder *substantive jurisdiction* gemäß *s* 67 *Arbitration Act* 1996 verlieren, muß sie die Mangelhaftigkeit gleich zu Beginn des Verfahrens rügen.[720] Geht eine Partei daher irrigerweise davon aus, daß es sich nicht um einen *excess of jurisdiction* nach *s* 67 *Arbitration Act* 1996, sondern vielmehr um einen solchen nach *s* 68(2)(b) *Arbitration Act* 1996 handelt, und versäumt sie entsprechend eine Rüge gleich zu Anfang des Verfahrens, steht ihr unter Umständen keiner der beiden Rechtsbehelfe zur Verfügung.[721] Es wird sich in solchen Grenzfällen aus Gründen der Vorsicht daher anbieten, jedenfalls auch die *substantive jurisdiction* zu rügen. So wird das Recht aus *s* 67 "gesichert". Ferner ist es in solchen Fällen mitunter auch ratsam, einen alternativen Klageantrag zu formulieren, der sowohl *s* 67 als auch *s* 68 berücksichtigt.

3. Verletzung der substantive jurisdiction

Voraussetzung für ein Eingreifen der Gerichte nach *s* 67 *Arbitration Act* 1996 ist zunächst das Vorliegen eines Schiedsspruchs, der unter Verletzung der *substantive jurisdiction* des Schiedsgerichts zustandegekommen ist.[722] Anders anders bei *s* 69 *Arbitration Act* 1996 sind bei der Beurteilung nicht lediglich Rechts- sondern auch Tatsachenfragen zu berücksichtigen.[723] Die anfechtende Partei muß den (angeblichen) Zuständigkeitsmangel zudem rechtzeitig gerügt haben.

---

719 Vgl. *supra* in diesem Kapitel, D.II.2.c)bb).

720 Vgl. *s* 31(1) *Arbitration Act* 1996:
"An objection that the arbitral tribunal lacks substantive jurisdiction at the outset of the proceedings must be raised by a party not later than the time he takes the first step in the proceedings to contest the merits of any matter in relation to which he challenges the tribunal's jurisdiction."

721 Merkin, Arbitration Act 1996, S. 97.

722 Dies ist etwa der Fall, soweit keine (gültige) Schiedsabrede zustandekam, eine solche zwar vorliegt, jedoch nicht den fraglichen Streit umfaßt, oder aber soweit die Schiedsrichter nicht ordnungsgemäß bestellt wurden.

723 DAC, 1996-Report, para 143.

4. Entscheidung des Gerichts

Auf einen Antrag nach *s* 67(1) *Arbitration Act* 1996 kann das Gericht den Schiedsspruch bestätigen, abändern oder (teilweise) aufheben.[724]

IV. Anordnung von Begründungen

Nach *s* 1(5)(6) *Arbitration Act* 1979 konnte der mit der Prüfung der Zulassung eines *appeals* befaßte High Court anordnen, daß das Schiedsgericht einen Schiedsspruch nachträglich eingehender begründete.[725]

S 52(4) *Arbitration Act* 1996 schreibt nunmehr eine grundsätzliche Begründungspflicht der Schiedsgerichte vor. Eine Ausnahme gilt nur, soweit die Parteien hierauf verzichten. *S* 70(4) *Arbitration Act* ersetzt *s* 1(5)(6) *Arbitration Act* 1979. Die Vorschrift lautet:

> *"If on an application it appears to the court that the award-*
> *(a) does not contain the tribunal's reasons, or*
> *(b) does not set out the tribunal's reasons in sufficient detail to enable the court properly to consider the application or appeal,*
> *the court may order the tribunal to state the reasons for its award in sufficient detail for that purpose."*

Neu ist im Vergleich zum alten Recht, daß das Gericht nicht nur die Befugnis hat, Begründungen im Falle eines *appeals* gemäß *s* 69 *Arbitration Act* 1996 anzuordnen. Diese Befugnis erstreckt sich vielmehr nun auch auf die "Rechtsmittel" nach *ss* 67 *Arbitration Act* 1996 ("*substantive jurisdiction*") und 68 *Arbitration Act* 1996 ("*serious irregularity*").[726]

V. Anordnung von Sicherheitsleistungen für ein Verfahren nach ss *67 - 69*

Nach *s* 70(6) *Arbitration Act* 1996 können die Gerichte eine Partei, die nach den ss 67 - 69 gegen den Schiedsspruch vorgehen möchte, zur Leistung einer entspre-

---

724 *S* 67(3) *Arbitration Act* 1996 lautet:
"On an application under this section challenging an award of the arbitral tribunal as to its substantive jurisdiction, the court may by order-
(a) confirm the award,
(b) vary the award,
(c) set aside the award in whole or in part."

725 Vgl. *supra* in diesem Kapitel, B.II.2..

726 Die *ss* 22 und 23 *Arbitration Act* 1950 sahen kein entsprechendes Recht vor.

chenden Sicherheit für die Verfahrenskosten verpflichten.[727] Gemeint ist nicht das Recht, Sicherheitsleistungen für die Kosten des *Schieds*verfahrens aufzuerlegen. Ein solches Recht steht nach dem *Arbitration Act* 1996 ausschließlich den Schiedsgerichten zu.[728] Die Sicherheit dient einzig der Finanzierung des staatlichen Rechtsmittelverfahrens.

Nach *s* 70(7) sind die Gerichte ferner befugt, eine nach dem Schiedsspruch zu zahlende Summe für die Dauer des gerichtlichen Rechtsmittelverfahrens als vom Gericht zu verwahrende Sicherheit einzufordern.[729]

E. Zwischenergebnis

Das neue englische Recht der Aufhebungs- und Abänderungsbefugnisse bringt eine teilweise Modernisierung des bisher geltenden Rechts mit sich. Es bleibt in entscheidenden Fragen jedoch hinter den Erwartungen an ein wirklich modernes Schiedsrecht zurück.

Enttäuschend ist zunächst, daß sich der englische Gesetzgeber nicht zu einer grundlegenden Reform des *right of appeal on a point of law* hat durchringen können. Hierzu Rokison: [730]

> *"Regarding the question of the courts' review of arbitrator's decisions in law, the 1996 Act has not on the face of it done much to reduce potential court intervention and has not apparently given full effect to the presumed intention of the parties that all aspects of the merits of their dispute should be decided by their chosen tribunal and not by the court."*

---

727 *S* 70(6) *Arbitration Act* 1996 lautet:
"The Court may order the applicant or appellant to provide security for the costs of the application or appeal, and may direct that the application or appeal be dismissed if the order is not complied with.
The power to order security for costs shall not be exercised on the ground that the applicant or appellant is-
(a) an individual ordinarily resident outside the United Kingdom, or
(b) a corporation or association incorporated or formed under the law of a country outside the United Kingdom, or whose central management and control is exercised outside the United Kingdom."

728 Vgl. *supra* Kapitel 8, C..

729 *S* 70(7) *Arbitration Act* 1996 lautet:
"The court may order that any money payable under the award shall be brought into court or otherwise secured pending the determination of the application or appeal, and may direct that the application or appeal be dismissed if the order is not complied with."

730 Arb.Int'l 363.

Entgegen Beteuerungen des Gegenteils[731] bringt der *Arbitration Act* 1996 keinen radikalen Bruch mit der Tradition des englischen Schiedsverfahrensrechts.[732] Durch die Übernahme des *rights of appeal* in den *Arbitration Act* 1996 wurde die Möglichkeit vertan, der Ursache für die vielgeübte Kritik am englischen Recht gleich an der "Wurzel" zu begegnen.[733]

Andererseits darf die englische Argumentation, daß solche Kontrollbefugnisse unter bestimmten Voraussetzungen der einzige Garant für ein "gerechtes" Ergebnis sein können, nicht leichtfertig in den Wind geschlagen werden.[734] Hier schließt sich jedoch der zweite Kritikpunkt an *s* 69 *Arbitration Act* 1996 an. Denn wenn man schon ein limitiertes *right of appeal on a point of law* beibehalten wollte, dann wäre es erforderlich gewesen, dieses klar zu begrenzen. Dies aber ist nicht geschehen. Durch die Übernahme der Nema-/Antaios-Richtlinien wurden auch die weiten Ermessensbefugnisse der Gerichte übernommen, über die Zulassung eines *appeals* zu befinden. Tatsächlich hat sich in diesem Punkt also nicht viel geändert.

Zumindest einen "Lichtblick" hat die Reform des *right of appeal on a point of law* jedoch gebracht. So sind die Parteien nunmehr ohne Einschränkungen zu einem Ausschluß des genannten Rechts berechtigt. Den Schiedsparteien steht es somit frei, durch Vereinbarung ein modernes englisches Schiedsverfahrensrecht zu schaffen. Diese Möglichkeit sollte nicht unterbewertet werden. Sie ermöglicht den Parteien die Wahl und ist damit Ausdruck der Parteiautonomie.

Die Reform der *ss* 22 und 23 *Arbitration Act* 1950 ist überwiegend positiv zu bewerten. Durch den *Arbitration Act* 1996 wurde endlich das ungeliebte, weil uferlose Tatbestandsmerkmal des *misconduct* abgeschafft. Es wurde ersetzt durch das der *serious irregularity*. Indem dieses in *s* 68(2) *Arbitration Act* 1996 eine abschließende Definition erfahren hat, verlieren die Gerichte zu einem großen Teil ihre bislang nahezu unbeschränkten Ermessensbefugnisse. Dies gilt allerdings unter dem Vorbehalt einer nicht unbedeutenden Ausnahme. So wird den Gerichten durch den Verweis von *s* 68(2)(a) *Arbitration Act* 1996 auf *s* 33 *Arbitration Act* 1996 ("*general duty of tribunal*") wiederum ein großzügiger Ermessenspielraum zur Beurteilung schiedsgerichtlichen Fehlverhaltens eingeräumt.

Der Vergleich des neuen englischen Rechts mit dem Modellgesetz ergibt in Teilbereichen zwar deutliche Ähnlichkeiten. Er macht aber auch deutlich, daß der *Arbitration Act* 1996 eben kein Modellgesetz ist. Der Hauptunterschied beider Rechtsordnungen liegt nach wie vor darin, daß das englische Recht die Möglich-

731 Harris/Planterose/Tecks, S. 1.
732 Rokison, Arb.Int'l 364.
733 Herrmann, Arb.Int'l 1994, 187.
734 Bernstein, Arbitration 1993, 5 f.

keit eines *appeal on a point of law* vorsieht. Das Modellgesetz ermöglicht eine Angreifbarkeit des Schiedsspruches ausschließlich auf Grundlage von Verfahrensverstößen. Jedenfalls vor dem Hintergrund der weiten und unbestimmten Ermessensbefugnisse zur Zulassung eines *appeals* erscheint die Lösung des Modellgesetzes in diesem Punkt vorzugswürdig.

Von *s* 69 *Arbitration Act* 1996 abgesehen weisen die Rechtsordnungen ansonsten nunmehr deutliche Ähnlichkeiten auf. Die Verfahrensverstöße, die zu einer gerichtlichen Kontrolle berechtigen, sind zu einem großen Teil, wenngleich unterschiedlich formuliert, vergleichbar. Beide Rechtsordnungen sehen enumerative Aufzählungen vor und bedingen dadurch ein hohes Maß an Rechtssicherheit und Vorhersehbarkeit. Hierzu stellt nur *s* 68(2)(a) *Arbitration Act* 1996 eine Ausnahme dar, indem die staatlichen Kontrollbefugnisse über den Verweis auf *s* 33 *Arbitration Act* 1996 an so vage Begriffe wie "Fairness" oder "Angemessenheit" gekoppelt werden. Es ist zum jetzigen Zeitpunkt nicht absehbar, ob und in welchem Umfang die englischen Gerichte *s* 68(2)(a) *Arbitration Act* 1996 im Sinne einer extensiven Kontrolle ge- bzw. mißbrauchen werden. Der Gesetzestext jedenfalls läßt einen solchen Mißbrauch zu. Sicherheit kann hier erst herrschen, wenn das House of Lords für entsprechende Klarheit sorgt.

Kapitel 11
Anerkennung und Vollstreckung

A. *Einführung*

Im internationalen Handelsgeschäft ist die Schiedsgerichtsbarkeit vielleicht die effizienteste Möglichkeit der Streitentscheidung. Anerkennung und Vollstreckung von Schiedssprüchen spielen zwangsläufig eine wichtige Rolle. Bei einer Untersuchung von ICC-Schiedssprüchen wurde ermittelt, daß mehr als 90 % aller Schiedssprüche freiwillig umgesetzt werden.[735] Jeder einzelne Schiedsspruch, dem die Anerkennung oder Vollstreckung versagt wird, stellt jedoch die Schiedsgerichtsbarkeit in Frage.[736] Denn der Wert eines Schiedsverfahrens bestimmt sich auch dadurch, ob der Schiedspruch nötigenfalls zwangsweise durchgesetzt werden kann.

Die Bedeutung der Anerkennung und Vollstreckung von Schiedssprüchen spiegelt sich auch in der Beachtung wieder, die dieses Thema weltweit in der Li-

735 De Vries, Tulane L.Rev. 1982, 43.
736 Vgl. auch die Ausführungen von Ungar, Colum.J.Transnat'l.Law 1987, 718 f.

teratur gefunden hat.[737] Die nachfolgenden Ausführungen orientieren sich schwerpunktmäßig an der Frage, unter welchen Vorausetzungen die englischen Gerichte und diejenigen der Modellgesetzstaaten Anerkennung und Vollstreckung eines Schiedsspruchs versagen können.

B. Art. 35 und 36 Modellgesetz

I. Einführung

Das Modellgesetz regelt die Anerkennung und Vollstreckung von Schiedssprüchen in Art. 35 und 36 Modellgesesetz.[738] Art. 35 Modellgesesetz regelt die grundsätzliche Pflicht der Gerichte zur Anerkennung und Vollstreckung sowie das betreffende Verfahren.[739] Art. 36 Modellgesesetz nennt die Voraussetzungen, unter denen die Gerichte Anerkennung und Vollstreckung versagen dürfen. Art. 36 ist - wie auch Art. 34 - eng an das New Yorker UN-Übereinkommen angelehnt.

Daraus folgt, daß die einzelnen Versagungsgründe von Art. 36 Abs. 1 mit denen aus Art. 34 Abs. 2 nahezu identisch sind.[740] Diese wurden bereits dargestellt.[741] Die nachfolgenden Untersuchungen beschränken sich deshalb im Wesentlichen auf die Unterschiede zwischen den Art. 35, 36 Modellgesesetz und Art. 34 Modellgesesetz einerseits bzw. Art. 35, 36 und dem New Yorker UN-Übereinkommen andererseits.[742]

---

737 Vgl. statt anderer Böckstiegel, in: Sanders (Hrsg.), Arbitration 1987, 177; Harnik, Am.J.Comp.L. 1983, 703; Lew, Int'l Bus.Lawy. 1976, 425; Mustill, Arkiv for Sjorett 1976-77, 321; Sandrock/Hentzen, Transnat'l Law. 1989, 49; Shenton, Int'l Bus.Lawy. 1980, 35.

738 Vgl. generell zum Thema Vollstreckung nach dem Modellgesetz Dore, S. 130 ff; Herrmann, Arb.Int'l, 6, 26 ff; Ungar, Colum.J.Transnat'l Law. 1987, 717.

739 Zum Umfang dieser Pflicht vgl. auch Herrmann, in: Lew (Hrsg.), Contemporary Problems, S. 169.

740 Holtzmann/Neuhaus, S. 1006, führen hierzu aus:
"This similarity with the New York Convention was not simply a drafting convenience. Rather, it is a basic policy of the Model Law that the Law be consistent with this successful and widely accepted international treaty".

741 Vgl. *supra* Kapitel 10, B.II..

742 Siehe auch Cole, Ohio St.J.Disp.Res. 1986, 365.

II. Keine Trennung nach in- und ausländischen Schiedssprüchen

Art. 35 Abs. 1 Modellgesetz lautet:

> "Ein Schiedsspruch ist unabhängig davon, in welchem Land er erlassen worden ist, als bindend anzuerkennen und auf schriftlichen Antrag an das zuständige Gericht zu vollstrecken, vorbehaltlich dieses Artikels und des Artikels 36."

Das Modellgesetz unterscheidet - anders als das New Yorker UN-Übereinkommen - hinsichtlich Anerkennung und Vollstreckung nicht nach in- oder ausländischen Schiedssprüchen. Die Vollstreckungsgerichte wenden vielmehr für alle Schiedssprüche, die in den Anwendungsbereich des Modellgesetzes fallen,[743] das gleiche Kontrollsystem an. Es wird nicht danach unterschieden, ob der zu vollstreckende Schiedsspruch in einem Modellgesetzstaat ergangen ist oder nicht. Im Sinne einer erstrebenswerten internationalen Harmonisierung des Schiedsrechts ist diese Regelung des Modellgesetzes grundsätzlich zu begrüßen. Der Verzicht auf eine Differenzierung zwischen in- und ausländisch ergangenen Sprüchen impliziert jedoch, daß eben auch die inländisch nach dem Modellgesetz ergangenen Schiedssprüche einer Vollstreckungskontrolle unterzogen werden. Calavros hält Art. 35 Abs. 1 daher für eine "rückschrittliche Lösung".[744]

Anders als das New Yorker UN-Übereinkommen weist Art. 35 keine Reziprozitätsklausel auf. Herrman verweist darauf, daß es den Modellgesetzstaaten freistünde, eine entsprechende Regelung aufzunehmen.

III. Doppelkontrolle

Bedingt durch die Identität der Aufhebungsgründe in Art. 34 und der Versagungsgründe in Art. 36 kann es nach dem Modellgesetz zu einer sog. "Doppelkontrolle" des Schiedsspruches kommen. So stehen den Parteien eben nicht nur die Möglichkeiten nach Art. 34 im Aufhebungsverfahren zu; sie können den Schiedsspruch vielmehr nochmals wegen exakt der gleichen Gründe im Exequaturverfahren überprüfen lassen. Diese doppelte Überprüfung ist möglich, weil der Streitgegenstand des Aufhebungsverfahrens nicht mit dem des Exequaturverfahrens identisch ist.[745] Nur dann, wenn der Schiedsspruch aufgehoben wird, kann es notwendigerweise nicht zu einer weiteren Kontrolle nach Art. 36 kommen. Dies gilt auch dann, wenn die Verfahren in unterschiedlichen Modellgesetzstaaten durchgeführt werden. Denn die Aufhebung hat - anders als die Versagung der

---

743 Vgl. Art. 1 Modellgesetz.

744 S. 170.

745 Schwab, Schiedsgerichtsbarkeit, S. 186 f.

Exequatur - zur Folge, daß der Schiedsspruch universell in seinem Bestand vernichtet wird.

Fallen Aufhebungs- und Vollstreckungshinderungsverfahren zeitlich zusammen, hat das Vollstreckungsgericht nach Art. 36 Abs. 2 die Möglichkeit, sein Verfahren bis zum Ergehen der Entscheidung im Verfahren nach Art. 34 auszusetzen.

Es ist viel über das für und wider der Doppelkontrolle geschrieben und gestritten worden.[746] Das "Problem" der Doppelkontrolle ist jedoch recht akademischer Natur. Es existiert keine überzeugende Alternative hierzu. Die Rechte der unterlegenen Partei würden unzulässig verkürzt, wenn diese einzig auf das zeitlich befristete Aufhebungsverfahren angewiesen wäre.[747] Die Doppelkontrolle besitzt zudem auch nur eine geringe praktische Relevanz. Sind Forumstaat und Exequaturstaat identisch und wurde ein erfolgloses Aufhebungsverfahren durchgeführt, wird regelmäßig ein Verfahren nach Art. 36 gar nicht erst angestrengt oder aber zügig entschieden. Sind Forum- und Exequaturstaat nicht identisch, ist die Doppelkontrolle schon wegen des unterschiedlichen *ordre public* der Staaten unverzichtbar.

IV. Hinderungsgründe nach Art. 36

1. Ermessen

Art. 36 S. 1 lautet:

> "Die Anerkennung oder Vollstreckung eine Schiedsspruchs darf, unabhängig davon, in welchem Land er erlassen worden ist, nur versagt werden: [es folgen die einzelnen Gründe]."

Die Fassung des Art. 36 ist das Ergebnis einer Grundsatzdiskussion zum Ermessensspielraum der Gerichte. So war ursprünglich eine Fassung vorgesehen, die den Gerichten die Versagung der Anerkennung oder Vollstreckung verbindlich vorgeschrieben hätte ("shall *be refused*").[748] Dem lag die Einschätzung der Arbeitsgruppe zugrunde, daß eine solche Fassung "*for the sake of certainty and predictability*" sinnvoll sei.[749] Daß Art. 36 letztlich als Ermessensvorschrift

746 Vgl. nur Calavros, S. 172 ff; Hüsslein-Stich, S. 197 ff; Nöcker, S. 170 ff.
747 Vgl. Hüßlein-Stich, S. 198.
748 UN-Doc. A/CN.9/233, para 140.
749 *Ibid.*

("darf") verabschiedet wurde, wirft die Frage nach dem Umfang des gerichtlichen Ermessens auf.[750]

Den *travaux préparatoires* sind hierzu keine Anhaltspunkte zu entnehmen. Doch ist sicherlich die Annahme nicht verfehlt, daß bei Vorliegen eines Versagungsgrundes die Versagung der Regelfall sein dürfte. Nur soweit unter besonderer Berücksichtigung der Fallumstände die Rechtsfolge der Versagung als gänzlich unangemessen einzustufen ist, wird man deshalb davon ausgehen dürfen, daß die Gerichte die Versagung der Vollstreckung verweigern.

2. *Die einzelnen Hinderungsgründe*

a) *Subjektive Schiedsunfähigkeit und Ungültigkeit des Schiedsvertrags*

Art. 36 Abs. 1(a)(i) weist gegenüber seinem Pendant Art. 34 Abs. (2)(a)(i)[751] keinerlei Besonderheiten auf. Beide Vorschriften knüpfen mangels einer anderslautenden Parteivereinbarung an das Recht des Forumstaates an. Auch im Rahmen des Art. 36 Abs. 1(1)(a) ist auf die Rechtsfolge der Art. 16 Abs. 2 i.V.m. Art. 4 Modellgesetz hinzuweisen, wonach die Parteien mit der Einrede der Unzuständigkeit ausgeschlossen sein können.[752]

b) *Verletzung des rechtlichen Gehörs und Überschreitung der Entscheidungskompetenz*

Es ergeben sich keine Besonderheiten zu Art. 34 Abs. 2(a)(ii) bzw. zu Art. 34 Abs. 2(a)(iii).

c) *Verstoß gegen die Vorschriften und die Schiedsabrede über die Bildung des Schiedsgerichts und das Schiedsverfahren*

Art. 36 Abs. 1(a)(iv) entspricht zwar Art. 5 Abs. 1(d) des New Yorker UN-Übereinkommens, weicht damit aber erheblich von seinem Gegenstück in Art. 34 Abs. 2(a)(iv) ab.[753] Die Vorschrift lautet:

---

750 Das Ermessen bezieht sich lediglich auf die Frage, ob die Gerichte bei Vorliegen eines Versagungsgrundes dennoch anerkennen und vollstrecken dürfen. Unstreitig kein Ermessen haben die Gerichte bei *Nicht*vorliegen eines Versagungsgrundes. Hier müssen sie anerkennen bzw. vollstrecken.

751 Vgl. *supra* Kapitel 10, B.II.1..

752 *Ibid.*

753 Vgl. *supra* Kapitel 10, B.II.4.

"[Anerkennung und Vollstreckung darf nur bei Beweis darüber versagt werden,] daß die Bildung des Schiedsgerichts oder das schiedsrichterliche Verfahren der Vereinbarung der Parteien oder, mangels einer solchen Vereinbarung, dem Recht des Landes, in dem das schiedsrichterliche Verfahren stattfand, nicht entsprochen hat [...]"

Es bietet sich an dieser Stelle an, folgende Stellungnahme von Holtzmann/Neuhaus zu zitieren:[754]

"The distinction between Articles 34(2)(a)(iv) nd 36(1)(a)(iv) is, of course, an exception to the general policy of harmony between these two Articles [...] While the rationale for the distinction is nowhere completely stated, it would appear to have been motivated by the following considerations. First, the need to align the Model Law with the New York Convention is most pressing with respect to provisions on recognition and enforcement, in order to help create a unified, worldwide system for these functions. The alignment between Articles 34 and 36 serves a different purpose, which is to diminish the importance of the place of arbitration in international commercial arbitration as between domestic and foreign arbitrations. The Working Group at times suggested that this second purpose - identity of treatment between foreign and domestic awards - while important, might be less important than harmony of treatment in recognizing and enforcing awards under both the Model Law and the New York Convention [...] As a result, it was more desirable to make the change in Article 34 than to retain a complete alignment between that Article and Article 36."

Es darf bezweifelt werden, ob die Arbeitsgruppe die richtige Entscheidung getroffen hat, als sie in Art. 36 Abs. 1(1)(iv) Modellgesetz den Art. 5 Abs. 1(d) New Yorker UN-Übereinkommen übernahm. Denn diese Vorschrift warf immer dann erhebliche Probleme auf, wenn die Parteivereinbarung gegen das zwingende Recht des Forumstaates verstieß. Es fragte sich, was in diesem Falle Vorrang haben sollte: Das Prinzip der Vertragsfreiheit oder das Gebot der Beachtung der zwingenden Vorschriften? Beide Ansichten sind vertreten worden. Es ist schwer, eine herrschende Meinung auszumachen.[755] Gleich welcher Ansicht gefolgt wird, bleibt das Ergebnis unbefriedigend. Folgt das Schiedsgericht der Parteivereinbarung und verstößt so gegen zwingende Verfahrensvorschriften, kann der Schiedsspruch nach Art. 34 Modellgesetz aufgehoben werden. Damit wären dann auch Anerkennung und Vollstreckung hinfällig. Werden hingegen die zwingenden Vorschriften beachtet, besteht die Möglichkeit, daß dem Schiedsspruch nach Art. 36 Abs. 1(a)(iv) Anerkennung und Vollstreckung versagt werden.

---

754 Holtzmann/Neuhaus, S. 1060 f.
755 Vgl. Quigley, Y.L.J. 1961, 1068; Martinez, Int'l.Law. 1990, 500.

d) Keine rechtliche Verbindlichkeit

Kein Gegenstück in Art. 34 hat - notwendigerweise - Art. 36 Abs. 1(a)(v). Denn dieser bezieht sich eben auf Art. 34 als Voraussetzung. Er lautet:

> "[Anerkennung und Vollstreckung darf nur bei Beweis darüber versagt werden,] daß der Schiedsspruch für die Parteien noch nicht verbindlich geworden ist, oder daß er von einem Gericht des Landes, in dem oder nach dessen Recht er ergangen ist, aufgehoben oder in seinen Wirkungen einstweilen gehemmt ist [...]"

Die Vorschrift ist Art. 5(1)(e) des New Yorker UN-Übereinkommen nachgebildet. Der Schiedsspruch darf danach für die Parteien noch nicht "verbindlich" geworden sein. Das wirft die Frage nach dem Zeitpunkt des Eintritts der Verbindlichkeit auf. Nach dem Willen UNCITRALs richtet sich dieser nach dem Recht des Forum-Staates.[756] Die Orientierung am Wortlaut des Art. 5 Abs. 1(e) ("*binding*") - im Gegensatz zu dem von Art. 1 der Genfer Abkommen zur Vollstreckung ausländischer Schiedssprüche vom 26.09.1927 (englisch: "*final*") - läßt Rückschlüsse auf den relevanten Zeitpunkt zu. Diese Unterscheidung kann nur bedeuten, daß Verbindlichkeit bereits dann vorliegen soll, wenn noch außergewöhnliche Anfechtungsmöglichkeiten, also etwa diejenige eines Aufhebungsverfahrens, bestehen.[757] Diese Ansicht wird durch Art. 36 Abs. 2 Modellgesetz gestützt. Danach steht es den Gerichten frei, ob sie bei laufendem Aufhebungsverfahren ihr Exequaturverfahren unterbrechen oder nicht. Ein Schiedsspruch ist somit zumindest dann noch nicht verbindlich, wenn die Parteien die Möglichkeit eines ordentlichen Rechtsmittels (vor einem anderen Schiedsgericht) vereinbart haben.

Anerkennung und Vollstreckung muß nach Art. 36 Abs. 1(a)(v) Modellgesetz ferner dann versagt bleiben, wenn der Schiedsspruch aufgehoben oder in seiner Wirkung einstweilen gehemmt ist.

e) Objektive Schiedsunfähigkeit und Verstoß gegen den ordre public

Bei der Beurteilung von Art. 36 Abs. (b) Modellgesesetz ergeben sich keine Besonderheiten gegenüber Art. 34 Abs. 2(b) Modellgesesetz.[758]

---

756 UN-Doc. A/CN.9/263, Art. 35, para 2.
757 Sanders, Int'l Law. 1979, 275.
758 Vgl. *supra* Kapitel 10, B.II.5. und 6..

V. Zwischenergebnis

Im Ergebnis ist das Anerkennungs- und Vollstreckungsrecht nach den Art. 35 und 36 als äußerst schiedsfreundlich und modern zu bewerten. Die grundsätzliche Pflicht der Gerichte zur Anerkennung und Vollstreckung - und dies unabhängig vom Schiedsort - sowie der enge Ausnahmekatalog in Art. 36 garantieren einen reibungslosen Ablauf des Verfahrens. Sie gewährleisten zudem ein Mindestmaß an verbleibenden Kontrollbefugnissen, die zur Verhinderung offensichtlich untragbarer Ergebnisse erforderlich sind.

C. Das englische Recht vor 1997

I. Einführung

Die Anerkennung und Vollstreckung von Schiedssprüchen nach dem englischen Recht stellte im Gegensatz zur Anfechtung von Schiedsprüchen im Regelfall kein praktisches Problem dar. In diesem Bereich existiert nur wenig Fallrecht. Dies hat vor allem zwei Gründe. Zum einen war England immer schon "*an exporter rather than an importer of arbitral awards.*"[759] Der überwiegende Anteil an englischen Schiedssprüchen wurde also nicht in England vollstreckt. Zum anderen waren aber diejenigen Schiedssprüche, die in England ergingen und auch vollstreckt werden sollten, Gegenstand eines umfangreichen Anfechtungs- und Revisionsrechts bevor es überhaupt zur Vollstreckung kommen konnte. Schiedssprüche, die zuvor unbeschadet das "Nadelöhr" dieser gerichtlichen Kontrolle passiert hatten, konnten in dem großzügigeren Vollstreckungskontrollverfahren kaum noch erfolgreich angegriffen werden.

Auch hinsichtlich der Anerkennung und Vollstreckung von Schiedssprüchen unterschied das englische Recht zwischen *domestic* und *foreign* bzw. *international awards*. Während *domestic awards* nur nach dem *common law* (*action on the award*)[760] oder nach dem verkürzten Verfahren (*summary enforcement*) der *s* 26 *Arbitration Act* 1950[761] vollstreckt werden konnten, stand für die Vollstreckung von *foreign* bzw. *international awards* ein komplexes Regelwerk an internationalen Verträgen und Konventionen zur Verfügung.[762]

---

759 Samuel, in: Knoepfler (Hrsg.), S. 122.
760 Vgl. in diesem Kapitel, C.II..
761 *Ibid.*
762 Es bestanden - je nach Art des Verfahrens und Herkunft der Parteien - folgende Vollstreckungsmöglichkeiten:

Von überragender praktischer Bedeutung war der *Arbitration Act* 1975, welcher das New Yorker UN-Übereinkommen in englisches Recht umsetzte.[763] Die anderen Übereinkommen spielten daneben eine vergleichsweise unbedeutende Rolle.[764] Die nachfolgenden Untersuchungen beschränken sich deshalb auf das *common law* und *s* 26 *Arbitration Act* 1950 einerseits bzw. den *Arbitration Act* 1975 andererseits.

II. Action on the award *nach dem* common law

Von zentraler Bedeutung für das Verständnis des englischen Vollstreckungsrechts war das Konzept der *obligation.*[765] Ein Schiedspruch verkörperte die Pflicht der unterlegenen Partei, diesen umzusetzen. Diese Pflicht war wie jede andere vom englischen Recht anerkannte vertragliche Pflicht einklagbar.[766] Das Konzept der *obligation* vermied eine Überprüfung des Zustandekommens des Schiedsspruchs nach materiellem Recht ("*on the merits*").[767] Vollstreckt wurde nicht der eigentliche Schiedsspruch, sondern das Recht, welches dieser begründete.

Mit dem Begriff *action on the award* ist die Klage der obsiegenden Partei auf Umsetzung des Schiedsspruches gemeint. Das mit der Klage befaßte Gericht konnte hierauf entweder den Schiedsspruch für vollstreckbar erklären[768] oder aber die unterlegene Partei zur Zahlung von Schadensersatz wegen Vertrags-

---

- nach dem Genfer Abkommen von 1927 wie in Teil II des *Arbitration Act* 1950 rezipiert;
- nach dem New Yorker UN-Übereinkommen in der Fassung des *Arbitration Act* 1975;
- nach Teil II des *Civil Jurisdiction and Judgements Act* 1982;
- nach Teil II des *Administration of Justice Act* 1920;
- nach Teil I des *Foreign Judgments (Reciprocal Enforcement) Act* 1933;
- nach dem *Arbitration (International Investment Disputes) Act* 1966, durch welchen das Washingtoner Übereinkommen zur Beilegung von Investitionsstreitigkeiten zwischen Staaten und Angehörigen anderer Staaten vom 18.03.1965 rezipiert wurde.

763 Vgl. auch Deshpande, Arb.Int'l 1991, 123.

764 So ist etwa die Genfer Abkommen von 1927 in weiten Teilen durch das New Yorker UN-Übereinkommen abgelöst worden und hat nur noch in Restbereichen eigenständige Bedeutung. Nach dem *Arbitration (International Investment Disputes) Act* 1966 erging im Schnitt lediglich ein Schiedsspruch pro Jahr (vgl. Samuel, in: Knoepfler (Hrsg.), S. 107).

765 Samuel, in: Knoepfler (Hrsg.), S. 105.

766 Cheshire & North, S. 338 f.

767 *Goddard v. Grey* (1870) 6 Q.B. 139.

768 *Beswick v. Beswick* [1968] A.C. 58.

bruchs verurteilen.[769] Das Ergebnis war aus Sicht der Parteien zumeist das gleiche.[770] Die klagende Partei unterlag der Beweispflicht hinsichtlich folgender Umstände: Es mußte eine Schiedsvereinbarung vorgelegen haben, ein Schiedsspruch mußte ergangen, dieser mußte nach Art und Umfang von der Schiedsabrede gedeckt und schließlich mußten die Schiedsrichter rechtmäßig ernannt worden sein.[771]

In direktem Zusammenhang hierzu standen auch die Gründe, bei deren Vorliegen Anerkennung und Vollstreckung nach dem *common law* versagt werden konnten. Nach Dicey & Morris waren dies folgende:[772]

> *"A[n] [...] arbitration award [...] will [...] not be recognised or enforced in England if*
> *(1) under the submission agreement and the law applicable thereto the arbitrators had no jurisdiction to make it*[773]*; or*
> *(2) it was obtained by fraud*[774]*; or*
> *(3) its recognition, or as the case may be enforcement, would be contrary to public policy; or*
> *(4) the proceedings in which it was obtained were opposed to natural justice."*

Die einzelnen Versagungsgründe entsprachen im wesentlichen den oben dargestellten Aufhebungsgründen.[775] Sie bedürfen an dieser Stelle deshalb keiner nochmaligen Untersuchung. Die Bezugnahme auf *natural justice* macht deutlich, daß die englischen Gerichte bei der Versagung der Anerkennung oder Vollstrekkung keinen strengen Schranken unterworfen waren. Ihnen war vielmehr ein freier Ermessenspielraum eröffnet.

---

769 *Dalmia Dairy Industries Ltd. v. National Bank of Pakistan* [1978] 2 Lloyd's Rep. 223 (273).

770 Man wird auch nicht falsch liegen, die Klage einfach als Zahlungsklage zu bezeichnen (*Coastal States Trading (UK) Ltd. v. Mebro Mineralölhandels GmbH* [1986] 1 Lloyd's Rep. 465 (467)).

771 *Christopher Brown Ltd. v. Genossenschaft Österreichischer Waldbesitzer Registrierte Genossenschaft mbH* [1954] 1 Q.B. 8.

772 S. 613; Dicey & Morris beziehen sich zwar in erster Linie auf *foreign arbitration awards*, doch galten die Versagungsgründe ebenso für *domestic awards*.

773 *Kianta Osakeyhtio v. Britain and Overseas Trading Co. Ltd.* [1954] 1 Lloyd's Rep. 247.

774 *Oppenheim & Co. v. Mahomed Haneef* [1922] 1 A.C. 482 (487).

775 Vgl. *supra* Kapitel 10, C.III.4..

III. Summary enforcement

Eine weitere Möglichkeit der Vollstreckung von Schiedssprüchen sah *s* 26 *Arbitration Act* 1950 vor. Die Vorschrift lautete:

> *"An award on an arbitration agreement may, by leave of the High Court or a judge thereof, be enforced in the same manner as a judgment or order to the same effect, and where leave is so given may be entered in terms of the award."*

S 26 sah damit zwei verschiedene Vollstreckungsmethoden vor. Einerseits konnte die obsiegende Partei zum einen eine Vollstreckbarkeitserklärung beantragen (Alt. 1). Damit war der Schiedsspruch *wie* ein Urteil vollstreckbar, ohne daß es hierzu eines Urteils bedurft hätte. Andererseits konnte auf Antrag auch ein Urteil gleichen Inhalts wie der Schiedsspruch ergehen. Soweit es um eine Vollstreckung in England ging, bestanden zwischen den beiden Methoden keine Unterschiede. Soweit der Schiedsspruch jedoch von einem ausländischen Gericht anerkannt oder vollstreckt werden sollte, empfahl sich mitunter die Wahl der zweiten Methode, da die Vollstreckung ausländischer Urteile teils einfacher war als die ausländischer Schiedssprüche.

Bei *s* 26 handelte es sich weniger um ein eigenes Vollstreckungsverfahren, als vielmehr um ein summarisches Verfahren zur Vollstreckung eines Schiedsspruches nach dem *common law*, also um ein verkürztes *action on the award*-Verfahren. Die materiellen Voraussetzungen wie auch die Verteidigungs- und Eingriffsmöglichkeiten der Gerichte waren daher die gleichen. Die Gerichte unterlagen somit keinen Ermessensbeschränkungen. Die Bedeutung von *s* 26 erschöpfte sich deshalb darin, eine einfachere, schnellere und kostengünstigere Alternative zum Klageverfahren anzubieten.[776] Ausreichend war ein Antrag der obsiegenden Partei, der mit den Originalen der Schiedsvereinbarung und einer Ausfertigung des Schiedsspruches versehen war. Ging die unterlegene Partei nicht innerhalb von 28 Tagen gegen den Schiedsspruch vor, konnte der High Court den Schiedsspruch jederzeit für vollstreckbar erklären.[777] Grundsätzlich konnten alle Schiedssprüche, die auf eine schriftliche Schiedsabrede ergingen, nach *s* 26 vollstreckt werden. Voraussetzung für die Vollstreckung nach *s* 26 war jedoch, daß die Fälle "*reasonably clear*"[778] waren, und daß kein "*real ground for doubting*

776 Mustill/Boyd, S. 419 mit Verweis auf *Coastal States Trading (UK) Ltd. v. Mebro Mineralölhandels GmbH* [1986] 1 Lloyd's Rep. 465.

777 Lew, Int'l.Law. 1976, 428.

778 *Re Boks & Co. and Peters Rushton & Co. Ltd.* [1919] K.B. 491 (497); *Grech v. Board of Trade* (1923) 130 L.T. 15; *Frank Jehr & Co. v. Kassam Jivraj & Co. Ltd.* (1949) 82 Ll.L.R. 673).

the validity of the award" ersichtlich war.[779] Denn nur in diesen Fällen erschien der implizierte Verzicht auf eine Anhörung der Parteien angemessen.[780]

IV. Der Arbitration Act *1975*

Die ganz überwiegende Anzahl aller *non-domestic awards* wurde nach dem *Arbitration Act* 1975 vollstreckt. Durch diesen hatte England das New Yorker UN-Übereinkommen in staatliches Recht übernommen. Daneben spielte auch die Vollstreckung nach *common law*, soweit es um *non-domestic* awards ging, keine nennenswerte Rolle mehr.[781] Ebenso war der Anwendungsbereich des durch Teil II des *Arbitration Acts* 1950 in das englische Recht rezipierten Genfer Abkommens von 1927 wegen des Anwendungsvorangs des *Arbitration Acts* 1975 stark eingeschränkt.[782]

Gemäß *s* 3(1) *Arbitration Act* 1975 war ein "*[c]onvention award*" in England vollstreckbar "*either by action or in the same manner as the award of an arbitrator is enforceable by virtue of section 26 of the Arbitration Act 1950*". Auch unter *s* 3(1) *Arbitration Act* 1975 sollte die Vollstreckung entsprechend *s* 26 *Arbitration Act* 1950 (*summary enforcement*) den Regelfall bilden. Der Unterschied zu den *non-convention awards* ergab sich einerseits aus *s* 4 *Arbitration Act* 1975. Danach mußte der Kläger lediglich beglaubigte Ausfertigungen von Schiedsvereinbarung und Spruch vorlegen, war ansonsten aber in keiner Weise beweispflichtig.

Der entscheidende Unterschied lag jedoch in der abschließenden Auflistung der Gründe, nach denen Anerkennung und Vollstreckung versagt werden durften, in *s* 5 *Arbitration Act* 1975. Diese waren identisch mit denen in Art. 5 des New Yorker UN-Übereinkommens und somit weitgehend auch mit denen aus Art. 36 Modellgesetz.[783]

---

779 Lew, Int'l.Law. 1976, 428 mit Verweis auf *Middlemiss and Could v. Hartlepool Corporation* (1973) 1 All E.R. 172 (175).

780 *Ibid.*

781 Samuel, in: Knoepfler (Hrsg.), S. 121, zufolge kam dem *common law* im Bereich der *non-domestic awards* nur noch eine Auffangfunktion zu, soweit der *Arbitration Act* 1975 etwa wegen des Schriftformerfordernisses nicht anwendbar war (vgl. etwa *Dallal v. Bank Mellat* [1986] Q.B. 441).

782 Shenton, Int'l Bus.Lawy. 1980, 35; vgl. auch Deshpande, J.Int'l Arb. 1987, 41.

783 Vgl. die Ausführungen *supra* in diesem Kapitel, B.IV.2.; vgl. ferner die Ausführungen bei Thomas, Lloyd's Mar. & Com. L.Q. 1981, 34 ff.

V. Zwischenergebnis

Eine Anerkennung und Vollstreckung von Schiedssprüchen erfolgte nach dem alten englischen Recht weitgehend unproblematisch. Soweit es hierbei um *foreign* oder *international awards* ging, garantierte dies bereits die Anwendbarkeit des New Yorker UN-Übereinkommens. Verstöße gegen das Gebot von *natural justice* wurden bei *convention-awards* scheinbar nur selten als Vollstreckungseinwand akzeptiert. Ähnlich restriktiv wurden auch Verstöße gegen *public policy* angenommen.[784]

Keiner solchen Ermessenbeschränkung unterlagen die Gerichte bei der Anerkennung und Vollstreckung von *domestic awards*. Die Gerichte waren bei Ihrer Entscheidung hierüber grundsätzlich frei. Dies galt sowohl für das Verfahren nach *s* 26 *Arbitration Act* 1950 als auch nach dem *action on the award*-Verfahren. Zumindest theoretisch war das englische Recht in diesem Punkt damit als rückständig anzusehen. In der Praxis wurde allerdings auch *domestic awards* nur in Ausnahmefällen eine Anerkennung und Vollstreckung versagt. Gleichwohl bleibt festzustellen, daß in solchen Fällen Verschleppungsmanöver unwilliger Schiedsparteien nicht ausgeschlossen werden konnten.[785]

D. Der Arbitration Act 1996

Der *Arbitration Act* 1996 ändert das englische Anerkennungs- und Vollstreckungsrecht nur unwesentlich. Die gleichwohl erfolgten Änderungen haben zumeist klarstellenden Charakter und schreiben lediglich bereits vorher geltendes *common law* fest.

I. Action on the award *nach dem* common law

Nach wie vor ist es möglich, Anerkennung und Vollstreckung über ein *action on the award*-Verfahren zu erreichen. Das Verfahren richtet sich weiterhin nach *common law*. Änderungen ergeben sich nicht. Von dieser Möglichkeit wird im Regelfall jedoch nur dort Gebrauch gemacht werden, wo die einfachere Voll-

---

784 Samuel, in: Knoepfler (Hrsg.), S. 127 f; differenzierend Harris/Meisel, Lloyd's Mar. & Com.L.Q. 1998, 568 ff; allgemein vgl. Böckstiegel, in: Sanders (Hrsg.), S. 177.

785 Vgl. etwa *Westacre Investments Inc. v. Judoimport-SDPR Co. Ltd. and Others* [1998] 2 Lloyd's Rep. 111.

streckung nach *s* 66 oder 99 - 104 *Arbitration Act* 1996 nicht möglich ist oder abgelehnt wird.[786]

II. Summary enforcement

S 66 *Arbitration Act* 1996 ersetzt nunmehr *s* 26 *Arbitration Act* 1950. Der Wortlaut der Vorschriften ist nahezu identisch. *S* 66(1)(2) *Arbitration Act* 1996 lautet:

> *"(1) An award made by the tribunal pursuant to an arbitration agreement may, by leave of the court, be enforced in the same manner as a judgment or order of the court to the same effect.*
> *(2) Where leave is so given, judgment may be entered in terms of the award."*

Inhaltliche Änderungen zu *s* 26 *Arbitration Act* 1950 ergeben sich nicht. Das Verfahren ist das gleiche, so auch der Ermessenspielraum der Gerichte. Letzterer erfährt in *s* 66(3) *Arbitration Act* 1996 allerdings eine Einschränkung. Darin heißt es:

> *"Leave to enforce an award shall not be given where, or to the extent that, the person against whom it is sought to be enforced shows that the tribunal lacked substantive jurisdiction to make the award."*

Soweit sich also nachträglich die Unzuständigkeit des Schiedsgerichts herausstellt, sind die Gerichte zur Versagung von Anerkennung oder Vollstreckung verpflichtet.[787] Der Zuständigkeitsmangel ist tatsächlich aber nur einer unter mehreren denkbaren Verfahrensverstößen, welche die Versagung zur Folge haben.

Bei den Beratungen zum Entwurf des *Arbitration Acts* 1996 war ursprünglich angedacht worden, eine Liste von Versagungsgründen in *s* 66 *Arbitration Act* 1996 aufzunehmen.[788] Diese Überlegung wurde jedoch unter dem Gesichtspunkt verworfen, daß eine solche Liste Mißverständnisse hervorrufen könnte. So wurde die Gefahr gesehen, daß die Liste fälschlicherweise als abschließend hätte verstanden werden können.[789] Dieser Eindruck aber sollte vermieden werden. Es war zu keinem Zeitpunkt beabsichtigt, in diesem Punkt dem Beispiel des Art. 36 Abs. 2 Modellgesetz zu folgen. Nach dem Willen des DAC soll die Verweige-

---

786 Lord/Salzedo, S. 51; *International Bulk Shipping and Services v. Minerals and Metals Trading Corp. of India* [1996] 1 All E.R. 1017.

787 Ein Mangel der Zuständigkeit beurteilt sich nach den *ss* 30 - 32 *Arbitration Act* 1996.

788 Merkin, Arbitration Act 1996, S. 95.

789 *Ibid.*

rung von Anerkennung und Vollstreckung grundsätzlich in allen Fällen möglich bleiben, in denen sie für angemessen erachtet würde.[790] Somit werden es voraussichtlich die gleichen Gründe wie schon vor 1997 sein, die zu einer Vollstrekkungsversagung führen.[791] Dies wird in *s* 81(1)(a)(c) *Arbitration Act* 1996 für die Fälle der mangelnden Schiedsfähigkeit und des Verstoßes gegen *public policy* auch ausdrücklich angeordnet.[792]

III. Schiedssprüche im Anwendungsbereich internationaler Konventionen

Die Vollstreckung von Schiedssprüchen, die in den Anwendungsbereich der bereits zuvor nach dem englischen Recht anwendbaren internationalen Konventionen fällt, bleibt erwartungsgemäß unverändert. Die *ss* 99 - 104 *Arbitration Act* 1996 übernehmen insoweit die Regelungen von Teil II *Arbitration Act* 1950 bzw. den *Arbitration Act* 1975.[793]

IV. Zwischenergebnis

Bei der Beurteilung des Vollstreckungsrechts des *Arbitration Acts* 1996 muß nach zwei Kategorien unterschieden werden. Soweit die zu vollstreckenden Schiedssprüche in den Anwendungsbereich internationaler Konventionen - vor allem in den des New Yorker UN-Übereinkommens - fallen, weist das englische Recht zwangsläufig keine Besonderheiten gegenüber anderen Schiedsrechten auf. Die Vollstreckung ist zumeist unproblematisch gewährleistet. Die Befugnisse der Gerichte sind klar definiert.

Soweit die Vollstreckung nach *s* 66 *Arbitration Act* 1996 erfolgen soll, gilt dies nur eingeschränkt. In diesen Fällen steht den Gerichten ein Ermessensspielraum zu. Wenngleich aufgrund der Erfahrungen mit *s* 26 *Arbitration Act* 1950 hiervon zwar nicht auszugehen ist, kann doch nicht ausgeschlossen werden, daß die Gerichte ihre weiten Eingriffsbefugnisse im Sinne einer verstärkten Kontrolle der Schiedssprüche gebrauchen könnten.

---

790 1996-Report, paras 371 - 376.

791 Harris/Planterose/Tecks, S. 244; vgl. *supra* in diesem Kapitel C..

792 *S* 81(1)(a)(c) *Arbitration Act* 1996 lautet:
"Nothing in this Part shall be construed as excluding the operation of any rule of law consistent with the provisions of this Part, in particular, any rule of law as to-
(a) matters which are not capable of settlement by arbitration; [...]
(c) the refusal of recognition or enforcement of an arbitral award on grounds of public policy."

793 Vgl. *supra* in diesem Kapitel ,C.III. und IV..

E. Zwischenergebnis

Wie sich aus den vorstehenden Ausführungen ergibt, unterscheidet sich das neue englische Vollstreckungsrecht nur unwesentlich vom alten. Uneingeschränkt gilt dies hinsichtlich der in den Anwendungsbereich internationaler Abkommen fallenden Schiedssprüche, zumindest weitgehend aber auch für alle anderen Schiedssprüche. Indem der Gesetzgeber sich in *s* 66 *Arbitration Act* 1996 - wie bereits zuvor in *s* 26 *Arbitration Act* 1950 - gegen nahezu jegliche Beschränkung der gerichtlichen Ermessensbefugnisse enschieden hat, wurde eine Chance zur Modernisierung des Schiedsverfahrensrechts vertan.

Dieser Kritikpunkt fällt auch bei einem Vergleich des neuen englischen Rechts mit dem Modellgesetz ins Gewicht. Dabei darf nicht übersehen werden, daß sich das Modellgesetz nach seinem Anwendungsbereich einzig auf internationale Schiedsverfahren bezieht,[794] während primärer Anwendungsbereich von *s* 66 *Arbitration Act* 1996 *domestic awards* sind. Ansonsten ist das neue englische Recht dem Modellgesetz vergleichbar.

794 Vgl. Art. 1 Abs. 1 Modellgesetz.

Zusammenfassung der Ergebnisse

Der Rechtsvergleich zwischen dem alten und neuen englischen Schiedsverfahrensrecht sowie zwischen dem neuen englischen Recht und dem Modellgesetz ergibt ein gemischtes Bild:

Mit *s* 1(c) *Arbitration Act* 1996 sieht das englische Recht erstmalig eine ausdrückliche Beschränkung der gerichtlichen Eingriffsbefugnisse auf die explizit im *Act* genannten vor. Die Vorschrift wurde jedoch nur als Sollvorschrift ausgestaltet. Ihre praktische Bedeutung hängt damit wesentlich von der Interpretation der Gerichte ab. Die vergleichbare Vorschrift des Modellgesetzes, Art. 5, geht weiter. Durch den verbindlichen Ausschluß aller nicht ausdrücklich genannten gerichtlichen Befugnisse erreicht Art. 5 Modellgesetz ein Höchstmaß an Vorhersehbarkeit und Rechtssicherheit. Sie ist deshalb vorzugswürdig.

S 9 *Arbitration Act* 1996 stellt eine durchweg gelungene Reform des zuvor in *s* 4 *Arbitration Act* 1950 und *s* 1 *Arbitration Act* 1950 geregelten Rechts zur Durchsetzbarkeit der Schiedsvereinbarung dar. Der Wegfall der Unterscheidung nach *domestic* und *non-domestic* und damit einhergehend auch der Wegfall der teils erheblichen Ermessensbefugnisse ist zu begrüßen. Nur noch in eng umrissenen Ausnahmefällen dürfen die Gerichte die Durchsetzung der Schiedsvereinbarung versagen. Die Regelungen des *Arbitration Acts* 1996 und des Modellgesetzes sind vergleichbar. Vor- oder Nachteile sind nicht erkennbar. Beide Regelungen werden den Anforderungen an ein modernes Schiedsverfahrensrecht gerecht.

S 12 *Arbitration Act* 1996 sieht wie bereits zuvor *s* 27 *Arbitration Act* 1950 das Recht der englischen Gerichte vor, ein von den Parteien vereinbartes Zeitlimit für die Einleitung des Schiedsverfahrens zu verlängern. Tatbestandliche Voraussetzung ist einzig das Vorliegen von *injustice*. Das Modellgesetz sieht keine entsprechende Regelung vor.

Anders als noch der *Arbitration Act* 1950 sieht der *Arbitration Act* 1996 keine Befugnis der Gerichte vor, die Ungültigkeit der Schiedsvereinbarung anzuordnen. Die zuvor in den *ss* 24(2) und 25(2)(b) *Arbitration Act* 1950 vorgesehenen Befugnisse wurden ersatzlos gestrichen. Diese Streichung ist zu begrüßen. Die Ausübung der vorgenannten Befugnisse stand nahezu im freien Ermessen der Gerichte. Sie war unkalkulierbar und stand außer Verhältnis zur beabsichtigten Rechtsfolge. Im Ergebnis ist das englische Recht in diesem Punkt mit dem Modellgesetz identisch.

Die als unkontrovers einzustufende Befugnis zur Ersatzbestellung von Schiedsrichtern bleibt nach dem *Arbitration Act* 1996 im wesentlichen unverändert. Die Befugnisse zur Abberufung von Schiedsrichtern wurden dagegen beschnitten. Vor allem der Wegfall der in *s* 1 *Arbitration Act* 1950 geregelten weiten Ermessensbefugnis zur *revocation of authority* ist fortschrittlich. Dennoch ist es nicht gelungen, die Abberufungsbefugnisse wirklich einzugrenzen und vorhersehbar zu machen. Das in *s* 24(1)(d)(i) *Arbitration Act* 1996 vorgesehene Tatbestandsmerkmal des *unproper conducts* läßt nach wie vor weitgehende Eingriffe zu. Im Vergleich zum Modellgesetz schneidet der *Arbitration Act* gleichwohl besser ab, da das Modellgesetz in Art. 14 ein nahezu uneingeschränktes Ermessen zur Abberufung von Schiedsrichtern einräumt.

Mit den *ss* 30 - 32 *Arbitration Act* 1996 erkennt das englische *statutory law* erstmals die *doctrines* der *separability* und der Kompetenz-Kompetenz an. Diese Anerkennung ist ein Kernstück der Reform. Das Ergebnis ist mit der Regelung des Modellgesetzes in Art. 16 inhaltlich nahezu identisch.

Das englische Recht zur Beweiserhebung hat sich nur unwesentlich durch den *Arbitration Act* 1996 geändert. Es bleibt dabei, daß Schiedsgerichte keinerlei Zwangsmaßnahmen anordnen dürfen. Die entsprechende Regelung des Art. 27 Modellgesetz ist dem englischen Recht weitgehend vergleichbar.

Der *Arbitration Act* 1996 weist nunmehr viele der Befugnisse zur Anordnung einstweiliger Maßnahmen, welche vormals einzig den Gerichten zugewiesen waren, primär den Schiedsgerichten zu. Das kommt der Autonomie des Schiedsverfahrens zugute. Die Regelungen des *Arbitration Acts* 1996 sind detaillierter als die entsprechende Regelung in Art. 16 Modellgesetz. Inhaltlich sind die Regelungen weitgehend vergleichbar.

Wie bereits das alte englische Recht sieht auch der *Arbitration Act* 1996 in *s* 45(4) das Recht der Gerichte zur *determination of a preliminary point of view* vor. Voraussetzung ist insofern jedoch die Zulassung durch das Schiedsgericht (oder die Zustimmung aller Parteien). Der Gefahr eines Mißbrauchs für Verschleppungsmanöver wird damit wirksam begegnet. Vor diesem Hintergrund ist die Beibehaltung der Möglichkeit zur Einholung einer gerichtlichen Rechtsfindung im Vorfeld des Schiedsspruchs sinnvoll. Das Modellgesetz sieht keine vergleichbare Regelung vor.

Der *Arbitration Act* 1996 behält in *s* 69 das zuvor in *s* 1 *Arbitration Act* 1979 vorgesehene *right of appeal on a point of law* bei. Es unterscheidet sich damit in einem wesentlichen Punkt vom Modellgesetz, welches keine entsprechende Möglichkeit vorsieht. Immerhin ist es den Parteien nach dem neuen englischen Recht nunmehr erstmalig möglich, einen generellen Ausschluß des *right of appeal* zu vereinbaren. Darin liegt ein wesentlicher Fortschritt gegenüber dem alten Recht. Soweit die Parteien von diesem Recht Gebrauch machen, ergeben sich keine Unterschiede zum Modellgesetz. Die Lösung des Modellgesetzes ist gleichwohl vorzugswürdig. Sie garantiert in jedem Falle den Ausschluß von Verschleppungsmanövern durch den Gang vor die staatlichen Gerichte.

Ganz überwiegend positiv ist dagegen die Reform der *ss* 22 und 23 *Arbitration Act* 1950 zu beurteilen. Indem das unbestimmte Tatbestandsmerkmal des *misconduct* durch das der näher definierten *serious irregularity* ersetzt wurde, wird das gerichtliche Ermessen zur Aufhebung und Abänderung von Schiedssprüchen wegen Verfahrensverstoßes erheblich eingeschränkt.

Das neue englische Recht der Anerkennung und Vollstreckung von Schiedssprüchen unterscheidet sich nicht wesentlich vom alten. Nach wie vor wird zwischen Schiedssprüchen, welche in den Anwendungsbereich internationaler Abkommen fallen, und anderen Schiedssprüchen unterschieden. Hinsichtlich der ersteren sind die Regelungen des englischen Rechts und des Modellgesetzes weitestgehend vergleichbar. Für letztere steht den englischen Gerichten wie zuvor ein weiter Ermessensspielraum zu.

Ausblick

Der *Arbitration Act* 1996 modernisiert das englische Schiedsverfahrensrecht. Den Prinzipien der Parteiautonomie und Effizienz des Schiedsverfahrens wird über weite Strecken konsequent Rechnung getragen. Damit ist das neue englische Schiedsverfahrensrecht dem Modellgesetz in vielen Punkten vergleichbar. In Teilbereichen ist es mitunter vorzugswürdig. In entscheidenden Fragen bleibt es allerdings hinter den kompromißloseren Lösungen des Modellgesetzes zurück. An erster Stelle ist hier die grundsätzliche Beibehaltung des *rights of appeal on a point of law* zu nennen. Bedauerlich ist auch, daß das neue englische Recht keine, dem Art. 5 Modellgesetz (verbindlicher Ausschluß gerichtlicher Befugnisse) entsprechende Vorschrift vorsieht sondern nur eine entsprechende *Soll*vorschrift.

Gleichwohl stellt der *Arbitration Act* 1996 eine überwiegend gelungene Reform des englischen Schiedsverfahrensrechts dar. Die Balance zwischen schiedsgerichtlicher Autonomie und staatlichen Kontrollbefugnissen wurde neu definiert. Der neue *Act* hat das Potential, dem Schiedsstandort England wieder "zu altem Glanz" zu verhelfen. Der Erfolg oder Mißerfolg des *Acts* wird jedoch entscheidend von der Einstellung der anwendenden Gerichte abhängen. Mit den Worten von Briner:[795]

"I feel the 1996 Act is the proper and necessary step in [the right] direction, but the final proof of the pudding will lie in the way the courts of England interpret the new Act and to what extent they are willing to interpret it in a pro-arbitration way, allowing the parties and, especially, the arbitrators, to draw the maximum benefit from the liberalization it will bring about [...]"

795 Arb.Int'l 1997, 159.

Schriftenreihe der August Maria Berges Stiftung für Arbitrales Recht

Herausgegeben von Dr. Hubertus W. Labes

Band 1 August Maria Berges – Ausgewählte Schriften zum Schiedsrecht. Herausgegeben von der August Maria Berges Stiftung für Arbitrales Recht. 1998

Band 2 Iris Koch: Außergerichtliche Streitbeilegung im japanischen Wirtschaftsverkehr unter besonderer Berücksichtigung der Schiedsgerichtsbarkeit. 2000.

Band 3 Hans-Claudius Scheef: Der einstweilige Rechtsschutz und die Stellung der Schiedsrichter bei dem Abschluß von Schiedsvergleichen nach dem deutschen und englischen Schiedsverfahrensrecht. Eine rechtsvergleichende Untersuchung. 2000.

Band 4 Dominik Lentz: Die internationale Wirtschaftsschiedsgerichtsbarkeit in der Russischen Föderation. Darstellung und Analyse anhand der Praxis des internationalen Handelsschiedsgerichts bei der Handels- und Industriekammer der Russischen Föderation. 2000.

Band 5 Torsten Lörcher: Neue Verfahren der internationalen Streiterledigung in Wirtschaftssachen. Verfahren vor dem Internationalen Seegerichtshof, WTO-Panelverfahren, ICSID-und WIPO-Schiedsverfahren. 2001.

Band 6 Julia Tief: Discovery und Informationspflichten der Parteien in der Internationalen Schiedsgerichtsbarkeit. Ein deutsch-amerikanischer Vergleich. 2000.

Band 7 Richard Happ: Schiedsverfahren zwischen Staaten und Investoren nach Artikel 26 Energiechartavertrag. Eine Studie zum Wandel der Streitbeilegung im Investitionsschutzrecht unter den Bedingungen einer globalen Weltwirtschaft. 2000.

Band 8 Jörn Schämann: Schiedsgerichte unter staatlicher Kontrolle. Das englische Recht und das UNCITRAL-Modellgesetz. 2001.

Julia Tief

Discovery und Informationspflichten der Parteien in der Internationalen Schiedsgerichtsbarkeit

Ein deutsch-amerikanischer Vergleich

Frankfurt/M., Berlin, Bern, Bruxelles, New York, Oxford, Wien, 2000. 140 S.
Schriftenreihe der August Maria Berges Stiftung für Arbitrales Recht. Bd. 6
Herausgegeben von Hubertus W. Labes
ISBN 3-631-36492-X geb. DM 54.–*

Bei dem Verfahren der Discovery handelt es sich um einen Kernpunkt des aus den Systemunterschieden zwischen kontinental-europäischem und anglo-amerikanischem Recht entstandenen Streits. Diese Abhandlung gewährt zunächst einen Überblick über die unterschiedlichen Verfahrenssituationen hinsichtlich der Discovery und der Informationspflichten der Parteien im Rahmen des Zivilprozesses in den USA und in der Bundesrepublik Deutschland. Anschließend wird aufgezeigt, wie sich der Konflikt zwischen den Rechtskreisen auf die Internationale Schiedsgerichtsbarkeit auswirkt. In diesem Zusammenhang erfolgt eine Darstellung der einschlägigen Normen der gängigen Schiedsverfahrensordnungen. Den Abschluß bildet schließlich eine Erörterung verschiedener Lösungsmöglichkeiten und deren Konsequenzen für die Handhabung der Problematik in der Praxis der Internationalen Schiedsgerichtsbarkeit.

Aus dem Inhalt: Der Zivilprozeß in den USA und in Deutschland – Discovery in der nationalen Schiedsgerichtsbarkeit – Discovery in der internationalen Schiedsgerichtsbarkeit – Konsequenzen für die Handhabung der Problematik in der Praxis.